Planting Churches among the City's Poor

An Anthology of Urban Church Planting Resources

VOLUME ONE:
THEOLOGICAL AND MISSIOLOGICAL
PERSPECTIVES FOR CHURCH PLANTERS

Edited by Rev. Dr. Don L. Davis

TUMI Press
3701 East Thirteenth Street North
Wichita, Kansas 67208

Planting Churches among the City's Poor:
An Anthology of Urban Church Planting Resources
Volume One: Theological and Missiological Perspectives for Church Planters

© 2015. The Urban Ministry Institute. All Rights Reserved. Copying, redistribution, and/or sale of these materials, or any unauthorized transmission, except as may be expressly permitted by the 1976 Copyright Act or in writing from the publisher is prohibited. Requests for permission should be addressed in writing to:

The Urban Ministry Institute
3701 East 13th Street North
Wichita, KS 67208

ISBN: 978-1-62932-304-6

Published by TUMI Press
A division of World Impact, Inc.

The Urban Ministry Institute is a ministry of World Impact, Inc.

All Scripture quotations, unless otherwise noted, are from The Holy Bible, English Standard Version, copyright © 2001 by Crossway Bible. A division of Good News Publishers. Used by permission. All Rights Reserved.

This book is dedicated to

urban church planters around the world,

the valiant men and women who have sacrificed personal ease and safety
to minister to those who are the voiceless, the broken,
and the most neglected in human society.

They have responded with open hearts and willing souls,
are willing to engage these communities with love and grace,
and are fearless in prophesying the deliverance of Christ and his Kingdom
to those who have been chosen to be rich in faith,
and heirs of the Kingdom (James 2.5).

For their courage and sacrifice,
for their burden and energy,
for their passion and perseverance,
we thank our Lord and God.

May their "beautiful feet" continue to walk the streets and alley-ways
of the neediest cities of this world,
never failing to publish peace, bringing Good News of happiness,
publishing to city dwellers God's salvation
and declaring without fear and shame that Jesus Christ is Lord,
to the glory of God.

~ Isaiah 52.7 ~

Table of Contents

Prologue 11

Part I
Developing Urban Congregations:
A Framework for World Impact Church Planters . 19

Introduction.	21
World Impact and Church Planting	23
Theology of the Church	24
Modern Missions' History	28
Indigenous Churches	30
Multicultural Congregations	38
A Strategy for Planting Churches	43
Commission the Church-Planting Team	44
Cultivate the Community	50
Establish Discipling Fellowships	58
Form a Celebration Group	65
Plan the Finances	69
Provide Facilities	73
Constitute the Church	77
Church/Mission Relations	82
Conclusion	86
Bibliography	87

Part II
Theological and Missiological Principles and Insights: Toward a Theology of Church Planting 93

Christus Victor: A Theology of the City and the Poor . . 95

The Theology of the Poor for Team Leaders 97
Ethics of the New Testament:
Living in the Upside-Down Kingdom of God 109
Christus Victor:
An Integrated Vision for the Christian Life and Witness . . . 110
The Kingdom of God: Church Planting in a Universe at War . . 111
Christus Victor: Toward a Biblical Theology for the Urban Church 120
Once upon a Time:
Understanding Our Church's Place in the Story of God . . . 150
The Black Church and Church Planting:
World Impact Blog, February 2015 163

A Theology of the Kingdom and the Church 167

Living in the Already and the Not Yet Kingdom 169
Jesus of Nazareth: The Presence of the Future 170
A Theology of the Church in Kingdom Perspective 171
A Schematic for a Theology of the Kingdom and the Church . 172
Thy Kingdom Come! Readings on the Kingdom of God . . . 173
There Is a River: Identifying the Streams of a
Revitalized Authentic Christian Community in the City . . . 182
The Role of Sound Ecclesiology in Urban Mission 183
The Story of God: Our Sacred Roots 195
Substitute Centers to a Christ-Centered Vision: Goods and Effects
Which Our Culture Substitutes as the Ultimate Concern . . . 196
The Picture and the Drama:
Image and Story in the Recovery of Biblical Myth 197
Old Testament Witness to Christ and His Kingdom 198
The Theology of Christus Victor: A Christ-Centered Biblical
Motif for Integrating and Renewing the Urban Church . . . 199
The Theology of the Church for Team Leaders 200
Models of the Kingdom 209

A Theology of Christ and Culture 211

The Difference That Difference Makes:
Culture, Religion, and Diversity in Post-Modern Society . . . 213

Five Views of the Relationship between Christ and Culture . . 231

Interaction of Class, Culture, and Race 232

The Complexity of Difference: Race, Culture, Class 233

Cycle of Freedom 234

Authentic Freedom in Jesus Christ. 235

Too Legit to Quit: A Continuum of Cultural Practice . . . 236

Apostolicity:
The Unique Place of the Apostles in Christian Faith and Practice 237

Theological Diversity 238

Creedal Theology as a Blueprint for Discipleship and Leadership:
A Time-Tested Criterion for Equipping New Believers
and Developing Indigenous Leaders 241

Translating the Story of God 253

Cross-Cultural Church Planting Principles 254

The Missionary Vocation: Assessing Cross-Cultural Adaptability. 255

Targeting Unreached Groups in Churched Neighborhoods . . 256

Different Traditions of African-American Response:
Interpreting a Legacy, Shaping an Identity, and
Pursuing a Destiny as a Minority Culture Person 257

Paul's Team Members:
Companions, Laborers, and Fellow Workers 260

Jesus' Practice of Silence and Solitude. 263

Seven Essential Practices for the Priesthood of All Believers . . 264

On World Impact's "Empowering the Urban Poor" 265

Responding to God's Call to the Poor 271

The Bible in Chronological Order: A Narrative
Literary Telling of the Story of God in Both Testaments . . . 273

From Before to Beyond Time:
The Plan of God and Human History 274

Part III
Planting Urban Churches: Resources for Church Planters 277

Church Planting Movements Overview 279

Church Planting Overview 281
World Impact's Strategy for Church Planting 288
Mobilizing American Cities for Church Planting Movements . 292
Church Planting Movements, C1 Neighborhoods,
and 80% Windows: The Importance of Vision 320
Discerning Valid Urban Church Planting Movements:
Elements of Authentic Urban Christian Community . . . 326

The Church Planter and the Church Plant Team 327

How to PLANT a Church 329
Responsibilities of a Church Plant Team Leader 336
The Heartbeat of a Church Planter:
Discerning an Apostolic/Pastoral Identity 337
Practical Steps in Church Planting:
Knowing Your Call and Your Community 349
Traditions (*Paradosis*) 356
What Shall I Preach, How Shall We Grow:
The Urban Pastor's Dilemma 367
Forming the Church Plant Team and Understanding the Roles . 371
Discipling the Faithful:
Establishing Leaders for the Urban Church 375
Spiritual Service Checklist 376

Models of Church Planting. 377

Overview PLANT to Birth Models 379
Three Levels of Ministry Investment 380
Six Types of Neighborhoods 381
Advancing the Kingdom in the City:
Multiplying Congregations with a Common Identity. . . . 382
Church Planting Models 385

Overview of Church Plant Planning Phases	388
The Role of Women in Ministry	389
Ordination of Women Q and A	393
Defining the Leaders and Members of a Church Plant Team.	396

Engaging the Community 397

Selecting a Target Area.	399
Researching Your Community	405
The *Oikos* Factor: Spheres of Relationship and Influence	418
Receptivity Scale	419
Living as an *Oikos* Ambassador	420
Apostolic Band: Cultivating Outreach for Dynamic Harvest	421
Resources for Studying Your Community	422
Ideas about Neighborhood Evangelism	423
Canvassing Dos and Don'ts.	424
Door-to-Door: Starting the Conversation	426

Body Life and Spiritual Formation. 427

Using Wisdom in Ministry: The PWR Process	429
Getting a Good Team Rhythm: Time Management and Ministry Stewardship	439
Commissioning of Our Elders	442
Order of Service: Sample 1.	444
Order of Service: Sample 2.	445
Small Groups: Ten Principles and Their Implications for Open Christian Gatherings.	455
The Service of Believer's Baptism	457
Sample Follow-up Card.	464
Church Plant Team Responsive Reading	465
Key Roles of a Church Planting Team	467
The Power of Multiplication: The 2 Timothy 2.2 Principle	468
Developing Ears That Hear: Responding to the Spirit and the Word	469

Appendix
Twenty-five Years of Urban Church Planting among the Poor: A Report 471

An Abridged Church Planting Bibliography 511

The Urban Ministry Institute:
Polishing the Stones That the Builders Reject
How You Can Equip Leaders for Your Church and Ministry . 519

Prologue

What Is an Anthology?
An anthology is a group of resources or items, a collection of some sort, usually selected from a larger whole, most often done by various contributors, authors, or creators themed according to a particular period, but usually concerning a single subject. In other words, an anthology brings together a host of various contributions and reflections all hoping to shed light on the nature of a single theme or enterprise.

By this definition, the following work is in fact that kind of collection on the nature of planting churches, specifically leading teams and coaching planters, among people groups and communities which have historically been the product of benign evangelical neglect. In other words, peoples and communities which, because of their race, or poverty, or violence, or cultural distance, have not been our normal targets for evangelical mission. These documents, graphics, and essays are the result of decades of thought and practice done by urban missionaries among America's urban poor. In their totality they offer a historical snapshot into the various thinking, writing, and reflection that emerged within the World Impact Religious Missionary Order, a community dedicated to planting churches in the most dangerous and least targeted urban communities for the past forty years.

Why Plant Churches among the Urban Poor?
More than two years ago, I wrote a short essay about the phrase "urban poor," whether it was still legitimate to use the term, or perhaps, it should be abandoned as a demeaning and outmoded wording for more accurate and less offensive language (cf. *http://worldimpact.org/empowering-the-urban-poor.*) I wrote the following:

> Since our founding more than forty years ago, World Impact has spoken prophetically regarding God's election of the poor, the benign neglect of the evangelical church of America's inner city poor, and the need for evangelism, discipleship, and church planting in unreached urban poor communities. We believe that credible urban mission must demonstrate the Gospel, testifying in both the proclaimed word and concrete action. In light of this, we have emphasized living in the communities we serve, ministering to the needs of the whole person, as well as to the members of the whole urban family. We have sought this witness with a goal to see communities reached and transformed by Christ, believing that those who live in the city and are poor can be empowered to live in the freedom, wholeness,

and justice of the Kingdom of God fleshed out in local churches and viable urban church planting movements. All our vision, prayer, and efforts are concentrated on a particular social group, the "urban poor," and our commitment to "empower" them through all facets of our work.

As a missions organization that was founded on a burden to provide empowerment and liberation through the Gospel for the poor, we have wholeheartedly and unashamedly embraced the term. As I said in the essay, "While the phrase 'the urban poor' may be misunderstood or misused, we have chosen to employ it with our own stipulated meanings, informed by biblical theology as well as urban sociology. We employ the term to identify those whom God has commissioned us to serve, as well as to represent God's prophetic call to proclaim Good News to the poor, both to the church and to our society at large." Without any doubt or equivocation, we are committed to see the Kingdom come and advance among those who live in the city, and those whose lives are exposed and vulnerable because of a lack of resources, choices, and options because they are poor. Not only has God chosen them to be rich in faith, he has also declared them to be the very heirs of the forever Kingdom of God to come (James 2.5). To plant churches among the urban poor is to touch the very heart of God, to gather those tender sheaves for which he died, those grains that are ripe for harvest (Matt. 9.35-38).

This anthology brings together a selected grouping of some of the significant essays, graphics, course outlines, articles, and explanations utilized by urban missionaries that have resulted in planting healthy churches among the city's poor. They are not necessarily given in a linear order (according to the time in which they were done), but are rather organized and grouped according to the categories of theology and missiology, leading church plant teams, and coaching urban church planters. Anthologies can be unwieldy and not clean collections, and such is the case here. We have gathered from a wide selection of events, venues, research, and reflection to amass this grouping, and we are confident that the overlap in theme will not deter from the importance of the material within this work.

The sheer extent of venues and publishings that this work draws from is impressive. The list is broad and diverse. For instance, we have drawn materials for this collection from our booklet for cross-cultural church plant teams called *Leading and Feeding Church Planting Teams*, and from our conference for team leaders called *The Timothy Conference*. This compilation includes materials referenced in World Impact Regional and National leadership meetings, our *Winning the World* TUMI course on church plant movements around the world, and presentations from our *School of Urban Cross-Cultural Church Planting*. We have taken a smattering of graphics from our seminary-level modular series, *The Capstone Curriculum*, and from our World Impact missionary *Candidate Assessment Program*, as well as from actual church plants we have done in the past. We have drawn from many venues, and though full of useful resources, it is not exhaustive! It does represent, however, some of our best thinking from various courses, consultations and reflections on the nature of planting churches among the poor.

We have organized the references in *Planting Churches among the City's Poor* in two complimentary volumes: *Volume One, Theological and Missiological Perspectives for Church Planters*, and *Volume Two, Resources and Tools for Coaches and Teams*. Volume One contains a range of materials related to the whys and wherefores of a biblical theology of mission and church planting, especially how that theology touches upon urban missions, church planting, and the development of healthy congregations and movements.

Volume One, Part I: Developing Urban Congregations, is a reprint of our formative, seminal essay on urban church planting which served as the foundational biblical and theological piece which informed our initial forays into church planting among the poor in the city. *Volume One, Part II: Theological and Missiological Principles and Insights* provides a treasure of resources related to urban missions, ministry among the poor and oppressed, and church planting, including biblical theologies of the Church, retrieval of the Great Tradition among churches which serve the poor, and the role of color, class, and race in making disciples in underserved communities. The resources in *Volume One, Part III, Planting Urban Churches*, concern mainly the theory and practice of actually planting churches among the urban poor, with a focus on the calling, character, and competencies of the church planter, that God-called, Spirit-filled individual who has been led to plant outposts of the Kingdom for Christ among the city's poorest and most vulnerable populations.

Volume Two, Resources and Tools for Coaches and Teams, provides a toolkit, an asset depot containing various materials, tools, and helps to outfit the church plant coach or mentor to lead teams. Additionally, this volume contains numerous specific aids that the planter and his/her team will find invaluable as they engage in their church planting effort.

Volume Two, Part I: Coaching Urban Church Planters, addresses the specific nature of coaching and mentoring church plant leaders and their teams, and seeks to give a broad, compelling outline of the kinds of issues, concerns, and commitments necessary for mentors to understand and do as they coach teams that plant effective churches. And *Volume Two, Part II: The Church Planting Toolkit*, provides a potpourri of miscellaneous articles, graphs, documents, and information relevant to planting a church, including information about financial, state relations, leadership development, forming associations, and equipping for reproduction in church planting movements. In this section you will find abundant particular resources all meant to be helpful for planters, coaches, and associations who desire to plant healthy churches among the poor, both cross-culturally and intra-culturally. These many helps will readily inform your thinking about the nature of planting the individual congregation, forming the structures of a healthy church planting movement, empowering leadership for reproduction, and advancing the Kingdom among the poor in the city.

A Loosely Categorized Collection
In order to aid you in your search for articles and materials that can prove helpful to your inquiries, we have grouped the various items under categories for easier reference. However, because the graphics themselves relate to a host of questions and contexts, you may find that many of the materials can speak to a number of themes, and not merely the category under which they were originally placed.

While the categories are helpful, they ought not to be viewed as authoritative or final. For instance, many of the graphics will undoubtedly speak to a number of different concepts, overlapping between the fields of church planting and coaching church planters, and/or relevant to the design and argument of viable models and theologies that can help us engage the complexity and promise of our unreached urban neighborhoods.

So, when you are perusing this volume, remember to use the table of contents first as a good guide to provide direction to a particular grouping of resources, but also remember that the materials are grouped in a more-or-less generic fashion, and that the materials will have multiple applications, covering a wide range of issues and topics. Do not hesitate to explore different graphics and articles, reading them in new and different contexts than the one we suggest. As a good solid rule, check the table of contents first, but, as you actually look at the resource, think in terms of what other contexts this item might refer to and provide insight into the concepts you explore.

"What Is the Reference for This?"

One of the problems of an anthology of materials within a set community is that, if you do not know the special terms, acronyms, and references which the community is acquainted with, you can lose the original meaning. To comprehend the meaning, you need to know the referent, the initial object or thing to which the reference looks back to. Unfortunately, with more than thirty years having passed, many of the individual articles and the original referents no longer exist; page numbers may be superfluous, reference to articles and essays may be irrelevant, and specific mentionings of previous materials no longer have any foundation. While we have sought to make this perusal of material easier to digest by citing the original referents we could find, alas, there will be citations within many of the documents where the original is lost, misplaced, renamed, or subsumed into another document. Forgive us when you encounter this phenomenon; our desire is to help you access these materials, include the referents where we could, and hope that the original documents are clear enough to navigate through the materials.

One notable exception on the original referent has to do with the letters *CPM* which means "church planting movement(s)." Also, the citations about *C1*, *C2*, and *C3* refer to our thinking about the sub-strata of cultures that interact in the overall American context. (You can understand the original source for this thinking and discussion in a document entitled *Interaction of Class, Culture, and Race*.) The numerous references to the *C1* and related cultures go back to our forty-year use of this thinking grid to comprehend and discuss the implications of culture in urban missions. Please refer to this diagram for our most direct communication on these cultural interactions.

Another issue you should be aware of as you go through this Anthology relates to the use of **designations and terms**. Since *Planting Churches among the City's Poor* is essentially an anthology, we sought to preserve our earlier documents in their original form, and did not go back through the documents and revise the language used in our earliest schools. This is not a major difficulty, however, because although we use different terms than our earlier schools, we have maintained the same functions for the positions. Two terms need to be defined:

- In previous materials, the term used for the church planting supervisor or mentor to whom the team leader reported or received input from was called a *Multiple Team Leader* or *MTL*. Now, in this volume and in our schools, we refer to this role as *Coach*. All references to *MTL* or *Multiple Team Leader* in this volume or in *Planting Churches among the City's Poor* should be understand now as **Coach**.

- Also, in past schools we used the term *Team Leader* for the person in charge of the church plant team and church plant effort. Now, we refer to the person fulfilling this role as the **Church Planter**.

In terms of language, then, please remember that when you engage materials in the *Anthology* that cite *MTL* or *Multiple Team Leader*, they now ought to be understood as an equivalent terms to Coach, and, the designation *Team Leader* is equivalent now to the designation *Church Planter*.

How to Use This Book
Since the contents of *Planting Churches among the City's Poor* is essentially a collected group of resources on church planting, it lends itself to creative and varied uses. You could simply follow the graphics according to the categories listed, and reflect on the particular graphics and outlines in the order in which they have been organized. You can select particular items and reflect and re-think the subjects based on your own questions and research. Or, you may choose to add to this collection – rearranging, remixing, and re-conceiving the various theologies, approaches, missiological models, and practical protocols we list here, and change and amend them for your context and ministry. This work accumulates a group of materials meant to be processed, rethought, and applied.

Therefore, this work is a varied assortment, an assembly of our dialogues and practices that have informed the ways in which we have conducted ministry that resulted in leaders from the neighborhood who live to serve the neighborhood. Be free in your engagement and application of these materials. Go in any order. Realize, too, that the groupings under the categories are somewhat arbitrary. Frankly, all of the materials included relate in one way or the other to all of the categories given. Use them to help sharpen your own thinking, and provide you with suggestions and insights that can make your own church planting in underserved neighborhoods more biblical and in sync with God's purposes for the church.

In one sense, this collection is a sampler of our theological and ministry tools available for workers on our ministry websites (*www.tumi.org* and *www.worldimpact.org*). These works represent only a fraction of the tens of thousands of pages of curricula, graphics, and course material produced by World Impact missionaries and Institute scholars these last twenty years. We have learned much about what it means to display the light of the Kingdom in at-risk communities, and we thank God for his leading and direction. Still, we are ever-learning, ever-reforming, ever-willing to learn new things, to explore new directions, and be equipped to do greater things in the name of Christ, for the sake of the city and the poor. Our humble intent is to share the lessons we've learned, not to give the definitive thinking on these matters, but reveal the lessons we have gleaned through planting communities of the Kingdom in the city.

Your interest in this work reveals your connection to three great themes which inform a truly biblical theology of missions: the city, the poor, and the church. Until the Great King returns and makes righteousness roll down like a mighty stream among the nations of the world, we have a sacred obligation to finish the Great Commission (Matt. 28.18-20). While human life began in a garden, it will consummate in a city of God's own building, inhabited by those who were poor in spirit, and will therefore see God. Those from every kindred, tongue, people, and nation who make up the redeemed of God, his church, will live in a new heavens and earth where Christ is Lord. Until that day, we are charged with the task of prophesying deliverance in the name of the Lord to the nations of the earth, whose majority population live in urban communities. The kingdoms of this world will become the Kingdom of our Lord and of his Christ, and he will reign forever (Rev. 11.15).

Your research and engagement in this great mission can contribute to this grand biblical vision. Our prayer is that God will use this work to provide you with greater insight, illumination, and understanding as to how we can plant these outposts of kingdom life among the poorest of the poor in the cities of the world. This is our vision, and our desire is to see the church in America rediscover the fruitfulness and fire of planting churches of among the city's poor. As John Yoder has referred to them, the poor are the "grains of the universe," ripe for harvest. May God send forth qualified spiritual laborers worthy of the risen Christ to plant communities of the Kingdom in his urban harvest.

Rev. Dr. Don L. Davis
March 20, 2015

Part I
Developing Urban Congregations:
A Framework for World Impact Church Planters

The missional center of our urban ministry has undergone great change over the last forty years. After beginning with a focus on Bible clubs and children (the mid 60s to early 70s), we shifted to a discipleship focus on teens (mid 70s to early 80s), the formation of compassion and justice ministries (early 80s), with early Christian gatherings (mid to late 80s), and finally to indigenous church planting (since 1990). More than twenty-five years ago, World Impact announced its intent to plant self-governing, self-supporting, and self-reproducing indigenous churches among the urban poor in the city. This change was neither easy nor hassle-free, but it was organic and deeply life-changing.

Still, to shift in this drastic way seemed both natural and necessary. Our missional identity grew, deepening more and more as we realized that in order to truly empower the urban poor we would need to allow the Spirit to let them general his forces in their own communities. Thus, our journey in urban church planting began with a goal to empower indigenous people to transform their communities, and our desire to see new generations of urban poor leaders emerge to lead those congregations gave way to a dedicated organization that continues to marshal its resources for the sake of planting churches among the least and the lost in the city.

This essay deserves its own unique place in our anthology, since it was in fact the first and definitive statement on the nature, scope, and meaning of urban church planting for World Impact. It is the culmination of much thinking and research that led up to its creation, with many dialogues, consultations, reports, and discussions leading to its writing. Terry Cornett and Jim Parker are its authors, who, at the time of writing, were the Director and Assistant Director of Missions Studies for World Impact, located in Los Angeles. Both had been full-time community ministers in urban poor neighborhoods, and Jim had served as our World Impact Portland Director. Their keen intellects and rich experience were harnessed to pen this piece which represents some of our earliest and most formative writing on the nature of urban church planting. As editors of the anthology, we find it heartening that this seminal piece continues to resonate, providing insight into the promise and the challenge of urban church planting among the poor. We are equally convinced that its insights and clarifications will still prove useful for those planting churches among the poor in urban neighborhoods today.

Introduction

By the year 2010, racial and ethnic minorities will make up one-quarter to one-third of the American population. These groups will concentrate in inner cities. Some missions experts fear that the church will not be ready to address their needs. Church planting and training resources continue to flow from city to suburb during a time of tremendous need in the city.[1] Fortunately, crisis and opportunity are often two sides of the same coin. Although city churches will face undeniable challenges, it is possible "new models for evangelism, church planting and theological training will come from the cities."[2]

This paper is intended to prepare World Impact church planters to be effective urban church planters. It provides an overview of the history and theology of church planting. It outlines a working model to guide the planting of urban churches. It suggests ways to build successful church-planting teams and coordinate church/mission relationships.

A cautionary note is in order before beginning. The proverb "Give a man a fish and he eats for a day, teach a man to fish and he eats for a lifetime" in practice may become, "Give a man a fish and he eats for a day, teach a man to fish and he starves to death." A wide gap frequently exists between theory and application!

Therefore, we assume that the process of building churches is more dependent on the work of the Holy Spirit, the Spirit-given gifts of the church planter and the character of the converts than it is on the development and application of "perfect" models. The church-planting team must seek the guidance of the Holy Spirit for each decision. This will involve:

> . . . the acceptance of a trial and error methodology. No matter how hard missiologists try to make church planting a science, . . . it will always remain more an art than a science. Not that scientific methodology should not be used to gather data to understand the people and conditions in which the church planter works: every tool of the social sciences should be used. But the impression should not be given that if the church planter follows a definite type of methodology, and if conditions are right, the development of a

---

1   Harvie Conn, Urban Missions Newsletter, (Philadelphia: Westminster Theological Seminary), 28, Dec. 1990, 1-2

2   Harvie Conn, p. 2

> new church is guaranteed. In church planting, there are no guarantees of success, and the shock comes to new church planters when their "ideal" methodology does not immediately produce churches. . . . Churches are born as a result of the supernatural work of the Holy Spirit, who uses the skills of his servants, the church planters. And those skills are developed over the course of time, through trial and error and many tears, and there are few shortcuts to their achievement."[3]

We encourage church-planting teams to read this paper with an eye toward innovation and experimentation. Each church-planting team will face the crucial task of discovering how general principles apply to the specific situation they face. The principles and models contained in this paper will not supplant the guidance and work of the Holy Spirit, but will give structure and support to those called to the task of planting new congregations.

---

[3] Tom Eckblad, "Tips for Church Planters", *Urban Mission* 1.3, Jan. 1984, pp. 28-29

World Impact and Church Planting

Twenty-five years ago Keith Phillips began a Bible Club in a Watts housing project. From this starting point as an inner-city youth ministry, World Impact has evolved into a full-fledged urban mission with more than two hundred staff in seven cities and three training centers. The guiding goal of making disciples has led to the development of training programs, schools and churches.

God's leading is evident in World Impact's development as a national ministry. The work began with few material resources and a young staff. Much of the early work relied upon volunteers. Because they were the most accessible, children became the early focus of evangelism. Eventually the desire to make disciples led to an incarnational ministry that included teens and adults. This ushered in the development of a worship service and support services. Each city ministry developed differently depending on its staff and resources but the national focus of attention changed from one period to the next:[4]

1. Evangelism with focus on children, 1965-1974

2. Discipleship with focus on teens, 1975-1981

3. Support services with focus on meeting community needs (camps, schools, clinics, housing, etc.), 1982-

4. Celebration worship as initial step toward church planting, 1982-1990

5. Indigenous Church-planting, 1990-

In 1990 World Impact's Executive Board pointed toward the church-planting stage of our ministry development, announcing the goal of planting self-governing, self-supporting and self-reproducing indigenous churches in the inner city.

---

4 This does not suggest that the prior emphases were abandoned as each new stage began. Each phase constituted the foundation for the next phase of ministry and each phase is an ongoing and integral part of our current ministry. Youth and teen evangelism, discipleship and support services undergird and work alongside our church-planting ministries.

Theology of the Church

World Impact missionaries come to the inner city to represent Christ and advance His Kingdom. A key element in this process is the cycle of evangelism and church planting that calls people into the Kingdom of God and places them in a context where they are discipled to live out its commands. To fulfill this calling, church planters must be clear about the nature of the church as revealed in Scripture.[5]

The Community of the Kingdom
Rene Padilla says, "The New Testament presents the church as the community of the Kingdom in which Jesus is acknowledged as Lord of the universe and through which, in anticipation of the end, the Kingdom is concretely manifested in history."[6] The gospels present the Kingdom of God as God's rule or reign. It encompasses the places which God has claimed and where God's will is done (Matthew 4:17; 6:10, 12:38; Mark 4:26-29; Luke 10:9). Those who proclaim "Jesus is Lord" acknowledge its existence and its claims over them. Thus, the Kingdom of God is evident whenever Christians gather in community for worship, fellowship or witness.

In explaining his vision for the church at Colossae, Paul reminded the believers there that God ". . . has rescued us from the kingdom of darkness and brought us into the *kingdom of the Son* He loves" (Colossians 1:13). It is interesting to note that the Book of Acts, our primary New Testament source on the history of church planting by early Christians, both begins and ends with the Kingdom of God. Luke's first words following his introduction are to describe Jesus appearing to his disciples and speaking to them "about the *Kingdom of God*" (Acts 1:3). Luke then describes the activities of the Apostles in spreading the news of the Kingdom and concludes with a summary of Paul's message in its final verse by saying, "Boldly and without hindrance he preached the *Kingdom of God* and taught about the Lord Jesus Christ" (Acts 28:31).

The church is the place where God's kingdom becomes real on earth. It is where the Light breaks through the world's darkness. "God's intention is that every congregation of believers in Jesus be a surprising

---

5 World Impact-planted churches will be built on the doctrinal foundation of World Impact's Affirmation of Faith statement.

6 Padilla, pp. 189-190

revelation of the presence of the kingdom of God on earth. It is through the creation (or planting) of churches that God's kingdom is extended into communities that have not yet been touched by the precious surprise of the presence of the kingdom of God in their midst."[7]

The community of the kingdom is comprised of all who acknowledge the Lordship of Christ, who repent of their sins and obey Christ. When a person becomes a Christian, he enters into this fellowship with God and with other Christians.

The characteristics of the community of the kingdom can be organized into three major categories: discipleship, worship and witness.[8] The church is a community of family-like relationships: a fellowship of disciples (I John 1:3). The church is a worshipping community that gives praise, honor and thanks to God (Ephesians 5:19-20). And the church is a witnessing community that spreads the message of God's reign to others (Matthew 28:18-20). These categories, in balance, form the dynamic life of the church.

A Community of Discipleship

Jesus' band of disciples were a community of the Kingdom. Before his death, Jesus commissioned the disciples to love one another, to bear fruit, and to testify about him (John 15). Discipleship means equipping people to live for Christ. It involves the internal and external disciplines needed for training in obedience (Colossians 1:28; II Timothy 2:2). Jesus discipled his followers, thus enabling them to disciple others.

Following Jesus, the New Testament writers emphasized three ingredients of discipleship in the community of the kingdom: fellowship, sanctification and spiritual gifts. Fellowship is the supportive love relationship that bonds the disciples together in the Body of Christ. Sanctification is the process of being "set apart" for service to God. It involves maturing in Christ by showing the fruit of the Spirit (Galatians 5:22-26; I Peter 1:2). Spiritual gifts refer to the Spirit's enablement of each member of the Body to perform his or her function in building the church (Romans 12:4-8; I Corinthians 12:1-31). God uses the gifts of the Holy Spirit to build the community of believers in faith and obedience so it can witness of Jesus to the world (John 15:26-27).

---

7   David Shenk and Ervin Stutzman, *Creating Communities of the Kingdom: New Testament Models of Church Planting* (Scottsdale, AZ: Herald Press, 1988), p. 23

8   Howard A. Snyder, *Liberating the Church* (Downers Grove, Il: Inter-Varsity Press, 1983), p. 86

A Community of Worship

The church is also a worshiping community. From the beginning the church worshiped God as a natural outpouring of its life together. Paul taught the young church that worship should remain the church's focus (Ephesians 5:19-20). Worship is the church's response to the character and actions of God. When God's Word is taught and God's power and love are demonstrated, it calls forth worship from His people. This worship may take many forms including repentance (James 4:8-10), praise (Psalm 9:1), thanksgiving (Psalm 107:1), music and singing (Psalm 43:4, Psalm 89:1), physical expressions of respect or gratitude (Psalm 95:6; 134:2), offerings and vows (Psalm 76:11) and affirmations of God's character and position (Psalm 96:7-13). Worship also includes celebrating the entry of new believers into the community of faith by baptism and the remembrance of Christ's finished work of redemption through Communion.

Robert Webber, an authority on the history and practice of worship, says, "The public worship of God takes place in the community of the church, by the power of the Holy Spirit, in proclamation and enactment of the work of salvation, through visible and tangible signs."[9]

A Community of Witness

Finally, the church is a witnessing community. The church's witness includes evangelism, service and prophesy.[10] Evangelism is sharing the good news of Jesus and the Kingdom. Service means following the example of Christ in meeting the world's needs. Prophesy refers to the church's corporate witness to the world. "The church is prophetic when by its worship, community and witness it points toward and manifests the new age of the Kingdom."[11]

Individual disciples carry out the church's witness within the context of a community of disciples. Jesus sent his disciples out in pairs or as a group (Luke 9:1-6; 10:1). Orlando Costas affirms, "To be sure, evangelization is nourished and facilitated by individuals. It takes place, practically speaking, through individuals. But it is a witness that cannot be offered without the ecclesiastical community."[12]

---

9   Robert E. Webber, Worship Old & New (Grand Rapids, MI: Zondervan, 1982), p. 17

10 See Snyder, p. 90

11 Snyder, p. 91

12 Orlando E. Costas, *Liberating News: A Theology of Contextual Evangelization* (Grand Rapids: Eerdmans, 1989), p. 135

This prophetic witness of the church includes creating and sustaining a reconciling community of believers, recognizing the true enemy, renouncing the world's definition and practice of power, and working for justice in society.[13]

David Shenk and Ervin Stutzman, in their discussion on church planting, accent the church's prophetic role in standing against evil powers, especially in the inner city where oppression is rampant. They say,

> Authentic Christ-centered church planting is confrontational, not only with the host of spiritual forces, but also with people who control the centers of power. When people use those powers to the detriment of the poor or the exclusion of people from opportunity and justice, they are serving evil. Power encounters in church planting often require confronting those who exploit the poor and obstruct human rights. When we love the poor as Jesus loved them, we discover that the task of evangelism also includes the obligation of confronting those who trample the powerless, the poor, and the oppressed.[14]

Summary

Creating churches that function as a community of discipleship, worship and witness is a supernatural act. It depends upon the power of the Word of God and upon the creative work of the Holy Spirit. This model should guide the planning of church planters in the inner city, to insure the development of churches that evidence the the Kingdom of God.

---

13 Howard A. Snyder, *Community of the King* (Downers Grove, IL: InterVarsity Press, 1978), pp. 107-114

14 Shenk and Stutzman, p. 81

Modern Missions' History

An overview of modern Christian missions reveals that two very different church-planting strategies have been employed.

In the early 1800's, Protestant missions followed the "three-self strategy" which was geared to planting indigenous churches. In the later 1800's, in large part due to the effects of colonization, the mentality changed and a mission-controlled strategy predominated.

Mission-Controlled Strategy

The mission-controlled strategy established "mission stations" where missionaries conducted evangelism and service ministries, e.g., a school, a hospital and a church. Local children gathered in the school and a church congregation was formed from the children's families.[15]

These churches were run by missionaries. Indigenous Christians participated but were seldom allowed substantive leadership in the mission enterprise. Missionaries often attempted to change the culture of the converts so that they demonstrated a Western lifestyle. Frequently, the result was that indigenous Christians became socially isolated and could not project a Christian influence on their society.

This strategy produced converts, educated future national leaders in Christian values, alleviated human suffering and established a Christian presence in foreign countries, but it did not necessarily result in a widespread, growing Christian church. Rather it often created converts and churches that remained dependent upon foreign funds and mission leadership. Eventually these mission churches broke free of mission control, but the process frequently created bitterness and misunderstanding on both sides.

Indigenous Church Strategy

The second strategy of missionary church planting sought to create culturally conducive, self-sustaining indigenous churches that were not dependent upon the mission for leadership or finances. In this strategy missionaries accommodated themselves to the local culture and introduced Christ in a way that allowed indigenous Christians to develop their own culturally conducive Christian lifestyle under the Spirit's leading.[16]

---

15 See R. Pierce Beaver, "The History of Mission Strategy," *Perspectives on the World Christian Movement*, ed. Ralph D. Winter and Steven C. Hawthorne (Pasadena, CA: William Carey Library, 1981), p. 196

16 See Beaver, *Perspectives*, p. 201

This strategy created indigenous, self-sustaining and self-reproducing churches that were part of the local culture but like the mission station strategy, the indigenous church strategy faced lingering problems such as transporting Western denominationalism, syncretism with indigenous religions, and failure to balance evangelism and social action.[17] In spite of these difficulties, the indigenous church strategy has been extremely dynamic. It has produced healthy national churches and genuine indigenous leadership for those church bodies. Therefore, in the years following World War II, most faith missions have again adopted the strategy of "indigenous church planting."

The practice of indigenous church planting attempts to follow the example of the Apostle Paul in establishing self-multiplying indigenous churches. The Apostle Paul had amazing success in planting a network of self-sustaining churches, some of which were evangelized, taught and commissioned within a few months.

This was true even though Paul had no advantages over present-day missionaries.[18] He faced many of the same moral, social class and cultural barriers that we face. And he used the same resources available to us – God's Word and Spirit.

The Apostle Paul focused on a simple and brief content of preaching and teaching and exercised great faith in God and in his new converts. Paul trusted that God's Spirit would continue to teach the young church after he moved on and was unavailable to help them.

Modern missionaries who employ Paul's strategy emphasize several church-planting essentials: an absolute dependence upon the work of the Holy Spirit, the simple gospel message communicated with a view to transforming people who respond, the calling and church-planting vision of the church planter and the need to plant in fertile soil among people who are willing to embrace Christ. When these essentials are there, church-planting will result.[19]

---

17 See J. Herbert Kane, *A Concise History of the Christian World Mission* (Grand Rapids: Baker Book House, 1982), pp. 161-164

18 See Roland Allen, *Missionary Methods: St. Paul's or Ours?* (Grand Rapids, MI: Wm. B. Eerdmans Publishing Co., 1962), pp. 1-95

19 See Charles Brock, *The Principles and Practice of Indigenous Church Planting* (Nashville, TN: Broadman Press, 1981), pp. 21-28

Indigenous Churches

The goal of World Impact is to plant indigenous inner-city churches. "Indigenous" means "having originated in and being produced, growing or living naturally in a particular region or environment."[20] Such churches are composed of people who reside in the inner city. They share the life of their communities, and are controlled and financed by the people themselves, not by outsiders.

Alan Tippet supplies six identifying characteristics of an indigenous church.[21]

1. It has an indigenous self-image.
2. It is self-functioning.
3. It is characterized by self-determination.
4. It provides self-support.
5. It is self-propagating.
6. It is self-giving.

The aim in planting indigenous churches is to develop congregations that share an inner-city culture and are able to govern themselves, support themselves and reproduce themselves. The term `self' when applied to the indigenous church does not imply a negation of the Holy Spirit's role in forming the church. It simply means that institutions or people from outside the culture do not control the indigenous church.

Self-Image
Church members see themselves as God's church in their community. They feel responsible as God's people in their city.

If the indigenous church looks, sounds and functions as part of the indigenous culture, its self-image will be positive. It will feel that it has a self-identity from God, not one passed down from some other culture. In a multi-cultural church body it is important to promote positive self-identity among each people-group represented. "Neighborhood people will expect to see some of their own forms of expression in

---

20 "indigenous", *Webster's New Collegiate Dictionary* (Springfield, MA: G. & C. Merriam Co., 1974)

21 Alan Tippet, *Introduction to Missiology* (Pasadena, CA: William Carey Library, 1987), pp. 377-381

liturgy and worship. Dialogue with and openness to indigenous peoples, old and new, are signs of a high-quality relationship between a church and its neighborhood."[22]

Self-Functioning

The church is a body where each member functions according to his/her gift (Ephesians 4:16). The church functions as an organism (relationships, personal support) and as an organization (structure, formal identity).

As an organism the church has different parts that fulfill important functions. The church is not fully functioning if only the pastor does the work of the church. To be a functioning organism every member of the church should participate and contribute according to their God-given gifts and abilities. Paul said, "*to each one* the manifestation of the Spirit is given for the common good" (I Corinthians 12:7).

The church is not self-functioning if it only responds to the missionary's directions. Every missionary church-planter must face the danger of dependency that will hinder indigenous self-functioning. The missionary's role is crucial in church planting. In indigenous church planting what the missionary *does not do* is just as important as what he *does*.

Wherever possible the missionary should use indirect leadership so the budding church does not depend upon him or her for spiritual direction and leadership. He or she should guide the young Christians to look to God and to themselves for leadership. The missionary is an advisor to the leaders chosen by the developing church. This process can begin even before the group is officially constituted as a formal church body. Even a home Bible study group can select its own informal leaders.

The missionary church-planter also "thinks reproducible" in all his/her dealings with the indigenous church. His/her teaching and example center on imparting the life of Christ in a way that is reproducible in the local culture. Charles Brock says, "Normally, he should not do anything which the people cannot do for themselves shortly after they are saved," and, "Do not use anything which the people cannot or will not provide for themselves."[23]

---

22 Clinton E. Stockwell, "Barriers and Bridges to Evangelization in Urban Neighborhoods," Signs of the Kingdom in the Secular City, Ed. David Frenchak and Clinton Stockwell (Chicago: Covenant Press, 1984), p. 104

23 Brock, p.58

These guidelines will help the church planter avoid creating dependency in the budding church. However, the church itself must exercise its gifts so it grows to become a fully self-functioning body. If the young church is taught to depend upon the Holy Spirit and to see Jesus as the head of the Body then self-functioning will likely result.

Self-Determination
The church makes its own decisions without outside interference or control. Decision-making occurs in ways that are culturally appropriate to church members.

Paul provided for self-determination in the churches he planted by appointing elders to lead each church (Acts 14:23). This formal leadership structure developed out of the informal organism of the church. As the church became self-functioning through the exercise of spiritual gifts, it soon became apparent which members were gifted to lead the church body. Those recognized as leaders in the informal network of community relationships then received formal recognition and leadership positions in the church.

One key to Paul's success in church planting was his willingness to appoint leaders quickly, trusting God for their growth and performance. Paul did not hold on to the strings of control indefinitely.

Developing indigenous leadership for the inner-city church is the church planter's first priority, following the initial work of evangelism. Ray Bakke believes, "The congregation can almost always provide whatever is needed for ministry in their own situation. The real difficulty is convincing them of their own power to act and make decisions for themselves."[24]

Building the decision-making capacity of a young church is like muscle-building. Making many small decisions builds the confidence needed to make larger decisions. Missionary church-planter Charles Brock asserts, "The church needs to begin making decisions as it develops. The three-week-old church need not have the knowledge of a ten-year-old church. The planter must be careful to act as counselor, yet not as a decision-maker."[25] Stanley Hallet echoes this attitude, "Experience shows that top-down authority tends to promote dependency, but that decentralized authority allows neighborhood people to begin to shape their own lives."[26]

---

24 Ray Bakke, *The Urban Christian* (Downers Grove, IL: Inter-Varsity Press, 1987), p. 95

25 Brock, p. 34

26 Stanley Hallet, "To Build a City," *Signs of the Kingdom in the Secular City*, p. 7

Missionaries who plant indigenous churches emphasize several distinctives of their church-planting strategy. First, a proper beginning is of utmost importance.[27] The first church planted in an area becomes a model for later churches that are "spun off." Therefore, it is especially important to set up indigenous self-government at an early stage.

The missionary first assumes the role of evangelist. Once a core group of believers is gathered, the missionary takes on the role of teacher. However, even in this early stage the indigenous leaders chosen by the church should hold church government roles. The missionary trains the church leaders who in turn govern the church. From the beginning the church is self-governing.

Self-Support
The church carries its own financial burdens and finances its own social service projects. An indigenous church regards the social problems of its local environment as its own concern and does not rely exclusively on outside resources in addressing needs.

Finances are necessary in church planting. Mission funds support church planters and undergird their initial efforts to gather a church. Nonetheless, finances must be handled carefully if the church is to become self-sustaining. The danger is that the church may become dependent upon outside finances unless the use of mission funds is administered wisely.

Financial considerations often determine the shape of church-planting strategy, especially in low-income areas where potential church members are poor. In discussing possible strategy options Jim Westgate, a church-planting specialist for the Evangelical Free Church, says, "Many house churches carry on with no financial outlay at all. . . when enough house churches are formed, they can merge together and buy a suitable facility. The key in this strategy is one coordinating pastor or leader with trained leaders ministering in the house churches with the intent of merging in the future . . . the house church provides flexibility for penetrating the mosaic of such an urban culture."[28] Others suggest variations of this option in which, ". . . one might encourage house churches in conjunction with a central church that meets once a week or once a month."[29]

---

27 Melvin L. Hodges, *The Indigenous Church* (Springfield, MO: Gospel Publishing House, 1953), pp. 22-23

28 James E. Westgate, "Emerging Church Planting Strategies for World Class Cities" *Urban Mission*, Nov. 1986, pp. 9-10

29 Roger Greenway and Timothy Monsma, *Cities: Mission's New Frontier* (Grand Rapids, MI: Baker Book House, 1989), p. 145

Poverty accents the danger of creating a relationship of continuous dependency where the new church depends upon mission finances instead of trusting God and their own initiative. Wise use of mission finances is essential to insure that they are doing good, not harm, to the new church. Roger Greenway suggests a guideline when he says,

> Mission subsidy and outside assistance do less damage to a young congregation when such funds are used to acquire church property. An unhealthy dependency results when financial subsidy is used to support pastors and programs. . . . This is because the delicate, sensitive relationship between pastor and congregation hinges on mutual trust and dependency. When foreign subsidy is introduced in any form that lessens the pastor's reliance on the congregation, serious damage is done to the pastor-church relationship. But when foreign money buys brick and mortar, or perhaps a city lot on which to erect a building, no long-term dependence is likely to develop; indeed, if a solid congregation is formed, this is frequently a wise use of mission money.[30]

Despite poverty-induced obstacles, urban Christians can finance their own churches. It will not look like a middle-class church. It may be housed in a storefront but it will be theirs. It will be built with their faith and sacrifice. This is important. God uses financial need to build faith in the young church. Church planters must keep the goal of a self-sustaining church in mind as they seek God's wisdom in the use of funds.

Self-Propagation
The indigenous church accepts the Great Commission as its personal responsibility and conducts evangelistic outreach and church expansion accordingly.

From its beginning on the day of Pentecost the church has been a witnessing community. Following Peter's sermon to the gathered multitude, "Those who accepted his message were baptized, and about three thousand were added to their number that day"(Acts 2:41). The early Christians witnessed not out of a sense of duty but from a heart of gratitude toward God and love toward people.

This Spirit-created desire to share Christ is a natural outflow of our new life in Christ. "Because it is a law of her being, the church spontaneously

---

30 Greenway and Monsma, p. 242

shares her faith with others."[31] This natural desire of Christians to share Christ leads to "the spontaneous expansion" of the church.[32] This Spirit-generated expansion begins with individuals and finds expression in the church community. The missionary must nurture this desire for witness from the earliest days of the new church's life together. George Patterson advises missionaries:

> Don't commit the missionaries' greatest sin – controlling the national churches. Keep out of the way. Let them work and grow. That's when you see the "spontaneous" dynamic. By "spontaneous" we mean that the impulse comes from the Body itself, indwelt by the Holy Spirit. The controlling impulse does not come from the missionary. You can share your vision to start the ball rolling, and then you've got to step back and let the Holy Spirit work.[33]

While the missionary should not try to control the church's witness, he/she should set an example of evangelism and church planting. A mission church's ability to reproduce itself once it is independent of the founding mission partly depends upon the model set by the founding missionaries. "A church's view of reproduction will be learned early. Every action of the church planter becomes part of a lesson learned by the church, even during its birth."[34]

As the church moves toward maturity, it must take responsibility for itself. It must plan seriously to reproduce its life in Christ. The church planter cannot insure that every church he plants will become a reproducing church, but he can do everything possible to leave the way open for such a self-reproducing church.

> The greater the nationalization from the beginning of a church planting project, the more likely the planted church will be a reproducing church. This means leadership by local people at their own level of ability and understanding, administering their chosen program to speak to the people in their language and culture. This is reproducible in any society.[35]

---

31 Dean Gilliland, *Pauline Theology and Mission Practice* (Lagos, Nigeria: Tryfam Printers Ltd., 1983), p. 188

32 Roland Allen, *The Spontaneous Expansion of the Church*, (Grand Rapids, MI: Eerdmans, 1962), p. 7

33 George Patterson, "The Spontaneous Multiplication of Churches," *Perspectives*, p. 608

34 Brock, p. 55

35 Brock, p. 60

If the young church sees the example of the missionary church-planter who is eager to grant independence in response to church maturity, the church will more likely accept church reproduction as its inheritance.

Self-Giving

The indigenous church seeks to serve the needs of its community. It sees itself as the hands and feet of Christ in its location.

When asked which was the greatest commandment Jesus replied that two commandments are equally great, "To love the Lord your God with all your heart . . . ," and to "Love your neighbor as yourself" (Mark 12:30-31). We cannot separate our relationship with God from our relationship with people.

Evangelism and social action are like the wings of an airplane. The gospel cannot fly without both wings being intact and operational. Jesus preached the good news, but he also healed the sick.

Rene Padilla asserts that good works are not just something added onto mission work, "rather, they are an integral part of the present manifestation of the Kingdom."[36] He concludes,

> Neither seeing nor hearing will always result in faith. Both word and deed point to the Kingdom of God, but no one can say 'Jesus is Lord' except by the Holy Spirit (I Corinthians 12:3). Every human need, therefore, can be used by the Spirit of God as a beachhead for the manifestation of his kingly power. That is why in actual practice the question of whether evangelism or social action should come first is irrelevant. In every concrete situation the needs themselves provide the guidelines for the definition of priorities.[37]

The need for ministry of both word and deed is especially important in the inner city. Veteran urban missionary Roger Greenway says, "Neither a deed-only nor a word-only strategy is adequate in the city. Poor people need more than bread and more than verbal truth if their lives are to be changed and made whole."[38]

---

36 C. Rene Padilla, *Mission Between the Times* (Grand Rapids: Eerdmans, 1985), p. 198

37 C. Rene Padilla, p. 198

38 Greenway and Monsma, p. 178

Social action, like evangelism, will happen on a person-to-person spontaneous basis. However, since many of the causes of poverty have an institutional basis, the church needs to prepare an institutional response as well.[39] The growing church must plan and organize to respond to needs inside and outside the church. This is the self-giving quality of the church.

Summary of Six Qualities

Each of these six qualities of the indigenous church is an end goal of the process. There are countless decisions of discernment, of give-and-take along the road that lead to a Body that is completely indigenous.

Some mission agencies have labored for decades without planting a single truly indigenous church. After twenty years, the Assembly of God mission in Central America concluded, "Our problem lies in the failure to work for an indigenous church."[40] Correction of that problem led to a spectacular move of God among their work in Latin America.

Even if this goal is in place, church planters must realize that it takes time to develop an indigenous church. It requires a balance between pushing indigeneity too fast and controlling the work too long.[41] However, as the balance of nurture and independence is achieved, a dynamic church can emerge. "When indigenous people . . . think of the Lord as their own, not a foreign Christ; when they do things as unto the Lord, meeting the cultural needs around them, worshiping in patterns they understand; when their congregations function in participation in a body, which is structurally indigenous; then you have an indigenous church."[42] This is World Impact's goal and prayer for the churches that are planted.

---

39 Greenway and Monsma, p. 181

40 Hodges, p. 13

41 Tippet, p.390 Tippet mentions three causes of failure when the mission pulls out too quickly. First is the failure to instill a vision for evangelism in the new church so that it does not reproduce itself once the missionaries have gone. Second is the failure to develop a solid leadership structure in the new church so that internal problems stifle the church life. And third is the failure to develop the stewardship dimension of the church so that it fails to support itself and its outreach. Each aspect of the indigenous church must be nurtured so that the young adult church is able to stand on its own.

42 Tippet, p. 381

Multicultural Congregations

One aspect of the indigenous inner-city congregation is so significant that it deserves special attention in planning. Many missionary church-planters work in a mono-cultural, rural village where they create a church that is indigenous to one group of people. However, because city neighborhoods are increasingly multiethnic, urban church planters may work with several different cultural groups, often tightly compressed into one geographic area. As a result, an indigenous inner-city church will have to think seriously about forming a multiethnic congregation. The church of Christ in an area should reflect the neighborhood's ethnic diversity.

Sound theology and insights from the social sciences lead to valuing diversity within church congregations. The apostolic witness presents a picture of the church in which rich and poor, slave and free, and people of varying nationalities worship together in unity (Romans 12:16; Colossians 3:11-16; James 2:1-12). Because this is good theology, it is also sound practice. Studies indicate that differences in a group facilitate moral development and leadership training.[43]

These benefits do not come without struggle. The early church was torn by conflicts between Jew and Gentile. The difficulties faced by a multicultural congregation are real. Nonetheless, ample evidence suggests that the church in the city has significant reasons to undertake the challenging task of forming bodies that combine diverse cultural and sub-cultural groupings.

A Prophetic Witness to the Kingdom of God

The reconciliation present in a multicultural congregation is a miracle of God's Spirit.

> In cross-cultural churches, there are opportunities to listen to other cultures, to affirm each one's place in the kingdom. A church that is open and secure in its own Christian identity is able to encourage the creative expression of constituent cultures in its life and liturgy. If the Gospel burns through racial and cultural barriers, then the presence of many nationalities in the neighborhood church reflects a microcosm of the kingdom.[44]

---

43 See Terry Cornett and Bob Edwards, "When is a Homogeneous Church Legitimate?", *Evangelical Missions Quarterly*, 20, Jan. 1984, 26-27

44 Stockwell, *Signs of the Kingdom*, p. 99

Because so many people in the city live in multicultural neighborhoods, the multicultural church has a unique opportunity to bear witness to God's plan for harmony and peace within that setting.

Respect for Cultural Groups
The urban church must respect people as individuals and as members of a cultural group. The ministry of the church must reflect this recognition of, and respect for, cultural heritage.[45]

The traditional American view of cultural diversity is that differing cultural groups should "blend in" with the dominant culture. America is viewed as a "melting pot" where people groups lose their distinctives in a common "American" culture. However, some American cities are more like a stew. The people groups mix, but maintain their identity as separate peoples.[46] Koreans interact with Italians, yet normally both retain their own cultural identity.

Churches too often ignore the importance of cultural heritage. "When we do perceive these groups we often do not appreciate and adequately value those things that define their peoplehood."[47] Multicultural churches must recognize the differences between people groups and minister to each group in ways that balance the conflicting needs for separate identity and common identity in Christ.

Alan Tippet advocates the Biblical picture of the church as different folds that are all part of one flock under one Shepherd (John 10:16).[48] Christ is the head of the flock but the flock comprises many different folds, which correspond to different ethnic groups in the church. This image communicates the unity amidst diversity which the multicultural church allows us to maintain and enjoy.

---

45 Church planters should acquaint themselves with the culture and history of ethnic groups they seek to evangelize. They should also explore, in depth, the religious history and existing religious traditions within that group. Two recommended books on black experience are: C. Eric Lincoln and Lawrence H. Mamiya, *The Black Church in African American Experience* (Durham, S.C.: Duke University Press, 1990) and Gayraud S. Wilmore, *Black Religion and Black Radicalism* (Maryknoll, N.Y.: Orbis Books, 1989).

46 See Clifton L. Holland, *The Religious Dimension in Hispanic Los Angeles: A Protestant Case Study*, (Pasadena, CA: William Carey Library, 1974), pp. 115-117

47 Charles L. Chaney, *Church Planting at the End of the Twentieth Century* (Wheaton: Tyndale Press, 1982) p. 134

48 Tippet, p. 367

Adaptability to the Needs of the City

Finally, a multicultural church has the potential to spread the gospel to many different people groups in the city. Harvie Conn speaks of this potential when he says, "The church needs to recognize that the gospel has spread and will continue to spread most naturally in the city through people groups. The evangelistic task should be seen not so much in terms of individuals or countries as in terms of peoples."[49] If the composition of the church represents the neighborhood, the church is likely to impact the entire community for Christ. Since ethnic composition of neighborhoods continually change, multiethnic churches have a distinct advantage in adapting to those changes.

Ethnic Sub-Cultures in the City

Whenever cultural groups converge, a process of `acculturation' or `assimilation' occurs. Acculturation refers to "the changes in cultures that arise from contact with other alien cultures."[50] Marvin Mayers says,

> Acculturation and assimilation differ in degree of adaptation to the new culture. Within the context of acculturation, people adapt to the degree they can effectively function within the context of the new culture. They assume they will leave the new culture at some time and return home. They are fully accepted and respected members of the new culture, yet in essence have a dual identity. . . . Assimilation is the more extreme process. It comes from the realization that one will never return to the society of origin. So one takes on the entire lifeway of the new.[51]

The process of acculturation produces many sub-cultures. Charles Chaney recognizes four divisions within ethnic people groups:

1. Nuclear Ethnics – those explicitly and self-consciously concerned about ethnic tradition.

2. Fellow Traveler Ethnics – those to whom ethnicity is a relatively important part of self-conscious identification.

---

49 Harvie Conn, *A Clarified Vision for Urban Mission* (Grand Rapids, MI: Zondervan, 1987), p. 216

50 Paul G. Hiebert, *Cultural Anthropology,* (Grand Rapids, MI: Baker Book House, 1983), p. 417

51 Stephen A. Grulan and Marvin K. Mayers, *Cultural Anthropology: A Christian Perspective*, (Grand Rapids: Zondervan, 1988), p. 81

3. Marginal Ethnics – those who occasionally think of themselves as ethnics.

4. Assimilated Ethnics – those who explicitly and self-consciously exclude themselves from ethnic collectivity.[52]

The presence of these subgroups will affect our outreach strategy. Chaney lists the implications for church planting as follows:[53]

1. The church should make every effort to win the `assimilated subgroup' to Christ and incorporate them into the English-speaking church.

2. To reach the "marginal" group for Christ requires adding a staff member from the marginal group and incorporating some of the marginal group's worship forms into the English service.

3. The "fellow traveler" ethnics require a bilingual or bicultural church. This subgroup may eventually require a new congregation. This may begin as a separate-language class that evolves into a separate congregation.

4. Unassimilated or `nuclear' ethnics, require a church indigenous in language, culture, and, as quickly as possible, leadership. They demand a church that looks, sounds, and functions as part of their culture.

Models of Multicultural Worship

A variety of models of church structure can accommodate a multicultural body that expresses unity in Christ and respect for cultural diversity.[54] Those that best suit cross-cultural urban church planting include:

1. *Single-language multicultural church.* There is one service in the predominate language for several different cultural groups. The

---

52 See Chaney, pp. 135-139 World Impact missionaries might note the high degree of correspondence between this concept of ethnicity and our model of C1, C2 and C3 ethnics.

53 Chaney, pp. 162-165

54 See Tetsunao Yamamori, "How to Reach Urban Ethnics", *Urban Mission* 1.4, March, 1984, pp. 29-35 and Jerry L. Appleby, *Missions Have Come Home To America: The Church's Cross-Cultural Ministry to Ethnics* (Kansas City: Beacon Hill Press, 1986), pp. 93-97 for a full discussion of these models.

services are often less formal and include the cultural forms of the groups represented in the church. This model could include assimilated and marginal ethnics.[55]

2. *Multilanguage classes church.* Here the English-speaking church begins Bible-study classes in different languages to reach various language groups in the community. These classes could meet in homes as cell groups or in the church facility as Sunday School classes. This model could be used to reach unassimilated ethnic groups where language barriers must be crossed.

3. *Multiworship church.* Here more than one worship service is held in the same facility as part of one church organization. The difference in the services may be cultural but is usually language based. This model could accommodate all the ethnic groupings (assimilated, marginal, fellow-traveler and nuclear) provided bi-cultural leaders are present.

4. *Multiethnic-mutually-autonomous churches.* In this model separate ethnic congregations with their own leadership and organization share a facility and cooperate in ministry. This is sometimes called the `umbrella' model. This model could conceivably include all the ethnic subgroups.

Obviously, many variations and combinations of these models can be used to meet the specific needs of an individual neighborhood. Which strategy of multicultural church ministry is suitable in a given situation depends upon the nature of the people group we are seeking to include in the church.

Note that language functions as a good guide to the degree of assimilation present. When dealing with multilanguage congregations, church planters should choose models that allow separate congregational life for each language group.

Generally, worship, communion, baptism and fellowship can be seen as multicultural, large congregation activities. Preaching, teaching, evangelism, discipleship, service and nurture should often be done within the context of the specific cultural group, especially if language barriers are involved. The general principle of respecting diversity while maintaining unity should continue to function as the church's overall guideline.

---

55 If the Multi-worship model or the Multi-ethnic-mutually-autonomous-churches model is used, this Single-language-multicultural-church model may be used as one of the separate congregations inside the larger structure.

A Strategy for Planting Churches

Strategy for an Urban Area

World Impact's goal is to use the principles of indigenous church planting to plant a cluster of churches in an urban area. It is not World Impact's desire to develop isolated, individual congregations, but rather, a network of mutually supporting congregations in proximity to each other.

There are four reasons to develop clusters of congregations.:

1. The large number of unchurched people in the inner city calls for a dynamic strategy that will reach multiple neighborhoods for Christ.
2. Newly planted churches need supportive networking with other churches.
3. Not every congregation will proceed to full-fledged-church identity. Some will fail or will combine with other near-by congregations.
4. A dynamic strategy insures greater indigenous-leadership development.

The following section describes a strategy for planting a single church in an inner-city area. Church planters will need to repeat these steps in each target area to create clusters of mutually supportive churches.

World Impact's church-planting strategy consists of seven steps.[56]

> A. Commission the Church Planting Team
>
> B. Cultivate the Community
>
> C. Establish Discipling Fellowships
>
> D. Form a Celebration Group
>
> E. Plan the Finances
>
> F. Determine Facilities
>
> G. Constitute the Church

---

56 We would like to acknowledge our indebtedness to Jack Redford's excellent book *Planting New Churches* (Nashville: Broadman Press, 1978) as a guideline for church-planting strategy. Although we have modified his steps to apply more directly to the cross-cultural missions situation, they serve as a framework for this section.

Commission the Church-Planting Team

Value of Team Strategy

Churches and mission agencies employ a variety of church-planting strategies.[57] Some strategies work best when planting churches in one's own culture. Such methods lead to expansion or extension of the church in a given culture. However, a mission organization does "bridging-growth" church planting across cultures.[58] The cross-cultural nature of missionary church planting calls for tested methods and strategies.

The strategy of using church-planting teams has proven effective in cross-cultural church planting.[59] The Apostle Paul functioned as the leader of a church-planting team commissioned by the church in Antioch (Acts:13:1-4). Paul continued the team approach throughout his years of church-planting ministry (Acts 16:6). Team church planting was not the only church-planting strategy employed in the New Testament church, but it was the predominant strategy.

Modern missions have often followed Paul's example of sending a team of missionaries to plant churches cross-culturally.[60] They cite several reasons for their use of the team strategy.[61] First, the team itself is a microcosm of the kingdom. The team's life together models the church to those converted through evangelism in the target community (John 13:35).

Second, culturally dissimilar team members can help when planting churches cross-culturally. Paul may have selected Timothy because he was a bi-cultural person who could help in reaching the Greeks (Acts 16:1-3). Luke also helped Paul in the cross-cultural ministry

---

57 See Elmer Towns, *Getting a Church Started*, (Lynchburg, VA: Church Growth Institute, 1985), pp. 69-116

58 James H. Feeney, *Church Planting By The Team Method*, (Anchorage: Abbott Loop Christian Center, 1988), p. 21

59 See Dan Bacon and William Goheen, "Should Mission Boards Send Teams as Well as Individuals?", *Perspectives on the World Christian Movement*, pp. 775-781

60 See David Hesselgrave, *Planting Churches Cross-Culturally*, (Grand Rapids: Baker Book House, 1980), pp. 135-154 and Charles J. Mellis, *Committed Communities: Fresh Streams for World Missions*, (Pasadena: William Carey Library, 1976), pp. 93-104

61 See Shenk and Stutzman, pp. 42-55

to Greeks. A culturally diverse church-planting team is especially effective in the cross-cultural mission.

Third, team members share power. This sharing of authority makes it easier to include indigenous converts in the decision-making structure of the newly forming church. If the team is multicultural, it helps the target people groups feel a sense of identification with the team and representation in the new church.

Fourth, team members provide care, support and community for one another. This aspect of team ministry was especially important for the Apostle Paul. In his letters Paul mentions by name thirty-eight partners in ministry.[62] This is a vital principle in urban missions where, because of the pressures and propensity toward "burnout," the "average length of service is not much more than four years."[63] Since "a major psychological factor [in burnout]. . . is loneliness and isolation"[64] the use of ministry teams is an important part of caring for the ministers so they in turn can care for others.

Kevin Dyer, who has helped send church-planting teams to four continents over the past twenty-five years summarizes the value of team ministry in church planting when he says, "We are thoroughly convinced of the value of the team effort. What can be accomplished together is so much greater than what can be accomplished by individuals working on their own."[65]

Forming the Team
Mission organizations that employ church-planting teams acknowledge "the success of a cross-cultural church-planting team is greatly influenced by the leadership/followership skills, gifts, and abilities of the team members."[66] Screening and selection of team members is an important first step in forming a church-planting team.

---

62 See Shenk and Stutzman, p. 49

63 David Claerbaut, *Urban Ministry* (Grand Rapids, MI: Zondervan, 1983), p. 205

64 David Frenchek, *Quoted in Urban Ministry*, p. 206

65 Kevin Dyer, "Crucial Factors in Building Good Teams", *Helping Missionaries Grow*, ed. Kelly and Michele O'Donnell, (Pasadena, CA: William Carey Library, 1988), p. 126

66 Thomas Graham, "How To Select the Best Church Planters", *Helping Missionaries Grow*, p. 46

Proper screening and selection begin with a clear statement of World Impact's philosophy and mission, a definition of the tasks that define this mission and a set of characteristics and qualifications needed in those who join undertaking the mission.[67]

Because the work is challenging and demanding, the biblical qualifications for leadership are stringent. The Bible lists twenty-eight separate qualifications for church leaders in the Epistles.[68] These include such character traits as being of good report, of good behavior, vigilant, temperate, hospitable, patient, and not being greedy or self-willed.

In addition to the character traits outlined in Scripture, the following characteristics are helpful to the prospective church planter: "A sense of call; spiritual maturity; submissive leadership; goal/performance orientation; discipling/nurturance skills; psychological maturity; functional intelligence; creativity; communication skills; cross-cultural adaptability; physical vitality . . ."[69]

These qualities are first seen in the team leader. Though the team shares authority, it is important to have a leader with the vision, gifts and experience to guide the team and make it effective. Vision is needed because the work is difficult. There are many obstacles, especially in cross-cultural church planting. Jack Redford says,

> Motivation is essential. Costs are often high and always an enormous amount of time is required on the part of the church planter. Forty-hour weeks will never get churches planted, nor will just going to meetings. Church planting is endless, tiresome, demanding, and extremely hard.[70]

In addition to having vision, the leader of the team also must be gifted as a church planter... Many believe the gift of being a church planter is akin to the biblical gift of apostle (Ephesians 4:11). This gift is the Spirit-inspired calling and ability to do pioneer church planting. Charles Chaney says, "I believe that church planting is very closely related to

---

67 See Graham, *Helping Missionaries Grow*, p. 48

68 See Feeney, p. 105-110

69 Graham, *Helping Missionaries Grow*, p. 50

70 Redford, p. 18

the apostolic gift. I fervently and regularly pray . . . that God will raise up apostles, gifted men and women, who can gather churches."[71]

Finally, "The team leader must see himself primarily as an enabler to the team. . . . He helps them reach their goals. When a team leader is primarily concerned with what he personally is going to do, the team is often less successful."[72]

In filling out the remainder of the team, it is important to select men and women who have the same high standards of Biblical character as the team leader. However, their gifts need not (and in most cases should not) be exactly the same as the team leader. It is in the diversity of the team that its primary advantages are seen. Balanced teams possess not only relational and evangelistic gifts but also administrative gifts and the gift of teaching. A varied background of culture and experiences among team members is usually helpful in cross-cultural church planting.

World Impact's teams will normally form around a core of two full-time church planters. These members commit to staying through the entire church-planting cycle. They may be either singles or couples. They will be supplemented by up to four support team members.[73] The support members may be World Impact staff who volunteer part-time to serve the church-planting effort. Alternatively, these staff may be assigned to the church-planting effort full-time for a specified period. They may be indigenous community members who have been discipled and are ready to support the effort. Seminary students or other volunteers may be used to supplement the team by assisting in research or other specialized tasks. Many combinations of staff, community and volunteer support team members may be used. The goal is to build teams that provide the support, giftedness and cross-cultural ability to accomplish the church-planting objective. Flexibility in adapting to the specific situation is essential.

Team members should see themselves as servants: first of Christ, then of the indigenous community and of each other. Loyalty to the team and its leadership, along with the disciplines of mutual submission and accountability, are commitments that need to be made and nurtured during the training process.

---

71 Chaney, p. 75

72 Dyer, p. 127

73 If church planting teams are too large, they become inefficient and incohesive. Large church planting teams may also inhibit indigenous leadership development.

Team formation and training follow the screening and selection process. A church-planting team should come together for a period of interaction and adjustment to develop group cohesion. This group-forming process often involves intensive cross-cultural training. Dayton and Fraser, in their book on planning mission strategy, acknowledge,

> The missions community recognizes that cross cultural training in communicating the gospel and planting the church is essential. . . . The task of on-site training of missionaries needs to be viewed as the highest missionary calling, not an interruption of the real task.[74]

Veteran missionaries advocate training through hands-on practical experience in cross-cultural ministry. Many believe a team formation training period is essential to establish effective church-planting teams. Kevin Dyer says,

> Training became the indispensable key to success for building and developing our teams. Since we began a six-month intensive training program, our casualty rate on the field has plummeted to four percent. . . . we have found that six months is about the optimum time. Most prospective missionaries can put on a spiritual front for about six weeks, but after that the cracks begin to appear under intense pressure. At about the four month stage, another crucial time is faced. The reality of what is ahead has clearly been faced and the team has or has not jelled.[75]

Once the team has been screened, selected, trained and formed into a cohesive unit, they are then commissioned and sent out with the support, prayers and direction of the mission. Commissioning is important to assure that the Holy Spirit is recognized as the author of the church-planting effort. Shenk and Stutzman affirm that,

> One's personal sense of call must be confirmed by the church. Otherwise, two serious problems may arise. First, it might be that the aspiring church planter has ulterior motives. Perhaps the idea to plant a church is of one's own making and not from the Lord. If the church planting ministry is not God's appointment, the church planter may become quickly discouraged and the effort will not bear

---

74 Edward R. Dayton and David A. Fraser, *Planning Strategies for World Evangelization*, (Grand Rapids: Eerdmans, 1990), p. 155

75 Kevin Dyer, "Crucial Factors in Building Good Teams", *Helping Missionaries Grow*, p. 127

lasting spiritual fruit. The second problem is that the church planter needs a praying community to provide encouragement. If the planter is a loner, long term survival is doubtful.[76]

Commissioning assures church planters of God's confirmation and the Body's support as they embark on the adventure of planting a new church in the inner city.

---

76 Shenk and Stutzman, p. 34

Cultivate the Community

Spiritual Warfare

The essence of church planting is taking territory for the reign of Christ. The church-planting team is invading areas falsely claimed by Satan with the good news of Christ's redemption and triumph. They intend to plant "communities of the Kingdom" which will change people and neighborhoods both now and in the years to come.

Obviously, Satan will not take this invasion lightly. Thus, the initial steps toward understanding and cultivating communities to receive the gospel are based on a recognition of spiritual realities. Every member of the church-planting team should understand that they have volunteered to engage in spiritual warfare of the highest and most crucial order.

The church-planting team should begin by gathering prayer support for their efforts that focuses on defeating Satan's forces and loosing the power of the Holy Spirit in their target area (Matthew 18:18-20). Supporting churches are an excellent resource for prayer support as are existing World Impact Celebration bodies, Bible studies, etc. Be creative and aggressive in enlisting groups of believers to pray consistently for the endeavor.

Second, the team itself should set aside a regular time to do spiritual warfare for the church-planting effort. This is the single most important part of the task and the priorities of the team should reflect this. This priority must be jealously safeguarded as the many urgent pressures created by the task of church planting clamor for the time and attention of the church planters.

Third, the team should work to increase its knowledge of effective spiritual warfare. Bible studies on this topic are critical. Study books on spiritual warfare.[77] Read, discuss and apply principles from missiological journals and missionary biographies.

Nowhere is it more true than in the task of church planting that "... our struggle is not against flesh and blood, but against the rulers, against the authorities, against the powers of this dark world and against the spiritual forces of evil in the heavenly realms" (Ephesians

---

77 A good starting point for this is the book *Taking Our Cities for God: How to Break Spiritual Strongholds by John Dawson* (Lake Mary, FL: Creation House, 1989)

6:12). The starting point for winning a community is to understand and battle the evil forces that seek to control it.

Researching Your Community
Church planting presumes a thorough understanding of Scripture and its commands. However, these commands are put into practice in a very concrete world. Our ability to obey Scripture is inseparably linked to our knowledge of the community in which we minister.

The church-planting team should focus its efforts on a specific community. Geographical boundaries and contacts within the community will influence the intial selection of a target community for church planting. However, later discoveries may modify this selection.

The task of the team is to discover as much as possible about the make-up of this community. This effort should start with a large map of the city. Detailed maps of a specific area of the city can often be obtained at no charge from the mayor's office, chambers of commerce, planning commission or highway department.

"The idea is to walk through the neighborhood and note on the map locations of agencies, institutions, places of employment, stores, parks and public places; to note the conditions of housing, parks, streets, and institutions; and to write down impressions about the tour and about places that might merit a second visit."[78] Mark existing churches on the map using symbols to denote specific denominations.[79] Identify and mark residential and business sections as well.

Study the population data available for the target area. Ethnic make-up of the area, education levels, age structure, types of housing and population mobility can be obtained through studying U.S. census reports, and by contacting city or county planning commissions. Collect these in written form and refer to them in all stages of planning. Where applicable, incorporate this information onto the map for easy visual reference. Professionally prepared demographic profiles and display maps for church planters, based on U.S. census data, are available for a fee.[80]

---

78 Stockwell, *Signs of the Kingdom*, pp. 101-102

79 You should obtain a handbook of denominations that will acquaint you with the basics of any church group with which you are not familiar. *Handbook of Denominations in the United States* (Nashville: Abingdon Press, Ninth Edition, 1990) by Frank S. Mead is one example of a useful guide to this area.

80 For more information on professionally prepared demographic information contact Church Information and Development Services, 3001 Redhill Ave, Suite 2-220, Costa Mesa, CA 92626, (800) 442-6277

The information obtained will help the church planters to anticipate the needs they will face and plan possible responses in advance. Taking this information seriously may influence the composition of the church-planting team, reveal the need for strategies that focus on certain age levels, suggest the inclusion of certain languages in worship services or ministry outreaches, or reveal specific residential complexes to visit. . . . It may even suggest the need to alter the geographical boundaries of the target church-planting area.

Data about the make-up of the community is a critical starting point but it is only a starting point. Church planters must move from a theoretical knowledge of the community to a knowledge based on actual human relationships.

Networking

To insure that this happens, urban missions specialist Ray Bakke suggests that pastors invest one day a week in "networking" their communities.[81] This networking involves several components.

First, there is the need for networking with other pastors. Bakke recounts the way in which he approached the problem.

> My first move was to meet all the other pastors. I started out to visit eighty-three churches, getting to forty-four in the first nine months. Fifty-three of them had services in languages other than English. I did not trouble myself with whether they were "sound" theologically or not and always used the opening speech. "My brother, my name is Ray Bakke. I am the new pastor of Fairfield Baptist Church and I want your help. I'm new to this community and I wonder if you could tell me the most important lesson you've learned about being a pastor here." I went to affirm my colleagues and learn from them.[82]

A letter may be used for contacting community churches. It provides a starting point for introducing them to your church-planting efforts. However, a visit should also eventually be made since the point is to create relational networks within the community. "Assurance should be given that the new churches do not desire to proselyte but want only to join hands with existing churches in seeking to reach the unchurched and to give a more adequate ministry to the community."[83] If the initial

---

81 See Bakke, pp. 100-11

82 Bakke, p. 111

83 Redford, p. 58

contact is met with suspicion, the pastor must respond graciously. Whenever possible he should try to discover the source of the person's complaint and ask them what he could do to alleviate it. "No church planter gains any ground when he appears to say, 'We've come to this community to show all you folks how to have a real, genuine church,' implying that the existing churches are not real and genuine."[84] The attitude of the church planter toward others must be humility, eagerness to serve and a willingness to learn.

If the church-planting effort is occurring in a city where World Impact already ministers, it is important to include other World Impact staff in this process as well. Schedule time with them and ask them what they have learned. The church-planting team should consciously tap the wealth of knowledge that exists inside the missionary community.

Extend this same process to social service agencies in the community, both public (police, firefighters, schools, hospitals, etc.) and private (food pantries, Legal Aid, etc.). Anyone with long term experience in the community is a valuable source of practical experience. They should be visited and informed of what the church-planting team is doing. The point is to discover what resources or services they provide, learn from their experience and let them know that the new church has an interest in them and the larger community.

Finally, contact garages, factories, financial institutions, shops; any place where potential church members may work, shop, recreate or socialize. Don't neglect informal leaders in this process. Many housing projects, for example, contain strong informal leaders who are instrumental in organizing life inside their communities. These informal leaders are critical links for understanding and gaining access to the community.

Bakke recounts the following results from one such investment.

> When I did this exercise, I visited forty-four local businesses in my first year. These included groceries, one-man businesses, garages and mechanics. I went to bars because they are centers of fellowship for the community, where people gather to pour their hearts out over drinks. One pastor I knew visited a bar and the manager complained about a drunken customer slobbering all over the bar and putting all the other customers off. The pastor reflected on this and offered the manager the presence of two people who would sit at the back of

---

84 Redford, p. 60

the bar in the evenings. When a troublesome customer came in the manager would say, "Here is a caring team who are willing to listen to you." The "carers" wore distinctive jackets with logos on them. The pastor was a Southern Baptist, and the congregation found it hard to understand when he and other members came in smelling as though they had fallen into a barrel of bad wine. But they had more baptisms from the taverns in one year than from many evangelistic missions.[85]

Spending time on personal contacts such as these may appear to use up precious ministry time in the short run but in the long run it provides invaluable relationships, updated information, linkage to resources and ministries that might otherwise be duplicated, and the ability to see the community from the viewpoint of the congregation.

As contacts are made with the community and the team comes to know its people, it is ready to begin the process of evangelization and church planting.

Evangelization
The Book of Acts recounts the evangelism of the early church. The Holy Spirit guided the first Christians to spread the message of Christ, "first in Jerusalem, and in all Judea and Samaria, and to the ends of the earth" (Acts 1:8). Ervin Hastey lists the methods of witnessing in the first century:

1. The public proclamation of the divine message.
2. The teaching from house to house, in public places, in forums, and in synagogues.
3. The informal witnessing – the gossiping of the gospel.
4. The healings, such as found in Acts 3, that opened the door for sharing Christ.
5. The miracles performed by Jesus, Paul, Peter and others.
6. The fellowshipping of the believers which testified to the love of God. People saw how Christians loved one another and were drawn to the fellowship.[86]

---

85 Bakke, pp. 116-117

86 See Ervin E. Hastey, "Reaching the Cities First: A Biblical Model of World Evangelization", Ed. Larry L. Rose, C. Kirk Hadaway, *An Urban World: Churches Face the Future*, (Nashville: Broadman Press, 1984), pp. 160-161

Michael Green summarizes the effective witness of these early Christians, saying, "When men have the will to speak of their Lord, they find no shortage of ways in which to do it. Indeed, it is the motivation of these men and women which impresses us more than their methods."[87] Likewise, the motivation for evangelism is more important than the methods of the church-planting team, although culturally appropriate methods are needed.

These methods reveal a Scriptural world view which sees evangelism as both proclamation and affirmation of the gospel. Proclamation is "an action through which the non-Christian receives a clear statement of the essential message" while affirmation is "a process of modeling and explaining the Christian message."[88] World Impact combines these aspects of evangelism when we say evangelism includes "everything we do that reveals the love of Christ to our neighbors."[89] This includes both our words and our actions.[90]

Through the years, World Impact's predominant method has been "incarnational evangelism." World Impact staff move into the target communities. They live in the inner-city neighborhood and relate to neighbors as fellow-residents of the community. Children's Bible clubs and teen clubs initiate access to neighborhood families. Adult home Bible studies provide an evangelistic forum for interested parents.

This incarnational strategy of evangelism is especially appropriate to the inner-city culture because it accents person-to-person relationships. Face-to-face communication and friendship is extremely important for communicating the gospel in the urban context. Immigrant and ethnic populations in the inner cities show a strong preference for communication via the spoken word within a context of relationship. Evangelism strategies must take this seriously.

World Impact's evangelism has also been family-oriented, including outreach to children and teens as well as adults. In communities where two-thirds of the residents are under the age of sixteen, this is a culturally

---

87 Michael Green, *Evangelism in the Early Church*, (Grand Rapids, MI: Eerdmans, 1970), p. 178

88 Jim Peterson, *Evangelism as a Lifestyle*, (Colorado Springs: NavPress, 1980), p. 22

89 *World Impact Mission Strategy*, (World Impact Staff Training Manual, 1980), p. 59

90 See Bruce Nicholls, *In Word and Deed: Evangelism and Social Responsibility*, (Grand Rapids, MI: Eerdmans, 1985)

appropriate methodology.[91] While churches cannot be built on a foundation of child evangelism, it must be understood that children are a major area of concern in the lives of inner-city people. Many people harbor frustration and guilt over their inability to parent effectively in the face of difficult situations. Others struggle with anxiety over the temptations facing their children and are actively seeking resources to help them prepare their children to overcome them. To effectively evangelize, missionaries must understand people in their role as parents and seek to address their needs and concerns. If done well, the result will be the evangelization of both parent and child.

World Impact's model of evangelism is also holistic, seeking to address the practical needs of families as well as spiritual needs. This is of special importance in physically impoverished areas. Ervin Hastey comments, "In today's cities it is being found that a holistic approach to witnessing to their inhabitants is giving good results. Hospitals, clinics, schools, food centers, halfway houses, and goodwill centers are more and more using their ministries not only to proclaim and teach the gospel but also to establish churches."[92]

Other evangelistic strategies have been used in the inner city: open air concerts and preaching, evangelistic films and door to door visitation. Many more strategies must be created as well as learned from other urban ministers. No matter which method is used to present the gospel, prayer must be central in both planning and implementation. Concluding a study of New Testament evangelism Harvie Conn says, "Biblical evangelizing is a twofold commission: to preach and to pray, to talk to people about God and to talk to God about people."[93]

Once contacts have been made, the gospel presented, and the first people converted through faith in Christ, they need encouragement to reach their networks of friends, family and co-workers. The first converts become "bridges" through which their relational network can be reached. Church planters can pray and expect that the gospel will spread along relational lines in the community.[94] These networks of

---

91 This is not a call to restrict our evangelism to these age levels but to continue to take them seriously in light of urban realities.

92 Hastey, p. 161

93 Harvie Conn, *Evangelism: Doing Justice and Preaching Grace*, (Grand Rapids, MI: Zondervan, 1982), p. 86

94 See Donald McGavran, *The Bridges of God*, (New York: Friendship Press, 1955), p. 31

"friends in Christ" become the foundation for cell groups that are the forerunners of the established church.

In summary, evangelism begins with motivation inspired by love for Christ and others that produces a zeal to obey the Great Commission. It is implemented through the use of culturally appropriate methods of communication.[95] And it is covered throughout by continuing, urgent prayer. The dynamic of evangelism: converts sharing their faith with family, friends, neighbors and co-workers, must continue throughout all the stages of church planting.

---

95 See David Hesselgrave, *Communicating Christ Cross-Culturally*, (Grand Rapids, MI: Zondervan, 1978)

Establish Discipling Fellowships

Once the first converts are won to Christ, the four steps of building discipling groups begin:

1. Start the initial cell group.
2. Recruit and train apprentice leaders.
3. Form new groups as soon as possible.
4. Meet regularly with cell group leaders.[96]

Start the Initial Cell Groups
The initial cell groups take on different characteristics according to the needs and distinctives of the target group. Bible study groups study the Word of God corporately and develop new relationships in the community. Contact groups are action-oriented, focusing on evangelization through special events such as concerts or other outreach activities. Task-oriented groups organize around a point of service, such as setting up a community food pantry, or ministering to the handicapped. Worship groups emphasize singing and prayer as primary activities. Forum groups discuss issues of community interest or concern, gaining biblical insights and awakening people's understanding of a Christian world view. Other groups could be created based on an understanding of the gifts, personalities and needs of the participants.[97] Regardless of the particular accent, each type of group should evidence the five activities mentioned in Acts 2:41-47: study, fellowship, worship, stewardship and witness.[98]

The initial meetings can occur in any suitable location: a home, school,[99] hotel, restaurant, store, park or community center. The church planters should choose a location that is not objectionable to those entering the

---

[96] Robert E. Logan, "How to Start a Growing and Reproducing Church", Taken from Peter Wagner course outline "Techniques of Planting New Churches" offered at Fuller Seminary (Robert E. Logan, 1988), p. 5

[97] See Redford, p. 64 and Robert C. Linthicum, *City of God, City of Satan: A Biblical Theology of the Urban Church*, (Grand Rapids, MI: Zondervan, 1991), pp. 274-277

[98] David Hesselgrave, *Planting Churches Cross-Culturally*, (Grand Rapids: Baker, 1980), p. 272

[99] Many schools are required by state or local ordinance to make their facilities available to community groups at no or minimal rental charges.

fellowship. World Impact staff homes can serve as a temporary starting point for the initial cell groups, but, to avoid dependency, other World Impact facilities will normally not be used.[100]

The meeting time should be selected to coincide with the availability of the new converts. Leaders should be sensitive to the group regarding the most suitable length of meetings. Cultural perceptions of time (e.g., whether the group has event- centered time orientation) must be taken seriously in organizing the meeting and deciding how flexible starting and ending times should be.

Church planters must have an outline of lessons so that the teaching in the early meetings is directed and effective. Because the church is "a fellowship of believers committed to obeying the Lord Jesus Christ," George Patterson advocates a focus on "obedience oriented teaching" that stresses practical accountability in order to verify application of what is learned. He suggests that the following scripturally prescribed areas be the foundation of the curriculum.

1. Faith and Repentance from sin
2. Baptism
3. Love
4. The Lord's Supper (Communion)
5. Prayer
6. Giving
7. Witnessing[101]

The centrality of the Kingdom of God, social justice, spiritual warfare and identity in Christ should also be taught early in this process.

As the initial fellowship group is taught and nurtured it is important to leave the door open to new converts. "Adjust the program of evangelism so as to encourage both converts from the world and converts from nominal Christian backgrounds to enter the new fellowship."[102] Such openness will encourage members to witness by inviting their friends to Christ and to the fellowship.

---

100 If special circumstances make the use of other World Impact facilities necessary, this should only be done with prior financial and phase-out agreements.

101 George Patterson, *Church Planting Through Obedience Oriented Teaching*, (Pasadena, CA: William Carey Library, 1981), p. 1

102 Hesselgrave, 1980, p. 271

Church planters are bound to encounter obstacles as they seek to form a cohesive mission fellowship. Troubled people may disrupt the group. Attendance may be sporadic. Children will need attention and care to allow parental participation.[103] The leader must move, with prayer and the Spirit's guidance, to overcome these obstacles to insure the success of the group.

Recruit and Train Leaders

Once the group is functioning, people are growing in Christ, and new members are being added, the leaders must concentrate on training the emerging indigenous leaders in the group. These emerging leaders will soon be called upon to lead the existing group so the church planters can focus on newly forming fellowships. One-on-one discipleship is a key tool for the missionary in training individual indigenous leaders.[104]

One-on-one discipleship has been the foundation of World Impact's ministry since its inception. World Impact's strategy statement affirms, "Our mission strategy is `to make God known' through evangelism, follow-up, discipleship and church planting."[105] This strategy is one which Mortimer Arias calls "discipleship evangelization."[106] The goal is not to make converts who give intellectual assent to the gospel and attend church but rather to produce disciples who are equipped to lead an indigenous church.

Discipleship, or training others to train others, begins with the selection of new Christians who show faithfulness during the follow-up process. Success in church-planting is directly linked to the identification and development of leaders from the indigenous community. These future leaders need to become the priority of the church-planter. It is here that the model of Christ and his disciples has its most direct application. The church planting team must spend significant amounts of time with these future leaders, not only in actual training for ministry but also personal and relational time in which the Christian life is modeled as well as taught.

---

103 Note that many cultures allow children to attend adult group meetings. The church planter should discover what is normative for the group of people that he works with.

104 See Keith Phillips, *The Making of a Disciple*, (Old Tappan, NJ: Fleming H. Revell Company, 1981)

105 *World Impact Mission Strategy*, 1991

106 Mortimer Arias, *Announcing the Reign of God: Evangelization and the Subversive Memory of Jesus* (Philadelphia, PA: Fortress Press, 1984), p. 101

When discipling indigenous leaders, church planters must proceed with "phase-out eyes."[107] As Jesus selected disciples to carry on the work of the Kingdom after his departure, so church planters must oversee development of indigenous leaders who can guide the church once the church-planting team departs. The end goal of missionary phase-out must be kept in the forefront of team planning.

It is important that the missionary spend time training group leaders, not only individually but also together so they can mutually equip and support each other. Because the discipling groups will eventually be combined into one church body, it is necessary that individual group leaders learn to function as a team.

The indigenous group leaders' practical training should include, not only character development and a study of the Word of God but also an instilling of the church-planting vision, and an understanding of the Biblical priority of justice for the poor and the church's role in that process.[108] It should also, at this stage, include in-depth work on witnessing and group leading as well as specific instruction on how to teach the curriculum utilized by the Fellowship groups. The growth and maturity of these emerging leaders is the key to developing new Fellowship groups.

Form New Groups

The goal is to multiply the groups as soon as possible. Splitting the groups helps to insure continued growth by making room for new converts and by allowing opportunity for the emergence of additional indigenous leadership. It is important to remember that many people in impoverished urban areas are reluctant to deal with institutions and have experience only in leadership roles involving small groups. While gifted leaders of large groups will undoubtedly emerge, the majority of the people encountered will probably be more comfortable in small group leadership roles. Thus, the embryonic church is much better off with ten discipling fellowships containing ten people each than with one group containing one hundred. "The responsibility given to each man must not exceed his strength, ability and time. A large group will

---

107 Tom A. Steffen, *Tribal and Peasant Church Planting: A Comprehensive Phase Out Model,* (unpublished doctoral dissertation, Biola University, 1990)

108 See Robert C. Linthicum, *City of God, City of Satan: A Biblical Theology of the Urban Church,* (Grand Rapids, MI: Zondervan, 1991) for a study on this theme.

quickly overload an untrained leader. On the other hand, a small group will stretch, but not break and discourage him."[109]

Meet Regularly with Cell Group Leaders

The church planters must pray for guidance about when to form new fellowship groups. They must insure that the separate units remain unified with each other and with the leaders. It is helpful to plan events such as picnics or pot-luck dinners that bring all the groups together for times that build a bond of love and trust.

Such activities build the organizational decision-making confidence of the developing leaders. This confidence is needed to move from discipling groups to a combined worship meeting. Urban Christians are often unaccustomed to making confident decisions within a group context.[110] Many feel powerless and victimized. The urban church planter must consciously build their decision-making confidence. Ray Bakke says, "You build decision-making as you build muscle – by gentle exercise. You use concrete, small, nonthreatening issues to start with. People cannot jump from paternalized, welfare-state dependency to democracy in one stride."[111]

David Claerbaut sees leadership development as a three-step process.[112] First, church planters must help new Christians in a holistic manner. Urbanites have many more problems than just spiritual ones. They lack money, proper housing, adequate education, legal protection. They are often plagued by relational or family problems, such as having a family member with a drug or alcohol problem."[113] Second, this help must proceed into the "mutually caring alliance" of the discipling group. Supportive group relationships must be available. Third, within this intimate setting, the new Christians must be encouraged to strengthen their gifts. Claerbaut notes "there is always a tendency for urban workers to see the poor as those with less education, less power, and

---

109 Ray Guy, "Pilgrimage Toward the House Church", *Discipling the City*, Ed. Roger Greenway, (Grand Rapids, MI: Baker Book House, 1979), p. 126

110 A valuable book on group decision-making is Em Griffin's *Getting Together: A Guide for Good Groups*, (Downers Grove, IL: Inter-Varsity Press, 1982)

111 Bakke, p. 95

112 See David Claerbaut, *Urban Ministry*, (Grand Rapids: Zondervan, 1983), p. 195

113 Claerbaut, p. 194

less wealth, and therefore as lesser people."[114] Leaders must overcome this attitude and draw out the distinctive gifts God has given each person.

In addition to the informal discipleship training provided by church planters, developing indigenous leaders also should include formal educational training. While such training will not be a requirement for church leadership, church planters should promote the benefit of formal Bible and theological education.[115] Suburban churches can be called upon to help with the costs of such training.

The apprentice leaders of the discipling groups become the focus of indigenous decision making in Celebration. These leaders form the nucleus of indigenous leadership for the emerging church. They are the interim "elders." Through this nucleus the church planters discern the timing of the move from discipling groups to Celebration.

Jack Redford says,"Hopefully the group will remain a mission fellowship until at least four groups are meeting in different parts of the community."[116] The following list of questions will help church planters know when to make the transition from mission fellowship to the next stage of forming a Celebration worship group.[117]

1. Is the adult nucleus large enough to staff a beginning worship service, Christian education program and basic church outreach?[118]

2. Is there unity and oneness of purpose that will insure a cohesive church?

3. Is there enough understanding of the basics of Christian living?

---

114 Claerbaut, p. 195

115 Church planters should explore the local availability of programs like the Center for Urban Theological Studies (C.U.T.S.) in Philadelphia or the Seminary Consortium for Urban Pastoral Education (S.C.U.P.E.) in Chicago which are designed to train urban Christian workers. Many Seminaries and Bible schools are now developing programs specifically designed to train indigenous leaders for ministry in the inner city.

116 Redford, p. 68

117 See Redford, p. 69

118 The nucleus must be large enough to manage 'indigenous' activities and programs. Church planters must not project suburban expectations on the emerging urban church.

4. Are there enough financial resources to allow the transition to a church structure?

5. Have the fellowship members committed themselves to beginning a new church?

If the answers to these questions are in the affirmative and if the Spirit's guidance is to move forward, then the team can proceed to the planting of a Celebration group.

Form a Celebration Group

Celebration is a weekly, large-group meeting for worship, body-life and outreach. It is the preliminary step toward self-sufficiency and independence. In the Celebration stage of church planting the emerging church grows from a network of small discipling groups into a more formal large-group identity. The emerging church takes primary responsibility for leadership, ministry and finances. The mission continues to offer guidance, leadership training, and supplemental financial support.

The move to begin Celebration includes the following steps:

1. Develop a philosophy of ministry.
2. Mobilize your nucleus in preparation for going public.
3. Take care of important administrative issues.
4. Develop goals for the first three years.[119]

Develop a Philosophy of Ministry
First, develop a written philosophy of ministry. C. Peter Wagner says, "The philosophy of ministry addresses two principal questions: who? and how?"[120] The answer to the "who?" question defines which people group the church is seeking to reach. This question is partially answered even before church planting begins, but it is redefined after the church nucleus has been formed. If a multi-ethnic ministry develops during the early stages of outreach, the strategy for developing a multi-ethnic church should be spelled out in the philosophy of ministry.

The answer to the "how?" question defines the details of the ministry approach used. Wagner suggests "you should have a detailed document of several pages that deals with things like . . . your expectation from the church members, your charismatic position, your ethical stands, your worship style, your musical program, your statement of faith, your fellowship groups, your budget process, and whatever else you consider important."[121] The discipling group leaders can determine these details in consultation with the church planting team. Ezra Jones encourages

---

[119] See Logan, p. 6

[120] C. Peter Wagner, *Church Planting for a Greater Harvest*, (Ventura, CA: Regal Books, 1990), p. 115

[121] Wagner, p. 116

mission-planted churches to also include any agreements that define the relationship between the mission and the new church. This will help to avoid misunderstanding or embarrassment later.[122]

During the Celebration stage of church planting the church is legally considered an outreach of the mission agency. The church does not have formal legal status until the final stage when it constitutes by submitting legal forms to the state. It is important that church members understand their identity in relation to the founding mission at each stage of the church-planting process. Church planters should work with the church on the financial and leadership phase-out schedule. This will help the church take ownership of the church-planting goals and vision.

Church planters need to exercise care in using many written documents in the congregation. Inner-city people often prefer verbal communication to formal written guidelines. It is valuable to have the guidelines in written form for occasional reference, but it is best to also verbally present written documents.

Mobilize Your Nucleus
A second step is to define the roles needed to begin Celebration. Two roles are essential: pastor/teacher and worship leader. Other roles might include music, counseling, child care, administration and holistic-care ministry. The church-planting team together with the indigenous leadership will normally form a "Celebration leadership team" which will share responsibility for these roles. The focus of the church-planting team is "indirect leadership" which trains and equips indigenous leaders to fill these roles.

Mobilizing the nucleus also means increasing community cultivation activity prior to the first Celebration. Redford advocates, "A new schedule of choir concerts, backyard-Bible clubs, ministries, and evangelistic visitation programs should immediately precede the formal Sunday services."[123] Such activity helps to galvanize the commitment of the discipling groups as they approach the move to formal large-group services.

Prepare for the Initial Service
A third step includes the details of determining a site for Celebration, setting the starting date, preparing the inaugural service, and training

---

122 See Ezra Earl Jones, *Strategies for New Churches*, (San Francisco: Harper and Row, Publishers, 1976), p. 100

123 Redford, p. 75

the apprentice leaders for their roles. The site should be as attractive as possible and appropriate to the lifestyle of the community. The starting date should not conflict with holidays or other scheduling competition. Publicity for the inaugural service, if desired, should be arranged ahead of time.[124]

A final step of preparation is prayer. Planning and prayer go together. The discipling groups should make prayer for the move to Celebration a major part of their activity in the weeks preceding the first service.

Once Celebration has begun the leaders must be careful not to schedule too many additional activities in the early stages. The discipling groups, however, should continue. Redford argues,

> The chapel should continue the [discipling] fellowship program. The units should not be discontinued abruptly but should continue as an evangelistic penetration group. Such groups help the congregation to cross more cultural and socioeconomic barriers within the same fellowship. The groups can serve as feeders to the Sunday morning activity and will accelerate growth if conducted carefully.[125]

Develop Goals for the First Three Years

The Celebration stage of church planting is a time of consolidation and growth for the emerging church. It allows the church to focus on study, fellowship, worship, stewardship and witness. It is helpful for church planters to set goals for the church to reach during this stage prior to complete independence.[126] One goal crucial to the success of the emerging church is to add new members.[127] Redford advocates an

---

124 See Towns, pp. 117-156 for complete list of details to consider.

125 Redford, p. 78

126 See Towns, p. 139

127 See Wagner, pp. 126-138. Wagner argues that the new church must decide early if it intends to remain a small church (under 200) or become a large church (over 200). The "200 member barrier" is the number of people who can maintain a face-to-face social solidarity. To grow larger than 200 requires a different kind of leadership than that required by the small church. The small church pastor is a "shepherd" who visits and counsels each member. But a large church pastor is a "rancher" who enables others to shepherd the various flocks that compose the congregation. The church that wants to assure rapid reproduction may need to begin with a "rancher" type pastor. In the inner city we will most likely encourage small face-to-face units, especially in a multicultural church. But a "rancher" type pastor could encourage unit and congregational reproduction. Also see Hesselgrave (1980), pp. 284-288 for a further discussion of optimum church size.

aggressive visitation program to encourage evangelism and outreach.[128] The natural "spontaneous" witness of new Christians can be channeled through a well-planned visitation program. Wagner says, "It is worthwhile to dedicate a considerable amount of the time available for outreach to following up the webs of social relationships of those already in your nucleus or in your church. This applies to all your members, but it is especially true of recent converts."[129]

Most church planters advocate the use of a well-prepared "prospect file" to guide the visitation activity.[130] Add names to the prospect file through community cultivation activities, personal contacts and visitors to the church. Continually update the file and use it to direct the church's outreach to prospective new members.

It is important to be organized and aggressive in visitation because the first few days after profession of faith often determine whether the new Christian continues with Christ into active church membership. Hesselgrave says, "Perhaps the two things most needed by new believers immediately following their conversion (whether individuals or groups) are clear instructions as to what God expects of His family members and caring Christian friendship."[131] These are things a well-planned visitation program can provide.

In summary,

> New local groups of believers will not become organized, integrated communities naturally and automatically. There must be a divine element – the operation of the Holy Spirit in the believing group. And a human element must be provided by the church-planter as the ultimate objective of glorifying Christ is made practical by means of clear and meaningful intermediate goals around which group members can rally their energies."[132]

---

128 Redford, p. 78-79

129 Wagner, p. 140

130 See Redford, pp. 78-79

131 Hesselgrave, (1980), p. 296

132 Hesselgrave (1980), p. 278

Plan the Finances

Finances can be either a blessing or a curse to the new congregation. "Carefully handled, finances are a source of pride and accomplishment... Badly handled, they become a source of debt, disgrace and division."[133] It is therefore essential that the financial dealings of the young church be conducted with integrity.

When the discipling fellowships move to begin Celebration there are three tasks to undertake:

1. Determine the church's financial needs.
2. Identify the financial resources.
3. Manage the money.

Determine the Church's Financial Needs

Celebration financial needs usually center on the costs of a temporary meeting place, support for leadership, ministries to the community and a permanent location for the new work.[134] The church must be flexible in determining a temporary meeting place. Often inconveniences must be tolerated in the early stages. It is advisable that no more than one third of the budget go toward renting a facility.[135]

The amount of the budget needed to support leadership depends upon the nature of the church's ministry. Often young churches do well with a part-time pastor. Bi-vocational lay leadership is the foundation of many church-planting strategies, especially in poor areas.[136] The strategy of World Impact calls for a team of church planters who partner with apprentice leaders from the community. Together they lead the church until the apprentice leaders can assume full leadership or until the church is ready to call a pastor who has been trained elsewhere.

Since the goal is to develop a self-supporting indigenous church, the church's needs and vision must be balanced with its financial ability. Determining needs will go hand-in-hand with identifying financial resources.

---

133 Redford, p. 82

134 See Jones, pp. 104-107 for detailed list of needs.

135 See Redford, p. 83

136 See Patterson, *Perspectives on the World Christian Movement*, p. 606

Identify the Financial Resources

The churches planted in the inner city will have two primary sources of income during the beginning stages of church planting: the congregation and World Impact. World Impact will support the core church planters throughout the church-planting cycle. It will also contribute toward initial facilities and program costs. This support will gradually diminish according to an agreed-upon schedule, so that every six months the church will shoulder more of the financial responsibilities.

For example, the church may begin paying 20% of its budget costs, increasing its share 20% every six months to become financially self-sustaining in two years. Such a schedule is important to give the church financial goals and to insure that a spirit of dependency does not develop. Redford says, "The phaseout is designed to foster healthy growth of the mission congregation and aims at building independence rather than fostering dependence."[137]

The church planters should focus on developing the financial resources within the congregation. We recognize at the start that most of our church members will be poor.

> A problem that many missionaries face is the extreme poverty of urban Christians. Coupled with this problem are (1) the danger of establishing a relationship of continuous dependency, and (2) the high cost of urban property and buildings, which often precludes a permanent edifice for the church.[138]

The poverty of church members does not negate their obligation to contribute according to their means. From the beginning of Celebration, biblical stewardship should be taught and members encouraged to tithe. Such giving will not only support the needs and programs of the church, but also will build the members' commitment to and vision for the church. Hesselgrave affirms, "If, for example, a person invests energy, money, and time in something, its perceived value goes up accordingly even though the intrinsic value does not change."[139] This "psychology of value" is an additional reason we should encourage members to invest in the church to the best of their ability. The more they give the more they will value the church.

---

[137] Redford, p. 86

[138] Greenway and Monsma, p. 150

[139] Hesselgrave (1980), p. 339

Financial Networking

The Apostle Paul taught the principle of equality and mutual support between the churches he planted:

> Our desire is not that others might be relieved while you are hard pressed, but that there might be equality. At the present time your plenty will supply what they need, so that in turn their plenty will supply what you need. Then there will be equality (II Corinthians 8:13-14).

There is a place for suburban Christians and churches to financially support new church planting in the inner city, but care must be taken to avoid dependency. The emerging church should pay for all of its own essential operations, including pastor's salary and ministry program costs.

Outside financial support is best used to provide resources and support such as formal education for pastoral trainees, scholarships for summer youth camps, food pantry programs, etc. Supporting churches should be encouraged to give, but their giving should be channeled to pay for services the church can live without if the outside funds dry up.

Manage the Money

At the beginning the church planters will manage whatever funds are necessary to establish the discipling fellowships. Once Celebration begins, the apprentice leaders should be trained to establish a budget and manage the church's money.

Shenk and Stutzman offer this list of guidelines for church money management:

1. At least two persons should collect and count the offering.

2. The congregation should see regular reports of the money received and the way in which it was used.

3. There should be an annual audit of the accounts of the church by a person not involved in any way in the receiving or distribution of the offerings.

4. As soon as possible, the church planter and the congregation should select a person other than the pastor to serve as treasurer of the congregation. Anyone receiving pay from the congregation should be disqualified as treasurer of the church.

5. Simple but adequate bookkeeping procedures are a must.

6. A group of persons appointed for that responsibility should make decisions concerning the allocation of funds.

7. Designated offerings should include prayer for the ministries for which the offering will be shared.

8. One should be cautious about borrowing funds for facility development or purchase.

9. The congregational leaders need to encourage the teaching of Christian stewardship.

10. It is important that the new congregation begin to experience the vision of giving right from the beginning.

11. Often new congregations designate the offering from its first public Sunday morning worship service explicitly for the purpose of sharing the gospel with people who have not yet heard of our Lord Jesus Christ.

12. Never develop a long-term dependency situation.

Following these principles will insure firm financial footing for the new church.

---

140 Shenk and Stutzman, pp. 203-205

Provide Facilities

There are two principles that guide the thinking about church facilities. First, "All congregations need a place (physical structure of some kind) that can serve as a tangible focal point, as well as provide a facility in which to gather and call new members."[141] And second, "The building should not absorb all of the time, energies, and finances of the members."[142]

It is difficult to maintain a sense of congregational identity if there is no central meeting place. However, if financing and maintaining a facility become the focus of church life, it can stifle the church members' zeal and vision. Maintaining proper balance in the area of facilities is essential to the healthy growth of the emerging church.[143]

Temporary Facilities

An initial step toward beginning Celebration is to locate a temporary meeting place. Redford says,

> The ideal process is for the mission chapel [Celebration] to start services in a temporary facility and remain there until sufficient stability and strength has been established. Mission congregations should have a minimum of a dozen families who are permanent residents and fully committed to the chapel before embarking on serious consideration of obtaining permanent facilities.[144]

There are many options for temporary facilities, some of which were mentioned in the discussion of mission fellowships. Every year new churches start in schools, community centers, auditoriums, storefronts and even mortuaries.

> Almost any facility can be used to house an embryo congregation. Storefronts are used but often are criticized by persons who have little or no experience in church planting. Several hundred new churches are planted each year in America in store buildings. Many

---

141 Jones, p. 131

142 Redford, p. 95

143 See Roger Greenway, "The Pros and Cons of Church Buildings", *Cities: Mission's New Frontier*, pp. 234-245, for a list of guidelines that will insure balance in the area of facilities.

144 Redford, p. 89-90

grow into strong, effective churches. When available, storefronts make effective and useful sites to temporarily house mission congregations.[145]

The possibility of joining with another congregation to share their building is also an option to consider, especially if the new congregation is composed of an ethnic group not being reached by the potential host church. The process of community cultivation will alert church planters to these possibilities.

Long-Term Options for Urban Churches
Roger Greenway, who has extensive experience with urban church planting in the U.S. and Mexico, asserts, "Building acquisition should never be made a fixed – that is, assumed and unquestioned – item in the overall mission strategy."[146] He further states, "The Holy Spirit can be relied upon to give urban congregations creativity to find solutions to the building problem."[147]

If the new congregation has the resources and the vision to engage in property acquisition and building construction, and if such a program would meet a need in the community and is in accordance with the Lord's leading, then such a course should be encouraged. However, the assumption is that, given the high cost of property in the inner city and the poverty of urban Christians, the new church should pursue other alternatives.

Many small congregations in the inner city never purchase property. They remain in rented facilities throughout their church life and this is entirely acceptable for their situation.[148] Because the inner city is constantly changing demographically, it may be wise to remain in "temporary" facilities to insure adaptability to changing conditions in the neighborhood. Generally a neighborhood proceeds through the cycle of growth, stabilization, transition, and renewal every fifty years. Many urban communities, however, experience the entire cycle in ten years.[149] The urban church must be adaptable to its rapidly changing

---

145 Redford, p. 90

146 Greenway and Monsma, p. 242

147 Greenway and Monsma, p. 243

148 Jones, p. 131

149 Redford, p. 94

neighborhood. Rented facilities may actually increase the urban churches' flexibility in this regard.

While some suburban church planters disparage the strategy of using home cell groups and house churches,[150] many urban church planters feel such a strategy is well suited to inner-city realities.[151] Roger Greenway says,

> To date, we have found no more effective way to promote growth, local leadership, and group identity than home cells and house churches. Big, united services are helpful, but home cells are the cutting edge of church growth and discipleship. Different configurations can be used to tie the cells together and rally believers periodically in larger gatherings. But in big cities nothing surpasses the small group for effective penetration of every apartment building, language group, social class, and neighborhood.[152]

The fact that the largest churches in the world, including Pastor Cho's 500,000 member church in Seoul, Korea, use the cell group strategy, is evidence of its effectiveness.[153] The strategy of multiplying small cell groups, tied together through periodic large-group meetings, is often called the cluster or network strategy.[154] This strategy provides a natural extension for discipling fellowships, assuming adequate indigenous leadership develops to lead diverse cell groups, and that a "rancher"[155] type pastor can be found to oversee the church.

Shenk and Stutzman portray their cell-group vision when they say,

> Every city block of every city on earth deserves at least one thriving cluster of loving, witnessing Christians. Surely every people and

---

150 See Wagner, p. 122

151 See C. Kirk Hadaway, Stuart A. Wright, Francis M. Dubose, *Home Cell Groups and House Churches: Emerging Alternatives for the Urban Church*, (Nashville: Broadman Press, 1987)

152 Greenway and Monsma, p. 244

153 See Paul Yonggi Cho, *Successful Home Cell Groups*. (South Plainfield, NJ: Bridge Publishing, 1981), and Elmer Towns, John Vaughan, and David Seifert, *The Complete Book of Church Growth*, (Wheaton: Tyndale House Publishers, Inc., 1989), pp. 61-68

154 See Westgate, Urban Mission (November 1986), p. 10

155 See Footnote 114 for a discussion of Wagner's concept of "rancher" pastors.

> language group in every city deserves at least one thriving cluster of redeemed people who point the way to salvation. . . . In order to evangelize the cities today, we must return to the New Testament model of urban evangelism. The approach used was to plant house churches or cell groups throughout entire metropolitan regions. Every urban congregation should be in the cell group planting business.[156]

Whichever solution the congregation pursues in answer to the need for permanent facilities, their focus on people must remain at the forefront of congregational life and ministry. Facilities exist only to serve a church's ministries and should never become the dominant consumer of the congregation's time or money.

---

[156] Shenk and Stutzman, p. 143

Constitute the Church

The phrase "constitute the church" means to make Celebration a spiritually and legally independent church.

Leadership Transition

The church becomes spiritually independent when the church planters formally withdraw by transferring leadership to indigenous leaders approved by the church.

> The service of constitution is the point at which the people who have been meeting together in worship, study, and planning groups officially become a church. It is at this point that they say to the community, 'We are now a fellowship of believers in Jesus Christ who have established a social institution for the purpose of worship, prayer, nurture, and service. Everyone who will may come.'[157]

This transition is seen in Acts 14:23 which says, "Paul and Barnabas appointed elders for them in each church and, with prayer and fasting, committed them to the Lord in whom they had put their trust." Paul withdrew from newly planted churches with confidence, saying, "He who began a good work in you will carry it on to completion until the day of Christ Jesus" (Philippians 1:6).

In commenting on this perspective, Philip Amerson reminds us that:

> Christians who undertake urban ministries are often far more concerned about gaining access to people than they are about leaving when the right time comes. Nevertheless, access by itself is not sufficient for discipleship. If discipleship is to progress, those who have come in the power of the Word must also retire so that faith can be directed to Christ and not to the message bearer. Retirement may be as crucial for Christian growth as access, because without retirement faith may be diverted to ministers with special skills, plans, or abilities. Access with retirement helps new believers to place their faith where it truly belongs – in the power of the Holy Spirit.[158]

---

157 Jones, p. 127

158 Philip Amerson, "Ministry on the Urban Frontier: Access and Retirement," *Signs of the Kingdom in the Secular City*, p. 87

The length of time required to bring a church to this point is a subject of much discussion in missionary research. The Apostle Paul normally spent between five and eighteen months in an area bringing his converts to a place where he could transfer control of the church to their elders.[159] Missionary efforts to constitute churches since then have ranged from a few months to hundreds of years.

The church planting team should have clear goals in this area. Ben Sawatsky shares the Evangelical Free Church's strategy in Malaysia when he says,

> The church planting strategy under consideration requires five years of training for each church planting team. In turn, the church planting team will work with a new church for a similar length of time [concurrently]. The assistance given each local church begins with the formation of the church planting team and continues to the stage where the new church has launched into the reproductive phase, assuming the role of a parent church giving birth to yet another church.[160]

Southern Baptist Charles Chaney, in speaking of a church-planting campaign in Illinois, says,

> . . . in forty-four months we counted exactly 100 new churches or church-type congregations. Of that 100, twelve either failed or did not follow through with official affiliation with IBSA and/or one of the thirty-four local associations within our state. At the end of the period, nine might legitimately have been called "Bible fellowships," not having reached the full phase of "mission" or "chapel" status.[161]

This campaign by an entire denomination took a little more than three and one half years.

Ezra Jones says that for mainline denominations doing church planting in the U.S., "Five years is the average time span for outside financial assistance."[162] Our goal in World Impact is a four year church-planting cycle with a possible one year extension.

---

159 See Allen, 1962, pp. 84-85

160 Ben A. Sawatsky, "A Church Planting Strategy for World Class Cities", *Urban Mission* 3.2, Nov. 1985, pp. 7-18

161 Chaney, p. 47

162 Jones, p. 102

The timing for constituting is important. The congregation risks collapse if the spiritual and leadership foundations are not secure. Redford advises that,

> Formal constitution of a mission congregation into a self-governing church should be deferred until everyone concerned is convinced the group is spiritually mature and sufficiently stable to govern themselves. Countless instances can be cited of mission churches which died because they were constituted prematurely.[163]

There are six checkpoints that will help the church determine the right time to constitute:

1. The congregation has a sense of fellowship with Jesus Christ and with each other.

2. The church has a true sense of its identity and mission.

3. The church is aware of community needs and has a vision for how they can help meet those needs.

4. The congregation is numerically and financially adequate to carry out its vision of ministry in the community.

5. The congregation has adequate training in church function, Christian doctrine, and stewardship. Church leaders are trained to fulfill their respective responsibilities.

6. The congregation has become self-supporting and is able to phase out all[164] outside help.[165]

Formal Independence
Constituting the church removes the last vestiges of mission leadership and financing, thus making the indigenous church fully self-determining and self-supporting. By assuming responsibility for itself the church takes a giant step toward spiritual maturity.

---

163 Redford, p. 97

164 This does not negate an ongoing mission/church relationship or suburban/urban church relationships that involve financial affairs. It does suggest however, that the church is now capable of being responsible for itself and enters into such partnerships voluntarily because it sees an opportunity to work more effectively to build the Kingdom of God.

165 See Redford, pp. 98-99

The process of constituting also makes the church legally independent. The following steps should be included in constituting the new church:

1. Formally request permission from the founding mission to constitute.

2. Choose a date for a formal constituting service.

3. Form a constitution committee to write a church constitution and bylaws including:

    ~ A preamble setting forth the purpose of the constitution.

    ~ The name of the church. This becomes the official, legal title.

    ~ The purposes of the church.

    ~ A church doctrinal statement. (The Articles of Faith)

    ~ The church covenant.

    ~ The government or polity of the church.

    ~ Denominational affiliation (if any).

    ~ Procedures to amend the constitution.

    ~ Bylaws including sections on membership, church officers, committees, organizations, ordinances, meetings and other general procedural matters.[166]

4. File incorporation forms with state and federal offices.[167]

While there is no law that requires churches to be legally incorporated, there are advantages to incorporation. Carl Moorhaus, who has planted over fifty independent Christian Churches, says,

> Legal incorporation is a necessity in my opinion. It will protect each member from the possibility of individual lawsuits. It makes the entire congregation a legal entity. To the best of my knowledge legal

---

[166] The following books contain sample Constitution and Bylaws:
– Towns (1985), pp. 167-176
– Carl W. Moorhous, *Growing New Churches: Step-By-Step Procedures in New Church Planting*, (Carl Moorhous, 1975), pp. 42-46
– Stanley J. Grenz, *The Baptist Congregation: A Guide to Baptist Belief and Practice*, (Valley Forge, PA, Judson Press, 1985), pp. 109-117

[167] See Redford, pp. 99-100

incorporation is necessary if the congregation is to purchase and hold title to real estate or intends to secure a loan from a recognized lending agency.[168]

It is advisable to consult an attorney to insure proper filing of incorporation papers required in the state where the church will be incorporated.

During the writing of a constitution and bylaws church leaders should re-evaluate the philosophy of ministry that was formulated when Celebration began.[169] Input should be gathered from the congregation to arrive at a document that reflects the vision and consensus of the congregation regarding church structure, procedures and mission.[170] The philosophy of ministry is the foundation of the constitution and bylaws and will determine their form. Close cooperation between the church and World Impact during the constituting phase will lay the foundation for a supportive relationship after the church becomes self-sustaining.

The constituting service should be a unique and memorable day for the new church and its founding mission. The service should be well organized in advance to convey the significance of constituting the church.

During the service the founding mission recommends independence for the church, the congregation formally adopts the constitution and bylaws and formally voices and approves the motion to incorporate. Letters of support from neighborhood churches or sister Celebration churches in other cities may be received and read at the service. The church proclaims its vision and recieves new members.

"If carefully prepared and carried out, the constitution service will have intense meaning. All churches, like all God's children, need milestones along the way for guidance and encouragement."[171]

---

168 Moorhous, p. 35

169 See Robert E. Logan and Jeff Rast, *Church Planters Checklist*, (Pasadena, CA: Charles E. Fuller Institute, 1987), p. 12

170 See Jones, p. 128-130

171 Redford, p. 100

Church/Mission Relations

Semi-Autonomous Teams

The church-planting strategy described in this paper calls for semi-autonomous teams which are trained and commissioned by World Impact to plant churches in inner-city communities within a period of five years. To accomplish such a goal, the teams must concentrate all their energies on the vision of planting a church.

The teams will therefore operate as special ministry units, planning their own ministry goals and schedules with the guidance of World Impact's national office and in coordination with other World Impact ministries in the area.

In some cases teams may be sent to establish churches in cities new to World Impact. In these circumstances the team itself will provide personal support for each member while external support is established through networking.

If the team operates where World Impact has a city ministry there will be cooperation between team members and city-ministry staff. If the city ministry operates a school close to the church-planters target community, the school and the new church will be mutually supportive. The relation between the church-planting effort and World Impact camps or clinics will be one of mutual support, cooperation and encouragement, but the basic autonomy of the teams will remain intact.

Cooperation and non-interference between city ministry and church planters is the goal. Veteran church planter Tom Eckblad confirms this perspective when he says, "It could be argued that all institutional ministries should be part of a total effort to plant the churches."[172] But he acknowledges the unique and specialized role of church planters when he says, "Institutional work by itself does not establish churches."[173] Schools or clinics can support church planting, but they cannot by themselves plant churches. All of our ministries must be seen as part of a supportive network that is building God's Kingdom in the inner city.

To insure smooth cooperation between the various aspects of World Impact's ministry in a city, directors must give their staff an overarching

---

172 Eckblad, p. 25

173 Eckblad, p. 25

picture of the ministry goals and strategy. Not all World Impact staff are gifted or called as members of a church-planting team, but each missionary fills a valuable role in building God's Kingdom in the inner city, whether involved in church planting or other types of community ministry.

Mission Support
World Impact's National Office will provide resources to help church planters.

This will include training church-planting teams, issuing written resource material and helping network the teams with each other and with outside resources.

When Celebration services begin, the office will provide sample bylaws which the Celebration body can revise and adopt. These bylaws will help regulate the relation between the emerging church and World Impact in the period prior to constituting. These bylaws will spell out responsibilities and describe the financial phase-out schedule.

World Impact will also be available to provide guidance for handling church finances and property acquisition. Once the church is ready to constitute, the National office will provide information about incorporation procedures. A sample constitution will also be provided for adaptation by the new church. Every effort will be made to insure a smooth transition to church independence.

If World Impact operates service ministries in the city where the new church is planted, these services will serve as a resource to the new church. Schools will seek to include children from the new church as space allows. World Impact camps will provide retreat opportunities for the church body. Clinics will include church members in their provision of medical services. Whatever services World Impact can provide in the city, whether job-training, housing referral, thrift shops, etc., will be available to support the church body and its ministry.

If staff and resources allow, the local World Impact city ministry may even originate ministry programs specifically designed to strengthen the network of churches that are planted. Theological Education by Extension (T.E.E.) and English as a Second Language (E.S.L.) are examples of such specialized programs which the mission is uniquely equipped to provide.

World Impact, as a mission agency, should remain available to help the new churches with their ongoing networking process. The networking begun by the church planters during community cultivation should be encouraged to continue once the church is established. This will strengthen the connection of the new church with other groups and will broaden its vision for the city.

Inter-Church Relationships

The goal of World Impact missionaries should be to pray and work toward the creation of a network of World Impact-planted churches, both locally and nationally. Rather than establishing isolated individual churches, teams should work to create an association of churches.

Some newly constituted churches may choose affiliation with an established denomination. Many denominations are presently seeking to establish urban congregations and are open to accepting World Impact-planted churches into their folds. The advantages and drawbacks of such association must be carefully weighed by church leaders. Others may choose to remain as independent community churches. In either case it is important that churches maintain supportive networks with other churches and with World Impact whenever possible.

Many missions experts advocate such networking. Melvin Hodges warns, "Small groups of individual believers that are cut off from all contact with other churches tend to become discouraged and inactive."[174] Shenk and Stutzman argue,

> In order for young congregations to thrive, it is usually wise to cluster new congregations together. Paul did not plant just one church in Asia minor, he planted a cluster of congregations. . . In each case, Paul trained a younger man to become overseer of these clusters of congregations after he left.[175]

In addition to networking between the newly planted churches, there is also a place for the churches to continue their relationship with World Impact. Hesselgrave comments that,

---

174 Hodges, p. 85

175 Shenk and Stutzman, pp. 168-169

The critical test of the work of a church-planter is the ability of the founded church to survive his departure and carry on the ministry. Nevertheless, a spiritual bond unites missionary and church, a bond which should find expression in some kind of continued relationship such as is exemplified in the New Testament.[176]

If a continued supportive relationship exists between the newly planted churches and World Impact, and if the churches work to support each other, it will more likely assure the church's stability and growth.

---

176 Hesselgrave, 1980, p. 418

Conclusion

This paper provides a framework for World Impact church planters. The framework includes practical principles and biblical perspectives. It mirrors World Impact's past experiences with church planting and also reflects recent missiological thinking about urban missions. Yet, even with this framework to guide them, World Impact church planters must still make many substantive decisions about how to apply these principles in their unique situation with their specific team.

We encourage each of you as church planters to dream big dreams for God. Then take the initiative, in faith, to bring them to reality so that:

> Those who were not told about Him will see, and those who have not heard will understand.
> ~ Romans 15:21

Bibliography

Allen, Roland. *Missionary Method's: St. Paul's or Ours?*. Grand Rapids: Eerdmans, 1962.

———. *The Spontaneous Expansion of the Church*. Grand Rapids: Eerdmans, 1962.

Amerson, Philip. "Ministry on the Urban Frontier: Access and Retirement" In *Signs of the Kingdom in the Secular City*, ed. David Frenchak and Clinton Stockwell, p. 83-94. Chicago: Covenant Press, 1984.

Appleby, Jerry L. *Missions Have Come Home to America: The Church's Cross-Cultural Ministry to Ethnics*. Kansas City: Beacon Hill Press, 1986.

Arias, Mortimer. *Announcing the Reign of God: Evangelization and the Subversive Memory of Jesus*. Philadelphia, PA: Fortress Press, 1984.

Bacon, Dan and William Goheen. "Should Mission Boards Send Teams as Well as Individuals?" In *Perspectives on the World Christian Movement*, ed. Ralph D. Winter and Steven C. Hawthorne, pp. 775-781. Pasadena, CA: William Carey Library, 1981.

Bakke, Ray. *The Urban Christian: Effective Ministry in Today's Urban World*. Downers Grove: Inter-Varsity Press, 1987.

Beaver, R. Pierce. "The History of Mission Strategy." In *Perspectives on the World Christian Movement*, ed. Ralph D. Winter and Steven C. Hawthorne, p. 191-205. Pasadena, CA: William Carey Library, 1981.

Brock, Charles. *The Principles and Practice of Indigenous Church Planting*, Nashville: Broadman Press, 1981.

Chaney, Charles L. *Church Planting at the End of the Twentieth Century*. Wheaton: Tyndale House, 1982.

Cho, Paul Yonggi. *Successful Home Cell Groups*. South Plainfield, NJ: Bridge Publishing, 1981.

Conn, Harvie. *A Clarified Vision for Urban Mission: Dispelling the Urban Stereotypes*. Grand Rapids: Zondervan, 1987.

———. Evangelism: *Doing Justice and Preaching Grace.* Grand Rapids: Zondervan, 1982.

———. *Urban Missions Newsletter* 28. Philadelphia: Westminster Theological Seminary (Dec. 1990): 1-2.

Claerbaut, David. *Urban Ministry.* Grand Rapids: Zondervan, 1983.

Cornett, Terry and Bob Edwards. "When Is a Homogeneous Church Legitimate?" *Evangelical Missions Quarterly* 20.1 (Jan. 1984): 22-28.

Costas, Orlando. *Liberating News: A Theology of Contextual Evangelization.* Grand Rapids: Eerdmans, 1989.

Dawson, John. *Taking Our Cities for God.* Lake Mary, FL: Creation House, 1989.

Dyer, Kevin. "Crucial Factors in Building Good Teams." In *Helping Missionaries Grow*, ed. Kelly O'Donnell and Michele O'Donnell, pp. 126-130. Pasadena: William Carey Library, 1988.

Eckblad, Tom. "Tips for Urban Church Planters." *Urban Mission* 1.3, (Jan., 1984): 24-29

Feeney, James H. *Church Planting by the Team Method.* Anchorage: Abbot Loop Christian Center, 1988.

Frenchak, David, and Clinton Stockwell, Compilers. Helen Ujvarosy, ed. *Signs of the Kingdom in the Secular City.* Chicago:Covenant Press, 1984.

Gilliland, Dean. *Pauline Theology and Mission Practice.* Lagos, Nigeria: Tryfam Printers, Ltd., 1983.

Graham, Thomas. "How to Select the Best Church Planters." In *Helping Missionaries Grow*, ed. Kelly O'Donnell and Michele O'Donnell, pp. 46-54. Pasadena: William Carey Library, 1988.

Green, Michael. *Evangelism in the Early Church.* Grand Rapids: Eerdmans, 1970.

Greenway, Roger, and Timothy Monsma. *Cities: Mission's New Frontier.* Grand Rapids: Baker, 1989.

Greenway, Roger, ed. *Discipling the City: Theological Reflections on Urban Mission.* Grand Rapids: Baker, 1979.

Grenz, Stanley J. *The Baptist Congregation: A Guide to Baptist Belief and Practice.* Valley Forge, PA: Judson Press, 1985.

Grunlan, Stephen A. and Marvin K. Mayers. *Cultural Anthropology: A Christian Perspective.* Grand Rapids: Zondervan, 1988.

Guy, Ray. "Pilgrimage Toward the House Church." In *Discipling the City,* ed. Roger Greenway, pp. 107-127. Grand Rapids: Baker, 1979.

Hadaway, C. Kirk, Stuart A Wright, and Francis M. Dubose. *Home Cell Groups and House Churches.* Nashville: Broadman Press, 1987.

Hallet, Stanley. "To Build a City." In *Signs of the Kingdom in the Secular City,* ed. David Frenchak and Clinton Stockwell, p. 3-7. Chicago: Covenant Press, 1984.

Hastey, Ervin E. "Reaching the Cities First: A Biblical Model of World Evangelization." In *An Urban World.* ed. Larry L. Rose and C. Kirk Hadaway, pp. 147-166. Nashville: Broadman Press, 1984.

Hesselgrave, David. *Communicating Christ Cross-Culturally.* Grand Rapids: Zondervan, 1978.

———. *Planting Churches Cross-Culturally.* Grand Rapids: Baker, 1980.

Hiebert, Paul G. *Cultural Anthropology.* Grand Rapids: Baker, 1983.

Hodges, Melvin. *The Indigenous Church.* Springfield: Gospel Publishing House, 1953.

Holland, Clifton L. *The Religious Dimension in Hispanic Los Angeles: A Protestant Case Study.* Pasadena, CA: William Carey Library, 1974.

Jones, Ezra Earl. *Strategies For New Churches.* San Francisco: Harpers Ministers Paperback Library, 1976.

Kane, Herbert J. *A Concise History of the Christian World Mission.* Grand Rapids: Baker, 1982.

Ladd, George Eldon. *A Theology of the New Testament.* Grand Rapids: Eerdmans, 1974.

Linthicum, Robert C. *City of God, City of Satan: A Biblical Theology of the Urban Church.* Grand Rapids: Zondervan, 1991.

Lincoln, C. Eric and Lawrence H. Mamiya. *The Black Church in the African American Experience*. Durhan, S.C: Duke University Press, 1990.

Logan, Robert E. "How to Start a Growing and Reproducing Church." Robert E. Logan, 1988.

Logan, Robert E. and Jeff Rast. *Church Planters Checklist*. Pasadena: Charles E. Fuller Institute, 1987.

McGavran, Donald. *The Bridges of God*. New York: Friendship Press, 1955.

Mellis, Charles J. *Committed Communities*. Pasadena: William Carey Library, 1976.

Moorhous, Carl W. *Growing New Churches: Step-By-Step Procedures in New Church Planting*. Carl Moorhous, 1975.

Nichols, Bruce, ed. *In Word and Deed: Evangelism and Social Responsibility*. Grand Rapids: Eerdmans, 1985.

O'Donnel, Kelly S. and Michele L. O'Donnel, eds. *Helping Missionaries Grow: Readings in Mental Health and Missions*. Pasadena: William Carey Library, 1988.

Padilla, C. Rene'. *Mission Between The Times: Essays on the Kingdom*. Grand Rapids: Eerdmans, 1985.

Patterson, George. "The Spontaneous Multiplication of Churches." In *Perspectives on the World Christian Movement*, ed. Ralph D. Winter and Stephen C. Hawthorne, pp.601-616. Pasadena: William Carey Library, 1982.

———. *Church Planting through Obedience Oriented Teaching*. Pasadena: William Carey Library, 1981.

Peterson, Jim. *Evangelism as a Lifestyle*. Colorado Springs: NavPress, 1980.

Phillips, Keith. *The Making of a Disciple*. Old Tappan: Fleming H. Revell Company, 1981.

Redford, Jack. *Planting New Churches: Nine Well-Tested Steps for Starting New Churches*. Nashville: Broadman Press, 1978.

Rose, Larry and C. Kirk Hadaway. *An Urban World*. Nashville: Broadman Press, 1984.

Sawatsky, Ben A. "A Church Planting Strategy for World Class Cities", *Urban Mission* 3.2, (Nov. 1985): 7-18.

Shenk, David W. and Ervin R. Stutzman. *Creating Communities of the Kingdom: New Testament Models of Church Planting*. Scottsdale: Herald Press, 1988.

Snyder, Howard. *The Community of the King*. Downers Grove: Inter-Varsity Press, 1977.

———. *Liberating the Church*. Downers Grove: Inter-Varsity Press, 1983.

Steffen, Tom A. *Tribal and Peasant Church Planting: A Comprehensive Phase Out Model*. Unpublished doctoral dissertation: Biola University, 1990.

Stockwell, Clinton E. "Barriers and Bridges to Evangelization in Urban Neighborhoods." In *Signs of the Kingdom in the Secular City*, ed. David Frenchak and Clinton Stockwell, pp. 95-104. Chicago: Covenant Press, 1984.

Tippet, Alan. *Introduction to Missiology*. Pasadena: William Carey Library, 1987.

Towns, Elmer. *Getting a Church Started*. Lynchburg: Church Growth Institute, 1985.

Towns, Elmer, John N. Vaughan, and David J. Seifert. *The Complete Book of Church Growth*. Wheaton: Tyndale House, 1989.

Wagner, C. Peter. *Church Planting for a Greater Harvest*. Ventura: Regal, 1990.

Westgate, James E. "Emerging Church Planting Strategies for World Class Cities." *Urban Mission* 4.2 (Nov. 1986): 6-13.

Webber, Robert E. *Worship Old and New*. Grand Rapids: Zondervan, 1982.

Wilmore, Gayraud S. *Black Religion and Black Radicalism: An Interpretation of the Religious History of the Afro-American People*. Maryknoll, N.Y.: Orbis Books, 1990.

Winter, Ralph D. and Stephen C. Hawthorne., eds. *Perspectives on the World Christian Movement*. Pasadena: William Carey Library, 1982.

Yamamori, Tetsunao. "How to Reach Urban Ethnics." *Urban Mission* 1.4 (March, 1984): 29-35.

Part II
Theological and Missiological Principles and Insights:
Toward a Theology of Church Planting

The resources in Part II specifically provide insight into the kinds of biblical, theological, and missional frameworks that give birth to effective missions among the city's unreached urban poor. Here you will find materials that provide suggestive reflection on the nature of the theological and missiological perspectives on the city and the poor, on the Kingdom of God and the Church, and on the ramifications of Christ and culture. Of course, these materials are meant to be suggestive as to the kind of theological and missiological insights we must have as we engage in God-honoring church planting efforts among the urban unreached poor around the country and beyond.

This part includes the following sections:

- *Christus Victor*: A Theology of the City and the Poor / p. 95
- A Theology of the Kingdom and the Church / p. 167
- A Theology of Christ and Culture / p. 209

Christus Victor: A Theology of the City and the Poor

The Theology of the Poor for Team Leaders

Rev. Terry Cornett • *The Timothy Conference: Building Church Plant Teams.* Wichita: The Urban Ministry Institute, 2005.

St. Lawrence the Deacon (d. 258 A.D.) is one of the great leaders and martyrs in the first 300 years of the Church.

I. Does Our Team Think of Our Mission Field as Hard or Easy?

  A. The affluent are difficult to evangelize and disciple.

  Deut. 8.12-14 – Otherwise, when you eat and are satisfied, when you build fine houses and settle down, and when your herds and flocks grow large and your silver and gold increase and all you have is multiplied, then your heart will become proud and you will forget the LORD your God, who brought you out of Egypt, out of the land of slavery (cf. Ps. 73.3-6; Prov. 30.8-9; Ezek. 16.49; Hos. 13.4-6).

  The New Testament teaching is far more explicit. Jesus surprises his disciples with the teaching that wealth has an inherent tendency to dull the spiritual senses and lead one to abandon God.

  > In the teaching of Jesus material possessions are not regarded as evil, but as dangerous.
  > ~ R.E. Dixon. New Bible Dictionary.

  Matt. 6.19-21 – Do not store up for yourselves treasures on earth, where moth and rust destroy, and where thieves break in and steal. But store up for yourselves treasures in heaven, where moth and rust do not destroy, and where thieves do not break in and steal. For where your treasure is, there your heart will be also.

  Jesus warns us that accumulation has an inevitable effect on our heart. There are things that we can do about it (reckless giving; associating with people of low status and poor reputation) but we cannot change the reality that wealth exerts a constant pull away from spirituality.

  Matt. 13.22 – The one who received the seed that fell among the thorns is the man who hears the word, but the worries of this life and the deceitfulness of wealth choke it, making it unfruitful.

Matt. 19.21-26 – Jesus answered, "If you want to be perfect, go, sell your possessions and give to the poor, and you will have treasure in heaven. Then come, follow me." When the young man heard this, he went away sad, because he had great wealth. Then Jesus said to his disciples, "I tell you the truth, it is hard for a rich man to enter the Kingdom of heaven. Again I tell you, it is easier for a camel to go through the eye of a needle than for a rich man to enter the Kingdom of God." When the disciples heard this, they were greatly astonished and asked, "Who then can be saved?" Jesus looked at them and said, "With man this is impossible, but with God all things are possible."

Luke 1.53 – He has filled the hungry with good things but has sent the rich away empty.

Luke 6.24-25 – But woe to you who are rich, for you have already received your comfort.

1 Tim. 6.9-11 – People who want to get rich fall into temptation and a trap and into many foolish and harmful desires that plunge men into ruin and destruction. For the love of money is a root of all kinds of evil. Some people, eager for money, have wandered from the faith and pierced themselves with many griefs. But you, man of God, flee from all this, and pursue righteousness, godliness, faith, love, endurance and gentleness.

1 Tim. 6.17 – Command those who are rich in this present world not to be arrogant nor to put their hope in wealth, which is so uncertain, but to put their hope in God, who richly provides us with everything for our enjoyment.

James 5.1-6 – Now listen, you rich people, weep and wail because of the misery that is coming upon you. Your wealth has rotted, and moths have eaten your clothes. Your gold and silver are corroded. Their corrosion will testify against you and eat your flesh like fire. You have hoarded wealth in the last days. Look! The wages you failed to pay the workmen who mowed your fields are crying out against you. The cries of the harvesters have reached the ears of the Lord Almighty. You have lived on earth in luxury and self-indulgence. You have fattened yourselves in the day of slaughter. You have condemned and murdered innocent men, who were not opposing you.

Heb. 13.5 – Keep your lives free from the love of money and be content with what you have, because God has said, "Never will I leave you; never will I forsake you."

Rev. 3.17 – You say, "I am rich; I have acquired wealth and do not need a thing." But you do not realize that you are wretched, pitiful, poor, blind and naked.

The specific teaching of the New Testament . . .

We cannot claim to be converted to God and not choose to be converted to the poor.

> Mary's Magnificat, her song of exaltation sung at the home of Zechariah and Elizabeth, clarifies her hope for the new Kingdom. . . . Five types of people are startled and surprised. In Mary's vision, those at the top of the social pyramid – the proud, the rich and the mighty topple. . . . Meanwhile, the poor and the hungry, those at the bottom of the social hill, take a surprise ride to the top. . . . A poor Galilean peasant girl, Mary expect the messianic Kingdom to flip her social world upside-down. . . . [but] the Kingdom of God isn't only upside down. It's also authoritative for our situation. Kingdom values address current issues and dilemmas.
>
> ~ Donald B. Kraybill. *The Upside Down Kingdom*, Rev. ed. Scottsdale, PA: Herald Press, 1990. pp. 17-21.

B. The poor are a receptive field for the Gospel.

The counterpoint to the New Testament teaching about the spiritual hardness of the wealthy is the teaching that the poor are the spiritually open. It is assumed throughout the Gospels that the poor are the natural examples of godliness. For example:

- The Poor Widow's Offering, Mark 12.41-44
- The Parable of Lazarus and the Rich Man, Luke 16.19-31
- The Widow who is Denied Justice, Luke 18.1-8
- The Guests at the Wedding Feast, Luke 14.16-24

And as you might expect, the direct propositional statements of Jesus completely reinforce what the stories imply to us.

Luke 4.18-19 – The Spirit of the Lord is on me, because he has anointed me to preach good news to the poor. He has sent me to proclaim freedom for the prisoners and recovery of sight for the blind, to release the oppressed, to proclaim the year of the Lord's favor.

Luke 6.20 – Looking at his disciples, he said: "Blessed are you who are poor, for yours is the Kingdom of God."

C. "Working with the grain of the universe."

> Mennonite theologian John Howard Yoder speaks about following the commands of the New Testament even when it runs counter to popular wisdom or does not appear on the surface to be achieving the results that we expect or desire. Yoder speaks about seeing the bigger picture behind the day-to-day battles and failures. He says that when we take the teachings of the New Testament seriously, we are "working with the grain of the universe."
>
> ~ Stanley Hauerwas. "Remembering John Howard Yoder." December 29, 1927-December 30, 1997. *First Things* 82 (April 1998): p. 15-16.

When your teams take the Gospel to the poor that is exactly what they are doing. They are "working with the grain of the universe." Your fields are receptive, they are "ripe for harvest."

Key Team Leader Virtue: Open thankfulness that the team's mission is in a spiritually receptive field.

II. Is Our Team's Mission to the Poor Rooted in Our Understanding of Jesus?

We are not in mission on our own initiative, rather we are ambassadors who act and speaks as those representing someone else. Our mission is simply the continuation of Jesus' mission. Or to put it another way, Jesus' example and teaching are the standard for evaluating our claims to know and represent God's message.

John 14.23-24 – Jesus replied, "If anyone loves me, he will obey my teaching. my Father will love him, and we will come to him and make our home with him. He who does not love me will not obey my teaching. These words you hear are not my own; they belong to the Father who sent me."

1 John 2.4-6 – The man who says, "I know him," but does not do what he commands is a liar, and the truth is not in him. But if anyone obeys his word, God's love is truly made complete in him. This is how we know we are in him. Whoever claims to live in him must walk as Jesus did. For Jesus the Messianic mission was defined primarily as preaching liberating news to the poor and oppressed. The Gospel was the good news that the Kingdom had come to those who had no hope. We serve as representatives of Christ only to the extent that our mission conforms to his.

A. Jesus identified himself with the poor.

   2 Cor. 8.9 – For you know the grace of our Lord Jesus Christ, that though he was rich, yet for your sakes he became poor, so that you through his poverty might become rich.

   1. Born to poor parents

      Luke 2.22-24 – When the time of their purification according to the Law of Moses had been completed, Joseph and Mary took him to Jerusalem to present him to the Lord (as it is written in the Law of the Lord, "Every firstborn male is to be consecrated to the Lord"), and to offer a sacrifice in keeping with what is said in the Law of the Lord: "a pair of doves or two young pigeons."

> Levitical law provided that after the birth of a son a woman would be unclean for seven days leading up to the circumcision and that for a further thirty-three days she should keep away from all holy things . . . Then she should offer a lamb and a dove pigeon. If she was too poor for a lamb a second dove or pigeon sufficed instead. (Leviticus 12.6-13). Mary's offering was thus that of the poor.
>
> ~ Leon Morris. *The Gospel According to St. Luke.*
> *Tyndale New Testament Commentaries.*
> Grand Rapids: Wm. B. Eerdmans, 1983. p. 87.

   2. As a social outcast

      a. Born in a stable, Luke 2.7

      b. Under assumed illegitimacy, Luke 3.23

3. He lives the life of the poor.

   a. No place to lay his head, Matt. 8.20

   b. Oppressed by the established authorities – both religious and secular, Isa. 53.7-8; Matt. 21.46; 22.15-16; Mark 3.6; John 7.32.

   c. Supported by the contributions of others, Luke 8.3.

B. Jesus defined and validated his messianic mission by making the poor his central priority.

Luke 4.16-21 – He went to Nazareth, where he had been brought up, and on the Sabbath day he went into the synagogue, as was his custom. And he stood up to read. The scroll of the prophet Isaiah was handed to him. Unrolling it, he found the place where it is written: "The Spirit of the Lord is on me, because he has anointed me to preach good news to the poor. He has sent me to proclaim freedom for the prisoners and recovery of sight for the blind, to release the oppressed, to proclaim the year of the Lord's favor." Then he rolled up the scroll, gave it back to the attendant and sat down. The eyes of everyone in the synagogue were fastened on him, and he began by saying to them, "Today this Scripture is fulfilled in your hearing."

Matt. 11.2-6 – When John heard in prison what Christ was doing, he sent his disciples to ask him, "Are you the one who was to come, or should we expect someone else?" Jesus replied, "Go back and report to John what you hear and see: The blind receive sight, the lame walk, those who have leprosy are cured, the deaf hear, the dead are raised, and the good news is preached to the poor. Blessed is the man who does not fall away on account of me."

C. Jesus directly tied salvation and discipleship to a similar concern for the poor and oppressed.

Luke 19.2-10 – A man was there by the name of Zacchaeus; he was a chief tax collector and was wealthy. He wanted to see who Jesus was, but being a short man he could not, because of the crowd. So he ran ahead and climbed a sycamore-fig tree to see him, since Jesus was coming that way. When Jesus reached the spot, he looked up and said to him, "Zacchaeus, come down immediately. I must stay at your house today." So he came down at once and welcomed him gladly. All the people saw this and began to mutter, "He has gone to be the guest of a 'sinner.'" But Zacchaeus stood up and said to the Lord, "Look, Lord! Here and now I give half of my possessions to the poor, and if I have cheated anybody out of anything, I will pay back four times the amount." Jesus said to him, "Today salvation has come to this house, because this man, too, is a son of Abraham. For the Son of Man came to seek and to save what was lost."

Matt. 19.21-23 – Jesus answered, "If you want to be perfect, go, sell your possessions and give to the poor, and you will have treasure in heaven. Then come, follow me." When the young man heard this, he went away sad, because he had great wealth. Then Jesus said to his disciples, "I tell you the truth, it is hard for a rich man to enter the Kingdom of heaven."

Luke 12.32-34 – Do not be afraid, little flock, for your Father has been pleased to give you the Kingdom. Sell your possessions and give to the poor. Provide purses for yourselves that will not wear out, a treasure in heaven that will not be exhausted, where no thief comes near and no moth destroys. For where your treasure is, there your heart will be also.

Luke 14.12-14 – Then Jesus said to his host, "When you give a luncheon or dinner, do not invite your friends, your brothers or relatives, or your rich neighbors; if you do, they may invite you back and so you will be repaid. But when you give a banquet, invite the poor, the crippled, the lame, the blind, and you will be blessed. Although they cannot repay you, you will be repaid at the resurrection of the righteous."

Luke 11.41 – But give what is inside the dish to the poor, and everything will be clean for you.

Matt. 25.41-46 – Then he will say to those on his left, "Depart from me, you who are cursed, into the eternal fire prepared for the devil and his angels. For I was hungry and you gave me nothing to eat, I was thirsty and you gave me nothing to drink, I was a stranger and you did not invite me in, I needed clothes and you did not clothe me, I was sick and in prison and you did not look after me." They also will answer, "Lord, when did we see you hungry or thirsty or a stranger or needing clothes or sick or in prison, and did not help you?" He will reply, "I tell you the truth, whatever you did not do for one of the least of these, you did not do for me." Then they will go away to eternal punishment, but the righteous to eternal life.

Key Team Leader Virtue: Consistent reminders to the team that faithfulness to Jesus is inextricably linked to faithfulness to the poor.

III. Is Our Mission's Hope for the Poor Anchored in the Electing Grace of God?

eklegomai - to select: make choice, choose (out), chosen.

> To choose, select, choose for oneself, not necessarily implying the rejection of what is not chosen, but giving favor to the chosen subject, keeping in view a relationship to be established between the one choosing and the object chosen. It involves preference and selection from among many choices.
> ~ Spiros Zoddhiates. "eklegomai."
> *The Complete Word Study Dictionary: New Testament.*
>
> When used in relation to God's choosing it has special reference ". . . to those whom he has judged fit to receive his favors and separated from the rest of making to be peculiarly his own and to be attended continually by his gracious oversight."
> ~ *Thayer's Greek English Lexicon of the Bible.*

Luke 6.13 – When morning came, he called his disciples to him and chose [eklegomai] twelve of them, whom he also designated apostles.

Eph. 1.4-5 – For he chose [eklegomai] us in him before the creation of the world to be holy and blameless in his sight. In love he predestined us to be adopted as his sons through Jesus Christ, in accordance with his pleasure and will.

It is therefore significant that the Apostle James takes up the very same concept in regard to the poor.

James 2.5 – Listen, my dear brothers: Has not God chosen [*eklegomai*] those who are poor in the eyes of the world to be rich in faith and to inherit the Kingdom he promised those who love him?

When the theology of the Old Testament and the Gospels about the poor is held together with the theology of the poor in the Epistles, a remarkable picture emerges.

> Bestowed exclusively on Israel, the chosen people ('*am segullah*), as a mark of God's election-love the Shechinah now rested on the poor, who, as the new Israel would inherit its splendor in the coming messianic Kingdom.
> ~ James B. Adamson. "James 2.5." *The Epistle of James. The New International Commentary on the New Testament.* Grand Rapids: Eerdmans, 1976. p. 110.
>
> In the New Testament the poor replace Israel as the focus of the Gospel.
> ~ C. M. N. Sugden. New Dictionary of Theology.

Key Team Leader Virtues: Leads the team in a group prayer life that wrestles with God by reminding him of his own stated promises and purposes (Deut. 9.25-29; Ps. 74; Jer. 14.20-21; Luke 18.1-8). Guides the team into finding every opportunity for evangelism because of the confidence that the team is working among those whom God has chosen.

IV. Is Our Mission Among the Poor Characterized by Respect and Expectation?

> If you want to do something and have no power to do it, it is talauchi (poverty).
> ~ Nigeria
>
> When one is poor, she has no say in public, she feels inferior. She has no food, so there is famine in her house; no clothing, and no progress in her family.
> ~ a woman from Uganda.
>
> For a poor person everything is terrible - illness, humiliation, shame. We are cripples; we are afraid of everything; we depend on everyone. No one needs us. We are like garbage that everyone wants to get rid of.
> ~ a blind woman from Tiraspol, Moldova
>
> ~ "Voices of the Poor." PovertyNet.
> http://www.worldbank.org/poverty/voices/listen-findings.htm#1

A. Respect, Respect, Respect

I believe in the Aretha Franklin approach to a theology of the poor. "R-E-S-P-E-C-T find out what it means to me."

> One of the ways that St. Francis described his relationship with the poor (and others) was through the word *Cortesia*. "We use the word 'courtesy' to mean manners. Originally, it meant the behavior and etiquette expected of one who served at a noble court. . . . For St. Francis . . . *cortesia* was a way of seeing and acting towards others.
>
> ~ Lawrence Cunningham. St. Francis of Assisi. San Francisco: Harper and Row. 1981.

The example of Paul and Onesimus:

Philem. 1.10-17 – I appeal to you for my son Onesimus, who became my son while I was in chains. Formerly he was useless to you, but now he has become useful both to you and to me. I am sending him – who is my very heart – back to you. I would have liked to keep him with me so that he could take your place in helping me while I am in chains for the Gospel. But I did not want to do anything without your consent, so that any favor you do will be spontaneous and not forced. Perhaps the reason he was separated from you for a little while was that you might have him back for good – no longer as a slave, but better than a slave, as a dear brother. He is very dear to me but even dearer to you, both as a man and as a brother in the Lord. So if you consider me a partner, welcome him as you would welcome me.

Many scholars believe that this same Onesimus became a bishop in the early church!

> We have no idea how old Paul's Onesimus was when he wrote about him; but a young man in his later teens or early twenties at that time would be about seventy by the time of Ignatius's martyrdom – not an incredible age for a bishop in those day. . . .The preservation of this private letter [Book of Philemon] must be explained. That Onesimus did become the bishop of Ephesus is not improbable. If so . . . Onesimus could scarcely fail to get to know about [the collecting of the Pauline corpus], and would make sure that his Pauline letter found a place in it.
>
> ~ F. F. Bruce. *Epistles to the Colossians, to Philemon, and to the Ephesians. The New International Commentary on the New Testament.* Grand Rapids: Eerdmans, 1984. p. 202.

Every poor person is to be treated based on the potential inherent in their calling.

B. Expectation: the poor as actors rather than acted upon.

> Poverty is not so much the absence of goods as it is the absence of power – the capability of being able to change one's situation.
>
> ~ Robert C. Linthicum. Empowering the Poor:
> Community Organizing Among the City's 'Rag, Tag, and Bobtail.'
> Monrovia, CA: MARC, 1991. p. 10.

The Church must be the place where the poor are expected to take leadership. We must know this about the poor even before they know it about themselves. We must ensure that the requirements that are established for leaders are fully biblical but are not expressed in middle-class cultural forms.

Paternalism can take two equally deadly forms: not expecting the poor to lead or simply giving leadership that a person is not equipped for as a kind of tokenism.

1. The Upside-Down Kingdom

    Ps. 18.27 – You save the humble but bring low those whose eyes are haughty.

    Isa. 23.9 – The LORD Almighty planned it, to bring low the pride of all glory and to humble all who are renowned on the earth.

    Ezek. 21.26 – this is what the Sovereign LORD says: Take off the turban, remove the crown. It will not be as it was: The lowly will be exalted and the exalted will be brought low.

    Luke 6.20, 24 – Looking at his disciples, he said: "Blessed are you who are poor, for yours is the Kingdom of God. . . ." But woe to you who are rich, for you have already received your comfort.

    James 1.9-10 – The brother in humble circumstances ought to take pride in his high position. But the one who is rich should take pride in his low position, because he will pass away like a wild flower.

    Luke 1.52 – He has brought down rulers from their thrones but has lifted up the humble.

2. The Poor as Leaders

Acts 4.13 – When they saw the courage of Peter and John and realized that they were unschooled, ordinary (*idiotes*) men, they were astonished and they took note that these men had been with Jesus.

1 Cor. 12.7, 11 – Now to each one the manifestation of the Spirit is given for the common good. . . . All these are the work of one and the same Spirit, and he gives them to each one, just as he determines.

James 2.5 – Listen, my dear brothers: Has not God chosen those who are poor in the eyes of the world to be rich in faith and to inherit the Kingdom he promised those who love him?

Rev. 1.5-6 – and from Jesus Christ, who is the faithful witness, the firstborn from the dead, and the ruler of the kings of the earth. To him who loves us and has freed us from our sins by his blood, and has made us to be a kingdom and priests to serve his God and Father – to him be glory and power for ever and ever! Amen.

> I have my defense, but it consists in the prayers of the poor. The blind and the lame, the weak and the old, are stronger than hardy warriors.
> ~ St. Ambrose (340-397). "Sermon Against Auxentius."
> *Nicene and Post-Nicene Fathers*, Second Series, Vol. 10. p. 436.

Key Team Leader Virtues: Constantly vigilant against paternalism and responses to the poor that are based on "remedial Christianity." Constantly investing in, and entrusting authority to, faithful leaders among the poor as the means by which the church will be planted.

Ethics of the New Testament
Living in the Upside-Down Kingdom of God
Rev. Dr. Don L. Davis

The Principle of Reversal

The Principle Expressed	Scripture
The poor shall become rich, and the rich shall become poor	Luke 6.20-26
The law breaker and the undeserving are saved	Matt. 21.31-32
Those who humble themselves shall be exalted	1 Pet. 5.5-6
Those who exalt themselves shall be brought low	Luke 18.14
The blind shall be given sight	John 9.39
Those claiming to see shall be made blind	John 9.40-41
We become free by being Christ's slave	Rom. 12.1-2
God has chosen what is foolish in the world to shame the wise	1 Cor. 1.27
God has chosen what is weak in the world to shame the strong	1 Cor. 1.27
God has chosen the low and despised to bring to nothing things that are	1 Cor. 1.28
We gain the next world by losing this one	1 Tim. 6.7
Love this life and you'll lose it; hate this life, and you'll keep the next	John 12.25
You become the greatest by being the servant of all	Matt. 10.42-45
Store up treasures here, you forfeit heaven's reward	Matt. 6.19
Store up treasures above, you gain heaven's wealth	Matt. 6.20
Accept your own death to yourself in order to live fully	John 12.24
Release all earthly reputation to gain heaven's favor	Phil. 3.3-7
The first shall be last, and the last shall become first	Mark 9.35
The grace of Jesus is perfected in your weakness, not your strength	2 Cor. 12.9
God's highest sacrifice is contrition and brokenness	Ps. 51.17
It is better to give to others than to receive from them	Acts 20.35
Give away all you have in order to receive God's best	Luke 6.38

Christus Victor
An Integrated Vision for the Christian Life and Witness
Rev. Dr. Don L. Davis

Christus Victor
Destroyer of Evil and Death
Restorer of Creation
Victor o'er Hades and Sin
Crusher of Satan

For the Church
- The Church is the primary extension of Jesus in the world
- Ransomed treasure of the victorious, risen Christ
- *Laos:* The people of God
- God's new creation: presence of the future
- Locus and agent of the Already/Not Yet Kingdom

For Theology and Doctrine
- The authoritative Word of Christ's victory: the Apostolic Tradition: the Holy Scriptures
- Theology as commentary on the grand narrative of God
- *Christus Victor* as the core theological framework for meaning in the world
- The Nicene Creed: the Story of God's triumphant grace

For Spirituality
- The Holy Spirit's presence and power in the midst of God's people
- Sharing in the disciplines of the Spirit
- Gatherings, lectionary, liturgy, and our observances in the Church Year
- Living the life of the risen Christ in the rhythm of our ordinary lives

For Gifts
- God's gracious endowments and benefits from *Christus Victor*
- Pastoral offices to the Church
- The Holy Spirit's sovereign dispensing of the gifts
- Stewardship: divine, diverse gifts for the common good

For Worship
- People of the Resurrection: unending celebration of the people of God
- Remembering, participating in the Christ event in our worship
- Listen and respond to the Word
- Transformed at the Table, the Lord's Supper
- The presence of the Father through the Son in the Spirit

For Evangelism and Mission
- Evangelism as unashamed declaration and demonstration of *Christus Victor* to the world
- The Gospel as Good News of kingdom pledge
- We proclaim God's Kingdom come in the person of Jesus of Nazareth
- The Great Commission: go to all people groups making disciples of Christ and his Kingdom
- Proclaiming Christ as Lord and Messiah

For Justice and Compassion
- The gracious and generous expressions of Jesus through the Church
- The Church displays the very life of the Kingdom
- The Church demonstrates the very life of the Kingdom of heaven right here and now
- Having freely received, we freely give (no sense of merit or pride)
- Justice as tangible evidence of the Kingdom come

The Kingdom of God
Church Planting in a Universe at War
Rev. Dr. Don L. Davis

> **The Kingdom of God Has Come upon You**
> But Jesus knew their thoughts, and said to them: "Every kingdom divided against itself is brought to desolation, and every city or house divided against itself will not stand. And if Satan casts out Satan, he is divided against himself. How then will his kingdom stand? And if I cast out demons by Beelzebub, by whom do your sons cast them out? Therefore they shall be your judges. But if I cast out demons by the Spirit of God, surely the Kingdom of God has come upon you. Or else how can one enter a strong man's house and plunder his goods, unless he first binds the strong man? And then he will plunder his house. He who is not with me is against me, and he who does not gather with me scatters abroad."
> ~ Matthew 12.25-30

I. **God's Kingdom Rule (i.e., the Kingdom of God) Has Been Contested and Challenged.**

   A. The Triune God as Sovereign Lord over the heavens and the earth

      1. As the Maker and Sustainer of all things

         Isa. 40.21-31 (ESV) – Do you not know? Do you not hear? Has it not been told you from the beginning? Have you not understood from the foundations of the earth? It is he who sits above the circle of the earth, and its inhabitants are like grasshoppers; who stretches out the heavens like a curtain, and spreads them like a tent to dwell in; who brings princes to nothing, and makes the rulers of the earth as emptiness. Scarcely are they planted, scarcely sown, scarcely has their stem taken root in the earth, when he blows on them, and they wither, and the tempest carries them off like stubble. To whom then will you compare me, that I should be like him? says the Holy One. Lift up your eyes on high and see: who created these? He who brings out their host by number, calling them all by name, by the greatness of his might, and because he is strong in power not one is missing. Why do you say, O Jacob, and speak, O Israel, "My way is hidden from the Lord, and my right is disregarded by my God"? Have you not known?

Have you not heard? The Lord is the everlasting God, the Creator of the ends of the earth. He does not faint or grow weary; his understanding is unsearchable. He gives power to the faint, and to him who has no might he increases strength. Even youths shall faint and be weary, and young men shall fall exhausted; but they who wait for the Lord shall renew their strength; they shall mount up with wings like eagles; they shall run and not be weary; they shall walk and not faint.

2. As Sovereign Lord over all

Ps. 135.3-6 (ESV) – Praise the Lord, for the Lord is good; sing to his name, for it is pleasant! For the Lord has chosen Jacob for himself, Israel as his own possession. For I know that the Lord is great, and that our Lord is above all gods. Whatever the Lord pleases, he does, in heaven and on earth, in the seas and all deeps.

B. The mystery of iniquity: war in the heavenlies through Satanic rebellion, Isa. 14.12-17

C. The Fall: humankind's self-reliance, voluntary rebellion, and tragic disobedience, Gen. 3.1-7

1. The loss of freedom: the entrance of sin and Satanic bondage

2. The absence of wholeness: the inauguration of sickness and reality of death

3. The end of justice: the brokenness and fragmentation of human relationships

D. The *proto-evangelium*: the first telling of the Gospel

Gen. 3.15 (ESV) – I will put enmity between you and the woman, and between your offspring and her offspring; he shall bruise your head, and you shall bruise his heel.

II. God's Rule Has Been Inaugurated Through God's Covenant Promise Culminating in the Person and Work of Jesus Christ.

A. The Abrahamic covenant: Gen. 12.1-3.

1. For all the families of the earth (i.e., Yahweh is not a tribal Semitic God but the God of all peoples everywhere).

   Gen. 12.1-3 (ESV) – Now the Lord said to Abram, "Go from your country and your kindred and your father's house to the land that I will show you. And I will make of you a great nation, and I will bless you and make your name great, so that you will be a blessing. I will bless those who bless you, and him who dishonors you I will curse, and in you all the families of the earth shall be blessed."

2. For the Gentiles ("beyond the Jordan")

   Isa. 9.1-2 (ESV) – But there will be no gloom for her who was in anguish. In the former time he brought into contempt the land of Zebulun and the land of Naphtali, but in the latter time he has made glorious the way of the sea, the land beyond the Jordan, Galilee of the nations. The people who walked in darkness have seen a great light; those who dwelt in a land of deep darkness, on them has light shined.

B. The Story of God's glory: the unfolding of the narrative of Israel

   Heb. 1.1-4 (ESV) – Long ago, at many times and in many ways, God spoke to our fathers by the prophets, but in these last days he has spoken to us by his Son, whom he appointed the heir of all things, through whom also he created the world. He is the radiance of the glory of God and the exact imprint of his nature, and he upholds the universe by the word of his power. After making purification for sins, he sat down at the right hand of the Majesty on high, having become as much superior to angels as the name he has inherited is more excellent than theirs.

C. The Kingdom present in Jesus of Nazareth: The Presence of the Future

   1 John 3.8 (ESV) – Whoever makes a practice of sinning is of the devil, for the devil has been sinning from the beginning. The reason the Son of God appeared was to destroy the works of the devil.

   1. His mission: To destroy the works of the devil, 1 John 3.8

   2. His birth: The invasion of God into Satan's dominion, Luke 1.31-33

3. His message: The Kingdom's proclamation and inauguration, Mark 1.14-15

4. His teaching: Kingdom ethics, Matt. 5-7

5. His miracles: His kingly authority and power, Mark 2.8-12

6. His exorcisms: His defeat of the devil and his angels, Luke 11.14-20

7. His life and deeds: The majesty of the Kingdom, John 1.14-18

8. His resurrection: The victory and vindication of the King, Rom. 1.1-4

9. His commission: The call to proclaim his Kingdom worldwide, Matt. 28.18-20

10. His ascension: His coronation, Heb. 1.2-4

11. His Spirit: The *arrabon* (surety, pledge) of the Kingdom, 2 Cor. 1.20

12. His Church: The foretaste and agent of the Kingdom, 2 Cor. 5.18-21

13. His present session in heaven: The generalship of God's forces, 1 Cor. 15.24-28

14. His Parousia (coming): The final consummation of the Kingdom, Revelation

D. Church planting is nothing more than establishing outposts of the "already/not yet" Kingdom throughout the world to represent God's rule.

1. *Christus Victum*: Jesus as ultimate sacrifice for sin

2. *Christus Victor*: Jesus as conquering Lord over God's enemies

3. *Christus Vicar*: Jesus as exalted head of his Church

> God's Kingdom means the divine conquest over his enemies, a conquest which is to be accomplished in three stages; and the first victory has already occurred. The power of the Kingdom of God has invaded the realm of Satan – the present evil Age. The activity of this power to deliver men from satanic rule was evidenced in the exorcism of demons. Thereby, Satan was bound; he was cast down from his position of power; his power was "destroyed." The blessings of the Messianic Age are now available to those who embrace the Kingdom of God. We may already enjoy the blessings resulting from this initial defeat of Satan This does not mean that we enjoy the fullness of God's blessings, or that all that is meant by the Kingdom of God has come to us. . . . the Second Coming of Christ is absolutely essential for the fulfillment and consummation of God's redemptive work. Yet God has already accomplished the first great stage in his work of redemption. Satan is the god of This Age, yet the power of Satan has been broken that men may know the rule of God in their lives.
>
> ~ George Ladd. *The Gospel of the Kingdom*. p. 50.

III. God's Rule Is Invading This Present Evil Age through the Church Militant.

   A. The empowering presence of the Holy Spirit of God, Eph. 5.18

   B. The Church as Sign and Foretaste of the Kingdom, Eph. 5.25-32

      1. Commissioned as his witnesses to the ends of the earth, Acts 1.8

      2. Ambassadors of Christ and his Kingdom, 2 Cor. 5.18-21

      3. Showcase of God's Eschatological glory, 1 Pet. 2.9-10

      4. Deputies of Christ's authority, Matt. 28.18-20; 16.18-19

   C. God's intent in this Present Age: to empower and authorize his Church to do battle against his foes, bearing witness to God's rule today

      1. Jesus' authority now in heaven and earth is absolute: He has been raised to the position of Lord of all by the Father, cf. Matt. 28.18 with Phil. 2.9-11.

2. The strong man must be bound: Jesus' authority over Satan must be enforced (even though he is defeated), 1 Pet. 5.8 with James 4.7.

3. The Church is the Deputy and Agent of the Kingdom of God: she has been granted the right and authority to represent Christ authority in the earth, to do violence against all powers and entities which defy God's knowledge and authority, 2 Cor. 10.3-5.

4. Church planting is the insertion of God's troops into enemy territory. Satanic opposition to Christ's victory and authority is vehement and malicious; only those commissioned with his sovereign Word and Kingdom authority can stand in the evil day, Eph. 6.10-18.

> According to the Bible, our lives are lived in the midst of an invisible spiritual war. One of the most dangerous things we can do is simply to ignore this reality. We accept the Bible as true but we often live as though the battle existed on some far-off mission field, not here in our city. The fact is, there is a battle raging over your city and it is affecting you right now. . . . Every one of us faces demonic forces in our local environment, but as Christians we are called to a bigger battle. We are contending for our whole generation. We are called to act locally but to think globally.
>
> ~ John Dawson. *Taking Our Cities for God*. pp. 27, 29.

D. The weapons of our warfare, 2 Cor. 10.3-5

2 Cor. 10.3-5 (ESV) – For though we walk in the flesh, we are not waging war according to the flesh. For the weapons of our warfare are not of the flesh but have divine power to destroy strongholds. We destroy arguments and every lofty opinion raised against the knowledge of God, and take every thought captive to obey Christ.

1. The whole armor of God, Eph. 6.11

2. Authority (by identification and organic unity with Christ), Eph. 1.13

3. The Word of God, Eph. 6.17

4. The Shield of Faith, Eph. 6.16

5. The Blood of Christ and the word of their testimony, Rev. 12.10-11

E. Soon, God's rule will consummate in the Age to Come at the Second Coming of Jesus Christ, Rom. 16.20.

IV. Implications for Church Plant Team Leaders

A. You must be a submitted disciple under the authority of Christ in order to represent his rule.

1. Others will follow you as you follow Christ.

    1 Cor. 11.1 (ESV) – Be imitators of me, as I am of Christ.

2. When disciples are fully trained they will be like the one who trained them.

    Luke 6.40 (ESV) – A disciple is not above his teacher, but everyone when he is fully trained will be like his teacher.

B. The battle is not yours personally, but the Lord's; church planting is simply his people responding together God's commands as he leads and empowers by the Holy Spirit.

Exod. 14.13-16 (ESV) – And Moses said to the people, "Fear not, stand firm, and see the salvation of the Lord, which he will work for you today. For the Egyptians whom you see today, you shall never see again. The Lord will fight for you, and you have only to be silent." The Lord said to Moses, "Why do you cry to me? Tell the people of Israel to go forward. Lift up your staff, and stretch out your hand over the sea and divide it, that the people of Israel may go through the sea on dry ground.

C. Only God-called people should apply for church planting: you cannot effectively face spiritual darkness in your own name and power; only those called and gifted by God are authorized to represent him in the battle.

1. The sons of Sceva, Acts 19.13-17

2. Singing saints: Paul and Barnabas at Philippi, Acts 16.19-33

D. Jesus Christ is the Lord of the harvest; don't confuse your role and responsibility with his.

1. He alone determines where his warriors serve; he alone reserves the right to dispense his troops where and when as he wills, John 21. 20-23.

   John 21.20-23 (ESV) – Peter turned and saw the disciple whom Jesus loved following them, the one who had been reclining at table close to him and had said, "Lord, who is it that is going to betray you?" When Peter saw him, he said to Jesus, "Lord, what about this man?" Jesus said to him, "If it is my will that he remain until I come, what is that to you? You follow me!" So the saying spread abroad among the brothers that this disciple was not to die; yet Jesus did not say to him that he was not to die, but, "If it is my will that he remain until I come, what is that to you?"

2. The Lord Jesus Christ possesses all authority and power over the enemy; we only represent his will and desires in the fight, Matt. 28.18; Phil. 2.9-11.

   Phil. 2.9-11 (ESV) – Therefore God has highly exalted him and bestowed on him the name that is above every name, so that at the name of Jesus every knee should bow, in heaven and on earth and under the earth, and every tongue confess that Jesus Christ is Lord, to the glory of God the Father.

3. The Lord Jesus Christ alone coordinates his infantry in all spiritual warfare; our responsibility is to be prayerful and deployable, Matt. 9.35-38.

   Matt. 9.35-38 (ESV) – And Jesus went throughout all the cities and villages, teaching in their synagogues and proclaiming the Gospel of the Kingdom and healing every disease and every affliction. When he saw the crowds, he had compassion for them, because they were harassed and helpless, like sheep without a shepherd. Then he said to his disciples, "The harvest is plentiful, but the laborers are few; therefore pray earnestly to the Lord of the harvest to send out laborers into his harvest."

E. Regardless of the outcome of any particular battle, campaign, or fight, in the end Jesus Christ will reign over all.

> Rev. 11.15-18 (ESV) – Then the seventh angel blew his trumpet, and there were loud voices in heaven, saying, "The kingdom of the world has become the kingdom of our Lord and of his Christ, and he shall reign forever and ever." And the twenty-four elders who sit on their thrones before God fell on their faces and worshiped God, saying, "We give thanks to you, Lord God Almighty, who is and who was, for you have taken your great power and begun to reign. The nations raged, but your wrath came, and the time for the dead to be judged, and for rewarding your servants, the prophets and saints, and those who fear your name, both small and great, and for destroying the destroyers of the earth."

> 1 Cor. 15.24-28 (ESV) – Then comes the end, when he delivers the Kingdom to God the Father after destroying every rule and every authority and power. For he must reign until he has put all his enemies under his feet. The last enemy to be destroyed is death. For "God has put all things in subjection under his feet." But when it says, "all things are put in subjection," it is plain that he is excepted who put all things in subjection under him. When all things are subjected to him, then the Son himself will also be subjected to him who put all things in subjection under him, that God may be all in all.

The Bottom Line: _____

Christus Victor
Toward a Biblical Theology for the Urban Church
Rev. Dr. Don L. Davis

> **Come, Enter into the Entire Sweep of History as We Glorify Christ the Risen One!**
>
> The Christian community gathers to remember and to enact its particular identity as those called out by God in Christ. Because all ministries are rooted in the redemptive presence and activity of Christ in the world, the church's sense of time and place is oriented toward God's self-giving in the whole person and work of Jesus Christ. Christian worship involves the gathering of a baptized people who are commissioned and empowered to serve the world. Such servanthood does not take place unless the church remembers with the whole sweep of Scripture and is enabled to hope for a real future in light of God's promises.
>
> ~ Doug E. Sailers. "The Origins of the Church Year."
> Robert Webber., ed. *The Services of the Church Year*.
> Nashville: Star Song Pub. Group, p. 92.
>
> Every culture, every religious tradition has its cycle of seasons, holy days (or holidays), and occasions of special commemoration. We know the earth's seasons of winter, spring, summer, and fall. In the United States, for example, people celebrate national holidays such as Independence Day and Memorial Day. The calendar of the Christian year marks the occasions that have to do with the life of Jesus: his conception, birth, baptism, teaching, ministry, suffering, death, resurrection, and ascension. Someone has said that the Church Year "is the life of Christ lived out again in liturgical time – in the time and in the memory of his Church."
>
> ~ Vicki K. Black. Welcome to the Church Year.
> Harrisburg, PA: Morehouse Publishing, 2004, pp. 2-3.

I. Introduction to the *Christus Victor* Motif: To Christ the Victory!

> The *Christus Victor* motif offers an alternative perspective on the work of Christ, viewing the cross and resurrection from the standpoint of conflict and victory over Satan, sin and death rather than ceremonial sacrifice for sins. It is a perspective that sees the plight of Israel and humankind as bondage to a power rather than laboring under guilt (though these are not ultimately exclusive perspectives). The cross and resurrection form the climax of the paradoxical battle that engages spiritual and human forces within Israel, with the cross, the harsh symbol of coercive Roman power, transformed into the symbol of Christ's victory.
>
> In the words of Paul, "having stripped off the powers and authorities, he made a public spectacle of them, and led them in triumphal procession on the cross" (Col. 2:15). In his resurrection from the dead he has vanquished the ancient enemy: "Death has been swallowed up in victory. "Where, O Death, is your victory? Where, O Death, is your sting?" (1 Cor. 15:54-55 NIV; cf. Hos 13:14). Since Jesus has triumphed over his enemies, "God has highly exalted him" (Phil. 2:9) as cosmic Lord. He is pictured both as presently subduing his enemies (1 Cor. 15:24-26) and as reigning in triumph over his enemies, who are now "under his feet" (Eph. 1:19-22; cf. Ps. 110:1). And he will come again in visible power and glory to vanquish the last embodiment of evil (2 Thess. 2:1-12) and establish his kingdom (1 Cor. 15:25-28).
>
> ~ Leland Ryken, et. al. *The Dictionary of Biblical Imagery, Elec. Edition.*

A. Gustaf Aulen's *Christus Victor*: three views of the Atonement (i.e., the work of Christ on the Cross)

1. *The Satisfaction motif*: Anselm of Canterbury (1033-1109). The sin of humanity had offended the honor of God, bringing disharmony and injustice into God's created order. Atonement is the debt payment necessary to restore God's honor and to restore justice back into the universe.

    a. Propitiation in response to God's honor defiled

    b. Expiation in response to the guilt and penalty of sinners

2. *The Moral Influence motif*: Abelard (1079-1142), the problem of the atonement was not to change God's mind to us, but to

enable sinful humankind to see how loving God was and is. Jesus died as a demonstration of God's love to humankind.

3. *Christus Victor motif*: called the "classic" view of the atonement. This view stresses the image of cosmic battle between good and evil, between God's forces and Satan's. "In that fray God's son Jesus Christ was killed, an apparent defeat of God and victory by Satan. However, Jesus' resurrection turned the seeming defeat into a great victory, which forever established God's control of the universe and freed sinful humans from the power of sin and Satan" (J. Denny Weaver, *The Nonviolent Atonement*, Grand Rapids: Eerdmans, 2001, pp. 14-15).

   a. Called "classic" as the prevailing view of the early Church

   b. A number of variations (none either biblical or convincing!)

      (1) Ransom price paid to Satan in exchange for freeing sinners he held captive

      (2) Satan was deceived because he failed to perceive the presence of God (i.e., the deity of Christ) hidden under his flesh

   c. The native language of the Apocalypse, the early Church, and the general sense of Scripture: *Christ has come to die for sins, rescind the curse, defeat Satan and the powers, destroy the devil's works, and to reestablish the reign of God in the earth!*

B. Why did the biblical *Christus Victor* motif lose favor, after nearly 1,000 years of acceptance?

   1. Aversion to the idea of Satanic rights that God might need to respect

   2. Discomfort with the military and battle symbolism it produces

   3. Modern cosmological problems with defining the Story in terms of malevolent, sentient evil personages which must be subdued

4. Gnawing theodicy issues: if Christ is victor, what has gone wrong with the world?

5. A perceived dualistic framework: God or the devil understanding, with little room for ambiguities or grayness

C. Jesus' presence as the "presence of the future" in the here and now

1. The distinctiveness of Jesus' gospel: "The Kingdom is at hand," Mark 1.14-15

2. Jesus and the inauguration of the Age to Come into this present age

   a. The coming of John the Baptist, Matt. 11.2-6

   b. The inauguration of Jesus's ministry, Luke 4.16-21

   c. The confrontation of Jesus with demonic forces, Luke 10.18ff.; 11.20

3. The teaching of Jesus and his claim of absolute authority on earth, Mark 2.1-12; Matt. 21.27; 28.18

> Christ's death for our sins – His payment of the penalty declared against us – was His legal victory whereby He erased Satan's legal claim to the human race. But Christ also won dynamic victory. That is, when He was justified and made alive, adjudged and declared righteous in the Supreme Court of the universe, Satan, the arch foe of God and man, was completely disarmed and dethroned. Christ burst forth triumphantly from that age-old prison of the dead. Paul says that He "spoiled principalities and powers" and "made a show of them openly, triumphing over them in it" (Colossians 2.15)."
>
> ~ Paul Billheimer. Destined for the Throne. p. 87.

4. "The Kingdom has come and the strong man is bound," Matt. 12.28, 29

   a. The kingdom of God "has come" – *pleroo*

   b. The meaning of the Greek verb: "To fulfill, to complete, to be fulfilled, as in prophecy"

c. The invasion, entrance, manifestation of God's kingly power

5. Jesus as the binder of the strong man

Matt. 12.25-30 (ESV) – Knowing their thoughts, he said to them, "Every kingdom divided against itself is laid waste, and no city or house divided against itself will stand. And if Satan casts out Satan, he is divided against himself. How then will his kingdom stand? And if I cast out demons by Beelzebul, by whom do your sons cast them out? Therefore they will be your judges. *But if it is by the Spirit of God that I cast out demons, then the kingdom of God has come upon you.* Or how can someone enter a strong man's house and plunder his goods, unless he first *binds the strong man*? Then indeed he may plunder his house. Whoever is not with me is against me, and whoever does not gather with me scatters."

6. Jesus defeats humankind's infernal enemy, the devil.

1 John 3.8 – Whoever makes a practice of sinning is of the devil, for the devil has been sinning from the beginning. *The reason the Son of God appeared was to destroy the works of the devil.*

Gen. 3.15 – *I will put enmity between you and the woman,* and between your offspring and her offspring; *he shall bruise your head,* and *you shall bruise his heel.*

Heb. 2.14 – Since therefore the children share in flesh and blood, he himself likewise partook of the same things, *that through death he might destroy the one who has the power of death,* that is, the devil.

Col. 2.15 – *He disarmed the rulers and authorities* and *put them to open shame,* by triumphing over them in him.

a. Blinds the minds of those who do not believe, 2 Cor. 4.4

b. Functions through deception, lying, and accusation, John 8.44

c. Animates the affairs of nations, 1 John 5.19

d. Distracts human beings from their proper ends, cf. Gen. 3.1.ff.

e. Oppresses human beings through harassment, slander, fear, accusation, and death, Heb. 2.14-15

f. Resists and persecutes God's people, Eph. 6.10-18

7. Two manifestations of the Kingdom of God: The Already/Not Yet Kingdom (Oscar Cullman, *Christ and Time*, George Ladd, *The Presence of the Future*)

   a. The *first* advent: the rebellious prince bound and his house looted and God's reign come in the presence of Jesus Christ

   b. The *second* advent: the rebellious prince destroyed and his rule confounded with the full manifestation of God's kingly power in a recreated heaven and earth

D. The Christo-centric order: Messiah Yeshua of Nazareth as centerpiece in both God's revelation and rule

> Jesus' message was the Kingdom of God. It was the center and circumference of all He taught and did. . . . The Kingdom of God is the master-conception, the master-plan, the master-purpose, the master-will that gathers everything up into itself and gives it redemption, coherence, purpose, goal.
>
> ~ E. Stanley Jones. *Is the Kingdom of God Realism?*

1. Messiah's *mission*: to destroy the works of the devil, 1 John 3.8

2. Messiah's *birth*: invasion of God into Satan's dominion, Luke 1.31-33

3. Messiah's *message*: the Kingdom's proclamation and inauguration, Mark 1.14-15

4. Messiah's *teaching*: the ethics of the Kingdom, Matt. 5-7

5. Messiah's *miracles*: his kingly authority and power, Mark 2.8-12

6. Messiah's *exorcisms*: the defeat of the devil and his angels, Luke 11.14-20

7. Messiah's *life and deeds*: the majesty of the Kingdom, John 1.14-18

8. Messiah's *resurrection*: the victory and vindication of the King, Rom.1.1-4

9. Messiah's *commission*: the call to proclaim his Kingdom worldwide, Matt. 28.18-20

10. Messiah's *ascension*: his coronation, Heb.1.2-4

11. Messiah's *outpouring of the Holy Spirit*: the *arrabon* (surety, pledge) of the Kingdom, 2 Cor.1.20

12. Messiah's *Church*: The foretaste and agent of the Kingdom, 2 Cor. 5.18-21

13. Messiah's *session*: his generalship of his forces (1 Cor. 15.24-28), and his high priestly intercession and advocacy at the Father's right hand, Rom. 8.24; Rom. 8.27; Isa. 53.12; John 16.23; John 16.26-27; John 17.20-24; Heb. 4.14-15; Heb. 7.25; Heb. 9.24; 1 John 2.1-2

14. Messiah's *return*: the consummation of his Kingdom reign, Rev. 19.6-9; Zech. 14.5; John 14.3; Acts 1.11; 1 Thess. 4.14; 1 Thess. 4.16; 2 Thess. 1.5-9; 2 Thess. 2.1; 1 John 3.2; Rev. 1.7

E. What *Christus Victor* signifies in the assembly of believers

1. The *Shekinah* has reappeared in the midst of the Church, which now is the dwelling place of God as his temple, Eph. 2.19-22.

2. The people (*ecclesia*) of the living God congregates here: Christ's own from every kindred, people, nation, tribe, status, and culture, 1 Pet. 2.8-9.

3. God's *Sabbath* rest is enjoyed and celebrated here, freedom, wholeness, and the justice of God, Heb. 4.3-10.

4. The *Year of Jubilee* has come: forgiveness, renewal, and restitution, Col. 1.13; Matt. 6.33; Eph. 1.3; 2 Pet. 1.3-4.

5. Light has *shined upon the Gentiles*, who now are fellow heirs of the eternal splendor to come, Col. 1.27; Rom. 16.25-27; Eph. 3.3-5.

6. *The Spirit of the living God* indwells us (*arrabon*): God lives here and walks among us here, 2 Cor. 1.20.

7. We *taste the powers of the Age to Come*: Satan is bound in our midst, the Curse has been broken here, deliverance is experienced in Jesus' name, Gal. 3.10-14.

8. We experience *the shalom of God's eternal kingdom*: the freedom, wholeness, and justice of the new order are present among us, and visibly displayed to the world through our good works, Matt. 5.14-16; Rom. 5.1; Eph. 2.13-22.

9. We *herald the Good News of God's reign* (*evanggelion*): we invite all to join us as we journey to the full manifestation of the Age to Come, Mark 1.14-15.

10. Here we cry *Maranatha!*: our lives are structured by the living hope of God's future and the consummation, Rev. 22.17-21.

II. Implications of *Christus Victor* Theology for Our Life and Witness

> God's Kingdom means the divine conquest over His enemies, a conquest which is to be accomplished in three stages; and the first victory has already occurred. The power of the Kingdom of God has invaded the realm of Satan – the present evil Age. The activity of this power to deliver men from satanic rule was evidenced in the exorcism of demons. Thereby, Satan was bound; he was cast down from his position of power; his power was "destroyed." The blessings of the Messianic Age are now available to those who embrace the Kingdom of God. We may already enjoy the blessings resulting from this initial defeat of Satan. Yes, the Kingdom of God has come near, it is already present.
>
> This does not mean that we now enjoy the fulness of God's blessings, or that all that is meant by the Kingdom of God has come to us. . . . [T]he Second Coming of Christ is absolutely essential for the fulfilment and consummation of God's redemptive work. Yet God has already accomplished the first great stage in His work of redemption. Satan is the god of This Age, yet the power of Satan has been broken that men may know the rule of God in their lives. The evil

> Age goes on, yet the powers of the Age to Come have been made available to men. To the human eye, the world appears little changed; the kingdom of Satan is unshaken. Yet the Kingdom of God has come among men [sic]; and those who receive it will be prepared to enter the Kingdom of Glory when Christ comes to finish the good work He has already begun. This is the Gospel of the Kingdom.
>
> ~ George Eldon Ladd. *The Gospel of the Kingdom*.
> Grand Rapids: Wm. B. Eerdmans Publishing, 1959, pp. 50-51.

A. For the Church

1. As the people of God and the new humanity of God's new creation, the Church is *the people of the victory* of the risen Christ, the very embodiment of Jesus in the world.

2. Clarification

   a. The Church is the people of God, 1 Pet. 2.8-9.

   b. The Church is God's new creation, 2 Cor. 5.17-21.

3. Implication: The Church is *both the locus and agent* of the Kingdom, the proof positive of *Christus Victor* in the earth.

B. For theology and doctrine

1. As confession rooted in the apostolic tradition (i.e., the canonical Scriptures), theology and doctrine is the commentary on the grand narrative of God regarding his saving work in the person of Jesus of Nazareth, the Lord and Messiah, 2 Tim. 3.15-17.

2. Clarification

   a. The Great Tradition has authoritatively affirmed the truth of the Christ event, i.e., *Christus Victor* and its meaning in the world, John 5.39-40; Luke 24.27, 44-48.

   b. The Nicene Creed is an authoritative summary of the Story of God's triumphant grace in the person of Jesus of Nazareth.

3. Implication: *Christus Victor is the center and heart of all biblical theology and orthodox doctrine*, Phil. 2.5-11; Col. 1.15-20.

C. For spirituality

1. As experience, both personal and communal, of our union with Christ by faith, spirituality is the living expression of the Holy Spirit's power in the people of God as they remember, reenact, and reflect upon the mystery of God in *Christus Victor*, 2 Pet. 3.18; John 15.4-5.

2. Clarification

    a. It is captured in the ongoing disciplines rooted in deepening our knowledge of God in Christ, 1 Tim. 4.7-9.

    b. It is shaped by our gatherings, our lectionary, our liturgy, and our observances of the story of Jesus in the Church Year, Col. 3.1-11.

3. Implication: Participating and being transformed by the life of the risen Lord is *the core of authentic spirituality*, Heb. 1.1-4.

D. For worship

1. As the ongoing acknowledgment, reenactment, and remembrance of God's saving acts in *Christus Victor*, worship is the celebration of the gathered assembly of the people of God as they enter into his presence through the Word and the Table, Eph. 5.18-21; Col. 3.11-17; 1 Cor. 15.1-8.

2. Clarification

    a. It is captured in our remembrance, reenactment, and celebration of the Christ event in our worship and service, 1 Cor. 11.23-26.

    b. It is summarized and highlighted in our hearing and response to the Word of God, 2 Pet. 1.20-21.

    c. It is celebrated in our remembrance and transformation at the Table, the Lord's Supper, 1 Cor. 11.23-26.

3. Implication: Coming into the presence of the Father through the work of the Son in the power of the Spirit is the heart of worship.

E. For gifts

1. As tokens and emblems of the Holy Spirit's sovereign supply within the Body of Christ, spiritual gifts are God's gracious endowments and benefits flowing from the bounty won through the victory of *Christus Victor*, Eph. 4.7-10.

2. Clarification

    a. God has given pastoral offices to the Church in order that its members may be equipped for the work of the ministry, Eph. 4.11-16.

    b. The Holy Spirit sovereignly dispenses the gifts to the members of the body for the common good, 1 Cor. 12.1-11.

3. Implication: Stewarding our gifts together for the common good of the Church is the core of spiritual giftedness, 1 Pet. 4.10-11.

F. For evangelism and mission

1. As proclamation of the Gospel of Jesus Christ, evangelism and mission is the unashamed declaration of the victory of Christ over the powers of evil, the penalty of sin, of its effects in both the curse and death, and his restoration of creation through the Father's sovereign will and unmerited grace, Matt. 9.35-38.

2. Clarification

    a. The Gospel is the saving message of God regarding his saving work in Christ, who reigns now as *Christus Victor*, Rom. 10.9-10; Acts. 2.33ff.; Col. 2.15; cf. Gen. 3.15.

    b. We proclaim the coming of the Kingdom of God in Jesus Christ, and proclaim repentance and faith in his name, Col. 1.13-14; 1 John 3.8; Matt. 12.25-30.

    c. We are to obey the Great Commission to go into all the world and make disciples of Jesus among all people groups, Matt. 28.18-20; Mark. 16.15-18; Luke 24.47-48; John 20.21.

3. Implication: Proclaiming Christ as Lord and Messiah is the essence of heralding the good news of the Reign of God.

G. For justice and compassion

1. As a witness to the present reality of the reign of God in the world today, justice and compassion are the gracious and generous expressions of the Church of God in response to the glorious deliverance and benefits of *Christus Victor*, Gal. 6.10.

2. Clarification

    a. As the new creation of God, the Church displays the very life of the Kingdom in its relationships and practices, Matt. 5.13-16.

    b. As agents and ambassadors of Christ, we demonstrate in our words and deeds the ways of the citizenship of heaven, 2 Cor. 5.20; Phil. 3.20-21.

    c. As grateful members of God's incendiary fellowship, we joyfully share who we are and what we have with those less fortunate, as a joyous expression of our thanks to God for his goodness to us, 1 John 3.16-18; Matt. 22.34-40.

3. Implication: As the new creation of God, the Church gives tangible evidence in her good works of the reality of the Kingdom come through the victory of Jesus Christ over evil.

H. For the world

1. Even though Christ has defeated the devil, destroyed the power of evil, and paid the penalty for sin, we still live in a fallen world, subject to sin, decay, and death.

2. In this world believers will still experience tribulation, John 16.33.

3. The devil continues to roam about, seeking whom he may devour, 1 Pet. 5.8.

4. Though ultimate victory comes only when Christ consummates his work at the *Parousia*, we are called to proclaim his victory in the world, and demonstrate the

justice and righteousness of the Kingdom wherever and whenever we can.

a. We are the light of the world, and the salt of the earth, Matt. 5.13-16.

b. We are to be in the world but not of it, John 17.14-19.

c. We are to do good to all people, especially those of the household of faith, Gal. 6.10.

d. We are to be ready to give an answer of the hope that indwells us, 1 Pet. 3.15.

e. We are called to declare the excellencies of him who called us from darkness into the light, 1 Pet. 2.8-9.

f. We are ambassadors of Christ, citizens of the heavenly Kingdom, called to represent its interests with faithfulness and honor, 2 Cor. 5.20; Phil. 3.20-21; 1 Cor. 4.1-2.

III. Embodying and Displaying the Story of the Christ: Embracing a Lived Theology of *Christus Victor* through the Church Year

> [Gustaf Aulen's interpretation of Irenaeus' view of the Christ event in the world]. The Resurrection is for him first of all the manifestation of the decisive victory over the powers of evil, which was won on the cross; it is also the starting-point for the new dispensation, for the gift of the Spirit, for the continuation of the work of God in the souls of men [sic] "for the unity and communion of God and man." "The passion of Christ brought us courage and power. The Lord through His passion ascended up on high, led captivity captive, and gave gifts to men, and gave power to them that believe in Him to tread upon serpents and scorpions and upon all the power of the enemy – that is, the prince of the apostasy. The Lord through His passion destroyed death, brought error to an end, abolished corruption, banished ignorance, manifested life, declared truth, and bestowed incorruption."
>
> ~ Gustaf Aulen. *Christus Victor*. Trans. A. G. Hebert. Eugene, OR: Wipf and Stock Publishers, 2003, p. 32.

A. Advent: the Promised Messiah

1. *Biblical framework*: through the covenant promise of God, a seed of the woman, of Abraham, and of David would come, crushing the head of the serpent, and redeeming God's people.

2. Exemplar Scripture references

    a. For to us a child is born, Isa. 9.6-7 – For to us a child is born, to us a son is given; and the government shall be upon his shoulder, and his name shall be called Wonderful Counselor, Mighty God, Everlasting Father, Prince of Peace. Of the increase of his government and of peace there will be no end, on the throne of David and over his kingdom, to establish it and to uphold it with justice and with righteousness from this time forth and forevermore. The zeal of the Lord of hosts will do this.

    b. The days are coming, Jer. 23.5-6 – Behold, the days are coming, declares the Lord, when I will raise up for David a righteous Branch, and he shall reign as king and deal wisely, and shall execute justice and righteousness in the land. In his days Judah will be saved, and Israel will dwell securely. And this is the name by which he will be called: "The Lord is our righteousness."

    c. The One who is coming will reign in righteousness and peace, Isa. 11.1-10.

3. *Its meaning in Jesus' history*: the pre-incarnate Word, only begotten Son of God in glory

4. *The Season of the Church Year*: Advent, the Coming of Christ. Advent anticipates the First and Second Comings of our Lord. God's prophets foretold his Coming, and angels announced his birth to Mary and the shepherds. We affirm God's promise fulfilled in the arrival of Messiah in Bethlehem.

5. *As to Spiritual Formation*: As we await the One who is coming, let us proclaim and affirm our sure and certain hope of deliverance.

B. Christmas: the Word Made Flesh

1. *Biblical framework*: In the person of Jesus of Nazareth, the Lord God has come into the world; he is Immanuel, "God with us," Isa. 7.14.

2. Exemplar Scripture references

    a. Immanuel, Matt. 1.20-23 – But as he considered these things, behold, an angel of the Lord appeared to him in a dream, saying, "Joseph, son of David, do not fear to take Mary as your wife, for that which is conceived in her is from the Holy Spirit. She will bear a son, and you shall call his name Jesus, for he will save his people from their sins." All this took place to fulfill what the Lord had spoken by the prophet: "Behold, the virgin shall conceive and bear a son, and they shall call his name Immanuel" (which means, God with us).

    b. The Word made flesh, John 1.14-18 – And the Word became flesh and dwelt among us, and we have seen his glory, glory as of the only Son from the Father, full of grace and truth. (John bore witness about him, and cried out, "This was he of whom I said, 'He who comes after me ranks before me, because he was before me.'") And from his fullness we have all received, grace upon grace. For the law was given through Moses; grace and truth came through Jesus Christ. No one has ever seen God; the only God, who is at the Father's side, he has made him known.

    c. The humility of the Son, Phil. 2.6-8 – who, though he was in the form of God, did not count equality with God a thing to be grasped, but made himself nothing, taking the form of a servant, being born in the likeness of men. And being found in human form, he humbled himself by becoming obedient to the point of death, even death on a cross.

3. *Its meaning in Jesus' history*: In the Incarnation, God has come to us. Jesus of Nazareth reveals to humankind the Father's glory in fullness, for the fullness of God dwelt in him, Col. 2.8-10.

4. *The Season of the Church Year*: Christmas, the Birth of Christ. Christmas celebrates the mystery of the incarnation of the Son of God, the Word made flesh. He enters the world to reveal the Father's love to humankind, to destroy the devil's work, and to redeem his people from their sins.

5. *As to Spiritual Formation*: O, Word made flesh, revealer of God come to us, help us to prepare our hearts for you to dwell within them.

C. Epiphany: the Son of Man

1. *Biblical framework*: As the promised King and divine Son of Man, Jesus reveals the Father's glory and salvation to the world.

2. Exemplar Scripture references

    a. A Star out of Jacob, Num. 24.17 – I see him, but not now; I behold him, but not near: a star shall come out of Jacob, and a scepter shall rise out of Israel; it shall crush the forehead of Moab and break down all the sons of Sheth.

    b. The King of the Jews, Matt. 2.2-6 – saying, "Where is he who has been born king of the Jews? For we saw his star when it rose and have come to worship him." When Herod the king heard this, he was troubled, and all Jerusalem with him; and assembling all the chief priests and scribes of the people, he inquired of them where the Christ was to be born. They told him, "In Bethlehem of Judea, for so it is written by the prophet: 'And you, O Bethlehem, in the land of Judah, are by no means least among the rulers of Judah; for from you shall come a ruler who will shepherd my people Israel.'"

    c. The Sunrise shall visit us, Luke 1.78-79 – because of the tender mercy of our God, whereby the sunrise shall visit us from on high to give light to those who sit in darkness and in the shadow of death, to guide our feet into the way of peace.

3. *Its meaning in Jesus' history*: as the Word that declares the Father's glory to the world, the divine Son of Man, Jesus, appears to the magi, and to the world

4. *The Season of the Church Year*: Epiphany, the Manifestation of Christ. Epiphany commemorates the coming of the Magi, who followed the star in search of the Christ child. The season emphasizes Christ's mission to and for the world. The light of God's salvation is revealed to all peoples in the person of Jesus, the Son of God.

5. *As to Spiritual Formation*: In Jesus, the divine Son of Man, the glory and salvation of God is revealed to the nations.

D. Lent: the Suffering Servant

1. *Biblical framework*: As Inaugurator of the Kingdom of God, Jesus demonstrates God's Reign as his Suffering Servant, showing the life of the Kingdom in his words, wonders, and works.

2. Exemplar Scripture references

    a. Matt. 12.25-30 – Knowing their thoughts, he said to them, "Every kingdom divided against itself is laid waste, and no city or house divided against itself will stand. And if Satan casts out Satan, he is divided against himself. How then will his kingdom stand? And if I cast out demons by Beelzebul, by whom do your sons cast them out? Therefore they will be your judges. But if it is by the Spirit of God that I cast out demons, then the kingdom of God has come upon you. Or how can someone enter a strong man's house and plunder his goods, unless he first binds the strong man? Then indeed he may plunder his house. Whoever is not with me is against me, and whoever does not gather with me scatters."

    b. Mark 1.14-15 – Now after John was arrested, Jesus came into Galilee, proclaiming the gospel of God, and saying, "The time is fulfilled, and the kingdom of God is at hand; repent and believe in the gospel."

    c. Luke 17.20-21 – Being asked by the Pharisees when the kingdom of God would come, he answered them, "The kingdom of God is not coming with signs to be observed, nor will they say, 'Look, here it is!' or 'There!' for behold, the kingdom of God is in the midst of you."

3. *Its meaning in Jesus' history*: His teaching, exorcisms, miracles, and mighty works done among the people

4. *The Season of the Church Year*: Lent, the Ministry of Christ. The Lenten season, a forty-day period starting on Ash Wednesday and ending on Thursday of Holy Week, calls us to reflect on Jesus' suffering, crucifixion, and death. Following our Lord, let us prepare ourselves on the way of the Cross for full obedience to God.

5. *As to Spiritual Formation*: In the person of Christ, the power of the reign of God has come to earth, and to the Church.

E. Holy Week: the Lamb of God

1. *Biblical framework*: As both High Priest and Paschal Lamb, Jesus offers himself to God on our behalf as a sacrifice for sin, and as victorious Lord who destroys death and the grave.

2. Exemplar Scripture references

   a. John 1.29 – The next day he saw Jesus coming toward him, and said, "Behold, the Lamb of God, who takes away the sin of the world!"

   b. 2 Cor. 5.18-21 – All this is from God, who through Christ reconciled us to himself and gave us the ministry of reconciliation; that is, in Christ God was reconciling the world to himself, not counting their trespasses against them, and entrusting to us the message of reconciliation. Therefore, we are ambassadors for Christ, God making his appeal through us. We implore you on behalf of Christ, be reconciled to God. For our sake he made him to be sin who knew no sin, so that in him we might become the righteousness of God.

   c. 1 John 3.8 – Whoever makes a practice of sinning is of the devil, for the devil has been sinning from the beginning. The reason the Son of God appeared was to destroy the works of the devil.

   d. Isa. 52-53

   e. 1 Tim. 2.3-6 – This is good, and it is pleasing in the sight of God our Savior, who desires all people to be saved and to come to the knowledge of the truth. For there is one God, and there is one mediator between God and men, the man Christ Jesus, who gave himself as a ransom for all, which is the testimony given at the proper time.

3. *Its meaning in Jesus' history*: As God's perfect Lamb, Jesus offers himself up to God as a sin offering on behalf of the world, and through his death, destroys death, the curse, the grave, and the works of the devil.

4. *The Season of the Church Year*: Holy Week, the Suffering and Death of Christ. Holy Week recalls the events of Christ's suffering and death. We recall his triumphant entry into Jerusalem on Palm Sunday, his giving of the commandments on Maundy (or "New Commandment") Thursday, his crucifixion on Good Friday, and the end the week with the solemn vigil of Saturday night before Easter Sunday.

5. *As to Spiritual Formation*: May those who share the Lord's death be resurrected with him.

F. Eastertide: the Victorious Conqueror

1. *Biblical framework*: In his resurrection from the dead and his ascension to the right hand of God, Jesus is verified, confirmed, and exalted as Victor over death and the restorer of creation.

2. Exemplar Scripture references

a. God raised up Jesus, and has made him both Lord and Christ, Acts 2.32-36 – This Jesus God raised up, and of that we all are witnesses. Being therefore exalted at the right hand of God, and having received from the Father the promise of the Holy Spirit, he has poured out this that you yourselves are seeing and hearing. For David did not ascend into the heavens, but he himself says, "The Lord said to my Lord, Sit at my right hand, until I make your enemies your footstool." Let all the house of Israel therefore know for certain that God has made him both Lord and Christ, this Jesus whom you crucified.

b. Christ is exalted as Head of the Church, Eph. 1.19-23 – and what is the immeasurable greatness of his power toward us who believe, according to the working of his great might that he worked in Christ when he raised him from the dead and seated him at his right hand in the heavenly places, far above all rule and authority and power and dominion, and above every name that is named, not only in this age but also in the one to come. And he put all things under his feet and gave him as head over all things to the church, which is his body, the fullness of him who fills all in all.

c. Every knee will bow, and every tongue will confess Jesus as Lord, Phil. 2.9-11 – Therefore God has highly exalted him and bestowed on him the name that is above every name, so that at the name of Jesus every knee should bow, in heaven and on earth and under the earth, and every tongue confess that Jesus Christ is Lord, to the glory of God the Father.

d. God desires that Jesus have first place in all things, Col. 1.15-20 – He is the image of the invisible God, the firstborn of all creation. For by him all things were created, in heaven and on earth, visible and invisible, whether thrones or dominions or rulers or authorities – all things were created through him and for him. And he is before all things, and in him all things hold together. And he is the head of the body, the church. He is the beginning, the firstborn from the dead, that in everything he might be preeminent. For in him all the fullness of God was pleased to dwell, and through him to reconcile to himself all things, whether on earth or in heaven, making peace by the blood of his cross.

e. He has conquered the principalities and powers, Col. 2.15 – He disarmed the rulers and authorities and put them to open shame, by triumphing over them in him.

3. *Its meaning in Jesus' history*: His resurrection, with appearances to his disciples and other witnesses, as well as his infallible proofs offered between the time of the resurrection and the ascension to the Father's right hand

4. *The Season of the Church Year*: Eastertide, the Resurrection and Ascension of Christ, and the outpouring of the Holy Spirit

a. On Easter Sunday we celebrate the resurrection of Jesus. He who was betrayed by his own disciple, crucified on a

Roman Cross, and buried in a borrowed tomb, rose triumphantly from death to life through the power of God. "Christ is risen! He is risen, indeed!"

    b. For fifty days, from Easter Sunday to Pentecost, we ponder the risen Jesus in his appearances to his disciples. Given all authority, Jesus ascends up to heaven to God's right hand, and sends to us the promise of the Father, the Holy Spirit.

    c. On Pentecost we commemorate the coming of the Holy Spirit to the people of God, the Church. Jesus is now present with his people in the person of the Spirit, to the glory of God the Father. We ponder this mystery together on Trinity Sunday.

5. *As to Spiritual Formation*: Let us participate by faith in the victory of Christ over the power of sin, Satan, and death

G. Kingdomtide (The Season after Pentecost): the Reigning Lord in Heaven, the Bridegroom, and Coming King

1. *Biblical framework*: Now reigning at God's right hand till his enemies are made his footstool, Jesus pours out his benefits on his body, the Church. Soon, at God's appointed time, the risen and ascended Lord will return to gather his Bride, the Church, and consummate his work–the reign of Christ, the King.

2. Exemplar Scripture references

    a. Matt. 28.18-20 – And Jesus came and said to them, "All authority in heaven and on earth has been given to me. Go therefore and make disciples of all nations, baptizing them in the name of the Father and of the Son and of the Holy Spirit, teaching them to observe all that I have commanded you. And behold, I am with you always, to the end of the age."

    b. Rom. 14.7-9 – For none of us lives to himself, and none of us dies to himself. If we live, we live to the Lord, and if we die, we die to the Lord. So then, whether we live or whether we die, we are the Lord's. For to this end Christ died and lived again, that he might be Lord both of the dead and of the living.

c. 1 Cor. 15.25 – For he must reign until he has put all his enemies under his feet.

d. Heb. 1.1-4 – Long ago, at many times and in many ways, God spoke to our fathers by the prophets, but in these last days he has spoken to us by his Son, whom he appointed the heir of all things, through whom also he created the world. He is the radiance of the glory of God and the exact imprint of his nature, and he upholds the universe by the word of his power. After making purification for sins, he sat down at the right hand of the Majesty on high, having become as much superior to angels as the name he has inherited is more excellent than theirs.

e. Rev. 5.9-10 – And they sang a new song, saying, "Worthy are you to take the scroll and to open its seals, for you were slain, and by your blood you ransomed people for God from every tribe and language and people and nation, and you have made them a kingdom and priests to our God, and they shall reign on the earth."

3. *Its meaning in Jesus' history*: the sending of the Holy Spirit and his gifts, Christ's present session in heaven at the Father's right hand, the harvest of God among the nations, the hope of his soon return

4. *The Season of the Church Year*: The Season after Pentecost, the Reigning Lord in heaven and the Judge and Coming Bridegroom

    a. During "ordinary time" (Kingdomtide), we consider God's saving acts through time. As Christus Victor, Jesus must reign until his enemies are put under his feet. He is the head of the body, the Church, and now he empowers his people to bear witness of his saving grace in the world.

    b. As Lord of the harvest, Jesus has commissioned the Church to go and make disciples of all nations. During this season let us consider how we may advance God's Reign as we show and tell of Christ's salvation to the world. This is a season of harvest.

c. As the dawn follows night, so our Lord will surely appear in power and glory to gather his own to himself, to make an end of war and sin, and to restore creation under God's will. This is a season of the hope of Christ's soon return.

d. According to Scripture, Christ will return and finish the work he began on the Cross, to judge the world and save his own. The Feast of Christ the King, the last Sunday before Advent, points to the day when Christ will reign supreme.

5. *As to Spiritual Formation*: Come, indwell us Holy Spirit and empower us to advance Christ's kingdom in the world. Let us live and work in expectation of his soon return, seeking to please him in all things.

IV. Benefits of Fleshing Out Christus Victor in our Worship and Mission

> A Christian is, in essence, somebody personally related to Jesus Christ. Christianity without Christ is a chest without a treasure, a frame without a portrait, a corpse without breath. Christ comes to each of us with an individual summons: 'Come to me', 'follow me'. And the Christian life begins as, however hesitantly and falteringly, we respond to his call. Then as we start following him, we discover to our increasing and delighted surprise, that a personal relationship to Christ is a many-sided, many-coloured, many-splendored thing. We find that he is our Mediator and our Foundation, our Life-giver and our Lord, the Secret and the Goal of our living, our Lover and our Model. Or, bringing together the prepositions we have been considering, we learn that to be a Christian is to live our lives through, on, in, under, with, unto, for and like Jesus Christ. Each preposition indicates a different kind of relationship, but in each case Christ himself is at the center, the symbol of Christ's victory.
>
> ~ John Stott. *Focus on Christ*.
> New York: William Collins Publishers, 1979, p. 155.

A. The answer to fragmentation and idiosyncratic emphases

1. *Christus Victor* saves us from the distraction of themes, concepts, and emphases which are more twigs than branches, trunk, or root, to the biblical story of God's love in Christ.

2. Supporting texts

   a. Don't be taken captive by substitute centers of emphasis, other than Christ, Col. 2.8-10 – See to it that no one takes you captive by philosophy and empty deceit, according to human tradition, according to the elemental spirits of the world, and not according to Christ. For in him the whole fullness of deity dwells bodily, and you have been filled in him, who is the head of all rule and authority.

   b. Teaching human tradition and not Jesus Christ, Mark 7.3-8 – (For the Pharisees and all the Jews do not eat unless they wash their hands, holding to the tradition of the elders, and when they come from the marketplace, they do not eat unless they wash. And there are many other traditions that they observe, such as the washing of cups and pots and copper vessels and dining couches.) And the Pharisees and the scribes asked him, "Why do your disciples not walk according to the tradition of the elders, but eat with defiled hands?" And he said to them, "Well did Isaiah prophesy of you hypocrites, as it is written, 'This people honors me with their lips, but their heart is far from me; in vain do they worship me, teaching as doctrines the commandments of men.' You leave the commandment of God and hold to the tradition of men."

B. The key to apostolic and biblical authority

   1. Jesus Christ himself is the key both to the subject and interpretation of the Scripture, and therefore of both spirituality, service, and mission.

   2. Supporting texts

      a. He came not to abolish the Law or the Prophets, but to fulfill them, Matt. 5.17-18 – "Do not think that I have come to abolish the Law or the Prophets; I have not come to abolish them but to fulfill them. For truly, I say to you, until heaven and earth pass away, not an iota, not a dot, will pass from the Law until all is accomplished.

      b. He interpreted the Scriptures as texts which referred to him.

(1) Luke 24.27 – And beginning with Moses and all the Prophets, he interpreted to them in all the Scriptures the things concerning himself.

(2) Luke 24.44-47 – Then he said to them, "These are my words that I spoke to you while I was still with you, that everything written about me in the Law of Moses and the Prophets and the Psalms must be fulfilled." Then he opened their minds to understand the Scriptures, and said to them, "Thus it is written, that the Christ should suffer and on the third day rise from the dead, and that repentance and forgiveness of sins should be proclaimed in his name to all nations, beginning from Jerusalem."

c. The Scriptures testify to him, John 5.39-40 – You search the Scriptures because you think that in them you have eternal life; and it is they that bear witness about me, yet you refuse to come to me that you may have life.

d. He quoted the Scripture as concerning himself, Heb. 10.5-7 – Consequently, when Christ came into the world, he said, "Sacrifices and offerings you have not desired, but a body have you prepared for me; in burnt offerings and sin offerings you have taken no pleasure. Then I said, 'Behold, I have come to do your will, O God, as it is written of me in the scroll of the book.'"

C. The fullness of shared spirituality

1. Spiritual wisdom and rootedness consists in being grounded in the person of Christ, united by faith to him in gathered assembly.

2. Supporting texts

a. Col. 2.1-3 – For I want you to know how great a struggle I have for you and for those at Laodicea and for all who have not seen me face to face, that their hearts may be encouraged, being knit together in love, to reach all the riches of full assurance of understanding and the knowledge of God's mystery, which is Christ, in whom are hidden all the treasures of wisdom and knowledge.

b. Col. 2.6-7 – Therefore, as you received Christ Jesus the Lord, so walk in him, rooted and built up in him and established in the faith, just as you were taught, abounding in thanksgiving.

c. 2 Pet. 3.18 – But grow in the grace and knowledge of our Lord and Savior Jesus Christ. To him be the glory both now and to the day of eternity. Amen.

d. John 17.3 – And this is eternal life, that they know you the only true God, and Jesus Christ whom you have sent.

e. Phil. 3.8 – Indeed, I count everything as loss because of the surpassing worth of knowing Christ Jesus my Lord. For his sake I have suffered the loss of all things and count them as rubbish, in order that I may gain Christ.

D. The freedom of cultural and tradition expression

1. The freedom Jesus won for his people means that all people, regardless of culture, ethnicity, background, or nationality, can experience the fullness of God in him.

2. Supporting texts

a. Christ died to set us free, Gal. 5.1 – For freedom Christ has set us free; stand firm therefore, and do not submit again to a yoke of slavery.

b. We were called to freedom, Gal. 5.13 – For you were called to freedom, brothers. Only do not use your freedom as an opportunity for the flesh, but through love serve one another.

c. Live as free people in God, 1 Pet. 2.16 – Live as people who are free, not using your freedom as a cover-up for evil, but living as servants of God.

d. The findings of the Jerusalem Council, Acts 15.22-29 – Then it seemed good to the apostles and the elders, with the whole church, to choose men from among them and send them to Antioch with Paul and Barnabas. They sent Judas called Barsabbas, and Silas, leading men among the brothers, with the following letter: "The brothers, both the apostles and the elders, to the brothers who are of the Gentiles in Antioch and Syria and Cilicia, greetings. Since we have heard that some persons have gone out from us and troubled you with words, unsettling your minds, although we gave them no instructions, it has seemed good to us, having come to one accord, to choose men and send them to you with our beloved Barnabas and Paul, men who have risked their lives for the sake of our Lord Jesus Christ. We have therefore sent Judas and Silas, who themselves will tell you the same things by word of mouth. For it has seemed good to the Holy Spirit and to us to lay on you no greater burden than these requirements: that you abstain from what has been sacrificed to idols, and from blood, and from what has been strangled, and from sexual immorality. If you keep yourselves from these, you will do well. Farewell."

e. Background and ethnicity are no longer obstacles to faith and spiritual maturity.

(1) Gal. 3.28 – There is neither Jew nor Greek, there is neither slave nor free, there is neither male nor female, for you are all one in Christ Jesus.

(2) Col. 3.11 – Here there is not Greek and Jew, circumcised and uncircumcised, barbarian, Scythian, slave, free; but Christ is all, and in all.

E. The visible display of the rule of God through the Church

1. As the people of the Resurrection, the Church of *Christus Victor* must concretely reveal through its worship, life, and service the tangible manifestations of the life of the Age to Come right here and now in the world today.

2. Supporting texts

a. We are the salt of the earth, and the light of the world, Matt. 5.13-16 – You are the salt of the earth, but if salt has lost its taste, how shall its saltiness be restored? It is no longer good for anything except to be thrown out and trampled under people's feet. "You are the light of the world. A city set on a hill cannot be hidden. Nor do people light a lamp and put it under a basket, but on a stand, and it gives light to all in the house. In the same way, let your light shine before others, so that they may see your good works and give glory to your Father who is in heaven.

    b. We are to shine like luminaries in the midst of this present twisted and off-center arrangement of society, Phil. 2.14-16 – Do all things without grumbling or questioning, that you may be blameless and innocent, children of God without blemish in the midst of a crooked and twisted generation, among whom you shine as lights in the world, holding fast to the word of life, so that in the day of Christ I may be proud that I did not run in vain or labor in vain.

    c. We are to live in such a way as to illumine the pathway to Christ and his kingdom through our tangible words and works of service, Eph. 5.8-14 – For at one time you were darkness, but now you are light in the Lord. Walk as children of light (for the fruit of light is found in all that is good and right and true), and try to discern what is pleasing to the Lord. Take no part in the unfruitful works of darkness, but instead expose them. For it is shameful even to speak of the things that they do in secret. But when anything is exposed by the light, it becomes visible, for anything that becomes visible is light. Therefore it says, "Awake, O sleeper, and arise from the dead, and Christ will shine on you."

    d. We are to do good to all people, especially those of the household of faith, Gal. 6.9-10 – And let us not grow weary of doing good, for in due season we will reap, if we do not give up. So then, as we have opportunity, let us do good to everyone, and especially to those who are of the household of faith.

F. The explosive power of multiplication and dynamic standardization

  1. Through a focus on the life and work of Jesus Christ of Nazareth, we now can train, equip, and empower an entire generation of believers for evangelization, justice, and mission.

2. Supporting texts

   a. We share fundamental practices for we are essentially one in Christ, Eph. 4.1-6 – I therefore, a prisoner for the Lord, urge you to walk in a manner worthy of the calling to which you have been called, with all humility and gentleness, with patience, bearing with one another in love, eager to maintain the unity of the Spirit in the bond of peace. There is one body and one Spirit – just as you were called to the one hope that belongs to your call – one Lord, one faith, one baptism, one God and Father of all, who is over all and through all and in all.

   b. We are one body, and members of each other, Rom. 12.4-5 – For as in one body we have many members, and the members do not all have the same function, so we, though many, are one body in Christ, and individually members one of another.

   c. We partake of the same bread, 1 Cor. 10.17 – Because there is one bread, we who are many are one body, for we all partake of the one bread.

   d. One body with many members, 1 Cor. 12.12-13 – For just as the body is one and has many members, and all the members of the body, though many, are one body, so it is with Christ. For in one Spirit we were all baptized into one body – Jews or Greeks, slaves or free – and all were made to drink of one Spirit.

   e. Many parts, one body, 1 Cor. 12.20 – As it is, there are many parts, yet one body.

   f. We were called by God into a single living entity, Col. 3.15 – And let the peace of Christ rule in your hearts, to which indeed you were called in one body. And be thankful.

> In the Introduction to this section, I described how, as a child, I always looked for the central piece of the puzzle (the same principle also applies to the central thread of a tapestry). There is also a centerpiece in the Christian faith. And that center, that focal point around which everything else is gathered, is the work of Christ. . . . I have shared with you how the Fathers took me back to the biblical idea that the victory of Christ over evil results in the recapitulation. His victory over evil is the key not only to the early Christian tradition but to the renewal of our personal faith, and to the renewal of the life of the church. I want to show how every aspect of the Christian life relates to Christ's victory over the power of evil and to the ultimate renewal of all things.
>
> The early church saw how faith centers in Christ. For them faith did not begin with the church, with worship, with Scripture, with theology, with spirituality, with education, with evangelism or social action. All these aspects of Christianity, important as they were, were servants of this central theme of the Scriptures: Christ became one of us in order to destroy the power of evil and restore us and the world to its original condition.
>
> I am firmly convinced that our whole life can be changed when we rediscover this radical vision of the work of Christ. A fuller view of Christ's work will form our vision of life and our acting out of that vision in the here and now. I believe the rediscovery of this vision is transforming the renewing congregations of our time. In this emerging church, whether Catholic, mainline Protestant, evangelical, or charismatic, the centrality of Christ's victory over the power of evil is the dynamic that breathes new life into the church.
>
> ~ Robert Webber. *The Majestic Tapestry.*
> Nashville: Thomas Nelson Publishers, 1986, pp. 36-37.

The Bottom Line: _____

Once upon a Time
Understanding Our Church's Place in the Story of God
Rev. Dr. Don L. Davis

> **Tick-Tock, Tick-Tock –
> Can You Sense Your Part in the Story (his-Story) of The LORD?**
>
> Our temporality is itself a feature of all human experience. We know that a family gains identity and deepens its life by keeping anniversaries and by knowing how to celebrate well the significant events which mark that family's history. Birthdays are kept with special rituals and celebrations; but so, too, in healthy families, are memories of deaths, transitions, and the characters and events of family history. At a family reunion the foods are brought and ordered, the stories of our grandparents, aunts, and uncles are told, the songs and entertainments are performed, and the memories recited and made real.
>
> Eating and drinking together in a family takes time. In everyday life we come to understand certain matters only after we have had meals on birthdays, after funerals, with all the children home and with them all gone, and during the subtly changing seasons of our lives. How much more, then, is our eating and drinking at the Lord's Table and our singing and hearing the Word of God this way. The meaning of our Eucharistic meal deepens as we mature in the times and places of such gathering.
>
> The way Christians keep time – or fail to keep time – is a theological expression of what is remembered and lived. "Why do they keep coming, Sunday upon Sunday, year upon year, just to hear me preach, to sing the same songs, and to pray together?" This startling question from a beleaguered pastor opens up our subject to the real issue of congregational faith and life. Why, indeed, do Christians continue, over time, to gather with such regularity? Obligation? Custom? Or could they be searching for a way of opening their temporal lives to God – a search, perhaps, for genuine transformation? The answer is: all of the above.
>
> ~ Doug E. Sailers. "The Origins of the Church Year."
> Robert Webber., ed. *The Services of the Church Year*.
> Nashville: Star Song Pub. Group, p. 92.

I. The Significance of Story: The Story of God's Glory

> The Christian gospel is a narrative. The Word did not become text or a series of abstracted propositions; the Word became flesh (John 1.14). Consequently Christian theology, if it is to be done appropriately, must take the form of a sustained engagement with the story rather then merely an engagement with the Church's propositional responses to the story. And, since we come to know by indwelling rather than in detachment, Christian theology appropriately attempted will take the form of an indwelling of this story, being drawn into its dramas, identifying with its characterizations, tracing the movements of its plot. And since appropriate knowledge should be appropriate to its specific object, and since God is the object (or rather the irreducible subject) of theology, this engagement with the gospel story which is the appropriate form of Christian theology is appropriately worshipful and prayerful. And it is precisely this manner of worshipful and prayerful indwelling that is enabled by the liturgy of the Christian Year.
>
> ~ John E. Colwell. *The Rhythm of Doctrine.*
> Colorado Springs, CO: Paternoster, 2007, p. 7.

A. Human beings operate according to their interpretive frameworks: human beings exist as "walking worldviews."

   1. Every human existence is basically a "story-ordered world."

   2. Myth-making as a primary act of human beings

   3. The role of culture: enabling us to compose our realities from scratch

B. Integrating the details: story and the need to live purposefully

   1. Purposeful mindset: relating all details to the whole

   2. Provisional mindset: relating to details as wholes

C. The problem of a reductionistic faith: substituting the part for the whole

   1. *Reductionism* – substituting a comprehensive religious vision of Christian faith for an alternative, smaller, usually culturally oriented substitute notion, activity, relationship, or element

2. *Rationalism* – spending the majority of time using modern scientific proofs and arguments to underwrite faith in Jesus, reducing Christian faith to holding of particular, contextualized doctrinal positions over against other contrary views

3. *Moralism* – reducing the Christian vision to personal and communal decency and ethics, e.g., living well in a nuclear family context, holding certain views on selected socially controversial moral issues

D. Elements of a comprehensive biblical story-ordered framework

1. The recovery of "Christian myth"

2. The Picture and the Drama: From Before to Beyond Time

3. Living in the Upside-Down Kingdom of God: The Principle of Reversal

4. Philosophical big picture: The Presence of the Future

E. Components of a guiding worldview: Arthur Holmes

1. It has a *holistic goal* (i.e., where we came from, and are going).

2. It is a *perspectival approach* (i.e., in terms of vantage point).

3. It is an *exploratory process* (i.e., how we manufacture meanings).

4. It is *pluralistic* (i.e., takes in the experience of others).

5. It has *action outcomes* (i.e., ramifications for our lives).

F. Elements in the wonder of story for us as human beings

1. The centrality of *human experience in the context of heaven's plan*

2. The richness of *human affections*

3. The use of *sanctified imagination*

4. The power of *concrete image, metaphor, action, and symbol*

5. The immediacy of *heightened reality*

6. The enjoyment of *artistic craftsmanship*

7. The power of *identification and participation*

G. Key propositions of story theology

William J. Bausch lists ten propositions related to story theology that help us understand the significance and importance of the study of stories in the understanding of Bible and theology. (William J. Bausch, *Storytelling and Faith*. Mystic, Connecticut: Twenty-Third Publications, 1984.)

1. Stories introduce us to *sacramental presences.*

2. Stories are always *more important than facts.*

3. Stories forever remain *normative (authoritative)* for the Christian community of faith.

4. *Christian traditions* evolve and define themselves through and around stories.

5. The stories of God *precede, produce, and empower* the community of God's people.

6. Community story implies *censure, rebuke, and accountability.*

7. Stories produce *theology.*

8. Stories produce *many theologies.*

9. Stories produce *ritual and sacrament.*

10. The stories in the canonical Scriptures are neither fiction nor invented; rather, *these stories are history.*

H. The importance of the biblical framework of the Kingdom

1. The canonical Scriptures are *the ultimate point of reference for truth*, and find their foci on God's revelation of himself in Jesus Christ.

2. Teaching on the kingdom story was *the heart of Jesus' teaching*.

3. The kingdom story is the *central focus* of biblical theology.

4. The kingdom story is *final criterion* for judging truth and value.

5. The kingdom story provides an *indispensable key* to understanding human history.

6. The kingdom story *coordinates and fulfills our particular lives* and destinies as they relate to God's reign.

II. Tua Da Gloriam: "The Story of God's Glory"

Ps. 115.1-3 – Not unto us, O Lord, not unto us, But to Your name give glory, Because of Your mercy, And because of Your truth. Why should the Gentiles say, "'Where now is their God?' But our God is in heaven; He does whatever He pleases."

> Christianity takes time seriously. History is where God is made known. Christians have no knowledge of God without time, for it is through actual events happening in historical time that God is revealed. God chooses to make the divine nature and will known through events that take place within the same calendar that measures the daily lives of men and women. God's self-disclosures take place within the same course of time as political events: "In the days of Herod king of Judea" (Luke 1.5 NEB), or "it took place when Quirinius was governor of Syria" (Luke 2.2 NEB). God's time is our time, too, marked by a temporal order called a calendar. . . . For Christianity, the ultimate meanings of life are revealed not by universal timeless statements but by concrete acts of God. In the fullness of time, God invades our history, assumes our flesh, heals, teaches, and eats with sinners.
>
> ~ Hoyt L. Hickman, et. al. *The New Handbook of the Christian Year*. Nashville: Abingdon Press, 1992, p. 16.

From Before to Beyond Time

Adapted from Suzanne de Dietrich, *God's Unfolding Purpose*. Philadelphia: Westminster Press, 1976.

A. ***Before Time*** (Eternity Past), Ps. 90.1-3

   1. The Eternal Triune God, Ps. 102.24-27

   2. God's Eternal Purpose, 2 Tim. 1.9; Isa. 14.26-27

      a. To glorify his name in all creation, Prov. 16.4; Ps. 135.6; Isa. 48.11

      b. To display his perfections in the universe, Ps. 19.1

      c. To draw out for himself a people for his pleasure, Isa. 43.7, 21

   3. The Mystery of Iniquity: the rebellion of the Dawn of the Morning (Lucifer), Isa. 14.12-20; Ezek. 28.13-17

   4. The emergence of the Principalities and Powers, Col. 2.15

B. ***The Beginning of Time*** (The Creation), Gen. 1-2

   1. The Creative Word of the Triune God, Gen. 1.3; Ps. 33.6, 9; Ps. 148.1-5

   2. The creation of the universe out of nothing (not from himself), Ps. 24.1-2; Ps. 50.12; Exod. 9:29; Exod. 19:5; Deut. 10.14; 1 Chron. 29.11; Job 41.11; Dan. 4.25; 1 Cor. 10.26

   3. The creation of Humanity: the Imago Dei (image of God), Gen. 1.26-27

C. ***The Tragedy of Time*** (The Fall and the Curse), Gen. 3

   1. The Fall and the Curse, Gen. 3.1-9

   2. The *protoevangelium*: the Promised Seed, Gen. 3.15

   3. The End of Eden and the beginning of the Reign of Death, Gen. 3.22-24

4. First signs of God's redeeming, ransoming grace, Gen. 3.15, 21

5. The judgment of humankind: Noah and the Flood, Gen. 6-9

6. The Tower of Babel and the scattering of peoples, Gen. 11

D. *The Unfolding of Time* (God's Plan Revealed through the People of Israel)

1. The Abrahamic Promise and the covenant of Yahweh (Patriarchs), Gen. 12.1-3; 15; 17; 18.18; 28.4

2. The Exodus and the Covenant at Sinai, Exodus-Deuteronomy

3. The Conquest of the inhabitants and the Promised Land, Joshua-2 Chronicles

4. Judges, Samuel, and the Kings: Saul, David, Solomon, 1 and 2 Samuel

5. The City, the Temple, and the Throne, Ps. 48.1-3; 2 Chron. 7.14; 2 Sam. 7.8ff. (The unified and divided Kingdoms of Judah and Israel)

    a. The role of the prophet: declaring the word of the Lord to the people of God, Deut. 18.15

    b. The role of the priest: representing God before his people, Heb. 5.1

    c. The role of the king: ruling with righteousness and justice in God's stead in his kingdom, Ps. 72

6. The judgment upon Israel: Assyrian captivity, cf. 2 Kings 15; Isa. 9

7. The Captivity of Judah, and the Babylonian Exile: Jeremiah, Lamentations, Daniel, Ezekiel, Esther

8. The Return of the Remnant: Ezra, Nehemiah, Malachi

E. *The Fullness of Time* (Incarnation of Christ Jesus), Gal. 4.4-6

1. The Word becomes Flesh, John 1.14-18; 1 John 1.1-4

2. The testimony of John the Baptist, Matt. 3.1-3

3. The Kingdom has come in the person of Jesus of Nazareth, Mark 1.14-15; Luke 10.9-11; 10.11; 17.20-21

    a. Revealed in his person, John 1.18

    b. Exhibited in his works, John 5.36; 3.2; 9.30-33; 10.37-38; Acts 2.22; 10.38-39

    c. Interpreted in his testimony, Matt. 5-7

4. The Secret of the Kingdom revealed, Mark 1.14-15

    a. The Kingdom is already present, Matt. 12.25-29

    b. The Kingdom is not yet consummated, Matt. 25.31-46

5. The Passion and Death of the Crucified King, Matt. 26.36-46; Mark 14.32-42; Luke 22.39-46; John 18.1ff.

    a. To destroy the devil's work: Christus Victor, 1 John 3.8; Gen. 3.15; Col. 2.15; Rom. 16.20; Heb. 2.14-15

    b. To make atonement for sin: Christus Victums, 1 John 2.1-2; Rom. 5.8-9; 1 John 4.9-10; 1 John 3.16

    c. To reveal the Father's heart of love and mercy, John 3.16; Titus 2.11-15

6. *Christus Victor*: The Resurrection of the Glorious Lord of life, Matt. 28.1-15; Mark 16.1-11; Luke 24.1-12

F. *The Last Times* (The Descent and Age of the Holy Spirit)

1. The *arrabon* of God: The Spirit as Pledge and Sign of the Kingdom's presence, Eph. 1.13-14; 4.30; Acts 2.1-47

2. "This is that which was spoken by the prophet": Peter, Pentecost, and the Presence of the Future

    a. The Church as foretaste and agent of the Kingdom of God, Phil. 2.14-16; 2 Cor. 5.20

b. The present reign of Messiah Jesus, 1 Cor 15.24-28; Acts 2.34; Eph. 1.20-23; Heb. 1.13

c. The ushering in of God's kingdom community "in-between the times"; Rom. 14.7

3. The Church of Messiah Jesus: Sojourners in the Already and the Not Yet Kingdom of God

   a. The Great Confession: Jesus is Lord, Phil. 2.9-11

   b. The Great Commission: Go and make disciples among all nations, Matt. 28.18-20; Acts 1.8

   c. The Great Commandment: Love God and your neighbor as yourself, Matt. 22.37-39

4. The Announcement of the Mystery: Gentiles as fellow-heirs of Promise, Rom. 16.25-27; Col. 1.26-28; Eph. 3.3-11

   a. Jesus as the Last Adam, the Head of a New Human Race, 1 Cor. 15.45-49

   b. God drawing out of the world a New Humanity, Eph. 2.12-22

5. In-between the times: Tokens of Age of Sabbath and of Jubilee, Acts 2.17 ff; cf. Joel 2; Amos 9; Ezek. 36.25-27

G. *The Fulfillment of Time* (The *Parousia* of Christ), 1 Thess. 4.13-17

1. Completion of World Mission: the evangelization of the world's ethnoi, Matt. 24.14; Mark 16.15-16; Rom. 10.18

2. The apostasy of the Church, 1 Tim. 4.1-3; 2 Tim. 4.3; 2 Thess. 2.3-12

3. The Great Tribulation, Matt. 24.21ff; Luke 21.24

4. The *Parousia*: the Second Coming of Jesus, 1 Thess. 4.13-17; 1 Cor. 15.50-58; Luke 21.25-27; Dan. 7.13

5. The Reign of Jesus Christ on earth, Rev. 20.1-4

6. The Great White Throne and Lake of Fire, Rev. 20.11-15

7. "For He Must Reign": The final placement of all enemies under Christ's feet, 1 Cor. 15.24-28

H. *Beyond Time* (Eternity Future)

1. The Creation of the New Heavens and Earth, Rev. 21.1; Isa. 65.17-19; 66.22; 2 Pet. 3.13

2. The Descent of the New Jerusalem: the abode of God comes to earth, Rev. 21.2-4

3. The Times of Refreshing: the Glorious Freedom of the Children of God, Rom. 8.18-23

4. The Lord Christ gives over the Kingdom to God the Father, 1 Cor. 15.24-28

5. The Age to Come: The Triune God as All-in-all, Zech. 14.9 and 2.10; Jer. 23.6; Matt. 1.23; Ps. 72.8-11; Mic. 4.1-3

III. Implications of the Drama of All Time

> Beginning with the affirmation of God as the one who comes (and who will come), the Church moves through the narrative of Christ's birth, of his baptism and revelation to the world, of his temptation and his journey to suffering and the Cross, of his resurrection and ascension, of his sending of the Spirit, and of his kingly reign together with all those made holy in him. Through prayers, canticles, readings, and responses the Church not only contemplates these stages of the story, it re-lives them, it enters into them, it is shaped by them. The Church journeys through the Christian Year with the Christ whose story is here narrated; the Church joins him in his journey and reaffirms his journey as its own journey, the journey by which it is defined and in which it participates. This is no detached propositional dogmatics, this is a repetition and an indwelling of the story that is deeply engaging and inherently transformative. . . . To celebrate the Christian Year is to engage in theological reflection that is narratival, doxological, and truly systematic.
>
> ~ John E. Colwell. *The Rhythm of Doctrine*. Colorado Springs, CO: Paternoster, 2007, p. 7.

A. The sovereign God underwrites all time and happenings in human history.

   1. Whatever he pleases, he does, Ps. 135.6.

   2. God's counsels and plans stand forever, to all generations, Ps. 33.11; Ps. 115.3.

   3. God declares the end of all things from the beginning, Isa. 46.10.

   4. Nothing and no one can withstand the plan of God for salvation and redemption, Dan. 4.35.

B. The LORD is the central character in the unfolding of the divine drama, Eph. 1.9-11.

   1. All things are being recapitulated in the person of Jesus Christ, the perfect Anti-type of the foreshadowings in the Hebrew Scriptures.

   2. As saints of God, we participate as characters in the epic and cosmic drama of God being played out on the stage of earth.

   3. As aliens and sojourners, our duty is to be God's counter-cultural community fleshing out the life of the Age to come in the here and now, 1 Pet. 1.13-21.

   4. As citizens of the heavenly realm and ambassadors of Christ, we are called to declare and demonstrate the life of heaven in the darkest, most dismal, and most dangerous places on earth, in every generation, 2 Cor. 5.18-21.

C. The Church bears witness of the Already/Not Yet Kingdom in its life and works, that reign which was lost at the beginning of time.

   1. God's sovereign rule, Mark 1.14-15

   2. Satan's infernal rebellion, Gen. 3.15 with Col. 2.15; 1 John 3.8

   3. Humankind's tragic fall, Gen. 3.1-8; cf. Rom. 5.5-8

4. Christ's victorious reclamation of all things in the name of God, cf. Eph. 1.10-11 with Col.2.15; 1 John 3.8; 1 Cor. 15.57

D. Making disciples among all nations and displaying the Kingdom's glory is fulfilling our role in the script of Almighty God!, Matt. 28.18-20.

1. To declare salvation to the nations, Ps. 96.3

2. To prophesy deliverance to the captives, Luke 4.18-19; cf. Isa. 61.1ff.

3. To be salt and light in the midst of corruption and darkness, Matt. 5.13-16

4. To be a dwelling place of God in the Spirit, with Christ as the cornerstone, Eph. 2.19-22

E. The Church is an eschatological community, being both the locus and agent of the Kingdom of God.

1. As *locus*, the Church is itself living proof, a concrete cosmic visual aid as to the splendor of God's grace, and as the very body of Jesus in the world: Churches are *concrete evidence* of the Heavenly Realm.

    a. We *recite* the story in our worship and praise.

    b. We *remember* the story in our remembrance through the Church Year.

    c. We *reenact* the story in our disciplines, festivals, and sacraments.

    d. We *embody* the story in our relationships as the new Israel of God.

2. As *agent*, the Church is the community of faithful witness, called to show and tell in concrete form what the Kingdom is and does in this in-between time: Churches are *outposts* of the Kingdom of God.

    a. We *unashamedly declare his glory* among the nations in sharing the Good News of the Kingdom of God.

b. We *multiply disciples* as we welcome and equip people groups in the fellowship of the body of Christ.

c. We *demonstrate in concrete, visible expression* the life of the Age to come through our good works, especially to the household of faith.

d. We *prophetically engage the powers* as we advocate the justice and righteousness of the Kingdom to others.

The Bottom Line: _____

The Black Church and Church Planting
World Impact Blog, February, 2015
Rev. Efrem Smith • www.worldimpact.org

The Black Church began with Church Planting and its future will depend on the recovery of this movement of reproduction, empowerment, and mission. Dr. Hank Voss, World Impact's National Director of Church Planting and I recently met with Elder Oscar Owens, an associate pastor at West Angeles C.O.G.I.C. (Church Of God In Christ) Church. The Church of God in Christ is one of the largest predominately African American denominations. During our visit we began to talk about a commitment to church planting that are the roots of the denomination and the Black Church more broadly. Until this moment, I had never truly reflected deeply on the Black Church and Church Planting. I must admit that I had seen Church Planting as a, mostly White Evangelical endeavor and that I was one of the few African Americans that had sensed a deep call to facilitating church planting movements. I thought a large part of my calling was to bring the spirit and the biblical theology of Church Planting to the Black Church. After my visit with Elder Owens, I realized my calling was more to be one of many voices assisting in helping the Black Church to recover something that is a deep part of its heritage and, an essential part of its future.

Some (like me for too long) have been led to believe that the White Church grows through Church Planting and the Black Church through Church Splitting. Not that Church splitting is not a reality in a significant segment of the Black Church and within the history of the White Church as well, but Church Planting is a major part of the Black Church narrative. There would be no Black Church if not for Church Planting. Not only must this heritage of Black Church Planting be recovered for the future Black Church, but also the context of how the first Black Churches were planted can serve as a gift to the whole body of Christ. This Black Church planting gift can inform a more missional approach to all Church Planting Movements.

The Black Church in America was birthed in the oppression, affliction, and suffering of slavery. The first Black Churches were planted illegally in the dark woods, away from the eyes and ears of slave owners who questioned if these church planters were even fully human. For Black people these church plants were much more than simply containing elements of worship, discipleship, and witness. These church plants were the organic spiritual communities in which the oppressed found the courage and strength to fight for personhood, deliverance, and liberation. There was no separation of evangelism and the social gospel in these church plants. Without formal institutions for credentialing and theological training, somehow Black Churches were planted. Without committed funding strategies, somehow Black Churches were planted. I believe these were both evangelistic and missional churches led by the indigenously oppressed of what was supposedly a Christian nation. The oppressed would have to seek a God beyond the God of the slave owners. The oppressed would have to repent to, seek salvation from, and be empowered by a Christ that looked different than the Christ of the slave owners and yet was more authentic to the Christ of the Scriptures they had to teach themselves to read and interpret in many cases. What a powerful church planting movement.

This Black Church planting heritage led to Black Churches that were leadership and community development centers during Jim Crow segregation. Black colleges, businesses, and social organizations would come into existence because of this Black Church planting heritage. The roots of this church planting movement provided fuel for what would eventually become the Civil Rights Movement.

The roots of Black Church planting could be the very medicine needed to be injected into today's Black Church that it may inform the broader body of Christ towards a more biblical and missional understanding. You see the roots of Black Church planting aren't very different from the church planting movements of Scripture. The first Christian Churches were planted under the oppression of the Roman Empire and religious power structures. Paul, when his name was Saul was known as a zealous religious Jew and Roman citizen who persecuted Christian church planters. Biblical Church Planting was done by a Jewish, multi-ethnic, multi-cultural, minority, and oppressed people. The roots of church planting biblically were about evangelism, discipleship, empowerment, and liberation. In many places on this planet this is exactly the kind of church planting movement we need today. In many under-resourced nations these types of indigenous movements are already taking place. My own nation must live into this more proactively. In the United States, church planting for the most part, seems to begin with the privileged and the resourced in mind. Black Church planting and biblical church planting seems to begin with the poor, oppressed, and marginalized.

At World Impact (www.worldimpact.org) we are about facilitating church planting movements among the unreached urban poor in the United States and beyond. We also see the empowerment and training of indigenous leaders as a key part of this endeavor. We don't' see this as some type of fringe movement, but as central to biblical church planting and as a way to recover the initial church planting DNA of the Black Church as well as some of the European immigrant history of church planting in this nation as well.

A Theology of the Kingdom and the Church

Living in the Already and the Not Yet Kingdom

Rev. Dr. Don L. Davis

The Spirit: The pledge of the inheritance (*arrabon*)
The Church: The foretaste (*aparche*) of the Kingdom
"In Christ": The rich life (*en Christos*) we share as citizens of the Kingdom

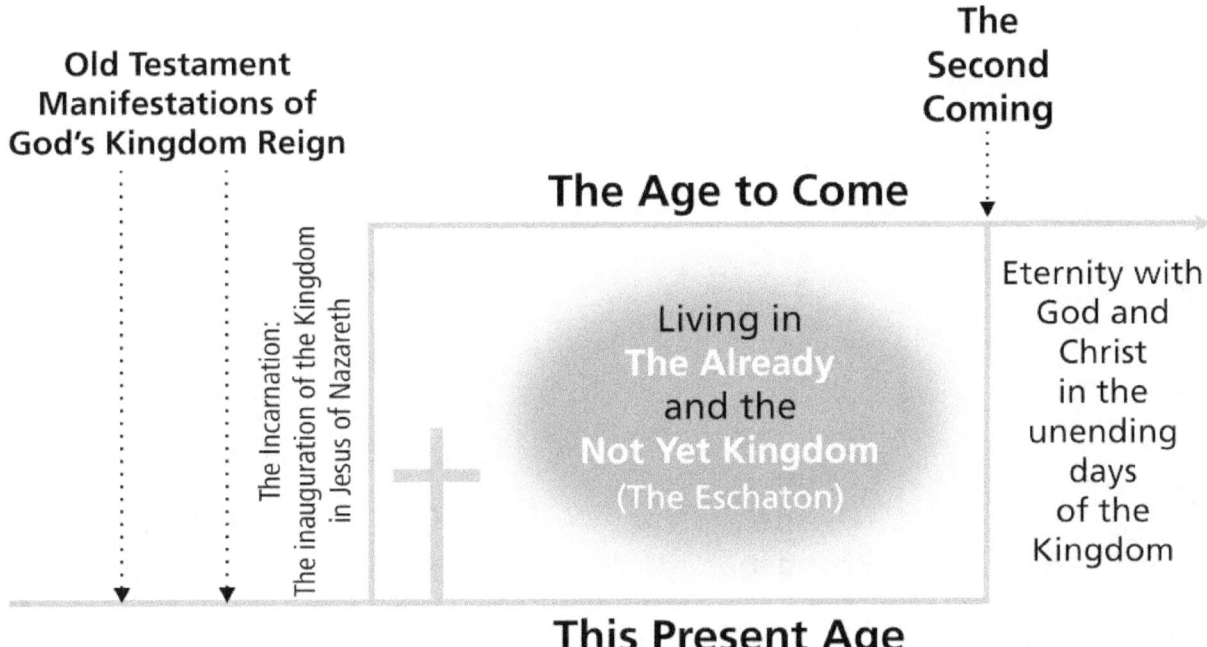

Internal enemy: The flesh (*sarx*) and the sin nature
External enemy: The world (*kosmos*) the systems of greed, lust, and pride
Infernal enemy: The devil (*kakos*) the animating spirit of falsehood and fear

Jewish View of Time

This Present Age   The Age to Come

The Coming of Messiah
The restoration of Israel
The end of Gentile oppression
The return of the earth to Edenic glory
Universal knowledge of the Lord

Jesus of Nazareth: The Presence of the Future
Rev. Dr. Don L. Davis

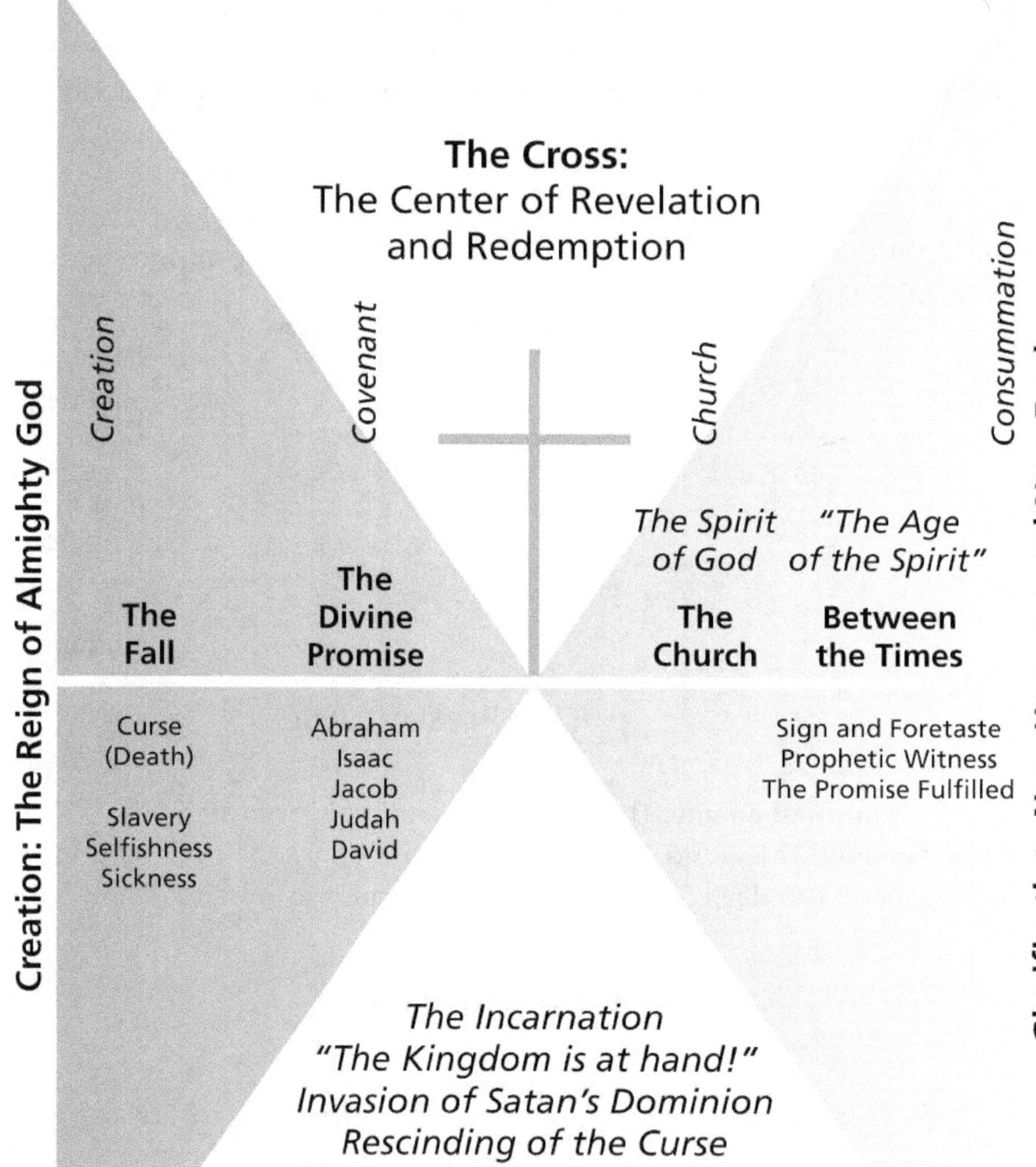

A Theology of the Church in Kingdom Perspective
Rev. Dr. Don L. Davis

A Schematic for a Theology of the Kingdom and the Church

The Urban Ministry Institute

The Father	The Son	The Spirit
Love - 1 John 4.8	Faith - Heb. 12.2	Hope - Rom. 15.13
Maker of heaven and earth and of all things visible and invisible.	Prophet, Priest, and King	Lord of the Church

Creation	Kingdom	Church
The triune God, Yahweh Almighty, is the Creator of all things, the Maker of the universe.	The Reign of God expressed in the rule of his son Jesus the Messiah.	The Holy Spirit now indwells the one, holy, catholic, and apostolic community of Christ, which functions as a witness to (Acts 28.31) and a foretaste of (Col. 1.12; James 1.18; 1 Pet. 2.9; Rev. 1.6) the everlasting Kingdom of God.

		*The Church Is a Catholic (universal), Apostolic Community Where the Word Is **Rightly Preached**. Therefore It Is a Community of:*
The eternal God, Yahweh Almighty, is the triune Lord of all, Father, Son, and Holy Spirit, who is sovereign in power, infinite in wisdom, perfect in holiness, and steadfast in love. All things are from him, and through him and to him as the source and goal of all things.	**Freedom** (Through the fall, the Slavery of Satan and sin now controls creation and all the creatures of the world. Christ has brought freedom and release through his matchless work on the Cross and the Resurrection, Rom. 8.18-21)	**Calling** - For freedom Christ has set us free; stand firm therefore, and do not submit again to a yoke of slavery. - Gal. 5.1 (ESV) (cf. Rom. 8.28-30; 1 Cor. 1.26-31; Eph. 1.18; 2 Thess. 2.13-14; Jude 1.1)
	Jesus answered them, "Truly, truly, I say to you, everyone who commits sin is a slave to sin. The slave does not remain in the house forever; the son remains forever. So if the Son sets you free, you will be free indeed." - John 8.34-36 (ESV)	**Faith** - ". . . for unless you believe that I am he you will die in your sins". . . . So Jesus said to the Jews who had believed in him, "If you abide in my word, you are truly my disciples, and you will know the truth, and the truth will set you free." - John 8.24b, 31-32 (ESV) (cf. Ps. 119.45; Rom. 1.17; 5.1-2; Eph. 2.8-9; 2 Tim. 1.13-14; Heb. 2.14-15; James 1.25)
O, the depth of the riches and wisdom and knowledge of God! How unsearchable are his judgments, and how inscrutable his ways! For who has known the mind of the Lord, or who has been his counselor? Or who has ever given a gift to him, that he might be repaid?" For from him and through him and to him are all things. To him be glory forever! Amen! - Rom. 11.33-36 (ESV) (cf. 1 Cor. 15.23-28; Rev. 21.1-5)		**Witness** - The Spirit of the Lord is upon me, because he has anointed me to proclaim good news to the poor. He has sent me to proclaim liberty to the captives and recovering of sight to the blind, to set at liberty those who are oppressed, to proclaim the year of the Lord's favor. - Luke 4.18-19 (ESV) (cf. Lev. 25.10; Prov. 31.8; Matt. 4.17; 28.18-20; Mark 13.10; Acts 1.8; 8.4, 12; 13.1-3; 25.20; 28.30-31)
	Wholeness (Through the Fall, Sickness [dis-ease] has come into the world. Christ has become our healing and immortality through the Gospel, Rev. 21.1-5!)	*The Church Is One Community Where the Sacraments Are **Rightly Administered**. Therefore It Is a Community of:*
	But he was wounded for our transgressions; he was crushed for our iniquities; upon him was the chastisement that brought us peace, and with his stripes we are healed. - Isa. 53.5	**Worship** - You shall serve the Lord your God, and he will bless your bread and your water, and I will take sickness away from among you. - Exod. 23.25 (ESV) (cf. Ps. 147.1-3; Heb. 12.28; Col. 3.16; Rev. 15.3-4; 19.5)
		Covenant - And the Holy Spirit also bears witness to us; for after the saying, "This is the covenant that I will make with them after those days, declares the Lord: I will put my laws on their hearts, and write them on their minds," then he adds, "I will remember their sins and their lawless deeds no more." - Heb. 10.15-17 (ESV) (cf. Isa. 54.10-17; Ezek. 34.25-31; 37.26-27; Mal. 2.4-5; Luke 22.20; 2 Cor. 3.6; Col. 3.15; Heb. 8.7-13; 12.22-24; 13.20-21)
		Presence - In him you also are being built together into a dwelling place for God by his Spirit. - Eph. 2.22 (ESV) (cf. Exod. 40.34-38; Ezek. 48.35; Matt. 18.18-20)
	Justice (Through the Fall, Selfishness now dominates the relationships of the world. Christ has brought his own justice and righteousness to the Kingdom, Isa. 11.6-9!)	*The Church Is a Holy Community Where Discipline Is **Rightly Ordered**. Therefore It Is a Community of:*
	Behold, my servant whom I have chosen, my beloved with whom my soul is well pleased. I will put my Spirit upon him, and he will proclaim justice to the Gentiles. He will not quarrel or cry aloud, nor will anyone hear his voice in the streets; a bruised reed he will not break, and a smoldering wick he will not quench, until he brings justice to victory. - Matt. 12.18-20 (ESV)	**Reconciliation** - For he himself is our peace, who has made us both one and has broken down in his flesh the dividing wall of hostility by abolishing the law of commandments and ordinances, that he might create in himself one new man in place of the two, so making peace, and might reconcile us both to God in one body through the cross, thereby killing the hostility. And he came and preached peace to you who were far off and peace to those who were near. For through him we both have access in one Spirit to the Father. - Eph. 2.14-18 (ESV) (cf. Exod. 23.4-9; Lev. 19.34; Deut. 10.18-19; Ezek. 22.29; Mic. 6.8; 2 Cor. 5.16-21)
		Suffering - Since therefore Christ suffered in the flesh, arm yourselves with the same way of thinking, for whoever has suffered in the flesh has ceased from sin, so as to live for the rest of the time in the flesh no longer for human passions but for the will of God. - 1 Pet. 4.1-2 (ESV) (cf. Luke 6.22; 10.3; Rom. 8.17; 2 Tim. 2.3; 3.12; 1 Pet. 2.20-24; Heb. 5.8; 13.11-14)
		Service - But Jesus called them to him and said, "You know that the rulers of the Gentiles lord it over them, and their great ones exercise authority over them. It shall not be so among you. But whoever would be great among you must be your servant, and whoever would be first among you must be your slave even as the Son of Man came not to be served but to serve, and to give his life as a ransom for many." - Matt. 20.25-28 (ESV) (cf. 1 John 4.16-18; Gal. 2.10)

Thy Kingdom Come!
Readings on the Kingdom of God

Edited by Terry G. Cornett and Don L. Davis • *The Kingdom of God. Module 2, The Capstone Curriculum.* Wichita: The Urban Ministry Institute, 2005.

A Tale of Two Kingdoms

Hear the parable of a kingdom, a usurper-prince of the realm of this world. By means of a masterful program of clever deception, he has managed to bring millions of subjects under his powerful rule. Granted, he has enticed them from the realm of another Monarch, but he considers them his. After all, they have been under his dominion for some considerable time now, and the Enemy hasn't yet taken them back. Yes, in the mind of this prince, these people are legally his people and this land his land. Possession is, after all, he says, nine-tenths of the law.

Suddenly, without much warning, the rival Government takes action. The Son of the Enemy Monarch is dispatched to the prince's very own turf (well, yes, he did steal it, but. . .) to take back those who would resubmit to his reign. The Monarch's plan is to draw these people out from under the prince's authority, philosophy, and life-style.

Most outrageous of all, the Monarch sets up his Government on the prince's own real estate. And instead of immediately removing his restored subjects from the country, he is keeping them there until a disease called *death* (a consequence of the prince's regime which eventually claims everyone) brings about a change in their state of existence. To make the matter even more aggravating, the Son even promises people that he will save them from death, and become the firstfruits by dying and coming back to life again himself.

Unsettled, but undefeated (he thinks), the prince launches an all fronts counterattack. Plainly, he is no match for the other King one on One. So he launches a renewed program of deception, simply lying to his citizens about the other Government. That doesn't always work, for the Monarch's Son keeps taking subjects back. Since they are such weak creatures, however, the prince sees no reason to give up hope for their eventual return. Consequently, even after they become citizens of that other kingdom, he keeps the pressure on.

Falsehood is the prince's most common weapon. He uses it at the most strategic points. Since the most committed people are the most dangerous, he attacks the zealots among his former subjects by spreading rumors about them and intimidating them by hints of his power. By and large his successes are few, however, for these people demonstrate an almost supernatural attachment to the Enemy Monarch.

Still, the prince in encouraged by one relatively small, though nonetheless significant, source of help he had not counted on.

There are some servants of the Monarch's Son, mostly honest and well intentioned, who mis-state his promises. These servants are so intent upon winning people back from the realm of the evil prince, that they leave out of their messages some very important facts concerning responsible citizenship in that Domain. They rarely, if ever, mention warfare, or the prince's subversive devices, or the residual effects of the dread diseases caught under his reign. Frankly, they portray the Son's Government as sort of a spiritual welfare state, where there are free goodies for all, with little work or responsibility. One gets the picture of a sort of laid-back paradise, with the Monarch running a giant handout program.

Gleefully, the wicked prince capitalizes on this unexplained chink in their armor. All he has to do is let them preach these omissions, and then cash in on the contradictions the people experience in their daily lives. After all, his best source of returnees just might turn out to be the disappointed hearers who listen to these enthusiastic servants.

~ Peter E. Gillquist. "The Agony and the Ecstasy."
Why We Haven't Changed the World.
Old Tappan, New Jersey: Fleming H. Revell Company, 1982. pp. 47-48.

The Kingdom as a Key to All of Scripture

Jesus was always full of surprises, even with his disciples. Perhaps the biggest surprise was his news about the Kingdom of God.

Jesus came announcing the Kingdom, creating a stir. Through a brief span of public ministry he kept showing his disciples what the Kingdom was really like. They understood only in part.

Later, risen from the dead, Jesus spent six weeks teaching his disciples more about the Kingdom (Acts 1.3). He explained that his own suffering, death and resurrection were all part of the kingdom plan foretold by Old Testament prophets (Luke 24.44-47).

Now, after the resurrection, his disciples ask, "Are you *finally* going to set up your Kingdom?" (paraphrasing Acts 1.6). How does Jesus respond? He says, in effect, "The time for the full flowering of the new order still remains a mystery to you; it's in God's hands. But. . . . the

Holy Spirit will give you the power to live the kingdom life now. So you are to be witnesses of the Kingdom and its power from here to the very ends of the earth" (Acts 1.7-8).

And so it was, and so it has been. Today we are finally nearing the fulfillment of Jesus' prophecy that "this gospel of the Kingdom will be preached in the whole world as a testimony to all nations" (Matt. 24.14 [NIV]).

And so, as never before, it is time to speak of God's Kingdom now!

This is no attempt to outguess God or pre-empt the sovereign mystery of the Kingdom. The Kingdom still and always remains in God's hands. So this book is not about "times or dates" (Acts 1.7) – a tempting but disastrous detour – but about the plain kingdom teachings which run throughout Scripture. My point is simply this: The Bible is full of teaching on the Kingdom of God, and the Church has largely missed it. But in the providence of God we may now have reached a time when the good news of the Kingdom can be heard and understood as never before. This is due not to any one person, not to any human wisdom or insight, but to God's own working in our day, bringing a new kingdom consciousness.

Thus the theme of this book: The Kingdom of God in Scripture and its meaning for us today.

The Kingdom of God is a key thread in Scripture, tying the whole Bible together. It is not the only unifying theme, nor should it replace other themes which are clearly biblical. Yet it is a critically important theme, especially today. And its recent resurgence in the Church is, I believe, one of the most significant developments of this century!

Once you begin to look in Scripture for the theme of God's reign or Kingdom, it turns up everywhere! Take an example I recently encountered in my own devotional study:

> All you have made will praise you, O LORD; your saints will extol you. They will tell of the glory of your kingdom and speak of your might, so that all men may know of your mighty acts and the glorious splendor of your kingdom. Your kingdom is an everlasting kingdom, and your dominion endures through all generations.
>
> ~ Psalm 145.10-13 (NIV)

This one psalm in fact contains a substantial theology of the Kingdom, stressing God's sovereign reign, his mighty acts, his compassion and nearness to those who seek him, his righteousness and justice.

The Kingdom is such a key theme of Scripture that Richard Lovelace can say, "The Messianic Kingdom is not only the main theme of Jesus' preaching; it is the central category unifying biblical revelation." And John Bright comments, "The concept of the Kingdom of God involves, in a real sense, the total message of the Bible. . . . To grasp what is meant by the Kingdom of God is to come very close to the heart of the Bible's gospel of salvation." As E. Stanley Jones wrote over four decades ago, Jesus' message "was the Kingdom of God. It was the center and circumference of all he taught and did. . . . The Kingdom of God is the master-conception, the master-plan, the master-purpose, the master-will that gathers everything up into itself and gives it redemption, coherence, purpose, goal."

True, seeing the Kingdom of God as the only unifying theme of Scripture could be misleading. Personally, I believe the overarching truth is the revelation of the nature and character of God (not merely his existence, which is clear from the created order – Romans 1.20). Here God's love, justice and holiness are central – the character of God's person in his tri-unity. Still the reign/rule of God is a key theme of Scripture, for the loving, just, holy God rules consistent with his character and in a way that produces the reflection of his character in all who willingly serve him.

So the Kingdom is indeed a key strand running through the Bible. If it seems less evident in Paul's writings, that is because Paul often speaks of the Kingdom in terms of the sovereign *plan* of God realized through Jesus Christ (as, for example, in Ephesians 1.10), and, for very good reasons, uses less kingdom language. But it is incorrect to say, as some have, that the kingdom theme "disappears" in Paul. . . .

The Bible is full of God's Kingdom. . . . We learn more about the Kingdom when we view all of Scripture as the history of God's "economy" or plan to restore a fallen creation, bringing all God has made – woman, man and their total environment – to the fulfillment of his purposes under his sovereign reign.

One evening my seven-year-old son and I walked through a little patch of woods and came out on an open field. The sun was westering; the sky was serenely laced with blue and gold. Birds flitted in the trees. We talked about peace, the future and the Kingdom of God. Somehow we both sensed, despite our differences in age and understanding, that God desires peace and that what he desires he will bring. Someday, we said and knew, all the world will be like this magic moment. But not without cost and struggle.

Jesus urges: "Enter through the narrow gate." For "small is the gate and narrow the road that leads to life, and only a few find it" (Matthew 7.13-14). The Kingdom of God is life in abundance (John 10.10), but the way to life is through the narrow gate of faith and obedience to Jesus Christ. If Christians today want to experience the peaceable order of the Kingdom, they must learn and live God's way of peace.

~ Excerpted from Howard A Snyder. *A Kingdom Manifesto*.
"Introduction and Chapter One."
Downers Grove: InterVarsity Press, 1985. pp. 11-25.

The Preaching and Teaching of Jesus
Summary of Teaching, Vic Gordon

1. The most important thing in life is to be a disciple of Jesus Christ. To do that we must learn from him and then obey what we hear. He must be our Teacher and Lord (Matthew 7.24-27; 11.29; 28.18-20; John 13.13).

2. Obviously, we cannot follow Jesus if we do not know what he taught. The main theme of his preaching and teaching was the Kingdom of God. Most Christians do not know this, yet they call him Lord and Master Teacher!

3. But we are then faced with an immediate problem. As soon as we know the main theme of his teaching, we automatically misunderstand it. Kingdom means something different in the biblical idiom (Hebrew, Aramaic, Greek) than in contemporary English. To us "Kingdom" means "realm" (a place over which a king rules) or "a group of people who live in a king's realm" (the people over whom a king rules). In the Bible, however, the primary meaning of "Kingdom" is "reign" or "rule." The Kingdom of God thus means the reign of God or the rule of God. The Kingdom of God is not a place nor a people, but God's active, dynamic rule. The Kingdom is an act of God, i.e. something he does.

4. The burden and purpose of Jesus' three year public ministry leading up to his death and resurrection was to preach, proclaim and teach about the Kingdom of God (Mark 1.14ff; Matthew 4.17, 23; 9.35; Luke 4.42ff; 8.1; 9.2, 6, 11; 10.1, 9; Acts 1.3; 28.31).

5. Jesus was the original proclaimer of the Gospel, and he proclaimed it originally in terms of the Kingdom of God (Mark 1.14ff; Matthew 4.23; 9.35; 24.14; Luke 20.1). The good news is about God's reign. Of course this is a metaphor, a word picture describing a profound reality.

6. Jesus' teaching on the Kingdom of God as we will see, determines the basic structure of all his teaching, and indeed the structure of the teaching of the entire New Testament.

7. Why did Jesus choose the word picture "Kingdom of God" to proclaim the good news of God to the world? Two basic reasons:

   a. *It was biblical.* While the exact phrase "Kingdom of God" never occurs in the Old Testament (maybe once in 1 Chronicles 28.5), the idea is everywhere present in the Old Testament. God is always and everywhere King in the Old Testament, especially in the prophets. His kingship is not always realized in this sinful world. In fact the major emphasis in the Old Testament, stated in hundreds of ways and different word pictures, is on God's future, coming reign. The hope of the Old Testament is that God himself will come and bring salvation to his people and judgment/destruction to his enemies. (See e.g. 1 Chronicles 29.11; Psalms 22.28; 96.10-13; 103.19; 145.11-13; Isaiah 25ff; 65ff; Daniel 2.44; 4.3, 34; 6.26; 7.13ff, 27.)

   b. *It was understood and meaningful to the first century Palestinian Jews to whom he proclaimed the Good News.* In fact, the phrase "Kingdom of God" had developed a great deal in the 400 years between the Old Testament and the coming of Jesus. Kingdom of God now summarized the entire Old Testament hope! The first century Jews were expecting God to come as king and reign over the entire world, destroying his enemies and giving all his blessings to his people, Israel. This concept was especially meaningful to the Jews who, on the one hand, strongly believed that their God Yahweh was the one and only true God who ruled over all the universe, and who, on the other, experienced over 700 years of foreign domination at the hands of pagan rulers from Assyria, then Babylon, then Persia, then Greece and finally Rome. Jesus never defines the Kingdom of God for them, because they all knew what it meant. This is a great example for us in our ministries. Jesus went to the people where they were (the incarnation!), was faithful to the biblical message, and spoke it to them in terms they could understand. (See e.g. Luke 1.32ff; 19.11; 23.51; Mark 11.10; 15.43; Acts 1.6.) The phrase

Kingdom of God summarized all of the Old Testament hope and promise. "All that God has said and done in Israel's history is brought to completion in the Kingdom of God" (Dale Patrick).

8. But Jesus offers a new understanding of an already understood concept. He pours his own authoritative meaning into the Kingdom of God and offers a definitive new interpretation of the Old Testament promise and teaching. He makes it certain that the "Kingdom of God" is the interpretive key for the Old Testament. He agrees with the Jews that the Kingdom is God coming into history and reigning by giving salvation to his people and judgment to his enemies. But Jesus goes far beyond this in providing a grand new interpretation of God's reign.

9. Jesus startles and stuns his hearers by saying the Kingdom of God which they have all been waiting for is now present (Mark 1.15). The time of the fulfillment of the Old Testament promises has now arrived. He goes even further than this by teaching that the Kingdom is present in his own person and ministry (Matthew 11.1-15; 12.28; Luke 10.23ff; 17.20ff). This teaching that the Kingdom of God has arrived or is here is radically new. No Jewish rabbi had ever taught such a thing (Luke 10.23ff).

10. But Jesus, like most of the Jews of his day, also taught that the Kingdom of God was still future, i.e. it was yet to come (e.g. Matthew 6.10; 8.11ff; 25.31-34; Luke 21.31; 22.17ff. Cf. Matthew 5.3-12; Mark 9.47).

11. The solution to this strange teaching is to realize that Jesus' new perspective on the Kingdom of God contains both elements: the Kingdom is present and future. Jesus taught two comings of the Kingdom. First, the Kingdom came partially in his own person and ministry in history. Second, Jesus taught that there will be a future complete coming of his Kingdom when he returns at the end of human history.

12. Now we can understand what Jesus meant by the "mystery of the Kingdom" (Mark 4.10ff). This strange, new perspective on the Kingdom of God taught that the Old Testament promises could be fulfilled without being consummated. Thus, the mystery of the Kingdom is fulfillment without consummation. *The Kingdom of God has come into history in the person and ministry of Jesus Christ without consummation.* This mystery has been hidden until now revealed in Christ.

13. In one way or another, all of Jesus' kingdom parables ("The Kingdom of God is like. . .") proclaim and/or explain this mystery. This understanding of the Kingdom is radically new. The first century Palestinian Jews needed to hear this message, understand it and believe it. This is the major concern of Jesus' preaching and teaching.

14. Thus, we can understand Jesus' teaching on the coming of God's Kingdom as being both present and future. The Kingdom is now and it is not yet. Jesus announces the presence of the future.

15. This chart of the Kingdom of God in the teaching of Jesus can help us see more clearly what he is saying. The chart is a time line from Creation into an eternal future (eternal in the Bible means unending time).

    a. The age of the Kingdom is the age to come. We now live in both this age and the age to come.

    b. The Kingdom of God has two moments, each one characterized by a coming of Jesus as the Messianic King to bring God's reign.

16. The Kingdom of God brings the blessings of God. As the people of the Kingdom live now in the tension of both the presence and the future of the Kingdom, some of the blessings have already arrived for us and some await the consummation of the Kingdom in the future.

    Present Blessings of the Kingdom
    a. The Gospel is proclaimed.
    b. The forgiveness of sin.
    c. The Holy Spirit indwells God's people.
    d. Sanctification has begun.

    Future Blessings of the Kingdom
    a. The Presence of God
    b. Resurrection bodies
    c. Full sanctification
    d. Shalom: peace, righteousness, joy, health, wholeness
    e. A new heaven and a new earth
    f. Judgment and destruction of all God's enemies including sin, death, the devil and his demons, all evil

17. Let us not overlook the obvious fact that for Jesus his preaching about the Kingdom is fundamentally a proclamation about God.

God brings his Kingdom as a seeking, inviting, gracious Abba Father. He also comes as judge to those who refuse his Kingdom.

18. The Kingdom of God is altogether God's work. He graciously comes into human history in the person of his Son Jesus Christ to bring his rule to the earth. The Kingdom is therefore completely supernatural and gracious. Humans cannot bring, build or accomplish the Kingdom. It is wholly God's act.

19. Jesus' miracles and exorcisms are signs that the Kingdom of God is present in him and his ministry (Matthew 11.1-6; 4.23; 9.35; 10.7ff; Luke 9.1, 2, 6, 11).

20. The Kingdom of God invades the kingdom of Satan when Jesus comes bringing the Kingdom (Matthew 12.22-29; 25.41; Mark 1.24, 34; Luke 10.17ff; 11.17-22).

21. The Kingdom of God is of great value, indeed the greatest thing by far in the whole world (Matthew 13.44-46). Therefore, we must ask, "How should we then respond to this Kingdom?" or "How do we receive this gift of the Kingdom of God?"

There Is a River
Identifying the Streams of a Revitalized Authentic Christian Community in the City*

Rev. Dr. Don L. Davis

Ps. 46.4 (ESV) - There is a river whose streams make glad the city of God, the holy habitation of the Most High.

	Tributaries of Authentic Historic Biblical Faith			
Recognized Biblical Identity	**Revived Urban Spirituality**	**Reaffirmed Historical Connectivity**	**Refocused Kingdom Authority**
The Church Is One	*The Church Is Holy*	*The Church Is Catholic*	*The Church Is Apostolic*
A Call to Biblical Fidelity Recognizing the Scriptures as the anchor and foundation of the Christian faith and practice	**A Call to the Freedom, Power, and Fullness of the Holy Spirit** Walking in the holiness, power, gifting, and liberty of the Holy Spirit in the body of Christ	**A Call to Historic Roots and Continuity** Confessing the common historical identity and continuity of authentic Christian faith	**A Call to the Apostolic Faith** Affirming the apostolic tradition as the authoritative ground of the Christian hope
A Call to Messianic Kingdom Identity Rediscovering the story of the promised Messiah and his Kingdom in Jesus of Nazareth	**A Call to Live as Sojourners and Aliens as the People of God** Defining authentic Christian discipleship as faithful membership among God's people	**A Call to Affirm and Express the Global Communion of Saints** Expressing cooperation and collaboration with all other believers, both local and global	**A Call to Representative Authority** Submitting joyfully to God's gifted servants in the Church as undershepherds of true faith
A Call to Creedal Affinity Embracing the Nicene Creed as the shared rule of faith of historic orthodoxy	**A Call to Liturgical, Sacramental, and Catechetical Vitality** Walking in the holiness, power, gifting, and liberty of the Holy Spirit in the body of Christ	**A Call to Radical Hospitality and Good Works** Expressing kingdom love to all, and especially to those of the household of faith	**A Call to Prophetic and Holistic Witness** Proclaiming Christ and his Kingdom in word and deed to our neighbors and all peoples

* This schema is an adaptation and is based on the insights of the *Chicago Call* statement of May 1977, where various leading evangelical scholars and practitioners met to discuss the relationship of modern evangelicalism to the historic Christian faith.

The Role of Sound Ecclesiology in Urban Mission

Rev. Dr. Don L. Davis • *World Impact's Candidate Assessment Program* (for missionary applicants). Wichita: World Impact.

Many questions are brewing about the church and its place in spirituality and mission:

- Can one be saved apart from the church?
- Is it possible to be in a right relationship with God and his people and yet not be a part of a local assembly of Christians?
- Is faith in the local church a "misplaced hope?"

> The point here is simply to recognize that if we place all our hope in the local church, it is a misplaced hope. Many well-intentioned pastors promote this perspective by proclaiming, "The local church is the hope of the world." Like most advertising slogans, this notion is emotionally appealing. The trouble is, the sentiment is not biblical. Jesus, and Jesus alone, is the hope of the world. The local church is one mechanism that can be instrumental in bringing us closer to him and helping us to be more like him. But, as the research data clearly show, churches are not doing the job. If the local church is the hope of the world, then the world has no hope.
> ~ George Barna. *Revolution*. Carol Stream, IL: Tyndale Publishers, 2005, p. 36.

The essence of sound ecclesiology: The Church of God in Jesus Christ is central in understanding and appreciating the saving acts of God in Christ throughout salvation history, in today's world, and in the age to come.

- The Church of God in Jesus Christ is critically important in salvation history.
- The Church of God in Jesus Christ is integral in its imagery in trinitarian theology.
- The Church of God in Jesus Christ has great implication for us in urban missions today.

I. The Church of God in Jesus Christ Is Critically Important in Salvation History.

    A. The Church is central in comprehending God's saving purpose for the universe.

1 John 3.8 – Whoever makes a practice of sinning is of the devil, for the devil has been sinning from the beginning. The reason the Son of God appeared was to destroy the works of the devil.

1. The universe is at war: the *proto-evangelium*, Gen. 3.15 (the two unequal halves of the canonical Scriptures).

    a. Gen. 3.15 – I will put enmity between you and the woman, and between your offspring and her offspring; he shall bruise your head, and you shall bruise his heel.

    b. Matt. 3.7 – But when he saw many of the Pharisees and Sadducees coming for baptism, he said to them, "You brood of vipers! Who warned you to flee from the wrath to come?

    c. Matt. 13.38 – The field is the world, and the good seed is the children of the kingdom. The weeds are the sons of the evil one.

    d. John 8.44 – You are of your father the devil, and your will is to do your father's desires. He was a murderer from the beginning, and has nothing to do with the truth, because there is no truth in him. When he lies, he speaks out of his own character, for he is a liar and the father of lies.

    e. 1 John 3.8 – Whoever makes a practice of sinning is of the devil, for the devil has been sinning from the beginning. The reason the Son of God appeared was to destroy the works of the devil.

2. The reign of God throughout history: The Capstone Theology of Time

    a. **BEFORE TIME** (Eternity Past) 1 Cor. 2.7 – But we impart a secret and hidden wisdom of God, which God decreed before the ages for our glory (cf. Titus 1.2).

    b. **BEGINNING OF TIME** (Creation and Fall) Gen. 1.1 – In the beginning, God created the heavens and the earth.

    c. **UNFOLDING OF TIME** (God's Plan Revealed Through Israel) Gal. 3.8 – And the Scripture, foreseeing that God would justify the Gentiles by faith, preached the gospel beforehand to Abraham, saying, "In you shall all the nations be blessed" (cf. Rom. 9.4-5).

    d. ***FULLNESS OF TIME*** (The Incarnation of the Messiah) Gal. 4.4-5 – But when the fullness of time had come, God sent forth his Son, born of woman, born under the law, to redeem those who were under the law, so that we might receive adoption as sons.

    e. **THE LAST TIMES** (The Descent of the Holy Spirit) Acts 2.16-18 – But this is what was uttered through the prophet Joel: And in the last days it shall be, God declares, that I will pour out my Spirit on all flesh, and your sons and your daughters shall prophesy, and your young men shall see visions, and your old men shall dream dreams; even on my male servants and female servants in those days I will pour out my Spirit, and they shall prophesy.

    f. ***THE FULFILLMENT OF TIME*** (The Second Coming) Matt. 13.40-43 – Just as the weeds are gathered and burned with fire, so will it be at the close of the age. The Son of Man will send his angels, and they will gather out of his kingdom all causes of sin and all law-breakers, and throw them into the fiery furnace. In that place there will be weeping and gnashing of teeth. Then the righteous will shine like the sun in the kingdom of their Father. He who has ears, let him hear.

    g. ***BEYOND TIME*** (Eternity Future) 1 Cor. 15.24-28 – Then comes the end, when he delivers the kingdom to God the Father after destroying every rule and every authority and power. For he must reign until he has put all his enemies under his feet. The last enemy to be destroyed is death. For "God has put all things in subjection under his feet." But when it says, "all things are put in subjection," it is plain that he is excepted who put all things in subjection under him. When all things are subjected to him, then the Son himself will also be subjected to him who put all things in subjection under him, that God may be all in all.

3. The glorious freedom of the children of God: God's redemptive purpose to set apart a people for his Son forever more, Rom. 8.19-21 – For the creation waits with eager longing for the revealing of the sons of God. [20] For the creation was subjected to futility, not willingly, but because

of him who subjected it, in hope [21] that the creation itself will be set free from its bondage to decay and obtain the freedom of the glory of the children of God.

B. The Church is central in understanding God's divine covenant of redemption.

    Gal. 3.8-9 – And the Scripture, foreseeing that God would justify the Gentiles by faith, preached the gospel beforehand to Abraham, saying, "In you shall all the nations be blessed." So then, those who are of faith are blessed along with Abraham, the man of faith.

    1. The promise of Abraham, Gen. 12.1-3 – Now the Lord said to Abram, "Go from your country and your kindred and your father's house to the land that I will show you. And I will make of you a great nation, and I will bless you and make your name great, so that you will be a blessing. I will bless those who bless you, and him who dishonors you I will curse, and in you all the families of the earth shall be blessed."

    2. The promise and plan in the history of Israel, Heb. 1.1-3 – Long ago, at many times and in many ways, God spoke to our fathers by the prophets, but in these last days he has spoken to us by his Son, whom he appointed the heir of all things, through whom also he created the world. He is the radiance of the glory of God and the exact imprint of his nature, and he upholds the universe by the word of his power. After making purification for sins, he sat down at the right hand of the Majesty on high.

    3. The incarnation, passion, death, resurrection, and ascension of Jesus as revelation to and redemption of the universe, John 1.14-18 – And the Word became flesh and dwelt among us, and we have seen his glory, glory as of the only Son from the Father, full of grace and truth. (John bore witness about him, and cried out, "This was he of whom I said, 'He who comes after me ranks before me, because he was before me.'") And from his fullness we have all received, grace upon grace. For the law was given through Moses; grace and truth came through Jesus Christ. No one has ever seen God; the only God, who is at the Father's side, he has made him known.

    4. The coming of the Spirit and the birth of the Church, Acts 2.16-21 (cf. Acts 2.14-21 – But Peter, standing with the eleven, lifted up his voice and addressed them, "Men of Judea and all

who dwell in Jerusalem, let this be known to you, and give ear to my words. For these men are not drunk, as you suppose, since it is only the third hour of the day. But this is what was uttered through the prophet Joel: "'And in the last days it shall be, God declares, that I will pour out my Spirit on all flesh, and your sons and your daughters shall prophesy, and your young men shall see visions, and your old men shall dream dreams; even on my male servants and female servants in those days I will pour out my Spirit, and they shall prophesy. And I will show wonders in the heavens above and signs on the earth below, blood, and fire, and vapor of smoke; the sun shall be turned to darkness and the moon to blood, before the day of the Lord comes, the great and magnificent day. And it shall come to pass that everyone who calls upon the name of the Lord shall be saved.'")

C. The Church lies at the heart of the mystery of God's final revelation in Christ.

Eph. 3.4-5 – When you read this, you can perceive my insight into the mystery of Christ, which was not made known to the sons of men in other generations as it has now been revealed to his holy apostles and prophets by the Spirit.

1. Mystery heretofore unrevealed to humankind, Rom. 16.25-27 – Now to him who is able to strengthen you according to my gospel and the preaching of Jesus Christ, according to the revelation of the mystery that was kept secret for long ages but has now been disclosed and through the prophetic writings has been made known to all nations, according to the command of the eternal God, to bring about the obedience of faith to the only wise God be glory forevermore through Jesus Christ! Amen.

2. The mystery's revelation: Gentiles as fellow heirs of the promise in the Church, Eph. 3.3-10 – How the mystery was made known to me by revelation, as I have written briefly. When you read this, you can perceive my insight into the mystery of Christ, which was not made known to the sons of men in other generations as it has now been revealed to his holy apostles and prophets by the Spirit. This mystery is that the Gentiles are fellow heirs, members of the same body, and partakers of the promise in Christ Jesus through the gospel. Of this gospel I was made a minister according to the gift of God's grace, which was given me by the working of his

power. To me, though I am the very least of all the saints, this grace was given, to preach to the Gentiles the unsearchable riches of Christ, and to bring to light for everyone what is the plan of the mystery hidden for ages in God who created all things, so that through the church the manifold wisdom of God might now be made known to the rulers and authorities in the heavenly places.

3. Christ in us Gentile followers of Jesus, the hope of glory, Col. 1.24-27 – Now I rejoice in my sufferings for your sake, and in my flesh I am filling up what is lacking in Christ's afflictions for the sake of his body, that is, the church, of which I became a minister according to the stewardship from God that was given to me for you, to make the word of God fully known, the mystery hidden for ages and generations but now revealed to his saints. To them God chose to make known how great among the Gentiles are the riches of the glory of this mystery, which is Christ in you, the hope of glory.

II. The Church of God in Jesus Christ Is Integral in its Imagery in Trinitarian Theology

A. The Church is figured and typified as *the family of God*.

Eph. 2.19 – So then you are no longer strangers and aliens, but you are fellow citizens with the saints and members of the household of God.

1. The necessity of regeneration, John 1.12-13 – But to all who did receive him, who believed in his name, he gave the right to become children of God, who were born, not of blood nor of the will of the flesh nor of the will of man, but of God.

2. The significance of adoption, Rom. 8.15-18 – For you did not receive the spirit of slavery to fall back into fear, but you have received the Spirit of adoption as sons, by whom we cry, "Abba! Father!" The Spirit himself bears witness with our spirit that we are children of God, and if children, then heirs heirs of God and fellow heirs with Christ, provided we suffer with him in order that we may also be glorified with him. For I consider that the sufferings of this present time are not worth comparing with the glory that is to be revealed to us.

3. The privilege of *oikos*: members of the household of God, 1 John 3.1-3 – See what kind of love the Father has given to us, that we should be called children of God; and so we are. The reason why the world does not know us is that it did not know him. Beloved, we are God's children now, and what we will be has not yet appeared; but we know that when he appears we will be like him, because we shall see him as he is. And everyone who thus hopes in him purifies himself as he is pure.

B. The Church is figured and typified as *the body and bride of Christ*.

1 Cor. 12.27 – Now you are the body of Christ and individually members of it.

2 Cor. 11.2 – I feel a divine jealousy for you, for I betrothed you to one husband, to present you as a pure virgin to Christ.

1. Our organic unity with Jesus by faith: we died, buried, raised, ascended, seated, suffering, glorified, returning, reigning in him, e.g., Rom. 6.1-10.

2. Interdependence and interconnection through the Holy Spirit

    a. 1 Cor. 12.12-13 – For just as the body is one and has many members, and all the members of the body, though many, are one body, so it is with Christ. For in one Spirit we were all baptized into one body Jews or Greeks, slaves or free and all were made to drink of one Spirit.

    b. Eph. 4.4-7 – There is one body and one Spirit just as you were called to the one hope that belongs to your call one Lord, one faith, one baptism, one God and Father of all, who is over all and through all and in all. But grace was given to each one of us according to the measure of Christ's gift.

    c. 1 Pet. 4.10-11 – As each has received a gift, use it to serve one another, as good stewards of God's varied grace: whoever speaks, as one who speaks oracles of God; whoever serves, as one who serves by the strength that God supplies in order that in everything God may be glorified through Jesus Christ. To him belong glory and dominion forever and ever. Amen.

3. Destined for the throne: the marriage Supper of the Lamb, Rev. 19.6-8

C. The Church is figured and typified as *the temple of the Holy Spirit*

Eph. 2.20-22 – built on the foundation of the apostles and prophets, Christ Jesus himself being the cornerstone, in whom the whole structure, being joined together, grows into a holy temple in the Lord. In him you also are being built together into a dwelling place for God by the Spirit.

1. Church as *typos* of the Temple, living stones making up God's habitation in the Spirit, 1 Pet. 2.4-10 (cf. 1 Peter 2.9-10 – But you are a chosen race, a royal priesthood, a holy nation, a people for his own possession, that you may proclaim the excellencies of him who called you out of darkness into his marvelous light. Once you were not a people, but now you are God's people; once you had not received mercy, but now you have received mercy.)

2. Consecrated and set apart for God's pleasure and purpose, 1 Cor. 3.16-17 – Do you not know that you are God's temple and that God's Spirit dwells in you? If anyone destroys God's temple, God will destroy him. For God's temple is holy, and you are that temple.

3. A community of the Spirit: the *shekinah* presence of God in the midst of God's people, Rom. 8.11 – If the Spirit of him who raised Jesus from the dead dwells in you, he who raised Christ Jesus from the dead will also give life to your mortal bodies through his Spirit who dwells in you. (Cf. Eph. 2.19-22 – So then you are no longer strangers and aliens, but you are fellow citizens with the saints and members of the household of God, built on the foundation of the apostles and prophets, Christ Jesus himself being the cornerstone, in whom the whole structure, being joined together, grows into a holy temple in the Lord. In him you also are being built together into a dwelling place for God by the Spirit.)

III. **The Church of God in Jesus Christ Has Great Implication for Us in Urban Missions Today.**

A. The Church stands out in urban mission as the *pillar and buttress of the truth*.

1 Tim. 3.15 – if I delay, you may know how one ought to behave in the household of God, which is the church of the living God, a pillar and buttress of truth.

1. To protect the canon (the Holy Scriptures) as interpreted by the Great Tradition, 2 Tim. 3.15-17 – and how from childhood you have been acquainted with the sacred writings, which are able to make you wise for salvation through faith in Christ Jesus. All Scripture is breathed out by God and profitable for teaching, for reproof, for correction, and for training in righteousness, that the man of God may be competent, equipped for every good work.

2. To guard the flock of God and the Gospel of Jesus Christ, Acts 20.28-30 – Pay careful attention to yourselves and to all the flock, in which the Holy Spirit has made you overseers, to care for the church of God, which he obtained with his own blood. I know that after my departure fierce wolves will come in among you, not sparing the flock; and from among your own selves will arise men speaking twisted things, to draw away the disciples after them.

3. To contend for the faith once for all delivered to the saints, Jude 1.3 – Beloved, although I was very eager to write to you about our common salvation, I found it necessary to write appealing to you to contend for the faith that was once for all delivered to the saints.

B. The Church stands out in urban mission as *the foretaste and trophy of God's saving acts in Christ*.

Eph. 3.10 – so that through the church the manifold wisdom of God might now be made known to the rulers and authorities in the heavenly places.

1. In the assembly of the faithful, we make the *Great Confession*: Jesus Christ is Lord to the glory of God the Father, Phil. 2.5-11. (Cf. Phil. 2.9-11 – Therefore God has highly exalted him and bestowed on him the name that is above every name, so that at the name of Jesus every knee should bow, in heaven and on earth and under the earth, and every tongue confess that Jesus Christ is Lord, to the glory of God the Father.)

2. In the body of believers, we obey the *Great Commandment*: Love God with all our hearts and our neighbors as ourselves, Matt. 22.37-40 – And he said to him, "You shall love the Lord your God with all your heart and with all your soul and with all your mind. This is the great and first commandment. And a second is like it: You shall love your neighbor as yourself. On these two commandments depend all the Law and the Prophets."

3. In the community of disciples, we fulfill the *Great Commission*: Go and make disciples among all nations, Matt. 28.18-20 – And Jesus came and said to them, "All authority in heaven and on earth has been given to me. Go therefore and make disciples of all nations, baptizing them in the name of the Father and of the Son and of the Holy Spirit, teaching them to observe all that I have commanded you. And behold, I am with you always, to the end of the age."

C. The Church stands out in urban mission as the *agent and ambassador of Christ and his Kingdom*.

2 Cor. 5.20 – Therefore, we are ambassadors for Christ, God making his appeal through us. We implore you on behalf of Christ, be reconciled to God.

1. To the Church alone is given the responsibility to do justice and love mercy in the name of Christ, Mic. 6.8; cf. 1 Pet. 2.9-10.

2. To the Church alone is given the task to evangelize the lost among all people groups, especially among the poor, Luke 4.18 – The Spirit of the Lord is upon me, because he has anointed me to proclaim good news to the poor. He has sent me to proclaim liberty to the captives and recovering of sight to the blind, to set at liberty those who are oppressed.

3. To the Church alone is given the role to catechize and disciple new converts, incorporating them into the family, the body, and the temple, 2 Pet. 3.15-18 – And count the patience of our Lord as salvation, just as our beloved brother Paul also wrote to you according to the wisdom given him, as he does in all his letters when he speaks in them of these matters. There are some things in them that are hard to understand, which the ignorant and unstable twist to their own destruction, as they do the other Scriptures. You

therefore, beloved, knowing this beforehand, take care that you are not carried away with the error of lawless people and lose your own stability. But grow in the grace and knowledge of our Lord and Savior Jesus Christ. To him be the glory both now and to the day of eternity. Amen.

4. To the Church alone is given the privilege to go into all nations and advance the Kingdom in planting churches to the ends of the earth, Acts 1.8 – "But you will receive power when the Holy Spirit has come upon you, and you will be my witnesses in Jerusalem and in all Judea and Samaria, and to the end of the earth."

A Sound Ecclesiology can answer our plaguing questions about the Church:

- The Lord is adding to the number of the Church each day!
- The presence of the Lord dwells in the assembly of his people!
- The church of God in Jesus Christ is the colony of God, his army advancing the Kingdom to the ends of the earth!

> The church exists today as resident aliens, an adventurous colony in a society of unbelief. As a society of unbelief, Western culture is devoid of a sense of journey, of adventure, because it lacks belief in much more than the cultivation of an ever-shrinking horizon of self-preservation and self-expression.
>
> . . . Our biblical story demands an offensive rather than a defensive posture of the church. The world and all its resources, anguish, gifts, and groaning is God's world, and God demands what God has created. Jesus Christ is the supreme act of divine intrusion into the world's settled arrangements. In the Christ, God refuses to "stay in his place." The message that sustains the colony is not for itself but for the world – the colony having significance only as God's means for saving the whole world. The colony is God's means of a major offensive against the world, for the world.
>
> ~ Stanley Hauerwas and William H. Willimon.
> *Resident Aliens: Life in the Christian Colony.*
> Nashville: Abingdon Press, 1989, pp. 49, 51.

The essence of sound ecclesiology: The Church of God in Jesus Christ is central in understanding and appreciating the saving acts of God in Christ throughout salvation history, in today's world, and in the age to come.

- The Church of God in Jesus Christ is critically important in salvation history.
- The Church of God in Jesus Christ is integral in its imagery in trinitarian theology.
- The Church of God in Jesus Christ has great implication for us in urban missions today.

> "... on this rock I will build my church, and the gates of hell shall not prevail against it."
>
> ~ Matthew 16.18

The Story of God: Our Sacred Roots
Rev. Dr. Don L. Davis

The Alpha and the Omega	Christus Victor	Come, Holy Spirit	Your Word Is Truth	The Great Confession	His Life in Us	Living in the Way	Reborn to Serve
The LORD God is the source, sustainer, and end of all things in the heavens and earth. All things were formed and exist by his will and for his eternal glory, the triune God, Father, Son, and Holy Spirit. Rom. 11.36.							
THE TRIUNE GOD'S UNFOLDING DRAMA — God's Self-Revelation in Creation, Israel, and Christ			THE CHURCH'S PARTICIPATION IN GOD'S UNFOLDING DRAMA — Fidelity to the Apostolic Witness to Christ and His Kingdom			
The Objective Foundation: The Sovereign Love of God — God's Narration of His Saving Work in Christ				The Subjective Practice: Salvation by Grace through Faith — The Redeemed's Joyous Response to God's Saving Work in Christ			
The Author of the Story	The Champion of the Story	The Interpreter of the Story	The Testimony of the Story	The People of the Story	Re-enactment of the Story	Embodiment of the Story	Continuation of the Story
The Father as Director	Jesus as Lead Actor	The Spirit as Narrator	Scripture as Script	As Saints, Confessors	As Worshipers, Ministers	As Followers, Sojourners	As Servants, Ambassadors
Christian Worldview	Communal Identity	Spiritual Experience	Biblical Authority	Orthodox Theology	Priestly Worship	Congregational Discipleship	Kingdom Witness
Theistic and Trinitarian Vision	Christ-centered Foundation	Spirit-Indwelt and -Filled Community	Canonical and Apostolic Witness	Ancient Creedal Affirmation of Faith	Weekly Gathering in Christian Assembly	Corporate, Ongoing Spiritual Formation	Active Agents of the Reign of God
Sovereign Willing	Messianic Representing	Divine Comforting	Inspired Testifying	Truthful Retelling	Joyful Excelling	Faithful Indwelling	Hopeful Compelling
Creator — True Maker of the Cosmos	Recapitulation — Typos and Fulfillment of the Covenant	Life-Giver — Regeneration and Adoption	Divine Inspiration — God-breathed Word	The Confession of Faith — Union with Christ	Song and Celebration — Historical Recitation	Pastoral Oversight — Shepherding the Flock	Explicit Unity — Love for the Saints
Owner — Sovereign Disposer of Creation	Revealer — Incarnation of the Word	Teacher — Illuminator of the Truth	Sacred History — Historical Record	Baptism into Christ — Communion of Saints	Homilies and Teachings — Prophetic Proclamation	Shared Spirituality — Common Journey through the Spiritual Disciplines	Radical Hospitality — Evidence of God's Kingdom Reign
Ruler — Blessed Controller of All Things	Redeemer — Reconciler of All Things	Helper — Endowment and the Power	Biblical Theology — Divine Commentary	The Rule of Faith — Apostles' Creed and Nicene Creed	The Lord's Supper — Dramatic Re-enactment	Embodiment — Anamnesis and Prolepsis through the Church Year	Extravagant Generosity — Good Works
Covenant Keeper — Faithful Promisor	Restorer — Christ, the Victor over the powers of evil	Guide — Divine Presence and Shekinah	Spiritual Food — Sustenance for the Journey	The Vincentian Canon — Ubiquity, antiquity, universality	Eschatological Foreshadowing — The Already/Not Yet	Effective Discipling — Spiritual Formation in the Believing Assembly	Evangelical Witness — Making Disciples of All People Groups

Substitute Centers to a Christ-Centered Vision
Goods and Effects Which Our Culture Substitutes as the Ultimate Concern

Rev. Dr. Don L. Davis

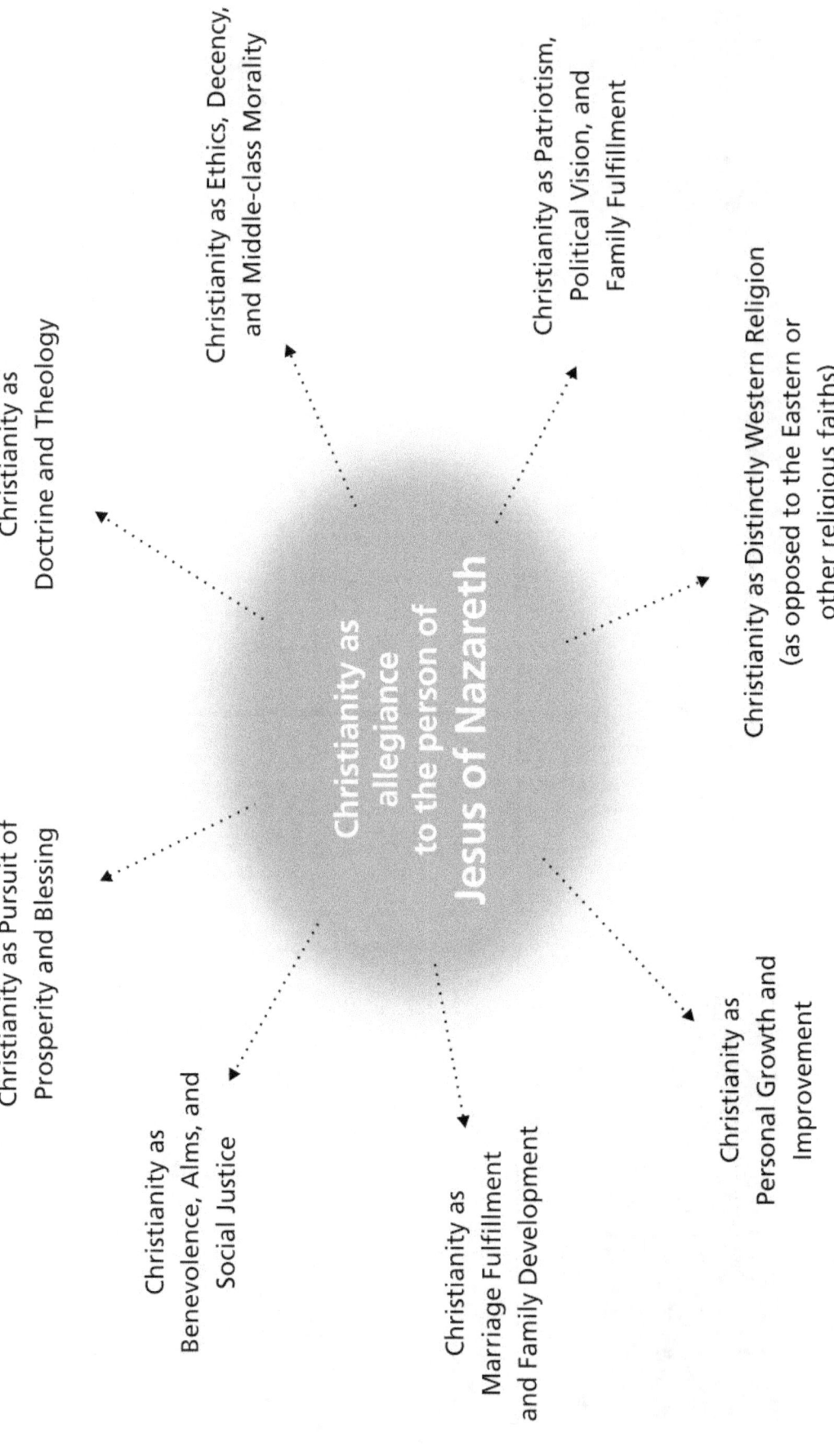

The Picture and the Drama
Image and Story in the Recovery of Biblical Myth

Rev. Dr. Don L. Davis

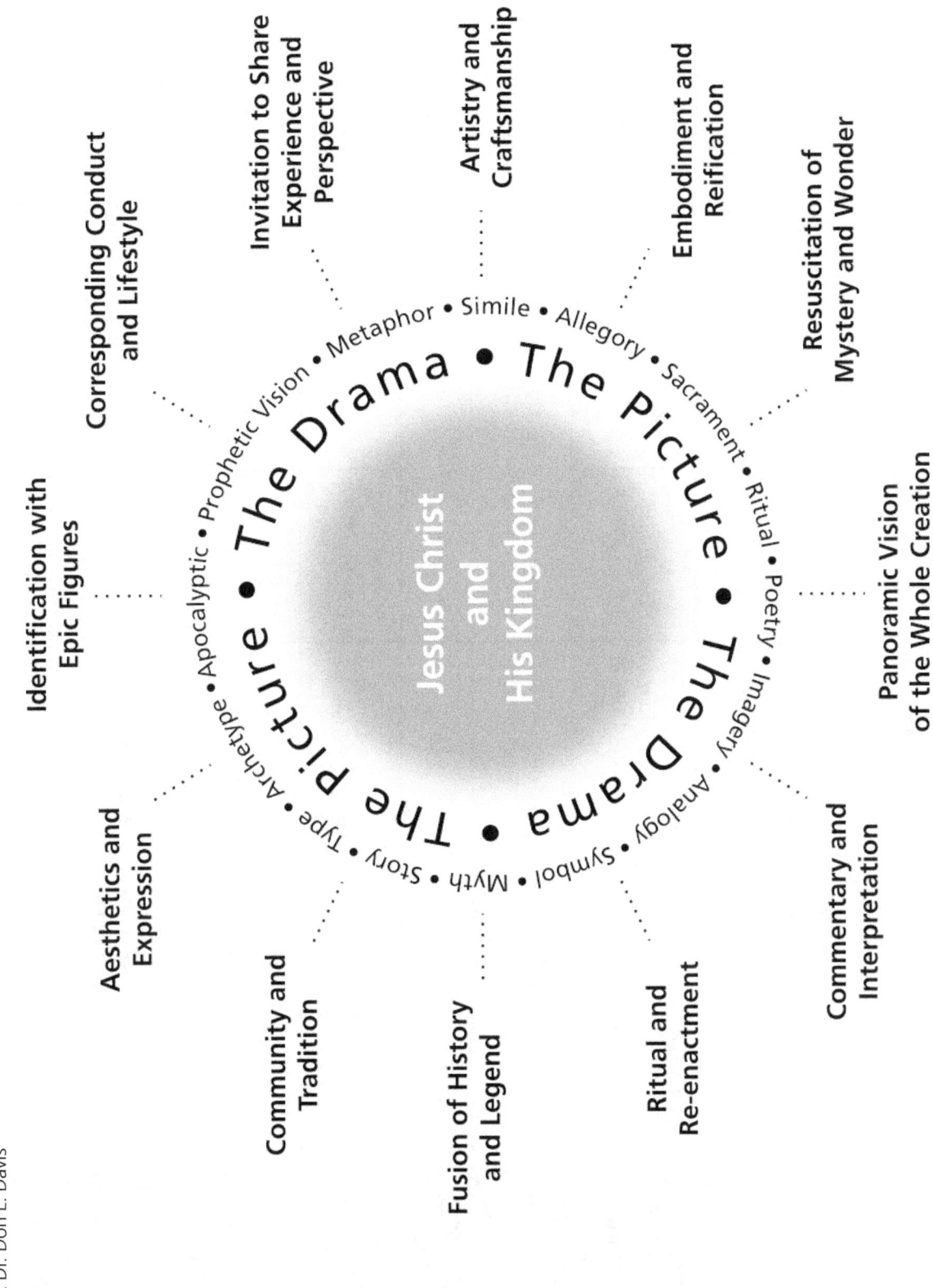

Old Testament Witness to Christ and His Kingdom
Rev. Dr. Don L. Davis

Christ Is Seen in the OT's:	Covenant Promise and Fulfillment	Moral Law	Christophanies	Typology	Tabernacle, Festival, and Levitical Priesthood	Messianic Prophecy	Salvation Promises
Passage	Gen. 12.1-3	Matt. 5.17-18	John 1.18	1 Cor. 15.45	Heb. 8.1-6	Mic. 5.2	Isa. 9.6-7
Example	The Promised Seed of the Abrahamic covenant	The Law given on Mount Sinai	Commander of the Lord's army	Jonah and the great fish	Melchizedek, as both High Priest and King	The Lord's Suffering Servant	Righteous Branch of David
Christ As	Seed of the woman	The Prophet of God	God's present Revelation	Antitype of God's drama	Our eternal High Priest	The coming Son of Man	Israel's Redeemer and King
Where Illustrated	Galatians	Matthew	John	Matthew	Hebrews	Luke and Acts	John and Revelation
Exegetical Goal	To see Christ as heart of God's sacred drama	To see Christ as fulfillment of the Law	To see Christ as God's revealer	To see Christ as antitype of divine typos	To see Christ in the Temple *cultus*	To see Christ as true Messiah	To see Christ as coming King
How Seen in the NT	As fulfillment of God's sacred oath	As *telos* of the Law	As full, final, and superior revelation	As substance behind the historical shadows	As reality behind the rules and roles	As the Kingdom made present	As the One who will rule on David's throne
Our Response in Worship	God's veracity and faithfulness	God's perfect righteousness	God's presence among us	God's inspired Scripture	God's ontology: his realm as primary and determinative	God's anointed servant and mediator	God's resolve to restore his kingdom authority
How God Is Vindicated	God does not lie; he's true to his word	Jesus fulfills all righteousness	God's fulness is revealed to us in Jesus of Nazareth	The Spirit spoke by the prophets	The Lord has provided a mediator for humankind	Every jot and tittle written of him will occur	Evil will be put down, creation restored, under his reign

The Theology of Christus Victor
A Christ-Centered Biblical Motif for Integrating and Renewing the Urban Church
Rev. Dr. Don L. Davis

	The Promised Messiah	The Word Made Flesh	The Son of Man	The Suffering Servant	The Lamb of God	The Victorious Conqueror	The Reigning Lord in Heaven	The Bridegroom and Coming King
Biblical Framework	Israel's hope of Yahweh's anointed who would redeem his people	In the person of Jesus of Nazareth, the Lord has come to the world	As the promised king and divine Son of Man, Jesus reveals the Father's glory and salvation to the world	As Inaugurator of the Kingdom of God, Jesus demonstrates God's reign present through his words, wonders, and works	As both High Priest and Paschal Lamb, Jesus offers himself to God on our behalf as a sacrifice for sin	In his resurrection from the dead and ascension to God's right hand, Jesus is proclaimed as Victor over the power of sin and death	Now reigning at God's right hand till his enemies are made his footstool, Jesus pours out his benefits on his body	Soon the risen and ascended Lord will return to gather his Bride, the Church, and consummate his work
Scripture References	Isa. 9.6-7 Jer. 23.5-6 Isa. 11.1-10	John 1.14-18 Matt. 1.20-23 Phil. 2.6-8	Matt. 2.1-11 Num. 24.17 Luke 1.78-79	Mark 1.14-15 Matt. 12.25-30 Luke 17.20-21	2 Cor. 5.18-21 Isa. 52-53 John 1.29	Eph. 1.16-23 Phil. 2.5-11 Col. 1.15-20	1 Cor. 15.25 Eph. 4.15-16 Acts. 2.32-36	Rom. 14.7-9 Rev. 5.9-13 1 Thess. 4.13-18
Jesus' History	The pre-incarnate, only begotten Son of God in glory	His conception by the Spirit, and birth to Mary	His manifestation to the Magi and to the world	His teaching, exorcisms, miracles, and mighty works among the people	His suffering, crucifixion, death, and burial	His resurrection, with appearances to his witnesses, and his ascension to the Father	The sending of the Holy Spirit and his gifts, and Christ's session in heaven at the Father's right hand	His soon return from heaven to earth as Lord and Christ: the Second Coming
Description	The biblical promise for the seed of Abraham, the prophet like Moses, the son of David	In the Incarnation, God has come to us; Jesus reveals to humankind the Father's glory in fullness	In Jesus, God has shown his salvation to the entire world, including the Gentiles	In Jesus, the promised Kingdom of God has come visibly to earth, demonstrating his binding of Satan and rescinding the Curse	As God's perfect Lamb, Jesus offers himself up to God as a sin offering on behalf of the entire world	In his resurrection and ascension, Jesus destroyed death, disarmed Satan, and rescinded the Curse	Jesus is installed at the Father's right hand as Head of the Church, Firstborn from the dead, and supreme Lord in heaven	As we labor in his harvest field in the world, so we await Christ's return, the fulfillment of his promise
Church Year	Advent	Christmas	Season after Epiphany Baptism and Transfiguration	Lent	Holy Week Passion	Eastertide Easter, Ascension Day, Pentecost	Season after Pentecost Trinity Sunday	Season after Pentecost All Saints Day, Reign of Christ the King
	The Coming of Christ	The Birth of Christ	The Manifestation of Christ	The Ministry of Christ	The Suffering and Death of Christ	The Resurrection and Ascension of Christ	The Heavenly Session of Christ	The Reign of Christ
Spiritual Formation	As we await his Coming, let us proclaim and affirm the hope of Christ	O Word made flesh, let us every heart prepare him room to dwell	Divine Son of Man, show the nations your salvation and glory	In the person of Christ, the power of the reign of God has come to earth and to the Church	May those who share the Lord's death be resurrected with him	Let us participate by faith in the victory of Christ over the power of sin, Satan, and death	Come, indwell us, Holy Spirit, and empower us to advance Christ's Kingdom in the world	We live and work in expectation of his soon return, seeking to please him in all things

The Theology of the Church for Team Leaders

Rev. Dr. Don L. Davis • *The Timothy Conference: Building Church Plant Teams*. Wichita, The Urban Ministry Institute, 2005.

> Christians discover in the Bible the "interpretive framework" by means of which our lives come together – make sense – as a unified whole. This interpretive framework is linked with the biblical narrative, the story of God at work in the world bringing creation to a glorious future goal. The Spirit addresses us through this narrative. Through it, he invites us to see our lives in the light of God's work. He summons us to link our personal stories with God's story and the story of God's people. Through the "old, old, story," the Holy Spirit calls us into God's new community. And the Spirit leads us to view our personal lives from the perspective of this ancient Gospel narrative. As we look at all of life from this vantage point, our lives begin to make sense. And we begin to see a unity within the variegated experiences that form the ingredients of our existence.
>
> ~ Stanley J. Grenz. *Created for Community*.
> Grand Rapids:Baker Books, 1998. p. 170.

I. **The Church Is the *Locus* (the Place) Where the Kingdom Power and Authority of God are Experienced and Displayed.**

The Church of Jesus Christ is God's anointed arena where his presence and power reside, and in the midst of this redeemed and redemptive society, the rule of the Kingdom of God is being experienced by his people.

A. The Church is the locus of God's revelation and salvation.

1. The Church is the custodian of the Gospel and the Word of God.

   1 Tim. 3.15 (NKJV) – but if I am delayed, I write so that you may know how you ought to conduct yourself in the house of God, which is the Church of the living God, the pillar and ground of the truth. And without controversy great is the mystery of godliness: God was manifested in the flesh, justified in the Spirit, seen by angels, preached among the Gentiles, believed on in the world, received up in glory.

2. The Church is the community where God's forgiveness and healing are experienced by the blood in the authority of Jesus Christ.

   Matt. 18.17 (NKJV) – And if he refuses to hear them, tell it to the church. But if he refuses even to hear the church, let him be to you like a heathen and a tax collector. Assuredly, I say to you, whatever you bind on earth will be bound in heaven, and whatever you loose on earth will be loosed in heaven. Again I say to you that if two of you agree on earth concerning anything that they ask, it will be done for them by my Father in heaven. For where two or three are gathered together in my name, I am there in the midst of them.

3. The Church as the physical gathering of the Body of Christ; salvation is merely incorporation by faith and the Spirit into the Church.

   Rom. 12.3 (NIV) – For by the grace given me I say to every one of you: Do not think of yourself more highly than you ought, but rather think of yourself with sober judgment, in accordance with the measure of faith God has given you. Just as each of us has one body with many members, and these members do not all have the same function, so in Christ we who are many form one body, and each member belongs to all the others.

   1 Cor. 12.12 (NKJV) – For as the body is one and has many members, but all the members of that one body, being many, are one body, so also is Christ. For by one Spirit we were all baptized into one body whether Jews or Greeks, whether slaves or free and have all been made to drink into one Spirit.

   1 Cor. 12.27 (NIV) – Now you are the body of Christ, and each one of you is a part of it.

B. The Church is the primary locus of the empowering presence of the Holy Spirit.

1. The Holy Spirit dwells in the Church as the supreme sign of God's Kingdom present in our age.

   Acts 2.14 (NKJV) – But Peter, standing up with the eleven, raised his voice and said to them, "Men of Judea and all who dwell in Jerusalem, let this be known to you, and heed my words. For these are not drunk, as you suppose, since it is only the third hour of the day. But this is what was spoken by the prophet Joel: "And it shall come to pass in the last days, says God, That I will pour out of my Spirit on all flesh; your sons and your daughters shall prophesy, your young men shall see visions, your old men shall dream dreams. And on my menservants and on my maidservants I will pour out my Spirit in those days; and they shall prophesy. I will show wonders in heaven above and signs in the earth beneath: blood and fire and vapor of smoke. The sun shall be turned into darkness, and the moon into blood, before the coming of the great and notable day of the Lord. And it shall come to pass that whoever calls on the name of the Lord shall be saved."

2. The Holy Spirit as pledge and *arrabon* of the Kingdom in the midst of God's people.

   Eph. 1.13 (NIV) – And you also were included in Christ when you heard the word of truth, the Gospel of your salvation. Having believed, you were marked in him with a seal, the promised Holy Spirit.

   2 Cor. 1.20 (NIV) – For no matter how many promises God has made, they are "Yes" in Christ. And so through him the "Amen" is spoken by us to the glory of God. Now it is God who makes both us and you stand firm in Christ. He anointed us, set his seal of ownership on us, and put his Spirit in our hearts as a deposit, guaranteeing what is to come.

3. The Church is animated and empowered by the Holy Spirit as the one providing life and direction in the Body of Christ.

   a. Provides gifts and endowments, 1 Cor. 12.3-11

   b. Appoints leaders and elders, Acts 13.1-3; cf. 20.28

   c. Prays with groanings too deep for utterance, Rom. 8.26

C. The Church is the concrete locus of authentic kingdom *Shalom*.

   1. In the community of believers is the place where God may become known and experienced in the midst of this god-forsaken world.

Eph. 2.19 (NIV) – Consequently, you are no longer foreigners and aliens, but fellow citizens with God's people and members of God's household, built on the foundation of the apostles and prophets, with Christ Jesus himself as the chief cornerstone. In him the whole building is joined together and rises to become a holy temple in the Lord. And in him you too are being built together to become a dwelling in which God lives by his Spirit.

2. In the community of believers, lives are transformed into wholeness in a broken world.

    1 Cor. 6.9 (NKJV) – Do you not know that the unrighteous will not inherit the Kingdom of God? Do not be deceived. Neither fornicators, nor idolaters, nor adulterers, nor homosexuals, nor sodomites, nor thieves, nor covetous, nor drunkards, nor revilers, nor extortioners will inherit the Kingdom of God. And such were some of you. But you were washed, but you were sanctified, but you were justified in the name of the Lord Jesus and by the Spirit of our God.

3. In the community of believers, God's justice can be experienced in the midst of an unjust world.

    James 2.1 (NKJV) – My brethren, do not hold the faith of our Lord Jesus Christ, the Lord of glory, with partiality. For if there should come into your assembly a man with gold rings, in fine apparel, and there should also come in a poor man in filthy clothes, and you pay attention to the one wearing the fine clothes and say to him, "You sit here in a good place," and say to the poor man, "You stand here," or, "Sit here at my footstool," have you not shown partiality among yourselves, and become judges with evil thoughts? Listen, my beloved brethren: Has God not chosen the poor of this world to be rich in faith and heirs of the Kingdom which he promised to those who love him?

    Col. 3.9 (NIV) – Do not lie to each other, since you have taken off your old self with its practices and have put on the new self, which is being renewed in knowledge in the image of its Creator. Here there is no Greek or Jew, circumcised or uncircumcised, barbarian, Scythian, slave or free, but Christ is all, and is in all.

II. The Church Is the Agent (the Deputy) Where the Authority and Power of the Kingdom of God Are Heralded and Enforced.

The Church of Jesus Christ is the Agent through which his kingdom authority and power are being exercised, and the Army through which his war is waged against his enemies. The Church of Jesus is the vehicle through which the Spirit of God announces the Good News of the Kingdom, and demonstrates its force in the midst of the contested ground of the earth.

A. The Church is the agent of apostolic witness and word.

1. We as the Church are called to be ambassadors of Christ to proclaim deliverance in Jesus name to the world, 2 Cor. 5.18-21.

2. We as Church are called to be stewards of God's mysteries to protect the faith.

   1 Cor. 4.2 (NKJV) – Moreover it is required in stewards that one be found faithful.

   Jude 1.3 (NKJV) – Beloved, while I was very diligent to write to you concerning our common salvation, I found it necessary to write to you exhorting you to contend earnestly for the faith which was once for all delivered to the saints.

3. In the Church we declare and protect the Apostolic witness to Jesus Christ.

   1 Cor. 15.1 (NKJV) – Moreover, brethren, I declare to you the Gospel which I preached to you, which also you received and in which you stand, by which also you are saved, if you hold fast that word which I preached to you; unless you believed in vain. For I delivered to you first of all that which I also received: that Christ died for our sins according to the Scriptures, and that he was buried, and that he rose again the third day according to the Scriptures.

   Gal. 1.8 (NKJV) – But even if we, or an angel from heaven, preach any other Gospel to you than what we have preached to you, let him be accursed. As we have said before, so now I say again, if anyone preaches any other Gospel to you than what you have received, let him be accursed.

1 John 1.1 (NKJV) – That which was from the beginning, which we have heard, which we have seen with our eyes, which we have looked upon, and our hands have handled, concerning the Word of life; the life was manifested, and we have seen, and bear witness, and declare to you that eternal life which was with the Father and was manifested to us; that which we have seen and heard we declare to you, that you also may have fellowship with us; and truly our fellowship is with the Father and with his Son Jesus Christ.

4. God reveals his eternal grace and loving-kindness through the witness of local assemblies of believers.

Eph. 3.4 (NASB) – And by referring to this, when you read you can understand my insight into the mystery of Christ, which in other generations was not made known to the sons of men, as it has now been revealed to his holy apostles and prophets in the Spirit; to be specific, that the Gentiles are fellow heirs and fellow members of the body, and fellow partakers of the promise in Christ Jesus through the Gospel, of which I was made a minister, according to the gift of God's grace which was given to me according to the working of his power. To me, the very least of all saints, this grace was given, to preach to the Gentiles the unfathomable riches of Christ, and to bring to light what is the administration of the mystery which for ages has been hidden in God, who created all things; in order that the manifold wisdom of God might now be made known through the Church to the rulers and the authorities in the heavenly places.

B. The Church as agent of good works which testify to the reality of the Kingdom.

1. As those who do good works, zealous for good deeds.

Eph. 2.10 (NIV) – For we are God's workmanship, created in Christ Jesus to do good works, which God prepared in advance for us to do.

Matt. 5.14 (NIV) – You are the light of the world. A city on a hill cannot be hidden. Neither do people light a lamp and put it under a bowl. Instead they put it on its stand, and it gives light to everyone in the house. In the same way, let your light shine before men, that they may see your good deeds and praise your Father in heaven.

Titus 2.14 (NIV) – who gave himself for us to redeem us from all wickedness and to purify for himself a people that are his very own, eager to do what is good.

2. Ministers of reconciliation, in word and deed, God to man, man to man.

2 Cor. 5.18 (NIV) – All this is from God, who reconciled us to himself through Christ and gave us the ministry of reconciliation: that God was reconciling the world to himself in Christ, not counting men's sins against them. And he has committed to us the message of reconciliation. We are therefore Christ's ambassadors, as though God were making his appeal through us. We implore you on Christ's behalf: Be reconciled to God.

3. The Church as an agent of freedom, wholeness, and justice.

    a. As an agent of freedom, we declare and demonstrate the freedom we have received in Christ through the blood of the New Covenant, Gal. 5.1; Rom. 8.21.

    b. As an agent of wholeness, we declare and demonstrate how union with Christ has made us well, whole, complete, Col. 2.6-10; Mark 2.17.

    c. As an agent of justice, we declare and demonstrate the justice of the Kingdom to come in all our dealings, both in the Church and with outsiders, 1 Cor. 6.1-10.

C. The Church is the agent of prophetic signs and wonders which display the power and glory of God's Kingdom.

1. Continuing signs to the Lordship of Christ are revealed in congregations of Spirit-filled believers.

    John 14.12 (NASB) – Truly, truly, I say to you, he who believes in me, the works that I do shall he do also; and greater works than these shall he do; because I go to the Father. And whatever you ask in my name, that will I do, that the Father may be glorified in the Son. If you ask me anything in my name, I will do it.

2. Deliverances, healings, and transformation: The Kingdom invades the demonic sphere in the presence and program of the Church.

   Matt. 16.18 (NASB) – And I also say to you that you are Peter, and upon this rock I will build my Church; and the gates of Hades shall not overpower it.

   Mark 16.17 (NASB) – And these signs will accompany those who have believed: in my name they will cast out demons, they will speak with new tongues; they will pick up serpents, and if they drink any deadly poison, it shall not hurt them; they will lay hands on the sick, and they will recover.

   Heb. 2.3 (NASB) – how shall we escape if we neglect so great a salvation? After it was at the first spoken through the Lord, it was confirmed to us by those who heard, God also bearing witness with them, both by signs and wonders and by various miracles and by gifts of the Holy Spirit according to his own will.

3. The empowering presence of the Holy Spirit in all we say and do.

   a. The power of the Spirit in the Body, 1 Cor. 12.3-11

   b. The powers of the world to come in the presence of the Holy Spirit, Heb. 6.4

   c. The filling and enriching of the Spirit in the community's life and through the community's ministry, Eph. 5.18ff.

D. Implications for Team Leaders

1. God in this age works within and through the Church; no Church, no word from the Lord, no Kingdom advance, no Gospel proclamation.

2. Planting healthy churches, therefore, is the most visible sign of Christ's Kingdom authority and power.

3. The Great Commission is synonymous with planting congregations of disciples.

4. A church plant team is merely one form of church which plants another form of church.

5. You cannot lead a church plant team if you have a low view of the Church of Jesus Christ.

6. Creating, strengthening, and reproducing churches is *raison d'etre* of apostolic ministry.

7. The Holy Spirit will supply all that is needed for every congregation of believers to grow, prosper, and multiply as Jesus Christ directs.

Models of the Kingdom

Howard A Snyder, March 2002. • *The Kingdom of God. Module 2, The Capstone Curriculum.* Wichita: The Urban Ministry Institute, 2005.

1. **The Kingdom as Future Hope – the Future Kingdom**
   This has been a dominant model in the history of the Church. The emphasis is strongly on the future: a final culmination and reconciliation of all things which is more than merely the eternal existence of the soul. The model draws heavily on NT material. While some of the following models also represent future hope, here the note of futurity is determinative.

2. **The Kingdom as Inner Spiritual Experience – the Interior Kingdom**
   A "spiritual kingdom" to be experienced in the heart or soul; "beatific vision." Highly mystical, therefore individualistic; an experience that can't really be shared with others. Examples: Julian of Norwich, other mystics; also some contemporary Protestant examples.

3. **The Kingdom as Mystical Communion – the Heavenly Kingdom**
   The "communion of saints"; the Kingdom as essentially identified with heaven. Less individualistic. Often centers especially in worship and liturgy. Examples: John of Damascus, John Tauler; in somewhat different ways, Wesley and 19th and 20th-century revivalistic and Evangelical Protestantism. Kingdom is primarily other-worldly and future.

4. **The Kingdom as Institutional Church – the Ecclesiastical Kingdom**
   The dominant view of medieval Christianity; dominant in Roman Catholicism until Vatican II. Pope as Vicar of Christ rules on earth in Christ's stead. The tension between the Church and the Kingdom largely dissolves. Traces to Augustine's City of God, but was developed differently from what Augustine believed. Protestant variations appear whenever the Church and Kingdom are too closely identified. Modern "Church Growth" thinking has been criticized at this point.

5. **The Kingdom as Counter-System – the Subversive Kingdom**
   May be a protest to #4; sees the Kingdom as a reality which prophetically judges the sociopolitical order as well as the Church. One of the best examples: Francis of Assisi; also 16th century Radical Reformers; "Radical Christians" today; Sojourners magazine. Sees Church as counter-culture embodying the new order of the Kingdom.

6. **The Kingdom as Political State – the Theocratic Kingdom**
Kingdom may be seen as a political theocracy; Church and society not necessarily to be organized democratically. Tends to work from O.T. models, especially the Davidic Kingdom. Constantinian model; Byzantine Christianity a good example. Calvin's Geneva, perhaps, in a somewhat different sense. Problem of Luther's "two kingdoms" view.

7. **The Kingdom as Christianized Society – the Transforming Kingdom**
Here also the Kingdom provides a model for society, but more in terms of values & principles to be worked out in society. Kingdom in its fullness would be society completely leavened by Christian values. Post-millennialism; many mid-19th-century Evangelicals; early 20th-century Social Gospel. Kingdom manifested progressively in society, in contrast to premillennialism.

8. **The Kingdom as Earthly Utopia – the Earthly Kingdom**
May be seen as #7 taken to extreme. This view of the Kingdom is literally utopian. Tends to deny or downplay sin, or see evil as purely environmental. The view of many utopian communities (Cohn, Pursuit of the Millennium) including 19th-century U.S. and British examples. In a different way, the view of many of America's Founding Fathers. Most influential 20th-century example: Marxism. Liberation theology, to some degree. In a starkly different way: U.S. Fundamentalist premillennialism, combining this model with #1, #2 and/or #3 -Kingdom has no contemporary relevance, but will be literal utopia in the future. Thus similarities between Marxism and Fundamentalism.

A Theology of Christ and Culture

The Difference That Difference Makes
Culture, Religion, and Diversity in Post-Modern Society
Rev. Dr. Don L. Davis • *Ministry in a Multicultural and Unchurched Society. Foundations for Ministry Series*. Wichita: The Urban Ministry Institute, 2007.

> Theology is a systematic description and explanation of the way things really are, the way God sees them, and we will speak of this as "Theology" with a capital T. At other times we use the term when we speak of human descriptions and explanations of reality that arise out of our study of the Bible. We will speak of this as "theology" with a small t. Too often we confuse the two. We think that our studies of the Bible are unbiased, that our own interpretations of the Scriptures are the only true ones. It disturbs us, therefore, when we begin to discover that theologies are influenced by culture. The very fact that we phrase our theology in English can prejudice our understanding of the Bible. There is no theologically unbiased language. The fact is, all theologies developed by human beings are shaped by their particular historical and cultural contexts - by the language they use and the questions they ask. All human theologies are only partial understandings of Theology as God sees it. We see through a glass darkly. . . . But the fact that we are humans and see through a glass darkly does not mean that we do not see at all. We can read the Scriptures and understand them. The central message of the gospel is clear: creation, sin, and redemption. Of these we can be certain. It is the fine details that we see less clearly.
>
> ~ Paul Hiebert, *Anthropological Insights for Missionaries*, p. 198.

Match the following cultural slang to the more proper English meaning equivalent	
"Your steez are mad ill!"	You are not nice at all
"What time it is!"	What a wonderful thing that was!
"You're so dill – you blow!"	I really like that song.
"That was the biz bizzom bomb!"	You are wrong on that point.
"You are all up in my grill."	I don't agree with that.
"That's completely whack!"	I have plenty of money.
"That last jam was fat."	Your clothes look really sharp.
"I'm kickin' you to the curb."	Hello, how are you doing?
"Poof you!"	I refuse to discuss this with you any further.
"Talk to the hand!"	You are too concerned with my affairs.
"I've got mad scrilla!"	Our relationship has to end now.
"None of that was fresh, you know what I'm sayin'?!"	That was not particularly fun.

Taking a Quick Tour of the World Today

I. **"What in the World Are We Doing?": The World Today**

   A. If the world were made up of 100 people . . .

   B. The world is becoming urban.

   1. Right now, there are 111,000 non-Christians becoming urban dwellers every single day (this number will triple within the next 30 years).

   2. In 1900 there were only 20 cities in the entire world over one million people; today, there are 360 cities with over one million people.

   3. By the year 2025, there will be 650 urban areas with more than one million people.

   4. In 1900, approximately 20 million people lived in urban slums; today, some 715 million are classified as urban slum dwellers. By 2025 over two billion people will live in urban slums and the total number of urban dwellers in poverty will be over three billion people.

   5. By the time I reach retirement age (i.e., 2025) one out of every three people on earth will be part of the urban poor, and three-fourths of the world's total population will live in cities.

II. **The World of the Future: Dramatically Diverse, Thoroughly Urban**

   A. More than 360 cities of more than one million inhabitants, 250 can be said to be of worldwide significance.

B. Center of human population: predicted numbers in terms of millions of the world's ten largest agglomerations by the year 2000

   1. Mexico City – 27.6 million people

   2. Sao Paulo – 26 million

   3. Tokyo/Yokohama – 24 million

   4. New York area – 23 million

   5. Shanghai – 23 million

   6. Beijing – 20 million

   7. Rio de Janeiro – 19 million

   8. Greater Bombay – 17 million

   9. Calcutta – 17 million

   10. Jakarta – 17 million

C. Impossible to think reasonably of modern civilization without referring to great cities of the world – Washington, New York, Seoul, Cairo, Brasilia, Istanbul, Moscow, Stockholm, London, Paris, Buenos Aires, Amsterdam, Los Angeles, and so on. Cities are significant because of their strategic import.

   1. Cultural cities (leading the world in fashion, trends, and ideas) e.g., Paris, Oxford, Boston, San Francisco

2. Political and Administrative cities (centers of worldwide decision making bodies, or which contain governments and their bureaucracies) e.g., Washington, Moscow, New Delhi

3. Industrial cities (noisy, blue-collar, factory centers host to central manufacturing industries) e.g., Bombay, Sao Paulo, Chicago-Gary Area)

4. Commercial cities (giant marketplaces or bazaars where goods and services are bartered and exchanged on a worldwide basis) e.g., New York, Hong Kong

5. Symbolic cities (cities where great struggles are fought and settled and symbolized, or which represent issues of division, oppression, warfare, religious hatred, or freedom within their countries or to the rest of the world) e.g., Soweto, Belfast, Berlin, Beirut, Jerusalem

6. Primary cities (cities which combine all of the preceding characteristics, and can be said to be the greatest of the great cities) e.g., Bangkok, Mexico City, London

D. The cities of America are microcosms of the globe, filled with all the world's complicated diversity.

1. Miami is the de facto capital of Latin America.

2. According to conservative estimates, at least one million Hispanics pour illegally over the 2400 mile border between Mexico and U.S. each year.

3. Los Angeles, with its 4.5 million Hispanics, is now the second largest Mexican city, while Houston is the fastest growing one.

4. Diverse populations make up the typical American city. Over 100 languages are spoken by the residents of Los Angeles, and four-fifths of all of Houston's schoolchildren are either Hispanic, Black, or Asian.

5. Twenty years ago, in May of 1982, a NY Times survey of Chinatown found refugees from every province of mainland China within a four block area in the middle of NY city.

6. Chicago has as many Native Americans as all but the very largest reservations in the country, and more Poles than virtually any other place with the exception of Warsaw.

7. Most American cities of any size (2 million or more) host diverse cultural and ethnic populations.

III. The Concept of Difference: Culture

"Culture is that integrated, well-established, and communally defined patterns of behavior and worldview which influences the cognitive, affective, and evaluative dimensions of its expression."

- Learned patterns
- Worldview and behavior
- Cognitive, affective, and evaluative dimensions

A. The Perils and Promise of ministry in a multicultural and unchurched society

1. Mind-boggling diversity

2. Formidable interpersonal barriers

3. Dramatic gaps in wealth and socio-economic reality

4. Complex patterns of kinship relations

5. Technological sophistication and richness

6. Shifting, volatile ethical visions of the human good

7. New Modern Dragons: the emergence of spiritually without God

B. "The Dimensions of Culture"

1. The Cognitive Dimension – "The knowledge shared by members of a group or society" (Hiebert, p. 30)

    a. Arrangement of knowledge, categories, systems of meaning

    b. What exists and what does not

    c. Worldview and conceptual frameworks: cultures as systems of relationships which compose and dictate what we consider to be possible and real

        (1) Ontology – the study of being

        (2) Cosmology – the study of creation

        (3) Epistemology – the study of knowing

    d. Assumptions and beliefs we make about reality, the nature of the world, and how it works

    e. Storage

(1) Print

(2) Oral

(3) Technology

(4) Story

(5) Art

2. The Affective Dimension – "feelings people have, with their attitudes, notions of beauty, tastes in food and dress, likes and dislikes, and ways of enjoying themselves or experiencing sorrow" (Hiebert, p. 32)

   a. Expression of emotions

   b. Ubiquitous – seen in virtually all areas of life

   c. "Expressive culture": art, literature, music, dance, drama

3. The Evaluative Dimension – "values by which [a culture] judges human relationships to be moral or immoral"

   a. Three spheres of evaluative judgment

      (1) Truth-falsehood claims

      (2) Beauty-ugliness claims

      (3) Right-wrong claims

   b. Moral codes: The power of ultimate concern, and sacredness in human society

C. Manifestations of Culture

1. Behavior – customs, products, and languages learned as symbol systems of forms and learned meaning

    a. Form

    b. Meaning

    c. Symbol

2. Products – material objects, lived environments

3. Explicit beliefs and value systems – all of those forms whereby we through practice, ritual, tradition, and structure embody, articulate, and celebrate our worldview

    a. Aesthetics

    b. Politics

    c. Religion

    d. Kinship relations

    e. Social organizations

    f. Economics

    g. Technology

    h. Etc.

IV. The Implications of Cultural Difference in Ministry to the Unchurched and to Diverse Populations

A. The differences between people are important (C1, C2, C3 contexts).

1. God created difference, Acts 17.

2. The Kingdom will reflect difference, Rev. 5.9-10.

B. The differences between people are real.

1. What we share in common (e.g., the imago Dei) is more significant than the superficial differences which separate us.

2. Our differences, nonetheless, are viewed as critical and significant, not to be ignored or eclipsed by some generic culture (cf. John 1.14-18).

C. The differences between people are significant.

1. These differences are more than cosmetic.

2. They have profound implications for how people think, act, feel, and what they value and strive for. (Example – white and black differences in perception during the O.J. Simpson trial).

D. The differences between people are not necessarily bad or wrong.

1. Every culture has elements that are moral, i.e. consistent with the way that God desires us to think and act (examples: punishment for murder, care for children, etc.).

2. Every culture has elements that are immoral, i.e. inconsistent with or opposed to the way that God desires us to think and act (examples: infanticide of female offspring, pursuit of material wealth as an ultimate value).

3. Every culture has elements that are amoral, i.e. differences arising from taste, custom, tradition, and habit (examples: eating tacos, wearing hats, speaking English, dancing at weddings).

E. The difference between people tend to alienate and divide groups.

1. Our differences tend to divide us because we are ethnocentric, we prefer our own culture and tend to judge others in light of it.

2. Anthropological roots of division

    a. The enormous power of enculturation

    b. The hidden nature of culture

    c. We love those who are like us.

    d. Culture Shock: The unsettling effects of operating outside of our own class, culture, or subculture

3. Theological roots of the division

    a. We tend to place ourselves at the center of the universe.

    b. We forget or ignore what God is doing in the world regarding the building of his kingdom on earth.

c. We fail to shift our loyalties from our own national, cultural, and class framework to the vision of God's new humanity in Christ.

4. We close off our hearts to God's love for all people.

5. We reject the notion that you need not change culture in order to become Christian and be Christ's people.

F. Our differences may erect barriers and cause us to treat people differently.

When differences are allowed to divide, we typically respond to others in three inappropriate ways.

1. We become paternalistic: "help the poor native syndrome".

   Our benevolent expression of assumed superiority often results in an attempt to modify the actions, and values of a differing group (example: missionaries issuing Western clothing to South Pacific islanders).

2. In suspicion, we isolate and separate ourselves from people who are different.

   The passive expression of my group's prejudice through the deliberate limiting of contact between my group and the people, actions, and values of the group that is different (example: segregated neighborhoods).

3. In hatred and malice, we reject the other culture as bad or evil or undeserving, and seek to undermine and persecute it.

   The active expression of my group's hatred for the people, actions, and values of the group that is different (example: ethnic cleansing in Bosnia or Rwanda, the Holocaust in Germany, etc.).

V. A Biblical Theology of Culture

A. Culture is intrinsic to the creation of God.

1. God as the author of human life (Gen. 1-2).

2. God's creation mandate as an intrinsic blessing of human creative cultural production.

    a. Be stewards of the earth: tools, technology, shaping environment.

    b. Go and multiply: kinship, social organization, structure.

B. The differences between peoples have now been acknowledged and reconciled in the ministry of Christ.

1. Our differences are now reconciled through the work of Christ on the cross.

    a. Between Jew and Gentile, slave and free, male and female, barbarian and Sycthian, Eph. 2; Col. 3.11; Gal. 3.28

    b. God is reconciled with all people now in his Son, 2 Cor. 5.18-21.

    c. We share in both the guilt and the glory, Rom. 3; 1.16-17.

2. The goal of redemption is Christlikeness, not cultural sameness. (The goal is always to help people become more like Jesus, not more like us.)

a. Colossians 3.11 and Galatians 3.28 do not advocate the obliteration of cultural identity, only the end of ungodly partiality.

b. Culture has been redeemed in the incarnation of Jesus, 1 John 1.1-3.

3. Our differences are displayed and celebrated in the one, holy, apostolic, and universal Church of Jesus Christ.

   a. A New Humanity in the Church

   b. Diverse, yet one: Although we are many members made up of every kindred, tribe, people, and nation, from every language and clan, from every class and culture, we nevertheless are one body in Christ. We are to strive to make this unity visible in our daily lives and relationships.

   c. In redemption God does not erase, shield, or obliterate our differences, but rather he acknowledges and rejoices in them, Acts 15.

   d. While we retain our differences, we now in Christ through the koinonia (fellowship) we have with God and each other.

      (1) We share a common parentage.

      (2) We share a common calling.

      (3) We share a common destiny.

4. Our differences are overcome in the unity of Christ for the purpose of the ministry of reconciliation.

a. We express the love of God in our reconciled relationships, making the gospel attractive to unbelievers, John 13.34-35.

b. We are reconciled to call the world to be reconciled to God in Christ, 2 Cor. 5.18-21.

c. Our differences allow us to penetrate every culture and people group with the gospel, and make disciples and plant churches wherever Christ has yet to be heard and followed.

C. The primacy of the Incarnation of the Son of God

1. Jesus' enfleshment demonstrates the moral neutrality of culture, John 1.14-18.

2. Jesus' complete identification with humankind at the most intimate level (e.g., he thought in Hebrew, Heb. 4.14ff.).

3. Jesus took on the nature of humanity in full for the sake of both revelation and redemption.

    a. Jesus as Perfect Revelation shows that humankind is a vessel through which God can be perfectly understood, Col. 2.6-10; John 1.18; 2 Cor. 4.6.

    b. Jesus as Perfect Redemption shows that humankind can offer to God in Christ what God demands, Phil. 2.5-11; 1 Pet. 3.18; 1 Tim. 2.5-6.

4. Jesus elevates the meaning of human culture; through the Incarnation, culture is embraced, John 4.

D. The significance of the Jerusalem Council

1. The Petrine faux pas: Cornelius's band and Gentile salvation, Acts 10-11

2. The Jerusalem Council rejoinder, Acts 15

    a. No need to shift cultures: God speaks in and through culture

    b. One can retain one's cultural distinctiveness while embracing the pursuit of Christlikeness

    c. All cultures are equally viable in the Christian worldview (culture is valid, cultures are relative)

> The biblical principle of cultural neutrality, which encouraged indigenous leadership in every culture, allowed the gospel of Christ to become universally applicable. It set the stage for the Church's worldwide missionary efforts. Soon Philip and Paul began to evangelize and plant churches among non-Jewish peoples who have never heard of Christ. Their example is relevant to our inner-city today.
>
> ~ Keith Phillips, *Out of Ashes*, p. 103.

E. The Apostolic Burden: becoming all things to all human beings

1. The burden is on the messenger, not those who receive the message to change, 1 Cor. 9.19-22.

2. God is already among people, having providentially arranged the peoples as he determined, Acts 17.

3. Receive others as Christ has received you, Rom. 15.6ff.

VI. Decoding and Encoding the Message of God in a Multi-Cultural and Unchurched Society

Correlating the timeless message of God with the timely task of embodying and proclaiming the Word of God effectively within contemporary society

A. Decode God's Meaning: Become a disciple of Jesus yourself.

Embracing and embodying the message of God thoroughly and completely in one's own life in preparation to teach others, Luke 6.40

1. The challenge of the fitness of the hearer and the messenger: who we are as individual disciples and as congregations in the society (i.e., her character, her competence, her compassion, her clarity, her calling)

    a. To be a living epistle, 2 Cor. 3

    b. To display the glory, Matt. 5

    c. To set the spiritual pace, 1 Cor. 11

    d. To watch herself and her teaching, 1 Tim. 4

2. The challenge of the broadness of the message: what we teach and proclaim to the world regarding Christ and his Kingdom

    a. The Word of God in the person of Jesus Christ

b. The Gospel of Grace

c. The Vision of the Kingdom of God

B. Encode God's Message: Become an ambassador for Christ where you are.

Communicating and enfleshing the truth of the Kingdom within a receiving culture in such a manner that they hear God's voice as you speak

1. Admit your own latent ethnocentrism; acknowledge and respect the differences that exist between us, Acts 10.

2. Pay the price to learn the language and symbol systems of those you serve and minister to, e.g., John 1.1.

3. Adopt a listening lifestyle and a learner's demeanor (i.e., do your homework by learning of the history and culture of the people you will serve), 1 Cor. 9.19ff.

4. Begin at the beginning. Start on a small scale with modest expectations (Reconciled relationships take prolonged time and effort.) Eph. 4.1-3.

5. Don't be overcome by initial suspicion and rejection. Your motives will be questioned, so don't give up, Gal. 6.7-10.

6. Recognize that relationship must be reciprocal; earn the right to be heard by not foisting your agenda on other peoples, 1 John 1.1-4.

7. Separate culture norms from biblical mandates, e.g., 1 Cor. 12-14.

8. Exercise prudence in speech and action. One cultural faux pas can have devastating consequences, Prov. 22.3.

9. Do not demand that people from other cultures join your own in order to be disciples of Christ, Gal. 5.1; 2 Cor. 3.17.

10. Live in biblical freedom: apply biblical principles, and do not elevate cultural platitudes (the 1 Corinthian 6-8-10 principles).

11. Recognize the universal nature of the Kingdom of God, and shift your loyalty. Get in step with what God's universal, global, and historical plan is for the Church of Jesus Christ. Become a world Christian while serving here in your local assembly, Matt. 28.18-20.

12. Pray that God will guide you in the process and enable you to be effective in understanding and service, Matt. 7.7.

Five Views of the Relationship between Christ and Culture

Based on *Christ and Culture* by H. Richard Niebuhr. New York: Harper and Row, 1951.

Christ against Culture	Christ and Culture in Paradox	Christ the Transformer of Culture	Christ above Culture	The Christ of Culture
Opposition	Tension	Conversion	Cooperation	Acceptance
Therefore come out from them and be separate, says the Lord. Touch no unclean thing, and I will receive you. ~ 2 Cor. 6.17 (cf. 1 John 2.15)	Give to Caesar what is Caesar's, and to God what is God's. ~ Matt. 22.21 (cf. 1 Pet. 2.13-17)	In putting everything under him, God left nothing that is not subject to him. Yet at present we do not see everything subject to him. ~ Heb. 2.8 (cf. Col. 1.16-18)	Indeed, when Gentiles, who do not have the law, do by nature things required by the law, they are a law for themselves. ~ Rom. 2.14 (cf. Rom. 13.1, 5-6)	Every good and perfect gift is from above, coming down from the Father of the heavenly lights, who does not change like shifting shadows. ~ James 1.17 (cf. Phil. 4.8)
Culture is radically affected by sin and constantly opposes the will of God. Separation and opposition are the natural responses of the Christian community which is itself an alternative culture.	Culture is radically affected by sin but does have a role to play. It is necessary to delineate between spheres: Culture as law (restrains wickedness), Christianity as grace (gives righteousness). Both are an important part of life but the two cannot be confused or merged.	Culture is radically affected by sin but can be redeemed to play a positive role in restoring righteousness. Christians should work to have their culture acknowledge Christ's lordship and be changed by it.	Culture is a product of human reason and is part of a God-given way to discover truth. Although culture can discern real truth, sin limits its capacities which must be aided by revelation. Seeks to use culture as a first step toward the understanding of God and his revelation.	Culture is God's gift to help man overcome his bondage to nature and fear and advance in knowledge and goodness. Human culture is what allows us to conserve the truth humanity has learned. Jesus' moral teaching moves human culture upward to a new level.
Tertullian, Menno Simons Anabaptists	Martin Luther Lutherans	St. Augustine, John Calvin Reformed	Thomas Aquinas Roman Catholic	Peter Abelard, Immanuel Kant Liberal Protestant

Interaction of Class, Culture, and Race
World Impact, Inc.

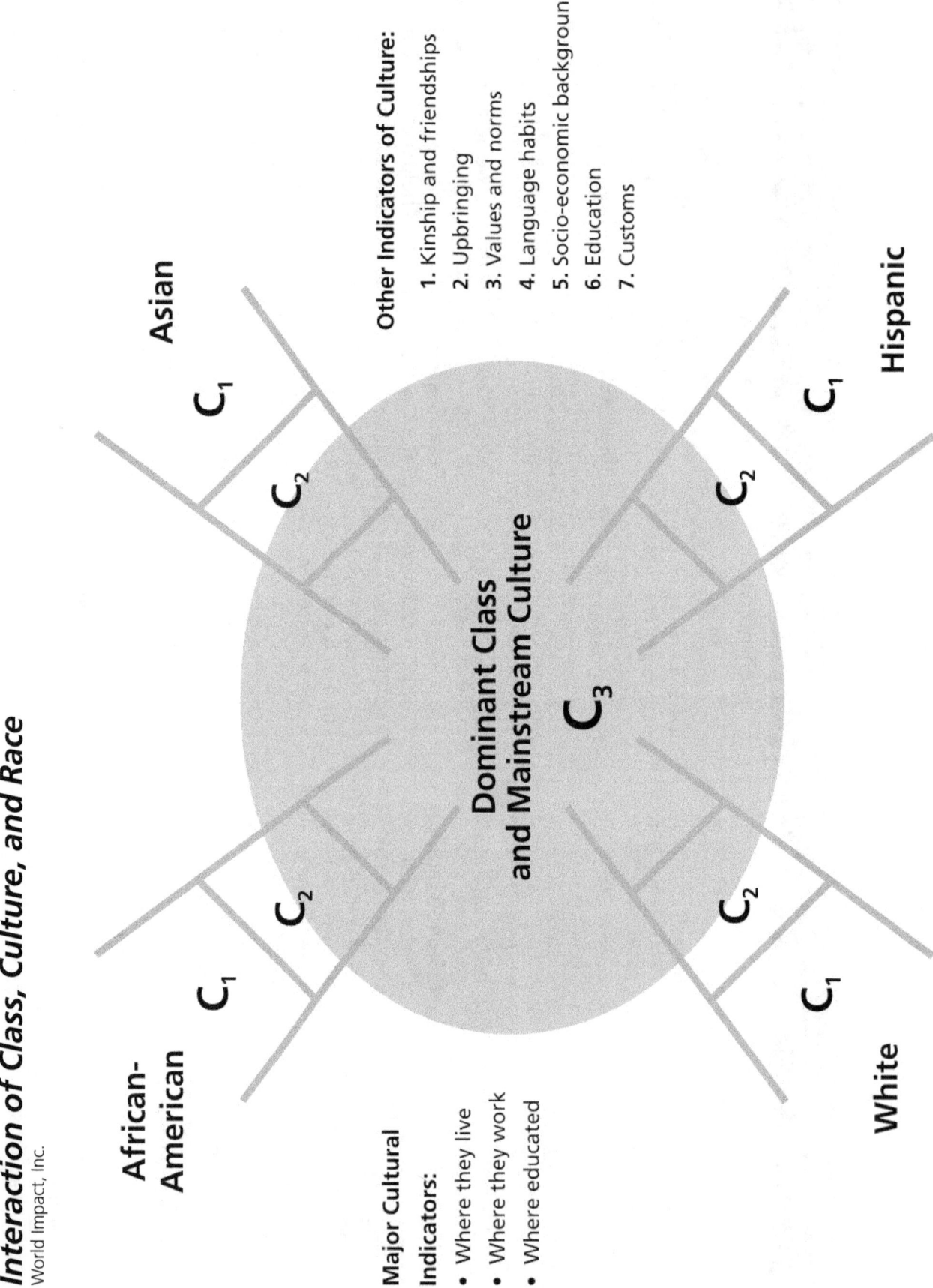

The Complexity of Difference: Race, Culture, Class
Rev. Dr. Don L. Davis and Rev. Terry G. Cornett

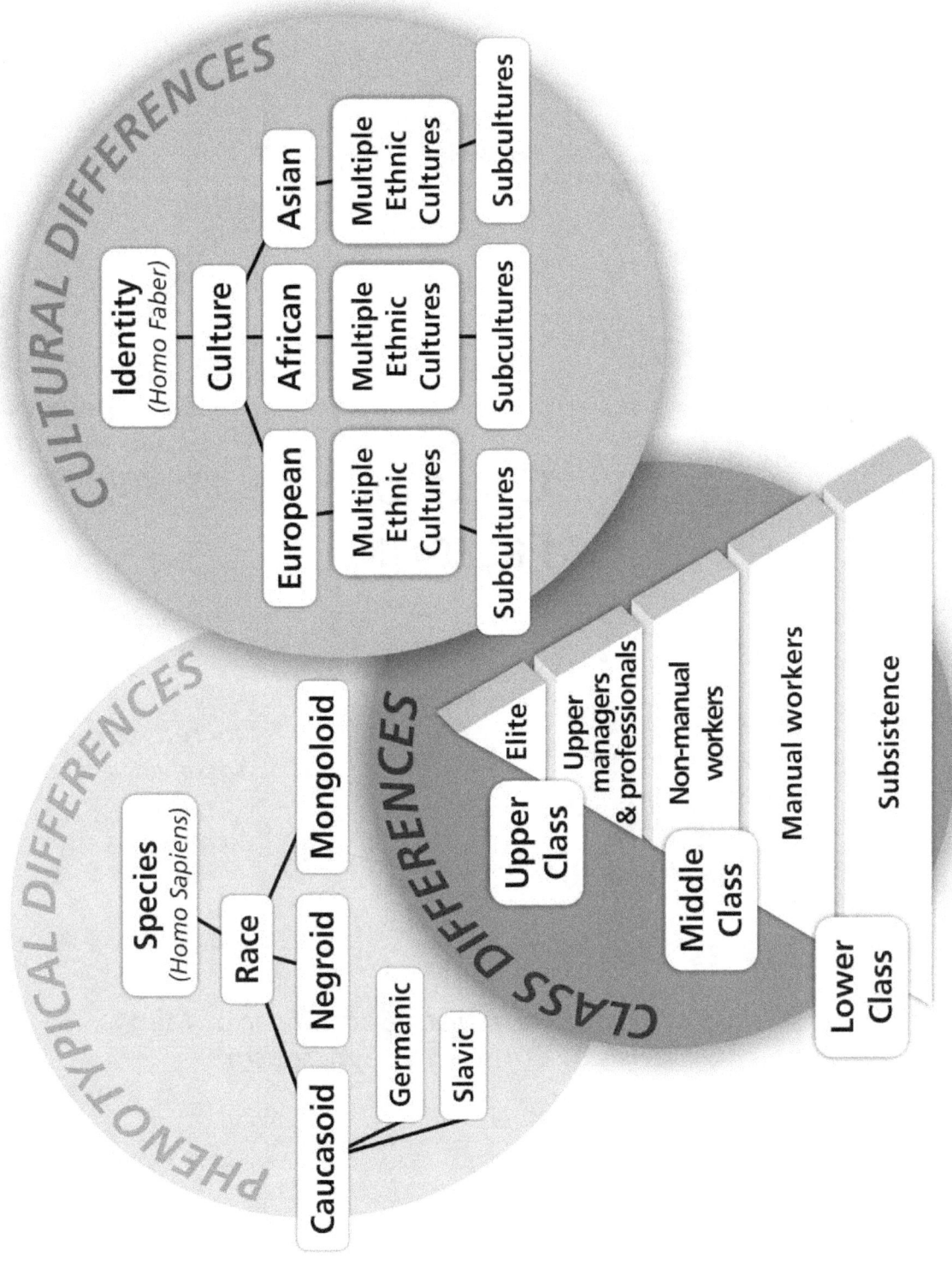

Cycle of Freedom
Rev. Dr. Don L. Davis

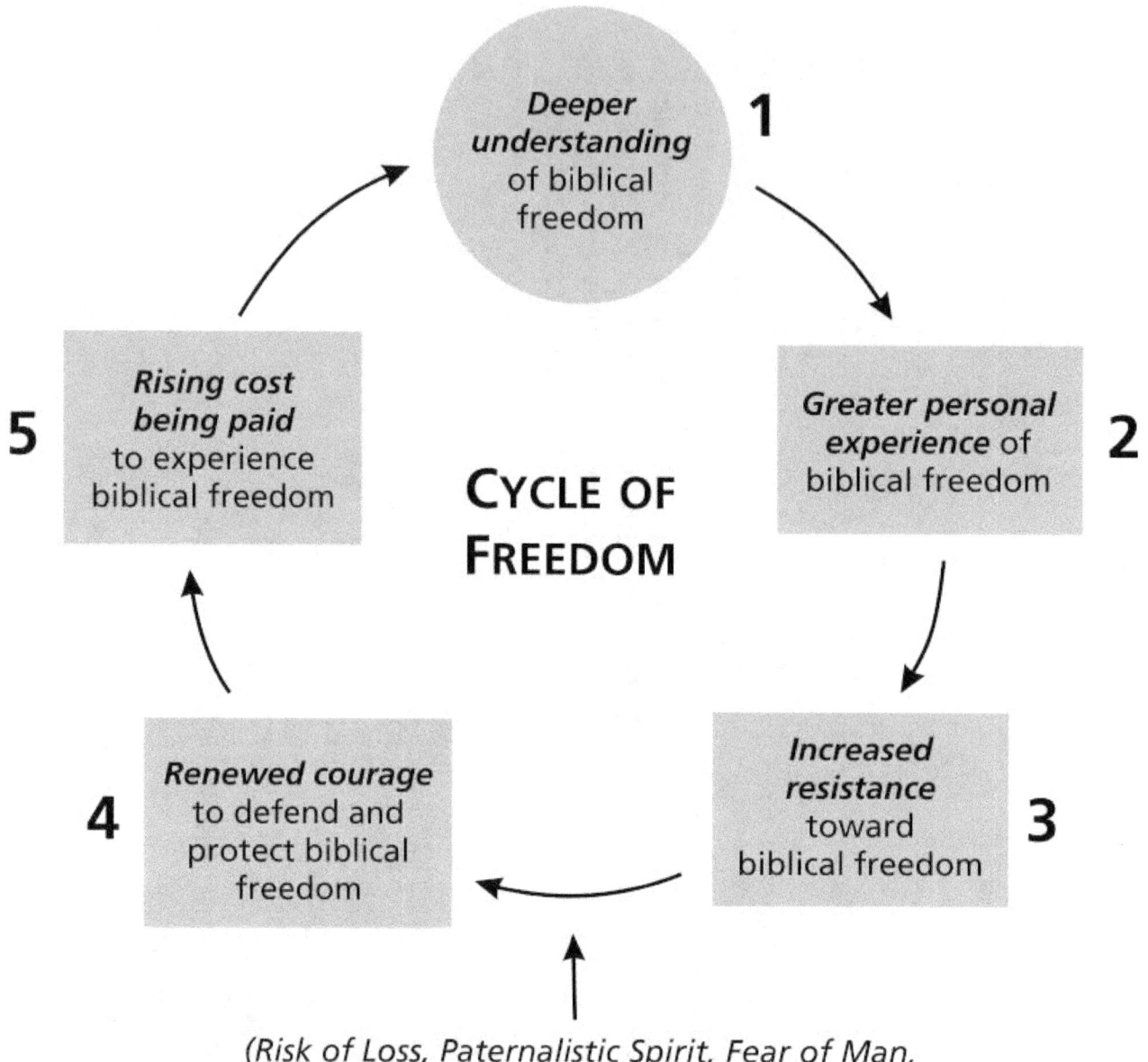

Authentic Freedom in Jesus Christ

Rev. Dr. Don L. Davis

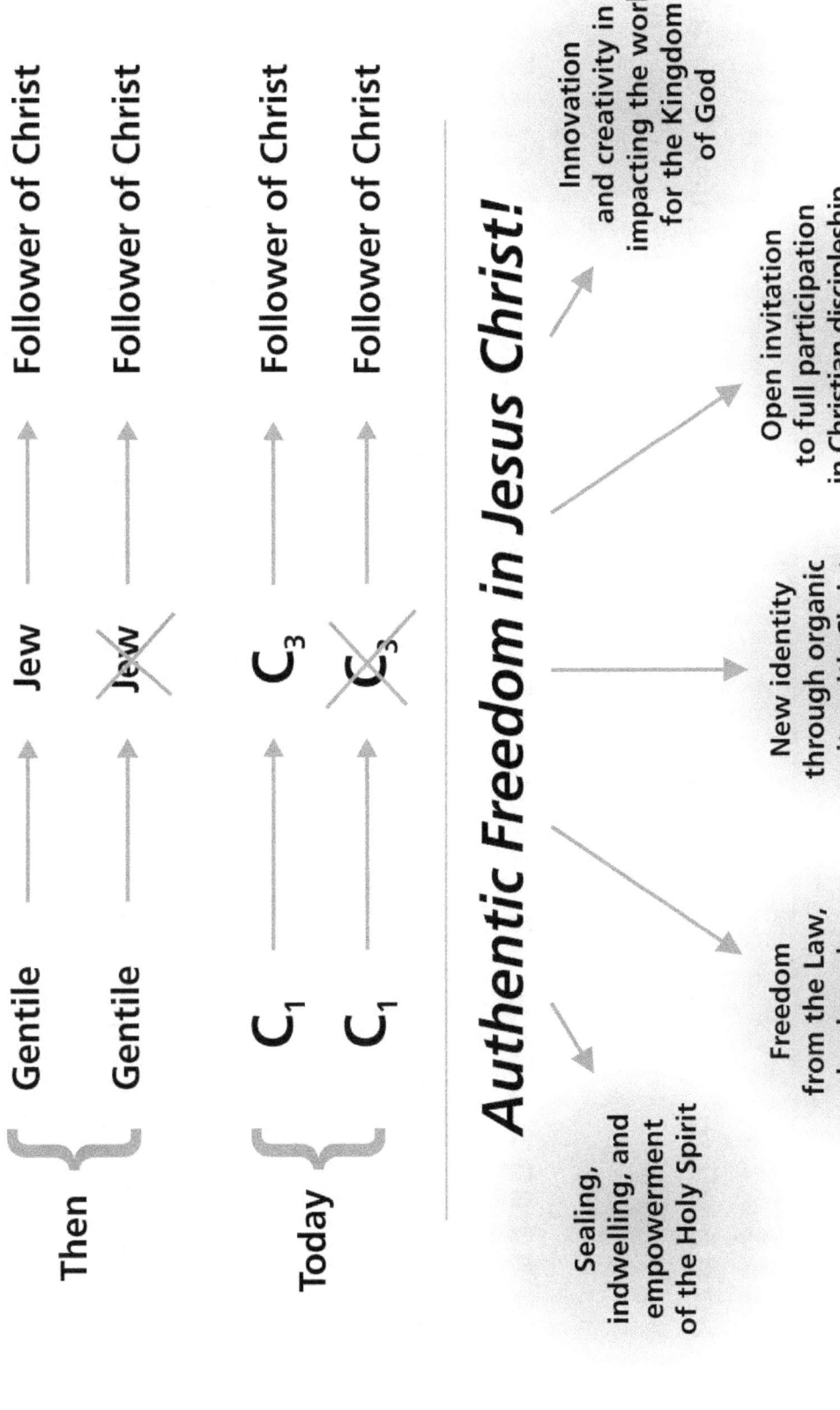

Too Legit to Quit: A Continuum of Cultural Practice
Rev. Dr. Don L. Davis

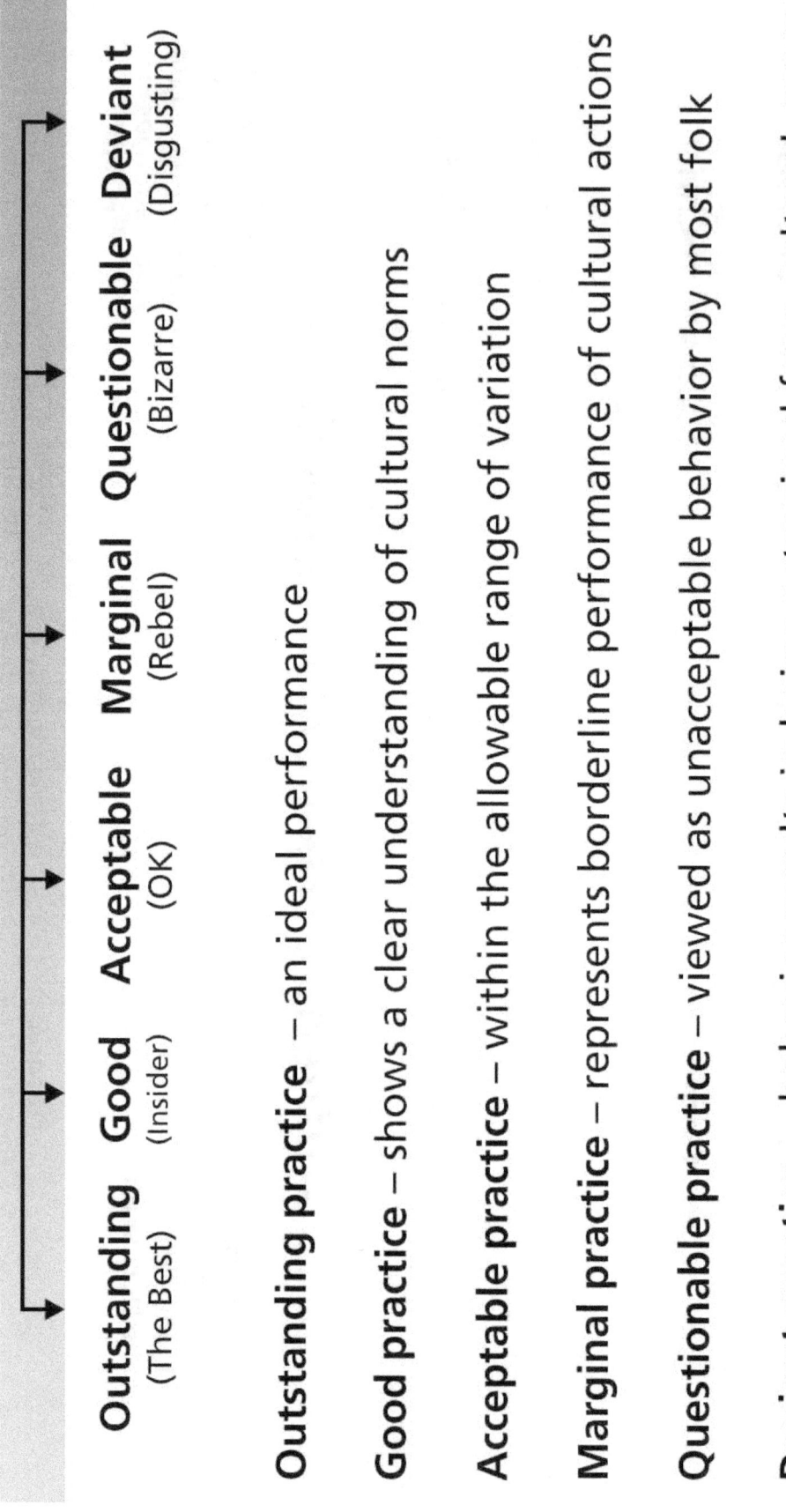

Outstanding **Good** **Acceptable** **Marginal** **Questionable** **Deviant**
(The Best) (Insider) (OK) (Rebel) (Bizarre) (Disgusting)

Outstanding practice – an ideal performance

Good practice – shows a clear understanding of cultural norms

Acceptable practice – within the allowable range of variation

Marginal practice – represents borderline performance of cultural actions

Questionable practice – viewed as unacceptable behavior by most folk

Deviant practice – behavior results in being ostracized from cultural group

Apostolicity
The Unique Place of the Apostles in Christian Faith and Practice
Rev. Dr. Don L. Davis

Gal. 1.8-9 – But even if we or an angel from heaven should preach to you a gospel contrary to the one we preached to you, let him be accursed. [9] As we have said before, so now I say again: If anyone is preaching to you a gospel contrary to the one you received, let him be accursed.

2 Thess. 3.6 – Now we command you, brothers, in the name of our Lord Jesus Christ, that you keep away from any brother who is walking in idleness and not in accord with the tradition that you received from us.

Luke 1.1-4 – Inasmuch as many have undertaken to compile a narrative of the things that have been accomplished among us, [2] just as those who from the beginning were eyewitnesses and ministers of the word have delivered them to us, [3] it seemed good to me also, having followed all things closely for some time past, to write an orderly account for you, most excellent Theophilus, [4] that you may have certainty concerning the things you have been taught.

John 15.27 – And you also will bear witness, because you have been with me from the beginning.

Acts 1.3 – To them he presented himself alive after his suffering by many proofs, appearing to them during forty days and speaking about the kingdom of God.

Acts 1.21-22 – So one of the men who have accompanied us during all the time that the Lord Jesus went in and out among us, [22] beginning from the baptism of John until the day when he was taken up from us— one of these men must become with us a witness to his resurrection.

1 John 1.1-3 – That which was from the beginning, which we have heard, which we have seen with our eyes, which we looked upon and have touched with our hands, concerning the word of life— [2] the life was made manifest, and we have seen it, and testify to it and proclaim to you the eternal life, which was with the Father and was made manifest to us— [3] that which we have seen and heard we proclaim also to you, so that you too may have fellowship with us; and indeed our fellowship is with the Father and with his Son Jesus Christ.

"Apostolicity"

- Focused on Messiah Jesus
- Infallible (Authoritative)
- Universally acknowledged among the churches
- Standard for NT canon
- Clear standard for credentialing ordained leaders

Theological Diversity

Rev. Dr. Don L. Davis • *World Impact's Candidate Assessment Program* (for missionary applicants). Wichita: World Impact.

I. **The Importance of Theology**

   A. It is critical to credible faith: Rom. 10.17 – So faith comes from hearing, and hearing through the word of Christ.

   B. It is critical to apostolic community: Jude 1.3-4 – Beloved, although I was very eager to write to you about our common salvation, I found it necessary to write appealing to you to contend for the faith that was once for all delivered to the saints. For certain people have crept in unnoticed who long ago were designated for this condemnation, ungodly people, who pervert the grace of our God into sensuality and deny our only Master and Lord, Jesus Christ.

   C. It is critical to godly leadership: Titus 1.9 – He must hold firm to the trustworthy word as taught, so that he may be able to give instruction in sound doctrine and also to rebuke those who contradict it.

II. **The Reality of Diversity in Christian Traditions**

   A. We are diverse in our *patterns of religious authority*: how we make decisions and recognize rulership

   B. We are diverse in our *hermeneutical methods*: how we read and interpret the Scriptures

   C. We are diverse in our *lived traditions*: how we worship and serve the same Lord of all

III. **The Essential Rule of Faith: The Nicene Creed**

   A. The Vincentian Rule of Theological Conviction: "All possible care must be taken that we hold that faith which has been believed everywhere, always, and by all" (Vincent of Lerins, "A Commonitory," *Nicene and Post-Nicene Fathers*).

B. The Significance of the Creed: Concise Summary of the Essentials

In the history of the church, the Nicene Creed has been the key statement of what is essential to Christian belief.

1. *Augustine* [says about the creeds] – Let thing contend with thing, cause with cause, reason with reason on the authority of Scripture, an authority not peculiar to either, but common to all. In this way, councils would be duly respected, and yet the highest place would be given to Scripture, every thing being brought to it as a test.

2. *John Calvin* - Thus those ancient Councils of Nicea, Constantinople, the first of Ephesus, Chalcedon and the like which were held for refuting errors, we willingly embrace, and reverence as sacred, in so far as relates to the doctrines of faith, *for they contain nothing but the pure and genuine interpretation of Scripture*, which the holy Fathers with spiritual prudence adopted to crush the enemies of religion who had then arisen (*Institutes* IV, ix. 8).

3. *John Wesley* – John Wesley accorded a fundamental status to the Nicene-Constantinopolitan Creed as both "a summary of the biblical faith" and as an interpretive web "for the reading of Scriptures" (Sen-King Tan, "The Doctrine of the Trinity in John Wesley's Prose and Poetic Works").

C. World Impact Affirmation of Faith Statement

1. Acknowledgment of the essentials

2. Affirms the "Great Tradition" (ie., theology of the core creedal statements)

3. Asserts the Reformer's central doctrinal claims

4. Addresses post-Nicea doctrinal issues

5. Anchored in broad evangelical perspective

D. The Power of Inter-denominationality: Peter Meiderlin (Rupertus Meldenius), 17th century Lutheran theologian and pastor

1. In essentials *unity*: never compromise the Great Tradition, Phil. 2.3; Jude 3.

2. In non-essentials *liberty*: allow for freedom on issues of conscience, Gal. 5.1.

3. In all things *charity*: practice love and charity in everything, John 13.34-35.

E. The Problem of Dogmatism: "Rabid Theology"

1. Dogmatists alone determine what are "the essentials."

2. Non-essentials do not exist; *all of their* beliefs are essential.

3. They love only those who agree with their view of "the essentials."

IV. Dealing with Disagreements

A. The Inevitability of *Disagreement*: expect conflict over doctrinal visions

B. The Importance of *Dialogue*: reason with principled conviction over matters of faith and doctrine

C. The Ingredient of *Demeanor*: maintain in all things a spirit of charity and respect

D. The Importance of *Deference*: defer to our denominational partners on non-essentials

V. Conclusions: The Importance of Theological Diversity

> In essentials, unity,
> In non-essentials, liberty,
> In all things, charity.
> ~ Peter Meiderlin (Rupertus Meldenius),
> 17th century Lutheran theologian and pastor

Creedal Theology as a Blueprint for Discipleship and Leadership
A Time-Tested Criterion for Equipping New Believers and Developing Indigenous Leaders

Rev. Dr. Don L. Davis • *The Timothy Conference: Building Church Plant Teams*. Wichita: The Urban Ministry Institute, 2005.

> "Creed" derives from the Latin credo, "I believe." The form is active, denoting not just a body of beliefs but confession of faith. This faith is trust: not "I believe that" (though this is included) but "I believe in." It is also individual; creeds may take the plural form of "we believe," but the term itself comes from the first person singular of the Latin: "I believe."
>
> ~ G. W. Bromiley. "Creed."
> *Elwell's Evangelical Dictionary Software*, 1998-99.

I. **What Is the Biblical Basis for Creedal Theology?**

   A. Creeds in the technical sense are not present in the Bible, but creeds do mean to express essential biblical data and truth.

   B. Creedal forms in Scripture

   1. The Shema of the Old Testament, Deuteronomy 6.4-9

   2. Little credo in Deuteronomy 26.5-9

   Deut. 26.5-9 (NKJV) – "And you shall answer and say before the Lord your God: 'My father was a Syrian, about to perish, and he went down to Egypt and sojourned there, few in number; and there he became a nation, great, mighty, and populous. But the Egyptians mistreated us, afflicted us, and laid hard bondage on us. Then we cried out to the Lord God of our fathers, and the Lord heard our voice and looked on our affliction and our labor and our oppression. So the Lord brought us out of Egypt with a mighty hand and with an outstretched arm, with great terror and with signs and wonders. He has brought us to this place and has given us this land, "a land flowing with milk and honey."

   3. New Testament references and occurrences to creedal material

a. Sources of creedal material

   (1) Traditions, 2 Thess. 2.15

   (2) Word of the Lord, Gal, 6.6

   (3) Preaching, Rom. 16.25 (In the technical sense, creeds are not present in the Bible, but they nevertheless express essential biblical data and truth.)

b. Baptismal creedal confessions, Acts 8.37; Matt. 28.19; Rom. 10.9-10

c. The Christological confession, Phil. 2.5-11

II. What Is the Instructional Basis for Creedal Theology?

A. Serves as *a syllabus for catechetical teaching* in Christian belief and doctrine in order to ground new believers in the faith

   1. Creed allows for variation (from "simple exposition to advanced theological presentation")

   2. E.g., from recitation of the Creed itself to the treatment of Langdon Gilkey's systematic theology based on the Creed (cf. the Catecheses of Cyril of Jerusalem in the fourth century)

   3. Sources show that candidates for baptism had to display some understanding of the profession they made in baptism (i.e., demanded intellectual comprehension as well as sincere heart commitment).

B. Serves as *a basis for doctrinal and theological education* for the Christian community at large, regardless of level of maturity

   1. Creeds forged out of theological controversy, the rise of heresies, and the need to protect the apostolic confession from admixture with falsehood

   2. The ministry of heresies: enabled early Christian pastors to expand their first rough confessions into more developed formulas

   3. Examples of creedal defense

a. "Maker of heaven and earth": probably to fight Gnostic idea of separation of the True God from creator

b. Teaching on the Virgin birth and Jesus' death: combats Gnostic claims against Jesus' authentic human nature

c. The Arian idea of Jesus as less than divine added to affirm Christ's absolute divinity

4. Creed slowly grew to function as both a proper understanding of the Scriptural story as well as test of the orthodoxy of the clergy.

C. Serves as *an important ingredient of the worship (liturgy)* of the community of believers (teaching in and through our worship)

1. Confession of faith, in song and sermon, is an essential part of all true Christian worship.

2. Nicene Creed was incorporated in the Eucharistic sequence (i.e., the Lord's Supper service), first in the East, then in Spain, and finally in Rome

3. Often was placed after the reading of the Scripture as a congregational response of faith to the Word of God

III. What Creeds Have Been Recognized as Prominent and Significant in the Church?

A. In Christian history, three creeds have taken superior place: The Apostles' Creed, the Nicene Creed, and the Athanasian Creed.

1. The Apostles' Creed

(Traditional English Version) I believe in God the Father Almighty, Maker of heaven and earth, and in Jesus Christ his only Son our Lord; who was conceived by the Holy Ghost, born of the Virgin Mary, suffered under Pontius Pilate, was crucified, dead, and buried; he descended into hell; the third day he rose again from the dead; he ascended into heaven, and sitteth on the right hand of God the Father Almighty; from thence he shall come to judge the quick and the dead. I believe in the Holy Ghost; the holy catholic Church; the communion of saints; the

forgiveness of sins; the resurrection of the body; and the life everlasting. Amen.

   a. Supposedly written by the apostles under inspiration, and therefore came to be called the Apostles' Symbol or Creed (Synod of Milan, 390 A.C.E.)

   b. Lorenzo Valla refuted the apostolic origin (which the East never accepted).

   c. Scholars attribute its origin to the Old Roman Creed (expounded by Rufinius in 404).

   d. Present form originates from the 8th century, and has been made of regular use in the West, especially by the Reformers in liturgies, confessions, and catechisms.

2. The Nicene Creed

We believe in one God, the Father Almighty, Maker of heaven and earth and of all things visible and invisible.

We believe in one Lord Jesus Christ, the only Begotten Son of God, Begotten of the Father before all ages, God from God, Light from Light, True God from True God, Begotten not created, of the same essence as the Father, through whom all things were made.

Who for us men and for our salvation came down from heaven and was incarnate by the Holy Spirit and the virgin Mary and became human. Who for us too, was crucified under Pontius Pilate, suffered and was buried. The third day he rose again according to the Scriptures, ascended into heaven and is seated at the right hand of the Father. He will come again in glory to judge the living and the dead, and his Kingdom will have no end.

We believe in the Holy Spirit, the Lord and life-giver, Who proceeds from the Father and the Son. Who together with the Father and Son is worshiped and glorified. Who spoke by the prophets.

We believe in one holy, catholic, and apostolic Church.

We acknowledge one baptism for the forgiveness of sin, and we look for the resurrection of the dead and the life of the age to come. Amen.

Note: The word "catholic" as used in the creed means "universal." It is significant because it reminds believers that there are many congregations but only one Church. No congregation is an end in itself, rather it is organically connected to the whole Church and must understand itself to be in unity with other believers both locally and around the world.

a. Despite its name, it should be distinguished from the creed of Nicea (325), has been debated whether it was recognized at Constantinople I (381), but was recognized by Chalcedon council in 451, and at Constantinople II in 553.

b. The West has added the one Latin clause called the "filioque clause" (i.e., and from the Son) as to the statement on the Holy Spirit, but the East never conceded the orthodoxy of the original drafts.

c. This is the undisputed primary confession of the Church in both the East and West; it is the primary Creed used in Eucharistic and catechetical contexts.

d. A concise, elegant, and beautiful statement of what the earliest pastors, theologians, and leaders of the Church considered to be the elemental essentials of Christian orthodoxy.

e. TUMI's most critical test of historic orthodoxy: fidelity to the teachings of the Nicene Creed.

> **What Is the Nicene Creed?**
>
> The original Nicene creed came out the first worldwide gathering of Christian leaders at Nicaea in Bithynia (what is now Isnik, Turkey) in the year 325. It was called to deal with a heresy called Arianism which denied that Jesus was God and taught that he was instead the greatest created being. The council at Nicaea hammered out language that bishops could use to teach their churches who Jesus was.
>
> A little over fifty years later new challenges were being faced. A modified form of the Arian heresy was making a comeback. And a new problem had also emerged. Some bishops and pastors had begun teaching that the Holy Spirit was not God (was not of the same substance as the Father) and was not really even a creature. He was thought of as a kind of power but not as a person of the Godhead.
>
> To resolve this problem, a council of 150 bishops of the Eastern Church were gathered in 381 at Constantinople (modern day Istanbul, Turkey). This council reaffirmed the fact that Jesus was

> fully God and then turned their attention to the question of the Holy Spirit which the Nicene council had left untouched (the original Nicene Creed read simply, "We believe in the Holy Spirit."). The council turned this simple statement into a paragraph which explained more fully the person and work of the Holy Spirit.
>
> This expanded version of the original Nicene creed is what is most commonly known as "The Nicene Creed" today, (although it is more technically correct to call it the "Niceno-Constantinopolitan Creed" or the "Creed of the 150 Fathers") It is universally acknowledged by Christians of all denominations. And it is used as a part of the worship service in many traditions, as well.
>
> ~ Terry Cornett, "What Is the Nicene Creed?"
> T2-105 Christian Theology: God the Holy Spirit.
> The Urban Ministry Institute, 1997.

3. The Athanasian Creed

   (Early Fifth Century) Whoever wills to be in a state of salvation, before all things it is necessary that he hold the catholic [apostolic/universal] faith, which except everyone shall have kept whole and undefiled without doubt he will perish eternally. Now the catholic faith is that we worship One God in Trinity and Trinity in Unity, neither confounding the Persons nor dividing the substance. For there is one Person of the Father, another of the Son, another of the Holy Spirit. But the Godhead of the Father, of the Son, and of the Holy Spirit, is One, the Glory equal, the Majesty coeternal. Such as the Father is, such is the Son, and such is the Holy Spirit; the Father uncreated, the Son uncreated, and the Holy Spirit uncreated; the father infinite, the Son infinite, and the Holy Spirit infinite; the Father eternal, the Son eternal, and the Holy Spirit eternal. And yet not three eternals but one eternal, as also not three infinites, nor three uncreated, but one uncreated, and one infinite. So, likewise, the Father is almighty, the Son almighty, and the Holy Spirit almighty; and yet not three almighties but one almighty. So the Father is God, the Son God, and the Holy Spirit God; and yet not three Gods but one God. So the Father is Lord, the Son Lord, and the Holy Spirit Lord; and yet not three Lords but one Lord. For like as we are compelled by Christian truth to acknowledge every Person by himself to be both God and Lord; so are we forbidden by the catholic religion to say, there be three Gods or three Lords. The Father is made of none, neither created nor begotten. The Son is of the Father alone, nod made nor created

> *but begotten. The Holy Spirit is of the Father and the Son, not made nor created nor begotten but proceeding. So there is one Father not three Fathers, one Son not three Sons, and Holy Spirit not three Holy Spirits. And in this Trinity there is nothing before or after, nothing greater or less, but the whole three Persons are coeternal together and coequal.*

    a. Creed often attributed to Athanasius around the 4th or 5th century

    b. Direct statement on the nature on the Trinity, more thorough

    c. Became a test of the orthodoxy and competence of the clergy in the West from the 7th century

    d. Differences between Apostles' and Nicene

        (1) More complex doctrinal character

        (2) More prosaic, less poetic

        (3) More as a plumb line of orthodoxy, less as a credo of faith

    e. Reformers highly accepted, some use among Anglicans, but the East did not recognize it; of significantly less importance in catechesis and liturgy.

> The dangers of creed-making are obvious. Creeds can become formal, complex, and abstract. They can be almost illimitably expanded. They can be superimposed on Scripture. Properly handled, however, they facilitate public confession, form a succinct basis of teaching, safeguard pure doctrine, and constitute an appropriate focus for the church's fellowship in faith.
> ~ G. W. Bromiley. "Creed."
> Elwell's Evangelical Dictionary Software, 1998-99.

IV. Why Can a Creedal Theology Be Critical for Establishing New Believers and Developing Indigenous Urban Christian Leaders?

While no commitment to any Creed can ever take away our responsibility to search the Scriptures daily in order to nurture and build our faith, nonetheless, a commitment to using the Creed as a safeguard for historic orthodoxy has great importance in grounding believers in the faith as well as training leaders for the urban church.

A. It represents *a historic, clearly defined outline summary* of the earliest Christian leaders' view of the Apostles' doctrine.

1. It is historic: the Nicene is nearly seventeen centuries old.

2. It is universally respected among traditions as an authoritative summary of the heart of the Apostles' teaching.

3. It has been used successfully throughout Church history as the curricula to ground new Christians and test emerging leaders as faithful disciples of Jesus Christ.

B. It can provide *a simple, memorable, and concise statement* of the substance of historic Christian belief.

1. Simple: not very wordy, provides essential summary

2. Memorable: becomes an easy instrument to serve as core of one's orthodox commitment

3. Concise: although abstract, it is extremely compact in its style but meaningful in its weight and concept

C. It lays *a foundation for determining an evangelical ecumenism*, a plumb line whereby we can judge what is essential for mutual fellowship and service.

1. The Nicene is a kind of universal statement of what Christians have believed on the core issues from the beginning.

2. Probably the most celebrated document that is recognized by virtually every tradition of Christian faith

3. It deals with the essential truths that Christians have historically counted to be bedrock truths of the faith.

D. It defines *the apostolic deposit that represents the defense of the Gospel* and full explication of Kingdom theology.

1. Focuses on the core teachings of the apostles about God and Christ

2. Deliberately drafted to deal with anti-Christ heresies of the day

3. Highlights the core teachings of the Church, especially against its fundamental Christ-centered background

E. It provides *the content of Christian multiplication and reproduction*, the bare minimum for equipping new leaders and giving catechesis for new members in the church.

1. A test of essential biblical conviction, accessible to everyone; the Nicene core is easily contextualized for both liturgy, confession of faith, and the Lord Supper

2. May be adapted easily as a standard for orthodoxy for Christian workers, ministers, pastors, and missionaries

3. Allows us to use a time-tested, Church endorsed rule for determining the doctrinal and theological credential for developing and emerging leaders

V. What Are the Implications for Church Plant Team Leaders?

A. Embrace the Creed as a kind of shorthand for the biblical Story; not a replacement for the Story but a concise summary and brilliant highlighting of its most salient points.

1 Tim. 3.14-16 (ESV) – I hope to come to you soon, but I am writing these things to you so that, if I delay, you may know how one ought to behave in the household of God, which is the Church of the living God, a pillar and buttress of truth. Great indeed, we confess, is the mystery of godliness: He was manifested in the flesh, vindicated by the Spirit, seen by angels, proclaimed among the nations, believed on in the world, taken up in glory.

1. The Creed is *essential*; it provides a summary of the Christian Narrative in bold relief.

2. The Creed is *Christo-centric*: the story of Jesus of Nazareth is the key to the entire self-consciousness of Christianity, and the key to understanding the hope of all twenty-first century disciples today.

3. The Creed is *confessional*: the Creed is meant to become a part of our conscience and hope, a statement of our deepest convictions regarding how we understand the nature of the world, God, life, and the afterlife.

4. The Creed is *celebratory*: it affirms in concise language we believe about God and Jesus, the Spirit, the Church, and the Age to Come we place ourselves in the sacred stream of men and women throughout history who have bled, suffered, and died on behalf of the biblical story.

B. Recognize *the sophistication of the Creed's teaching*: it can easily be adapted to ground the new believer to empowering the sophisticated theologian, pastor, or bishop.

1. Determine your audience and their need.

2. Relate your teaching to their context.

3. Link your presentation to the readiness and grittiness of the hearts and lives of your people.

    a. Show them why theology makes all the difference.

    b. Connect doctrine to attitude and to perspective.

    c. Use case studies to show how theological perspective bleeds into all fabrics of our psychological and social frameworks.

C. Allow the Creed to squire to help you defend the Apostles' witness to Jesus Christ against falsehood: the Creed is not as equal to Scripture, but serves as a historical statement of what the Church has contended for and defended for centuries.

Jude 1.3-4 (ESV) – Beloved, although I was very eager to write to you about our common salvation, I found it necessary to write appealing to you to contend for the faith that was once for all delivered to the saints. For certain people have crept in unnoticed who long ago were designated for this condemnation, ungodly people, who pervert the grace of our God into sensuality and deny our only Master and Lord, Jesus Christ.

1. Connect the struggles of your people with the struggles of Christians all over the world, and throughout all history.

2. Relate the teaching of the Creed in its big panoramic vision to what is taking place today.

3. Ground your people in the historical, worldwide, trans-cultural, multi-ethnic and multi-national movement of Jesus.

D. Be diligent *to consistently rehearse historic orthodoxy* with your church plant team, with your fledgling community, and with your developing leaders through the Creed.

2 Tim. 4.1-5 (ESV) – I charge you in the presence of God and of Christ Jesus, who is to judge the living and the dead, and by his appearing and his Kingdom: preach the word; be ready in season and out of season; reprove, rebuke, and exhort, with complete patience and teaching. For the time is coming when people will not endure sound teaching, but having itching ears they will accumulate for themselves teachers to suit their own passions, and will turn away from listening to the truth and wander off into myths. As for you, always be sober-minded, endure suffering, do the work of an evangelist, fulfill your ministry.

1. Do not hesitate to emphasize the critical, life-and-body shaping role of theology; show how theological perspective ultimately determines life outcome.

2. Challenge mentors always to connect specific details and issues to the great biblical narrative, which the creed summarizes and outlines.

3. Use the Creed to connect the faith and works of your people to the historic works of faith done from the apostles onward.

Eph. 4.4 – There is one body and one Spirit, just as you were called in one hope of your calling; one Lord, one faith, one baptism; [4.6] one God and Father of all, who is above all, and through all, and in you all.

4. Tell the stories which breathe life into the Creed, and allow the Creed to become a means by which you can ground the new believer, encourage the disciple, and enrich the tested soldier.

E. Finally, make *the study, recitation, and discussion of the Creed* a critical part of your church-planting life.

1. Use the Creed in your devotions and corporate worship.

2. Preach on the topics included in the Creed in the community of believers, and emphasize it within your Christian education.

3. Develop studies and curricula for your growing disciples and emerging leaders on the Creed as a criterion of doctrinal and theological necessity.

Translating the Story of God
Rev. Dr. Don L. Davis

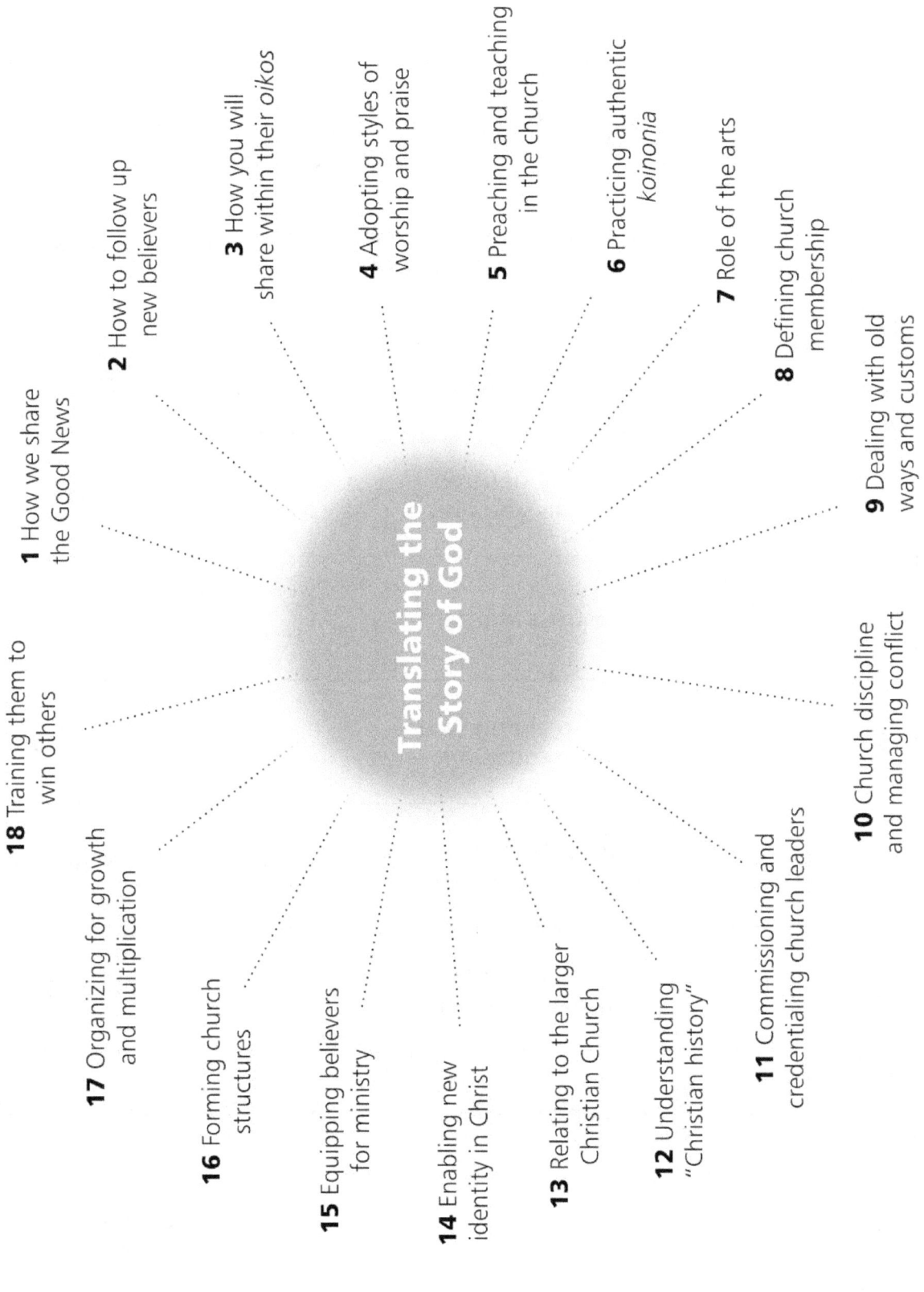

Cross-Cultural Church Planting Principles
World Impact

1	Jesus is Lord.	Matthew 9.37-38
2	Evangelize, Equip, and Empower unreached people to reach people.	1 Thessalonians 1.6-8
3	Be inclusive: Whosoever will may come.	Romans 10.12
4	Be culturally neutral: Come just as you are.	Colossians 3.11
5	Avoid a fortress mentality.	Acts 1.8
6	Continue to evangelize to avoid stagnation.	Romans 1.16-17
7	Cross ethnic, class, gender, and language barriers.	1 Corinthians 9.19-22
8	Respect the dominance of the receiving culture.	Acts 15.23-29
9	Avoid dependence.	Ephesians 4.11-16
10	Think reproducibility.	2 Timothy 2.2; Philippians 1.18

The Missionary Vocation: Assessing Cross-Cultural Adaptability
Rev. Dr. Don L. Davis

How do missionaries engage received cultures with the Gospel of Christ?

Hegemony

Ethnocentric Denial of Old Cultural Ways
(Uncritical dismissal)

→ Gospel perceived as foreign entity
Gospel rejected as denial of received culture

→ **Old Goes Underground**
Syncretism

Decode/Encode

Critically Engage Old Cultural Ways
(Critical Contextualization)

→ 1) Gather Info on the Old

→ 2) Study Biblical Teachings

→ 3) Evaluate Old in Light of Theology

→ 4) New Contextualized Christian Practice

Accommodation

Uncritically Accept Old Cultural Ways
(Uncritical endorsement)

→ Culture adopted without critique or reflection
Gospel is demoted and/or altered to accommodate culture

→ **Old eclipses biblical vision**
Syncretism

Targeting Unreached Groups in Churched Neighborhoods
Mission Frontiers

Many different peoples!

Many homogenous congregations.

The extent of normal "outreach": Incorporating and gathering according to culture.

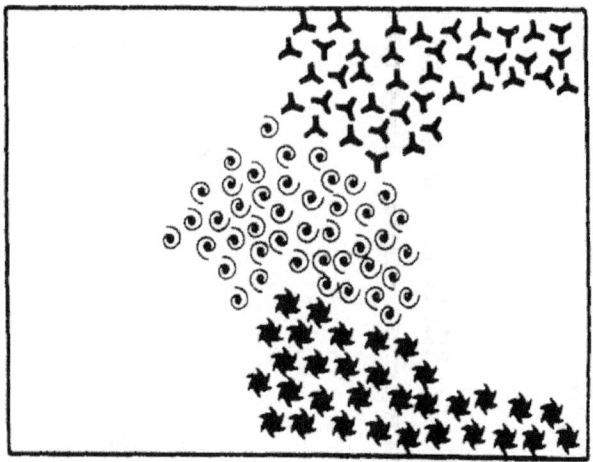

"So close and yet so far away": The unreached, unaffected neighbors.

Different Traditions of African-American Response
Interpreting a Legacy, Shaping an Identity, and Pursuing a Destiny as a Minority Culture Person

Rev. Dr. Don L. Davis, adapted from and informed by Cornel West's *Prophesy Deliverance*.

I. **Exceptionalism – Afro-centrism and superiority – "Above"**

   A. Definition – tendency to respond in terms of exalted, superior, and even romanticized view of one's own cultural and racial roots

   B. Example – Louis Farrahkan, W.E.B. DuBois

   C. Issues

   1. Pendulum swing: same bigotry as oppressive group, only inverted ("Same shoe, different foot")

   2. Isolationist and separatistic; have no desire to be in relationship with people of majority culture and/or race

   3. See separation and segregation as an essential step on the road to a full personhood as a minority group

   4. To gain one's own identity is the prime goal, not relating to people of another culture

II. **Assimilationism – Adopting the predominant culture as one's primary, and in some cases, only, culture – "Behind"**

   A. Definition – the tendency to ignore or bypass one's particular cultural roots in order to identify with a more general, broad, and accepted majority culture identity

   B. Example – Shelby Steele, Alan Keys

   C. Issues

   1. Advocate a full blown adoption of the predominant cultural identity (e.g., "I am not Black, but American")

2. Tends to ignore the specialness of difference

3. Need not be committed to obliterating culture, only ignoring difference in order that we may all meld into one common pot

4. Perpetually defers to the cultural mores and habits of the dominant culture

III. Marginalism – Inferiority, shame and hatred, denial – "Outside"

A. Definition – Tendency to deny, overlook, or even reject one's own cultural legacy as pathological, insignificant, and even detrimental to one's own growth and prosperity

B. Example – Joseph Washington, E. Franklin Frazier

C. Issues

1. Breeds contempt for oneself; self-deprecation is not viewed as a negative in reference to the overall badness of the culture

2. Ignores God's role in shaping culture

3. Oversimplifies one's own cultural legacy as either insignificant or immoral

IV. Integrationism – Modern-day multi-culturalism – "Among"

A. Definition – Tendency to strive for a multi-cultural integration of peoples within society that guarantees the rights and privileges of citizenry, equality, and justice

B. Example – Jesse Jackson, Thurgood Marshall, Traditional civil rights vision

C. Issues

1. Focus on attaining distributive justice within society among all the people groups within it ("equal treatment under the law", and "cut the societal pie correctly")

2. Seeks limited goods within the society of equality and fairness under the law, and does not focus (usually) on friendship but equal treatment

3. Appeals mainly to issues related to economic issues, distribution of wealth, and the overall benefits of society

4. May focus on establishing coalitions of people of different culture in order to sway the hand of government and society for equal and just treatment

5. Legislates its agenda, does not emphasize relationship

V. **Celebrationism – Acknowledgment, Delight, Critique and Relationship – "Alongside"**

A. Definition – Tendency to see all cultures as significant and unique, and intentionally celebrates the differences between cultures while 1) critiquing its immoral elements according to a biblical vision and, 2) arguing against exclusion and bigotry on the basis of the differences

B. Example – Martin Luther King, Jr.

C. Issues

1. Grounded in a Christian vision of God's creation

2. Ethic of a Christian community, and its prophetic message

3. Affirms culture as a distinctly human phenomenon

4. Attaches no pejorative connotation to cultural identity or preference

See *Targeting Unreached Groups in Churched Neighborhoods.*

Paul's Team Members
Companions, Laborers, and Fellow Workers
Rev. Dr. Don L. Davis

Achaicus, a Corinthian who visited Paul at Philippi, 1 Cor. 16.17.

Archippus, Colossian disciple whom Paul exhorted to fulfill his ministry, Col. 4.17; Philem. 2.

Aquila, Jewish disciple Paul found at Corinth, Acts 18.2, 18, 26; Rom. 16.3; 1 Cor. 16.19; 2 Tim. 4.19.

Aristarchus, with Paul on 3rd journey, Acts 19.29; 20.4; 27.2; Col. 4.10; Philem. 24.

Artemas, companion of Paul at Nicopolis, Titus 3.12.

Barnabas, a Levite, cousin of John Mark, and companion with Paul in several of his journeys, cf. Acts 4.36; 9.27; 11.22, 25, 30; 12.25; chs. 13, 14, and 15; 1 Cor. 9.6; Gal. 2.1, 9, 13; Col. 4.13.

Carpus, disciple of Troas, 2 Tim. 4.13.

Claudia, female disciple of Rome, 2 Tim. 4.21.

Clement, fellow-laborer at Phillipi, Phil. 4.3.

Crescens, a disciple at Rome, 2 Tim. 4.10.

Demas, a laborer of Paul at Rome, Col. 4.14; Philem. 24; 2 Tim. 4.10.

Epaphras, fellow laborer and prisoner, Col. 1.7; 4.12; Philem. 23.

Epaphroditus, messenger between Paul and the churches, Phil. 2.25, 4.18.

Eubulus, disciple of Rome, 2 Tim. 4.21.

Euodia, Christian woman of Philippi, Phil. 4.2

Fortunatus, part of the Corinthian team, 1 Cor. 16.17.

Gaius, 1) a Macedonian companion, Acts 19.29; 2) a disciple/companion in Derbe, Acts 20.4.

Jesus (Justus), a Jewish disciple at Colossae, Col. 4.11.

John Mark, companion of Paul and cousin of Barnabas, Acts 12.12, 15; 15.37, 39; Col. 4.10; 2 Tim. 4.11; Philem. 24.

Linus, a Roman Companion of Paul, 2 Tim. 4.21.

Luke, physician and fellow-traveler with Paul, Col. 4.14; 2 Tim. 4.11; Philem. 24.

Onesimus, native of Colossae and slave of Philemon who served Paul, Col. 4.9; Philem. 10.

Hermogenes, a team member who abandoned Paul in prison, 2 Tim. 1.15.

Phygellus, one with Hermogenes turned from Paul in Asia, 2 Tim. 1.15.

Priscilla (Prisca), wife of Aquila of Pontus and fellow-worker in the Gospel, Acts 18.2, 18, 26; Rom. 16.3; 1 Cor. 16.19.

Pudens, a Roman companion of Paul, 2 Tim. 4.21.

Secundus, companion of Paul on his way from Greece to Syria, Acts 20.4.

Silas, disciple, fellow laborer, and prisoner with Paul, Acts 15.22, 27, 32, 34, 40; 16.19, 25, 29; 17.4, 10, etc.

Sopater, accompanied Paul to Syria, Acts 20.4.

Sosipater, kinsman of Paul, Rom. 16.21.

Silvanus, probably same as Silas, 2 Cor. 1.19; 1 Thess. 1.1; 2 Thess. 1.1.

Sosthenes, Chief Ruler of the Synagogue of Corinth, laborer with Paul there, Acts 18.17.

Stephanus, one of the first believers of Achaia and visitor to Paul, 1 Cor. 1.16; 16.15; 16.17.

Syntyche, one of Paul's female "fellow workers" in Philippi, Phil. 4.2.

Tertius, slave and person who wrote the Epistle to the Romans, Rom. 16.22.

Timothy, a young man of Lystra with a Jewish mother and Greek father who labored on with Paul in his ministry, Acts 16.1; 17.14, 15; 18.5; 19.22; 20.4; Rom. 16.21; 1 Cor. 4.17; 16.10; 2 Cor. 1.1, 19; Phil. 1.1; 2.19; Col. 1.1; 1 Thess. 1.1; 3.2, 6; 2 Thess. 1.1; 1 Tim. 1.2, 18; 6.20; 2 Tim. 1.2; Philem. 1; Heb. 13.23.

Titus, Greek disciple and co-laborer of Paul, 2 Cor. 2.13; 7.6, 13, 14; 8.6, 16, 23; 12.18; Gal. 2.1, 3; 2 Tim. 4.10; Titus 1.4.

Trophimus, Ephesian disciple who accompanied Paul to Jerusalem from Greece, Acts 20.4; 21.29; 2 Tim. 4.20.

Tryphena and ***Tryphosa***, female disciples of Rome, probably twins, who Paul calls laborers in the Lord, Rom. 16.12.

Tychicus, a disciple of Asia Minor who accompanied Paul in various trips, Acts 20.4; Eph. 6.21; Col. 4.7; 2 Tim. 4.12; Titus 3.12.

Urbanus, Roman disciple and aid to Paul, Rom. 16.9.

Jesus' Practice of Silence and Solitude

Dr. Hank Voss

Event	Type	References
Jesus' preparation years were not necessarily solitude, but worth reflecting on. What was Jesus doing during this time?	Jesus spent thirty years in quietness. Consider also his weekly Sabbath practice during this time. He spent more than four years resting. (1,560 Sabbath days!)	(#27) Luke 3.23
Desert Month	Jesus spent forty days in solitude, prayer, and fasting in the wilderness	(#28) Matt 4.1-11 Mark 1.12-13 Luke 4.1-13
Lonely Hours	Jesus spent a block of time (3-4 hours?) in solitude and prayer. He had regular places he would go.	(#50) Mark 1.35-39 Luke 4.42-44 (cf. Luke 11.1)
Habitual Half Day	Jesus would "often slip away to the wilderness and pray."	(#52) Luke 5.16
All Night Vigil	"He went off to the mountain . . . he spent the whole night in prayer to God" (before a major decision).	(#63) Luke 6.12-16
Executive Team Retreat	"Come away by yourselves to a lonely place, and rest a while."	(#104) Mark 6.31-34
Habitual Half Day/Night	"He went up on the mountain by himself to pray; and when it was evening, he was there alone."	(#106) Matt 14.22-23 Mark 6.45-46 Luke 6.14-15
Friend Retreat	"He brought them up to a high mountain by themselves."	(#121) Matt 17.1-8 Mark 9.2-8 Luke 9.28-36a
All Night Vigil	"And he withdrew from them about a stone's throw, and he knelt down and began to pray."	(#226) Matt. 26.36-46 Mark 14.32-42 Luke 22.40b-46 John 18.1

#xx = Episode number in *A Harmony of the Gospels*, by Gundry and Thomas (1978)

Jesus took a "solitude" time at least three times a year (eight times in three-year period).

Seven Essential Practices for the Priesthood of All Believers
Dr. Hank Voss

Practice	Description	Key Texts
Baptism	A public covenant celebration of a believer's union with Christ. It emphasizes not only the believer's identification with the death of Christ, but also the new life now lived in Christ. Like Christ's baptism, a believer's baptism is a public commissioning to share in the ministry and mission of the royal priesthood.	Matt. 3.13-17; 28.19-20; Rom. 6.1-14
Prayer	The royal priesthood has the privilege and responsibility of crying out to our Father in heaven. Our prayer joins the intercession of Christ at the right hand of the Father and our praise joins with the worship of heaven.	Matt. 6.5-15; Psalms; Luke 18.1-15; 1 Thess. 5.17
Lectio Divina	The royal priesthood finds the Holy Spirit's power in the Word of God. The royal priesthood approaches God's Word with the fear of the Lord, humility, delight, and costly obedience. We daily listen to the Spirit's voice speaking through Scripture.	Matt. 4.1-11; Ps. 119
Ministry	Leaders have been given to the church to equip the members of the church to do the work of the ministry. As each member uses his or her gifts in love to build up the body, the body grows into maturity, into the fullness of Christ.	John 13; Eph. 4.11-16; Rom. 12; 1 Cor. 12; 1 Pet. 4.10-11
Church Discipline	Christ's bride is holy, but its members are broken by sin. The church instructs its members in the deceitfulness of sin, the need for speaking the truth in love (confrontation), the confession of sins, the giving and receiving of forgiveness, and the joyful restoration of the repentant.	Matt. 6.14-15; 18.15-20; 2 Cor. 2.1-11; 2 Thess. 3.13-15; Gal. 6.1
Proclamation	All members of the royal priesthood testify in word and deed to Christ and his Kingdom in the power of the Spirit for the glory of the Father. Through the power of the Holy Spirit the Church is empowered to faithfully witness to Christ in the world.	Matt. 4.23; 1 Pet. 2.9; Phil. 2.15-16; Acts 1.8
The Lord's Supper	A public celebration of the New Covenant inaugurated by Christ at the Last Supper ultimately consummated at the wedding feast of the Lamb. It is a practice with past, present, and future significance calling for remembrance, forgiveness, thanksgiving, covenant renewal, fellowship, nourishment, and anticipation	Matt. 22.2-14; 26.26-31; 1 Cor. 11.17-34; Rev. 19.6-9

On World Impact's "Empowering the Urban Poor"

Rev. Dr. Don L. Davis

Since our founding more than forty years ago, World Impact has spoken prophetically regarding God's election of the poor, the benign neglect of the evangelical church of America's inner city poor, and the need for evangelism, discipleship, and church planting in unreached urban poor communities. We believe that credible urban mission must demonstrate the Gospel, testifying in both the proclaimed word and concrete action. In light of this, we have emphasized living in the communities we serve, ministering to the needs of the whole person, as well as to the members of the whole urban family. We have sought this witness with a goal to see communities reached and transformed by Christ, believing that those who live in the city and are poor can be empowered to live in the freedom, wholeness, and justice of the Kingdom of God fleshed out in local churches and viable urban church planting movements. All our vision, prayer, and efforts are concentrated on a particular social group, the "urban poor," and our commitment to "empower" them through all facets of our work.

While the phrase "the urban poor" may be misunderstood or misused, we have chosen to employ it with our own stipulated meanings, informed by biblical theology as well as urban sociology. We employ the term to identify those whom God has commissioned us to serve, as well as to represent God's prophetic call to proclaim Good News to the poor, both to the church and to our society at large.

It must be conceded, of course, that the term "urban poor" may be easily misapplied and misused. The American city is dramatically diverse, profoundly complex in its mixtures of classes, cultures, and ethnicities. Amid so much diversity, a phrase like "the urban poor" may, at first glance, appear to be too denotative to be suitable as a summary designation of those whom we serve, being somewhat dry and academic. Without clearly stipulating what you mean when you use it, it can easily turn to mere labeling, which tends to reinforce stereotypes, encouraging generalizations about city dwellers which are either too vague or generic to be useful.

Further, some might even suggest that such language is used for its sensationalized impact, for "tear jerk" effect, largely used to elicit donor response without providing clear information on a particular communities or grouping. It is argued that language like "urban poor" encourages over-generalization, and, using such terms to describe thousands, even millions of discrete cultures and communities is demeaning, sloppy thinking, and generally belittling to urban folk. Others suggest that such terms as "urban poor" should be replaced with other terms more sensitive to urban people, suggesting alternative phrases as "the disenfranchised" or "the economically oppressed." Some might even suggest that using any language that asserts particular differences between and among urban dwellers on the basis of class is inappropriate, and unnecessarily creates division among those whom Christ died for.

While these and related arguments have some validity, especially for those who use phrases like this in an insensitive and unthinking manner, none of them, either separate or together, disqualify the legitimate use of that term. For more than four decades as a national missions organization, World Impact has boldly identified its target population as those who reside in the city who are socio-economically poor. We use the language of "the urban poor" in this light, informed by the demographics in the city and the teaching of the Scriptures regarding God's commitment to the poor.

Poverty in the United States continues to rise. In data gathered as late as 2010, the poverty rate has been increasing to 15.1 percent in 2010 from 14.3 percent in 2009 and 13.2 percent in 2008. According to the research think-tank, the Urban Institute, there were 46.2 million poor people in 2010 compared to 43.2 million in 2009, with the poverty rater looming higher than it has been since 1993 (Urban Institute, Unemployment and Recovery Project, September 13. 2011). Sluggish job markets, high unemployment, and rising poverty rates have dramatically impacted urban communities, with literally thousands of families lacking income and access to the basic resources to live and survive. World Impact unashamedly focuses its time and attention on evangelizing, equipping, and empowering those in communities hardest hit by our recessions, economic blight, and all the by-products of violence, crime, broken family, and the overall desperation that poverty and hopelessness brings.

We do not use the term "urban poor" only to clearly identify the population to which we have been historically called. We also use the term because of the prophetic meaning of the poor in Scripture. Many dozens of text in both Old and New Testaments reveal a consistent perspective regarding God and those who are poor. They show that God has always had a burden for those who lack power, resources, money, or the necessities of life. The standards God gave to his covenant people regarding the poor reveal his commitment to the destitute, and all groups and classes associated with them. It is clear that the Old Testament includes a number of groups in close proximity to the poor, including orphans, widows, slaves, and the oppressed (e.g., Deut. 15; Ruth; Isa. 1). Those who exploited and took advantage of the vulnerable because of their poverty and weakness would be judged, and mercy and kindness was exhorted as the universal standard of God's people on behalf of the poor. The Law provided numerous commands regarding the fair and gracious treatment of the poor and the needy, of the demand to provide the hungry and destitute with food, and for the liberal treatment of the poor (Deut. 15.11).

The New Testament reveals God's heart for the poor crystallized in the incarnation of Jesus. Jesus proclaimed in his inaugural sermon that he was anointed with God's Spirit to proclaim the Good News of the Kingdom to the poor (Luke 4.18; 6.20), and confirmed his Messianic identity to John the Baptizer with preaching to the poor, along with healings and miracles (Luke 7.18-23). The Lord declared Zacchaeus' justice to the poor as a sign of his salvation (Luke 19.8-10), and he identified himself unequivocally with those who were sick, in prison, strangers, hungry, thirsty, and naked (Matt. 25.31-45). Every facet of Jesus' life and ministry intersected with the needs of those who lacked resources and money, and therefore could be easily exploited, oppressed, and taken advantage of.

In the actions and writings of the Apostles, we also see clear statements regarding God's election of and care for those who are economically poor. James 2.5 says that God has chosen the poor in this world to be rich in faith and to inherit the Kingdom he promised to those who love him. Paul told the Corinthians that God has chosen the foolish things of the world to shame the wise, the weak things of the world to shame the strong, the lowly and despised things of this world to nullify the things that are, in order that no one might boast in his presence (1 Cor. 1.27-29). This text and others thicken our view of the poor as merely lacking goods, services, and resources: more than that, the poor are those who need make them vulnerable to the effect of their need and the world's exploitation, and are desperate enough to rely on God's strength alone.

In using the term "urban poor" we make clear both the target population that guides the decisions and outreaches of our ministry, as well as unashamedly testify to the biblical perspective of God's election of and commitment to the most vulnerable, needy, and exposed people within our society. Urban dwellers outnumber all other populations today, and our cities have been magnets for massive migrations of urban peoples looking for economic betterment. We believe that "empowering the urban poor" therefore is missionally strategic and prophetically potent. Missionally, the phrase is strategic because it rightly denotes the vast numbers of people who remain unreached with the Gospel of Christ who dwell in our cities. Prophetically, it is potent because it reveals our bold and unashamed call to follow in the footsteps of Jesus, our respect for the poorest of the poor, our belief that God is calling the poor to be members of his church, and our confidence that the urban poor have a significant place in raising up leaders who will reach the cities of our nation, and beyond.

What of the use of the term "urban poor" and World Impact's prayer partners and donors, and our friends and neighbors in the city? To begin with, we have used the term clearly and circumspectly to help anyone interested in our mission agency know precisely those whom God has called us to reach. We love the families and individuals that we serve in the city, and ought never use language (this phrase or any other) to shame or exploit our relationship with them. We do not use this term as a stereotyping label, some pejorative stamp to limit the potential of the communities where we live and work. Rather, we use the phrase in our materials in order to communicate clearly, forthrightly, and persuasively argue the priority of this long neglected field in evangelical mission. From the beginning we have unashamedly committed our lives and resources to making disciples and planting churches among America's urban poor. This is a stewardship, the outworking of our individual and corporate call as missionaries of Christ. God forbid that any one of us would use such language to denigrate the very ones for whom Christ died, those to whom we are called, and those which we believe are the key to future mission in America, and beyond! Speaking clearly regarding our calling is our duty, which never includes shaming or belittling any person to which we are called. For the sake of our mission, our donors, and those whom we serve, we must be unequivocal regarding our target population; likewise, we must never shame nor denigrate them in our use of any communication, ever.

"Empowering the urban poor," therefore, as our adopted language, is neither just a tag-line nor a catchy motto. Rather, for us it functions as a representation of our single vision, the integrating mission of our work as an interdenominational ministry in the city. We believe that empowerment is neither merely meeting needs, dealing only with the mere symptoms of underlying structures of poverty, nor is it being hegemonic patrons to the poor, making them forever dependent on our charity and service. As missionaries of Christ, we believe that the poor, like any other people, can be redeemed, transformed, and released to be the people of God in their own communities. When God wanted to empower his people, he sent his Holy Spirit upon the apostolic company, and formed a community which he entrusted with the life of God and the Word of life. The answer of God to systemic poverty and neglect was to form a people who embodied the very life of the Kingdom where freedom, wholeness, and justice reside. These communities are entrusted with a mission to gather the elect from among the poorest, most broken people on earth, and, through the power of the Spirit and Christian community, see the Kingdom come to earth in new relationships of hospitality, generosity, and righteousness, right where they live. Every healthy functioning church is an outpost of the Kingdom of God, and can be a place where true transformation takes place. Nothing "empowers" the poor like a simple assembly of believers, obedient to the Lordship of Christ!

Armed with this perspective, we wholeheartedly believe that no organization in the history of the world can recognize the dignity and value of the poor like the Church of Jesus Christ. In light of this conviction, World Impact strives to plant as many churches as fast as possible among the various cultures represented by the urban poor, in all of our cities and beyond. We are convinced that no other social organization has the endorsement of God, the headship of Christ, and the power of the Spirit like a healthy functioning local church. And, nothing empowers a community like facilitating church planting movements among the urban poor, where the life and power of the Gospel of Christ can reach and transform entire communities as outposts of the Kingdom. All that we do in mission and in justice (from our camps, our schools, our businesses, medical and dental clinics, our work in the jails and the prisons, and most important of all, our missionary church planting and leadership development efforts) contribute to this empowerment work. Rather than merely meet needs or serve as patrons to the poor, we believe that the Spirit of God can win them, raise up leaders, empower them to lead, and release them as laborers in their very own communities as ambassadors of Christ. More than being recipients of care, we believe they can receive investment to be God's servant leaders, transformers of their communities and co-laborers in God's Kingdom work.

In conclusion, while the phrase "empowering the urban poor" may be misused and misapplied, we at World Impact wholeheartedly embrace the phrase not only because it clarifies the target population of our mission, but also because it unequivocally states our prophetic call to represent God's unchanging commitment to the most vulnerable and least resourced among us. Let us allow Jesus' challenge given so many centuries ago to continue to be our model and vision of ministry today as we seek to fulfill the Great Commission among the world's urban poor:

> Then the King will say to those on his right, "Come, you who are blessed by my Father, inherit the kingdom prepared for you from the foundation of the world. For I was hungry and you gave me food, I was thirsty and you gave me drink, I was a stranger and you welcomed me, I was naked and you clothed me, I was sick and you visited me, I was in prison and you came to me." Then the righteous will answer him, saying, "Lord, when did we see you hungry and feed you, or thirsty and give you drink? And when did we see you a stranger and welcome you, or naked and clothe you? And when did we see you sick or in prison and visit you?" And the King will answer them, "Truly, I say to you, as you did it to one of the least of these my brothers, you did it to me."
>
> ~ Matthew 25.34-40 (ESV)

Responding to God's Call to the Poor
World Impact

"The harvest is plentiful, but the workers are few." - Matt. 9.37

World Impact is looking for highly committed people who have a calling from God to cross-culturally evangelize, equip, and empower the unreached urban poor. We nurture and train missionaries who join others to form a church plant team that seeks to establish an indigenously led, reproducing church.

Those who join our church plant teams do so with a commitment to "do whatever it takes" to get the church planted, despite a person's particular expertise or credentials. We believe that "who you are" (Christian character) is more important than "what you do" (what qualifications you bring).

Once the team is formed, God will equip team members with the gifts and burdens necessary to establish that particular church, just like the church itself (Rom. 12.5-8). Only the Holy Spirit knows which gifts and functions will be needed in that given context. For example, one church might have a heavy emphasis on adult addiction ministry, while another might begin through children's Bible clubs that create entre into adult relationships.

Because of the dynamic nature of each missionary endeavor, it is not important for you to come with a pre-determined role, gifting, or emphasis. What is needed is a calling from God and a willingness to serve in any way needed to penetrate whole families, disciple them, and hand over the leadership of the church (1 Cor. 9.23-27). What matters most is a commitment to contribute to the vision of establishing new churches.

Once a group of people is formed into a team, then the task of assigning roles begins (knowing that the initial assignments are likely to change). Some common functions that emerge in many church plants (this list is not exhaustive) include: adult ministry (men's, women's, marriage and family), children's and teen ministry, worship leading, organizing (projects and developing systems), and administration (keeps systems going). The most critical functions are evangelism, shepherding/nurturing believers, and communicating the Word of God (teaching and preaching).

Of course, the team's leader must assume certain functions that are not to be delegated to other team members, such as spiritual leadership of the team and vision-casting. The team leader must also serve as a role model to the emerging church in the critical functions (evangelism, shepherding, and communicating the Word of God).

Some tasks, especially evangelism, require all members' involvement from time to time. In fact, the team needs to be flexible enough to overlap into many, if not all areas. Since not everyone will be equally gifted or compelled in every area, the team must have a spirit of servanthood and openness as they assume various roles to accomplish the task.

In areas where a team consistently lacks expertise, a support team member can be enlisted to assist in that task. For example, if no one can lead worship well, a support team member could be asked to lead music until someone within the church takes over.

The Bible in Chronological Order
A Narrative Literary Telling of the Story of God in Both Testaments
Adaptation of Stanley M. Horton's arrangement of the Bible

Genesis 1-22	Psalms 64, 70	Isaiah 1-5	Mark
Job	2 Samuel 21-22	2 Chronicles 26.9-23	Matthew
Genesis 23-50	Psalm 18	Isaiah 6	Luke
Exodus	2 Samuel 23-24	2 Chronicles 27-32	John
Psalms 90	Psalms 4-9; 11-17, 19-22; 24-29; 31, 35-41; 53, 55, 58, 61, 62, 65, 68, 72, 86, 101, 103, 108-110; 138-141; 143-145	Isaiah 7-66	Acts 1-14
Leviticus		Hosea	James
Numbers		Micah	Acts 11
Deuteronomy		Nahum	Galatians
Psalms 91		2 Chronicles 33-34	Acts 16
Joshua		Zephaniah	Philippians
Judges	1 Kings 1-4	2 Chronicles 35	Acts 17.1-10
Ruth	Proverbs	Habakkuk	1 Thessalonians
1 Samuel 1-16.13	Song of Solomon	Jeremiah 1-6, 11-12, 26.7-10, 14-20, 35-36, 45, 25, 46-49, 13, 22-24, 27-29, 50, 51, 30-33, 21, 34, 37-39, 52, 40-44	2 Thessalonians
Psalms 23	1 Kings 5-11		Acts 17.11-12.11
1 Samuel 16.14-19.11	Ecclesiastes		1 Corinthians
Psalms 59	1 Kings 12-22		2 Corinthians
1 Samuel 19.12-21.15	2 Kings 1-14.25		Acts 18.12-20.1
Psalms 34, 56	Jonah	Lamentations	Ephesians
1 Samuel 22.1-2	2 Kings 14.26-29	2 Chronicles 36.1-8	Romans
Psalms 57, 142	Amos	Daniel	Acts 20.2-28.30
1 Samuel 22.3-23	2 Kings 15-25	2 Chronicles 36.9-21	Colossians
Psalms 52	Psalms 1-2, 10, 33, 43, 66, 67, 71, 89, 92-100; 102, 104-106; 111-125; 127-136; 146-150	Psalm 137	Hebrews
1 Samuel 23		Ezekiel	Titus
Psalms 54, 63		2 Chronicles 36.22-23	Philemon
1 Samuel 24-31		Ezra 1-5.1	1 Timothy
2 Samuel 1-7	1 Chronicles 1-16	Haggai	2 Timothy
Psalm 30	Psalms 42, 44-50; 73-85, 87,88	Zechariah	1 Peter
2 Samuel 8.1-14		Psalms 107	2 Peter
Psalm 60	1 Chronicles 17-29	Ezra 5.2-6	1 John
2 Samuel 8.15-12.14	2 Chronicles 1-21	Esther	2 John
Psalms 51, 32	Obadiah	Ezra 7-10	3 John
2 Samuel 12.15-15-37	2 Chronicles 22	Nehemiah	Jude
Psalms 3, 69	Joel	Malachi	Revelation
2 Samuel 16-20	2 Chronicles 23-26.8		

From Before to Beyond Time
The Plan of God and Human History
Adapted from Suzanne de Dietrich. *God's Unfolding Purpose*. Philadelphia: Westminster Press, 1976.

I. Before Time (Eternity Past) 1 Cor. 2.7
  A. The Eternal Triune God
  B. God's Eternal Purpose
  C. The Mystery of Iniquity
  D. The Principalities and Powers

II. Beginning of Time (Creation and Fall) Gen. 1.1
  A. Creative Word
  B. Humanity
  C. Fall
  D. Reign of Death and First Signs of Grace

III. Unfolding of Time (God's Plan Revealed through Israel) Gal. 3.8
  A. Promise (Patriarchs)
  B. Exodus and Covenant at Sinai
  C. Promised Land
  D. The City, the Temple, and the Throne (Prophet, Priest, and King)
  E. Exile
  F. Remnant

IV. Fullness of Time (Incarnation of the Messiah) Gal. 4.4-5
  A. The King Comes to His Kingdom
  B. The Present Reality of His Reign
  C. The Secret of the Kingdom: the Already and the Not Yet
  D. The Crucified King
  E. The Risen Lord

V. The Last Times (The Descent of the Holy Spirit) Acts 2.16-18
  A. Between the Times: the Church as Foretaste of the Kingdom
  B. The Church as Agent of the Kingdom
  C. The Conflict Between the Kingdoms of Darkness and Light

VI. The Fulfillment of Time (The Second Coming) Matt. 13.40-43
  A. The Return of Christ
  B. Judgment
  C. The Consummation of His Kingdom

VII. Beyond Time (Eternity Future) 1 Cor. 15.24-28
  A. Kingdom Handed Over to God the Father
  B. God as All in All

From Before to Beyond Time
Scriptures for Major Outlines Points

I. **Before Time (Eternity Past)**

1 Cor. 2.7 (ESV) – But we impart a secret and hidden wisdom of God, which God decreed before the ages for our glory (cf. Titus 1.2).

II. **Beginning of Time (Creation and Fall)**

Gen. 1.1 (ESV) – In the beginning, God created the heavens and the earth.

III. **Unfolding of Time (God's Plan Revealed Through Israel)**

Gal. 3.8 (ESV) – And the Scripture, foreseeing that God would justify the Gentiles by faith, preached the Gospel beforehand to Abraham, saying, "In you shall all the nations be blessed" (cf. Rom. 9.4-5).

IV. **Fullness of Time (The Incarnation of the Messiah)**

Gal. 4.4-5 (ESV) – But when the fullness of time had come, God sent forth his Son, born of woman, born under the law, to redeem those who were under the law, so that we might receive adoption as sons.

V. **The Last Times (The Descent of the Holy Spirit)**

Acts 2.16-18 (ESV) – But this is what was uttered through the prophet Joel: "'And in the last days it shall be,' God declares, 'that I will pour out my Spirit on all flesh, and your sons and your daughters shall prophesy, and your young men shall see visions, and your old men shall dream dreams; even on my male servants and female servants in those days I will pour out my Spirit, and they shall prophesy.'"

VI. **The Fulfillment of Time (The Second Coming)**

Matt. 13.40-43 (ESV) – Just as the weeds are gathered and burned with fire, so will it be at the close of the age. The Son of Man will send his angels, and they will gather out of his Kingdom all causes of sin and all lawbreakers, and throw them into the fiery furnace. In that place there will be weeping and gnashing of teeth. Then the righteous will shine like the sun in the Kingdom of their Father. He who has ears, let him hear.

VII. **Beyond Time (Eternity Future)**

1 Cor. 15.24-28 (ESV) – Then comes the end, when he delivers the Kingdom to God the Father after destroying every rule and every authority and power. For he must reign until he has put all his enemies under his feet. The last enemy to be destroyed is death. For "God has put all things in subjection under his feet." But when it says, "all things are put in subjection," it is plain that he is excepted who put all things in subjection under him. When all things are subjected to him, then the Son himself will also be subjected to him who put all things in subjection under him, that God may be all in all.

Part III
Planting Urban Churches:
Resources for Church Planters

The resources in Part III address four distinct areas relevant to leading teams as the church planter. First, materials are provided to give an overview of the church planting process, followed by the particular calling and character needed to plant a church, along with their primary duties and responsibilities. These materials are followed by a section that provide a look at some of the various models associated with church planting, and a collection of helpful tools that can be used as the leader and the team actually engages the community in evangelism, justice, and demonstration of the Gospel.

Because World Impact's church planting vision is not merely connected to planting individual churches in the city, but also facilitating church planting movements among the poor, the first section should be carefully read and reflected upon. The necessity of seeing the planting of individual congregations in connection with others in like-minded life and mission is essential for effective mission among the poor in the city. Planting individual congregations that have no link or tie to others has proven to be ineffective to bring about the kind of transformation so desperately needed among the communities of the under-served.

Note: In this anthology you will see multiple references to the "Team Leader" or "Church Plant Team Leader." All the citations that include these phrases (in all their varied usages) of team leader should now be understood as the "Church Planter." Additionally, all the references to "Multiple Team Leader" should now be understood in our updated language as "Coach."

This part includes the following sections:

- Church Planting Movements Overview / p. 273
- The Church Planter and the Church Plant Team / p. 321
- Models of Church Planting / p. 371
- Engaging the Community / p. 391
- Body Life and Spiritual Formation / p. 419

Church Planting Movements Overview

Church Planting Overview

Rev. Terry G. Cornett

> It has always been my ambition to preach the Gospel where Christ was not known, so that I would not be building on someone else's foundation. Rather, as it is written: "Those who were not told about him will see, and those who have not heard will understand."
>
> ~ Romans 15.20-21

I. What is the Biblical Pattern?

A. Is there a pattern?

"Does the Bible give principles or patterns of church-planting to go along with the command to plant churches?"

Missiologist David J. Hesselgrave rightly answers in the affirmative:

> And where could we find a pattern for these activities that is less likely to lead us into blind alleys than is the apostle Paul's missionary work. As A. R. Hay writes, "Paul's ministry and that of his companions is recorded in detail because he and they provide a typical example of the exceedingly important permanent ministry of church planting.
>
> ~ David J. Hesselgrave.
> *Planting Churches Cross-Culturally: North America and Beyond*, 2nd ed.
> Grand Rapids: Baker Book House, 2000. p. 46

B. How do we describe this pattern?

1. The Pauline Cycle

   *The "Pauline Cycle" terminology, stages, and diagram are taken from David J. Hesselgrave, **Planting Churches Cross-Culturally: North America and Beyond**, 2nd ed. (Grand Rapids: Baker Book House, 2000).*

- Missionaries Commissioned - Acts 13.1-4; 15.39-40; Gal. 1.15-16
- Audience Contacted - Acts 13.14-16; 14.1; 16.13-15; 17.16-19
- Gospel Communicated - Acts 13.17-41; 16.31; Rom. 10.9-14; 2 Tim. 2.8
- Hearers Converted - Acts 13.48; 16.14-15; 20.21; 26.20; 1 Thess. 1.9-10
- Believers Congregated - Acts 13.43; 19.9; Rom. 16.4-5; 1 Cor. 14.26
- Faith Confirmed - Acts 14.21-22; 15.41; Rom. 16.17; Col. 1.28; 2 Thess. 2.15; 1 Tim. 1.3
- Leadership Consecrated - Acts 14.23; 2 Tim. 2.2; Titus 1.5
- Believers Commended - Acts 14.23; 16.40; 21.32; (2 Tim. 4.9 and Titus 3.12 by implication)
- Relationships Continued - Acts 15.36; 18.23; 1 Cor. 16.5; Eph. 6.21-22; Col. 4.7-8
- Sending Churches Convened - Acts 14.26-27; 15.1-4

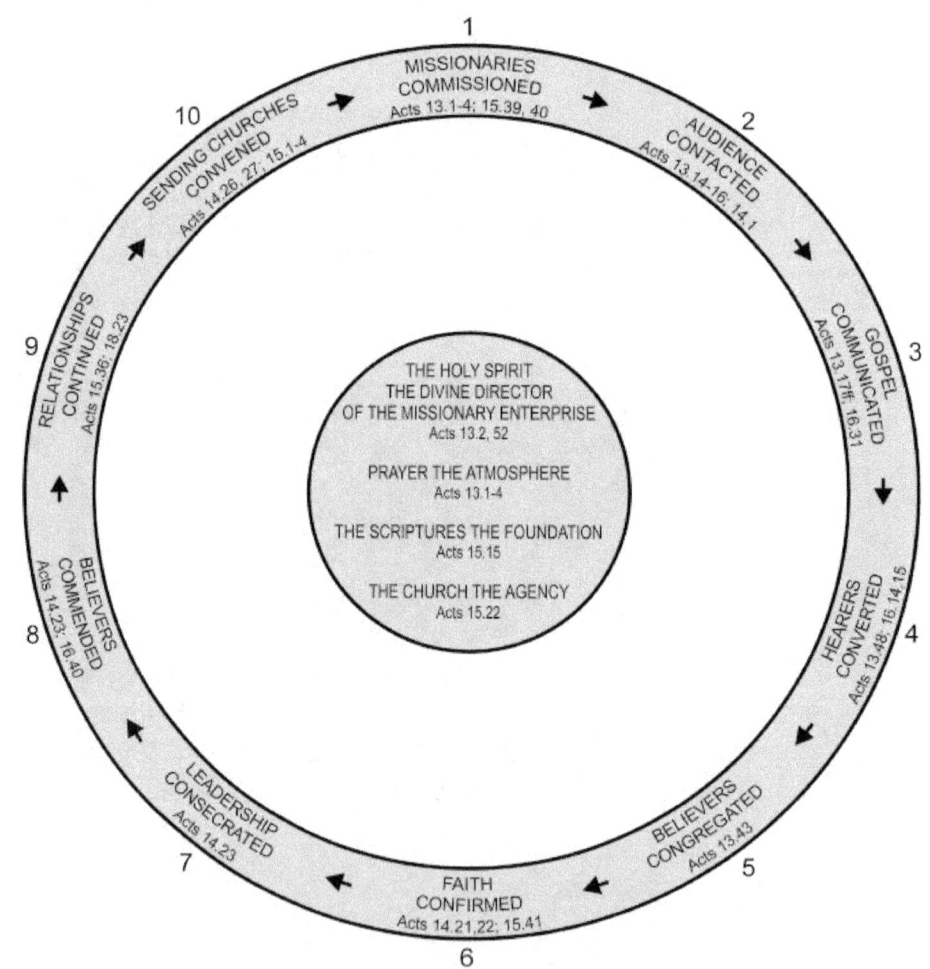

2. PLANT - The Stages of Missionary Activity

How to PLANT a Church across Cultural Barriers

PREPARE
- Form a church-plant team
- Pray
- Select a target area and population
- Do demographic and ethnographic studies

LAUNCH
- Recruit and train volunteers
- Make contact with the target population
- Share the Gospel (evangelistic events, door-to-door evangelism, relational evangelism, media, etc)

ASSEMBLE
- Form cell groups, Bible studies, etc. to follow-up new believers, to continue evangelism, and to identify and train emerging leaders
- Announce the birth of a new church to the neighborhood and meet regularly for pubic worship, instruction and fellowship

NURTURE
- Develop individual and group discipleship
- Fill key roles in the church; identify and use spiritual gifts

TRANSITION
- Transfer leadership to indigenous leaders so they become self-governing, self-supporting and self-reproducing (appoint elders and pastors)
- Finalize decisions about denominational or other affiliations
- Commission the church
- Foster association with World Impact and other urban churches for fellowship, support and mission ministry

Our PLANT acrostic is a way to organize the material found in Acts which Hesselgrave refers to as the Pauline cycle. It is easily memorized, easy to communicate and gives all World Impact church-planters a common language to use in discussing what may be very different types of church plants.

The most essential point about the PLANT model is this: It is a way to organize the BIBLICAL pattern. In other words, this is not "*World Impact's way of doing church planting*" but rather World Impact's way of describing how Pauline cross-cultural church planting is done.

Notice that while the nature of the task is defined by the PLANT acrostic, the way of accomplishing those goals is left open . . .

No model, whether circular or linear, will ever fully approximate reality. It helps us in our thinking and planning but it has limitations. Some things to remember while using the PLANT model include . . .

II. Key Issues for Team Leaders to Oversee

One of the key responsibilities of a church-plant team leader is knowing what questions to ask about their team at each stage of the church-planting process.

Have we met the basic PREPARE requirements?

- Is the team recruited and a team leader identified?
- Has a target area or people group been chosen?
- Will the church plant team be involved in any partnerships for the planting of this church? If so, which partnership model (one, two, three or four) will be followed? See *Models of World Impact Associations: Range of Partnership Responses*.
- If a partnership model is used, has a partnership agreement been written and agreed to by both parties?
- Has an MTL (Multiple Team Leader) been assigned to oversee the team?
- Has the team undergone the required training and received certification?
- Do the team members understand their roles (core, support, or volunteer) and what their primary tasks are?
- Do we have a plan for learning about the people and the culture we are called to serve among?
- Do we have a plan for the worship life of our church plant team?

Are we ready to LAUNCH?
- Does each team member understand the essential core of the Gospel message and feel confident in sharing it with others?
- Have we contextualized the message and the evangelism methods so that we are most likely to gain a hearing and have the Gospel understood?
- Have we identified the most receptive members of our target group?
- Have we agreed on the initial methods and outreaches we will use to make contact and begin sharing the Gospel?
- Do we have a plan for following up those who accept Christ as Lord and Savior?

Are we ready to ASSEMBLE for public worship?
- Do we have a core of genuine converts who have made a break with their old way of life confirmed by:
  ~ Verbal confession of Christ as Lord, Acts 2.21; 22.16.
  ~ Symbolic confession through baptism, Acts 16.15, 33; 18.8.
  ~ Behavioral confession through good works and a changed life, Acts 26.20.
- Are those converts evangelizing others and bringing them to the cell groups?
- Are there fledgling leaders who have already taken on responsibility and who can continue to be apprenticed as we move to public worship?

Have we focused on NURTURE?
- Do we have a plan for preaching and teaching the basics of the faith?
- Are we identifying and discipling (apprenticing) emerging leaders so that they are taking increasing levels of responsibility?
- Do we understand church discipline and are we holding people accountable to obey what they have learned?
- Are we identifying every member's gifts and are we including everyone in the work of the ministry?
- Are we teaching people how to listen to the Word and the Spirit?
- Are we recognizing and celebrating what God is doing among the people?

Are we ready to TRANSITION?

- Have called and gifted leaders been invested in through formal and informal discipleship?
- Has a church government structure been developed so that the church has a way to make decisions and choose future leaders?
- Is the church doctrinally sound on the essentials?
- Have decisions been made about affiliating with a denomination or association?
- Have missionaries planned a way to continue the relationships after withdrawal?

III. What about Cultural Differences?

> A Christian missions organization:
> - Crosses class and cultural barriers
> - To reach those unreached by the Gospel of Jesus Christ
> - And form culturally conducive churches among them.
>
> ~ *Missionary Orientation and Training Course: A Guide for New Missionaries with World Impact.* Los Angeles/Wichita: World Impact Press, 1996. p. 4

A. Indigenous Principles and the End Goal.

The end goal is to create a church that is completely at home in the culture of a people group and that is capable of functioning and reproducing without the missionaries.

The most important missiological principle that World Impact embraced in its early days as a ministry was the Acts 15 principle: People do not have to change cultures in order to become Christians.

Some implications:

Missiologists refer to this as the principle of indigeneity. See *Indigenous Churches*.

The idea of using an indigenous approaches is central to World Impact's understanding of how to take issues of class and culture seriously in the city.

Respect the dominance of the receiving culture
- Seek to discover how things are done in the culture.
- Defer to the wishes of indigenous people in regard to methods (What and Why are unchanging principles, How is a culturally determined application).

Pauline Model: Paul's circumcision of Timothy, Acts 16.1-3.

Avoid dependence
- Tell people that they have leadership gifts and potential.
- Tell people that you are not going to always be in charge.
- Plan absences.
- Point people to the Word and the Spirit.

Pauline Model: Ephesian Elders, Acts 20.24-32.

Think reproducibility
- Don't use things just because they are there. Ask, *"Is this likely to continue when the missionary team is gone?"*
- Always ask *"What person can work with me on this?"*
- *Do things the same way each time whenever possible* (establish habits) because it will be easier to train people when this is true.
- *Structured is more reproducible than unstructured* (assuming that the structure is not overly complex and that it is culturally conducive).

Pauline Model: All things to all people, 1 Cor. 9.19-23.

This type of church planting demands certain things from a team leader:
- Evangelistic
- Pastoral
- Flexible
- Called by God

World Impact's Strategy for Church Planting
Rev. Efrem Smith

"Crowns of Beauty: the indigenous and urban church planting initiative of World Impact."

Church Planting Purpose
Striving to plant as many churches as possible among the various cultures represented by the urban poor, in all of our cities and beyond.

1. **Credibility**
   - We are not a Para Church or Suburban Church coming into the city. We are an urban missions' organization with 40 plus years of incarnational, cross-cultural ministry experience.
   - Multiple staff that has over 20 years of Church Planting experience.
   - President and CEO, has extensive church planting, church planting training, and church planting design experience.
   - Significant research has been done on urban church planting through TUMI
   - We are unashamedly evangelical (Gospel, Christ, and Word-centered)
   - We are an interdenominational organization.

2. **Theology and Biblical Foundations**
   - Use Isaiah and Ezekiel to lift up significance of "Crowns of Beauty."
   - Embracing the Entire Epic of the Bible- "People of the Story"
   - Embracing the multi-ethnic, multicultural, urban, and liberating dynamic of the Bible.
   - Engaging the Kingdom of God and *Christus Victor*.
   - We are informed by the Great Tradition.
   - Planting urban churches which function as communities of theology, worship, discipleship, and witness.

3. **The Movement's Missional Design**
   - The overall church planting movement will be one which reflects a "Three-self" Missional Design (self-sustaining, self-reproducing, and self-governing).
   - We plant churches with World Impact staff that transition to indigenous leadership and churches which begin with indigenous leadership.
   - *The dynamics of our church planting movements will be known by shared spirituality, the ability to contextualize, and to create and sustain standardized practices and structures.*

4. **Values**
   - "The best way to restore Christians to vibrant theology, worship, discipleship, and outreach is to recapture the Church's identity as a People of the Story, through a re-connection to the Church's Sacred Roots." (Pg. 151- *Jesus Cropped from the Picture* by Allsman)
   - *Connecting the Great Tradition, The Urban Poor, and Urban Church Planting*
   - We plant church associations, facilitate movements, and engage collaborative partnerships.

5. **Principles**
   - P.L.A.N.T. Acrostic
   - Indigenous Urban Leader Commitment
   - Historic Commitment to the Urban Poor and to Cities
   - A Missional (incarnational) Approach
   - Honoring multi-ethnic, multicultural, ethnic specific, and first generation-immigrant focuses
   - Planting churches with the existing urban church

6. **Supplemental Initiatives**
   - Urban Church Associations (UCA's)
   - World Impact Associates (WIA's)
   - The Urban Ministry Institute (TUMI)
   - SIAFU (Chapters and Leadership Homes)

7. **Three Expressions (all include assessing, training, chartering, and resourcing)**
   - House Church (20-50 people)

     Can be understood as a small store in a shopping mall. Needs the connections to other small churches to both survive and thrive. Can meet virtually anywhere and can operate with a small footprint with little to no financial burdens. Can focus on a specific block, housing development, or network of families. A strong discipleship focus of indigenous leadership development can take place in this smaller connected group.

   - Community Church (60-150 people)

     Can be understood as a grocery or convenience store. Focuses on a particular geographic identity and proximity, highlighting both the affinity, connection, and unique context of the congregation and the surrounding community. Developed around a deep calling and connection to a particular neighborhood. Will need a semi-stable place to meet (park, community center, or school). Partnership with other community churches is important.

   - Mother Church (200+ people)

     Can be understood as a Walmart Superstore or Super Target. A missionally directed congregation that leverages its capabilities and gifts to be a . . .
     - Center of compassion, mercy, and justice ministries,
     - Nurturing headquarters for planting new churches, and
     - Incubator of other effective ministries among the unreached urban poor.
     - Note that a more rooted facility would be needed within this expression.

8. **Church Planting Framework**
   - Church Planting School (Events, Training, Resources)
   - A unified assessment, training, resourcing, and standardization strategy.
   - Training World Impact Staff as coaches, mentors, and co-pastors.
   - Assessing call and gifts of World Impact Staff/Indigenous Leaders. (school, assessment, charter)
   - Partnerships (local churches, denominations and organizations)

9. **Delivery and Support**
    - Charter Budget-$15,000-$75,000 per church over 3 years and based on location/expression
    - History and Current State- 72 churches planted and 45 active
    - Goal: Plant 300 churches over the next 7 years (Cost: $15 million, Initial injection of $1 million)
    - Target both C-1 and C-2 leaders.
    - *Church Resources Division will provide general oversight and Regions will implement.*
    - *Staff Needs – Begin with National Director, reporting to Don Davis and providing resourcing support to RVP's and EDM's.*
    - Fund development strategy – National Planting Fund – split between regions with administrative percent, Regional Partnering Churches, and Regional Operating Budgets
    - Factor in costs of Coaching, Church Plant in a Box ($100), Training, etc.
    - Include Member Care as needed.
    - Coaching and Mentoring Tools (Prepare, Work, and Review)
    - Potential Goal Management Tool (Goal Span-Jeff Hunt)
    - *Set Chartering Goals in the areas of Theology, Worship, Discipleship, and Witness.*

Mobilizing American Cities for Church Planting Movements
Issues and Concerns
Rev. Dr. Don L. Davis, from *Winning the World: Facilitating Urban Church Planting Movements*

> **I Keep Six Honest Serving-men**
>
> I keep six honest serving-men, (they taught me all I knew);
> Their names are What and Why and When, and How and Where and Who.
> I send them over land and sea, I send them east and west;
> But after they have worked for me, I give them all a rest.
>
> I let them rest from nine till five, for I am busy then,
> As well as breakfast, lunch, and tea, for they are hungry men.
> But different folk have different views. I know a person small –
> She keeps ten million serving-men, who get no rest at all!
>
> She sends 'em abroad on her own affairs, from the second she opens her eyes –
> One million Hows, two million Wheres, and seven million Whys!
>
> ~ Rudyard Kipling, from *The Elephant's Child*.

I. WHY Ought We Consider the Power of Church Planting Movements for Ministry and Mission in Today's American Inner-City Contexts?

A convincing and compelling case can be made that the American church and mission leaders must take seriously the responsibility to begin their church mobilization and church planting efforts in their own Jerusalems and Judeas, rather than thinking about the Samarias of other places: Acts 1.8 – "But you will receive power when the Holy Spirit has come upon you, and you will be my witnesses in Jerusalem and in all Judea and Samaria, and to the end of the earth."

Matt. 28.18-20 (ESV) – And Jesus came and said to them, "All authority in heaven and on earth has been given to me. Go therefore and make disciples of all nations, baptizing them in the name of the Father and of the Son and of the Holy Spirit, teaching them to observe all that I have commanded you. And behold, I am with you always, to the end of the age."

A. The American inner city represents a tough and difficult mission field: *40 million strong.*

James 2.5 (ESV) – Listen, my beloved brothers, has not God chosen those who are poor in the world to be rich in faith and heirs of the kingdom, which he has promised to those who love him?

1. America's inner city is not homogenous, but dramatic in its mind-numbing diversity and levels of cultural and class difference.

    a. Massive new immigration (legal and illegal)

    b. Push-pull theory of African-American migration

        (1) First migration: between World War I and II where nearly 4 million blacks left the South "pushed" out by racism and ostracism

        (2) Second migration: after the Civil Rights Act of 1965, the most serious abandonment of the inner city by businesses, professionals, educators, etc.

    c. Well-worn historical divisions between cultures and groups: Koreans, Blacks, Hispanics, poor Whites, etc.

    d. Linguistic and ethnic difference: 23 languages in LA for driver's license!

2. Dramatic class alienation in the American city, which impacts and affects life in urban poor neighborhoods throughout the country

    a. Unemployment and lack of education

    b. Dramatic levels of noninvolvement in political processes and community governance

    c. Economic separation between those living in the city and those in the suburbs

    d. Lack of government attention and care: a seriously developed "blame-the-victim" social view in the 80's and 90's

3. Rising levels of violence and involvement in the jurisprudential system (i.e., the police, the courts, and the prison systems – heavily weighted on urban needs and issues)

   a. Some stats as high as nearly one in three African American homes are touched by involvement in the jurisprudential system

   b. More AA men in prison than in college; nearly 600,000 Black men alone in prison today (Note: The Center for Disease Control actually recently placed Black men on the endangered list.)

4. Abandonment and benign neglect of the church

   a. Difficulty of many ethnic churches to reach their own neighbors cross culturally

   b. Evangelical church concentration on foreign fields: 10/40 Window

   c. Estimations by missions groups that America is basically "reached," and that scarce dollars and missionaries should be deployed to more needy fields

   d. Lack of unity and strategy among the American church to join forces to ignite new movements in American urban poor communities

B. God's heart for the poor, and the biblical mandates to care for them

1. OT clear sign of God's burden for the poor

   a. Isa. 58.5-7 (ESV) – Is such the fast that I choose, a day for a person to humble himself? Is it to bow down his head like a reed, and to spread sackcloth and ashes under him? Will you call this a fast, and a day acceptable to the Lord? Is not this the fast that I choose: to loose the bonds of wickedness, to undo the straps of the yoke, to let the oppressed go free, and to break every yoke? Is it not to share your bread with the hungry and bring the homeless poor into your house; when you see the naked, to cover him, and not to hide yourself from your own flesh?

    b. Ps. 41.1-3 (ESV) – Blessed is the one who considers the poor! In the day of trouble the Lord delivers him; the Lord protects him and keeps him alive; he is called blessed in the land; you do not give him up to the will of his enemies. The Lord sustains him on his sickbed; in his illness you restore him to full health.

    c. Prov. 19.17 (ESV) – Whoever is generous to the poor lends to the Lord, and he will repay him for his deed.

2. Jesus' unique identification with the poor

    a. Matt. 25.35-40 (ESV) – "For I was hungry and you gave me food, I was thirsty and you gave me drink, I was a stranger and you welcomed me, I was naked and you clothed me, I was sick and you visited me, I was in prison and you came to me." Then the righteous will answer him, saying, "Lord, when did we see you hungry and feed you, or thirsty and give you drink? And when did we see you a stranger and welcome you, or naked and clothe you? And when did we see you sick or in prison and visit you?" And the King will answer them, "Truly, I say to you, as you did it to one of the least of these my brothers, you did it to me."

    b. Luke 18.22 (ESV) – When Jesus heard this, he said to him, "One thing you still lack. Sell all that you have and distribute to the poor, and you will have treasure in heaven; and come, follow me."

3. The early Church's transparent commitment to the city, the poor, and the disenfranchised

    a. Heb. 13.16 (ESV) – Do not neglect to do good and to share what you have, for such sacrifices are pleasing to God.

    b. Rom. 12.13 (ESV) – Contribute to the needs of the saints and seek to show hospitality.

    c. 2 Cor. 9.12 (ESV) – For the ministry of this service is not only supplying the needs of the saints, but is also overflowing in many thanksgivings to God.

d. Gal. 6.10 (ESV) – So then, as we have opportunity, let us do good to everyone, and especially to those who are of the household of faith.

C. Growing sense of hopelessness, nihilism, and despair of America's urban poor, (i.e., those who are disenfranchised, alienated, and voiceless)

1. Failed social projects for America's poor

   a. Civil Rights Movement

   b. The Great Society

   c. Trickle-Down Economics

   d. No-Child-Left-Behind promises

2. Present-day stark examples of the gap between the haves and the have-nots: Hurricane Katrina

3. Breakdown of infrastructures, institutions

   a. Housing and urban development

   b. Health care and quality of life

   c. Lack of investment: deteriorating neighborhoods

   d. Broken public systems: education, medical care, political corruption, etc.

   e. Deep, growing animosity between city and city hall: the LA riots

4. The urban family's woes: shattered, broken, neglected, decaying

   a. Alienation: husbands from wives, parents from children, families from neighbors, neighbors from community

   b. 70% born out of wedlock

   c. Vast majority of prison populations of America from urban poor communities

d. Jurisprudential involvement as a way of life: Few urban families are not affected by the police, the courts, and the prison system.

D. Implications and conclusions

1. The US urban poor field is one of the largest, toughest, and most reachable fields on earth: They do not align or compare to many other urban fields.

2. Extreme difficulties posed by diversity, violence, shattered families, and spiritual alienation make American cities formidable and intimidating.

3. Church planting movements targeted to reaching the world's lost must seriously take advantage of the challenges represented by the American urban poor.

II. WHAT Are the Central Distinctives of American Inner-City Contexts, and How Might They Affect Our Understanding of Church Planting Movements for Them?

Discerning the particular, specific elements in American urban neighborhoods may greatly impact the ways in which we interpret and apply the various insights learned about the nature of spirituality, missions, church planting, church growth, and urban ministry.

1 Chron. 12.32 (ESV) – Of Issachar, men who had understanding of the times, to know what Israel ought to do, 200 chiefs, and all their kinsmen under their command.

Eph. 5.15-17 (ESV) – Look carefully then how you walk, not as unwise but as wise, making the best use of the time, because the days are evil. Therefore do not be foolish, but understand what the will of the Lord is.

A. Urban America is plagued by deep-rooted spiritual alienation and neglect.

1. "The root cause of all alienation – from God and from each other – is sin. The antidote to sin is a personal relationship with God through Christ. This leads to hope, reconciliation, and healing. God usually initiates a personal relationship

with an individual, and then nurtures it, through His Church" (Keith Phillips, *Out of Ashes*, p. 60).

2. America is not a Christian nation (cf. *Out of Ashes*, p. 61).

   a. Less than 20% of the population meet for worship on any given Sunday.

   b. For instance, in Miami only 7.9% of the population attend church, whether Catholic or Protestant.

   c. Immigration during the 80's exploded, with 90% of the population being non-European, and 15% being Muslim.

   d. One out of seven people in the US (roughly 32 million) speak a language other than English at home.

   e. The diversity of America is indicative of the same kind of diversity in the most unreached places on earth, i.e., the 10/40 Window.

3. This neglect is not a conspiracy against urban America: As of 2000, 419,000 Christian workers are serving God outside of their home countries (this number includes missionaries of all traditions, Catholic, Orthodox, Protestant, Anglican, independent, and marginal Christian). The U.S. is the largest mission sending and receiving country on earth, sending 118,200 missionaries to other countries and received 33,200.

4. Most workers go to the least needy fields, though over 60% of all people live in cities.

The real, demonstrated sending priorities apparently emphasize helping Christians become better Christians rather than helping non-Christians consider Christ—or helping Christians of one kind (essentially Catholic or Orthodox) become Christians of another kind (evangelical or Catholic or charismatic, and so on) rather than helping those who have not heard the gospel to hear it.

~ Michael Jaffarian. "The Statistical State of the Missionary Enterprise." *Missiology: An International Review.* Vol. XXX. No. 1, January 2002, p. 28.

5. Rise of spiritualism, relativism, secularism, and new age religions in American popular culture

B. Urban America's radical diversity is directly connected to racial, cultural, and ethnic suspicion, conflict.

1. Dramatic population growth in the world: Over six billion people; in 1900 there were only about 1.6 billion, and as recently as 1970, only 3.7 billion. Almost four times as many people in 2000 as 1900 (World Christian Encyclopedia, 2nd Edition, 2002, 1:4). Most populous continent is Asia 3,683 million, Africa, 784 million, Europe, 729 million, Latin America 519 million, North America 310 million, and Oceania 30 million. (Asia, Africa, and Latin America comprise 82% of the world's population!)

2. Complex, ethnic diversity in America: hundreds of distinct languages spoken, numbering well over 60 million people who have been drawn to urban areas for economic, social reasons

3. Race issues still matter: note the Hurricane Katrina aftermath

4. Old wounds still remain; unhealed, festering, ready to be ignited with the least amount of effort.

5. The interconnections of genuine race hatred and class conflict are complex and poignant in America (e.g., between poor Whites, Hispanics, Asians, Blacks, etc.).

C. Urban America is riddled with broken kinship relationships and decaying social networks among many of its varying ethnic groups.

1. The differences between people tend to alienate and divide groups.

2. Our differences tend to divide us because we are ethnocentric, we prefer our own culture and tend to judge others in light of it.

a. Anthropological roots of division

(1) The enormous power of enculturation

(2) The hidden nature of culture

(3) We love those who are like us.

(4) Culture Shock: the unsettling effects of operating outside of our own class, culture, or sub-culture

b. Theological roots of the division

(1) We tend to place ourselves at the center of the universe.

(2) We forget or ignore what God is doing in the world regarding the building of his Kingdom on earth.

(3) We fail to shift our loyalties from our own national, cultural, and class framework to the vision of God's new humanity in Christ.

(4) We close off our hearts to God's love for all people.

(5) We reject the notion that you need not change culture in order to become Christian and be Christ's people.

3. Our differences may erect barriers and cause us to treat people differently.

a. When differences are allowed to divide, we typically respond to others in three inappropriate ways.

b. We become paternalistic: "help the poor native syndrome": *Our benevolent expression of assumed superiority often results in an attempt to modify the actions, and values of a differing group. (Example – missionaries issuing Western clothing to South Pacific islanders.)*

c. In suspicion, we isolate and separate ourselves from people who are different: *The passive expression of my group's prejudice through the deliberate limiting of contact between my group and the people, actions, and values of the group that is different. (Example – Segregated neighborhoods.)*

d. In hatred and malice, we reject the other culture as bad or evil or undeserving, and seek to undermine and persecute it: *The active expression of my group's hatred for the people, actions, and values of the group that is different.* (Example – ethnic cleansing in Bosnia or Rwanda, the Holocaust in Germany, etc.)

4. Dramatic rise in out-of-wedlock births, broken alienated families are a norm

5. The stability of families in many of the countries we studied make it difficult to easily connect Garrison's research and claims to an American inner city context.

6. Individualism (one of America's main "isms" along with secularism and relativism) has created entire neighborhoods of elderly, poor, and troubled families which are essential lonely, alone, and vulnerable to whatever social influences their community gives rise to (e.g., gang proliferation: 100 percent of cities with populations greater than 250,000 reported gang activity in 2001; there were almost 800,000 people in gangs in the US in 2001, and in a recent survey, 31 percent said their communities refused to acknowledge the gang problem. Many only did so after high-profile gang incidents.)

D. Poverty, disenfranchisement, and a deeply developed class polarization

1. Poverty carries deep racial and ethnic meanings in America which are not present in many societies which, on the whole, are in fact even more poor than the American urban poor.

2. They work with people who prioritize their faith; they are hungry for change, p. 57.

3. They are a source for relationship-building, p. 58.

4. They create a "sense of exhilaration over the transformation," p. 58.

5. Poverty has increased the overall sense of alienation, isolation, and disconnection from the larger society: a cultural case in point, the underground cultures of urban America (e.g., punk, rap, emo, metal, etc.).

6. Ever increasing reality of despair, leading to out-of-control levels of violence in America's inner city (nearly half of the number of people killed in Vietnam conflict are murdered on American streets each year!)

E. Implications and conclusions

1. The elements of America's inner city must be factored into all discussions of church planting, growth, and mobilization, especially in applying models and approaches which have been used effectively in other places.

2. An effective approach to church planting models in America's inner city must seek to address and meet head on all elements of that context if it hopes to be effective.

3. Uncritical application of church planting models which fail to take into account these factors will only invite real failure in the missionaries and pastors, and real failure in the communities targeted and served by them.

4. Church planting movement insights, in order to be effective, must be contextualized both by the pastors who serve as well as missionaries who evangelize and plant churches.

III. WHO Will Be the Central Players in Igniting, Sustaining, and Multiplying Vital Church Planting Movements in American Inner-City Contexts?

In sync with all that we have learned of church planting movements abroad, all efforts toward creating, sustaining, and multiplying vital, healthy church planting movements in America's inner cities must begin and end with indigenous leadership development. The most effective evangelism, follow-up, discipleship, and church planting will be done by city people on behalf of city people through the resources of city people. All of our attention, planning, and effort must concentrate, therefore, on raising up urban men and women, urban families, and urban young people who will reach their own neighbors and webs with the Gospel of Jesus Christ.

Acts 14.21-23 (ESV) – When they had preached the gospel to that city and had made many disciples, they returned to Lystra and to Iconium and to Antioch, strengthening the souls of the disciples, encouraging them to continue in the faith, and saying that through many tribulations we must enter the kingdom of God. And when they had appointed elders for them in every church, with prayer and fasting they committed them to the Lord in whom they had believed.

A. The God-called cross-cultural missionary: apostolic ministry

1. God the Holy Spirit calls men and women to cross barriers and declare the Good News to the lost, Acts 13.1-3 (ESV) – Now there were in the church at Antioch prophets and teachers, Barnabas, Simeon who was called Niger, Lucius of Cyrene, Manaen a member of the court of Herod the tetrarch, and Saul. While they were worshiping the Lord and fasting, the Holy Spirit said, "Set apart for me Barnabas and Saul for the work to which I have called them." Then after fasting and praying they laid their hands on them and sent them off.

2. These specially gifted, particularly called persons are gifts of the Lord to the Church for the purpose of equipping the saints for the work of the ministry, Eph. 4.11-12 (ESV) – And he gave the apostles, the prophets, the evangelists, the pastors and teachers, to equip the saints for the work to ministry, for building up the body of Christ.

3. The role of gifted men and women who can entrust the Good News to faithful laborers can never be underestimated or substituted by any technology, model, or effort.

    a. Acts 20.24 (ESV) – But I do not account my life of any value nor as precious to myself, if only I may finish my course and the ministry that I received from the Lord Jesus, to testify to the gospel of the grace of God.

    b. 1 Cor. 4.1-2 (ESV) – This is how one should regard us, as servants of Christ and stewards of the mysteries of God. Moreover, it is required of stewards that they be found trustworthy.

    c. 2 Cor. 5.18 (ESV) – All this is from God, who through Christ reconciled us to himself and gave us the ministry of reconciliation.

    d. 2 Tim. 4.5 (ESV) – As for you, always be sober-minded, endure suffering, do the work of an evangelist, fulfill your ministry.

B. The indigenous ("home grown") leader: elder/pastor/bishop

1. Elders were to be selected to ground the new believers in the faith, Titus 1.5 (ESV) – This is why I left you in Crete, so that you might put what remained into order, and appoint elders in every town as I directed you.

2. Indigenous leaders are to be appointed and confirmed by those given the authority to establish the churches, Acts 14.23 (ESV) – And when they had appointed elders for them in every church, with prayer and fasting they committed them to the Lord in whom they had believed.

3. Ultimately, indigenous leaders are to be the ones who must take responsibility to both sustain the movement, as well as multiply the movement in natural and indigenous contexts, 2 Tim. 2.2 (ESV) – and what you have heard from me in the presence of many witnesses entrust to faithful men who will be able to teach others also.

4. Much of our training has little or nothing to do with urban contexts: "Few will deny that the United States is an "urban" nation whose most profound problems are on display daily in its metropolitan areas. Nonetheless, only one third of the Association of Theological School accredited seminaries in this country offer (much less require) courses concerned with "urban ministry." (Robert V. Kemper, "Theological Education for Urban Ministry: A Survey of U.S. Seminaries," *Theological Education*, Vol. 34, Number 1 [1997]: 51-72.)

C. The "*oikos*" networks of indigenous disciples of Christ will be the means through which the movements are created and thrive.

1. The dimensions of our relational webs

    a. Common kinship relationships (immediate, extended, and adopted families)

    b. Common friendships (friends, neighbors, special interests)

    c. Common associates (work relationships, special interests, recreation, ethnic or cultural alliances, national allegiances)

2. Why *oikos* (household) evangelism via relational webs are effective

    a. *Oikos* evangelism is biblical – Jesus and apostles ministered in this fashion.

    b. *Oikos* is our most natural and least threatening network of existing relationships (no cold calling, or the truest form of lifestyle and friendship evangelism).

    c. *Oikos* individuals are usually receptive to other members (builds on shared history, experience, and concerns).

    d. *Oikos* relationships are "built in" or resident mission fields.

    e. *Oikos* relationships make follow-up less strained and impersonal.

    f. *Oikos* allows entire family groups to be targeted.

    g. *Oikos* relationships constantly re-seed new contact base.

D. The healthy, vital indigenous church (whatever its form – community, mega, or house church network)

   1. Church will be critical in every dimension of urban church planting, regardless of the form it takes: community, mega-church, or house church network.

   2. No church planting movement will make a lasting impact unless its activities and structures make it possible for vital local churches to be both salt and light in their communities, demonstrating and advancing the Kingdom in ways that the indigenous community can both understand and respect, Matt. 5.14-16 (ESV) – You are the light of the world. A city set on a hill cannot be hidden. Nor do people light a lamp and put it under a basket, but on a stand, and it gives light to all in the house. In the same way, let your light shine before others, so that they may see your good works and give glory to your Father who is in heaven.

   3. The relationship between vital churches and godly leaders is indisputable, therefore, all missionary efforts must ultimately

dovetail into efforts of identifying and empowering leaders to continue the work, 2 Tim. 2.2.

E. The supportive church association network: denomination, regional, or shared vision/values

1. Denominational association: "churches of a distinct historical sense of identity and belonging"

2. Regional or locale church: e.g., "the churches of God in Christ in Judea," 1 Thess. 2.14 (ESV) – For you, brothers, became imitators of *the churches of God in Christ Jesus that are in Judea*. For you suffered the same things from your own countrymen as they did from the Jews.

3. The churches of shared vision/values: "churches allied in the Spirit"

4. Regional church networks are the key to ensuring long-term viability for urban church starts and plants.

F. Implications and conclusions

1. Church planting movements in urban America will demand those who are churchmen and churchwomen to lead the way in every respect.

2. The role of the cross cultural missionary is essential in igniting church planting movements, but, ultimately, all inroads into culture (and their *oikia*) will necessarily be done by indigenous workers and laborers.

3. Without indigenous workers, no people group will be able to be won.

IV. HOW Can Such Vital Church Planting Movements Be Wisely and Successfully Ignited in American Inner-City Contexts?

Our research has shown that churches are multiplied and grow when they are planted and mobilized within a particular linguistic, ethnic, and cultural identity (i.e., homogenous unit) which embrace together their own shared spirituality and vision (identity), and structure themselves in a connected and integrated manner (connectivity).

Acts 15.19-21 (ESV) – Therefore my judgment is that we should not trouble those of the Gentiles who turn to God, but should write to them to abstain from the things polluted by idols, and from sexual immorality, and from what has been strangled, and from blood. For from ancient generations Moses has had in every city those who proclaim him, for he is read every Sabbath in the synagogues.

Acts 15.28-29 (ESV) – For it has seemed good to the Holy Spirit and to us to lay on you no greater burden than these requirements: that you abstain from what has been sacrificed to idols, and from blood, and from what has been strangled, and from sexual immorality. If you keep yourselves from these, you will do well. Farewell.

A. Plant, grow, and sustain churches within a particular linguistic, ethnic, and cultural identity: the homogenous unit principle.

1. Culture is intrinsic to the creation of God.

2. God as the author of human life (Gen. 1-2)

3. God's creation mandate as an intrinsic blessing of human creative cultural production

    a. Be stewards of the earth: tools, technology, shaping environment.

    b. Go and multiply: kinship, social organization, structure.

4. The differences between peoples have now been acknowledged and reconciled in the ministry of Christ.

    a. Our differences are now reconciled through the work of Christ on the cross.

    b. Between Jew and Gentile, slave and free, male and female, barbarian and Sycthian, Eph. 2; Col. 3.11; Gal. 3.28

    c. God is reconciled with all people now in his Son, 2 Cor. 5.18-21.

    d. We share in both the guilt and the glory, Rom. 3; 1.16-17.

5. The goal of redemption is Christlikeness, not cultural sameness. (The goal is always to help people become more like Jesus, not more like us.)

a. Colossians 3.11 and Galatians 3.28 do not advocate the obliteration of cultural identity, only the end of ungodly partiality.

b. Culture has been redeemed in the incarnation of Jesus, 1 John 1.1-3.

6. Our differences are displayed and celebrated in the one, holy, apostolic, and universal Church of Jesus Christ.

    a. A New Humanity in the Church, Eph. 2.13-14 (ESV) – But now in Christ Jesus you who once were far off have been brought near by the blood of Christ. For he himself is our peace, who has made us both one and has broken down in his flesh the dividing wall of hostility.

    b. Diverse, yet one: although we are many members made up of every kindred, tribe, people, and nation, from every language and clan, from every class and culture, we nevertheless are one body in Christ. We are to strive to make this unity visible in our daily lives and relationships.

    c. In redemption God does not erase, shield, or obliterate our differences, but rather he acknowledges and rejoices in them (Acts 15).

    d. While we retain our differences, in Christ through the *koinonia* (fellowship) we have with God and each other:

        (1) We share a common parentage.

        (2) We share a common calling.

        (3) We share a common destiny.

7. Our differences are overcome in the unity of Christ for the purpose of the ministry of reconciliation.

    a. We express the love of God in our reconciled relationships, making the Gospel attractive to unbelievers, John 13.34-35.

b. We are reconciled to call the world to be reconciled to God in Christ, 2 Cor. 5.18-21.

   c. Our differences allow us to penetrate every culture and people group with the Gospel, and make disciples and plant churches wherever Christ has yet to be heard and followed.

B. Cultivate a shared communal spirituality where a sense of belonging, ownership, identity, and answerability are highlighted and emphasized.

   1. A shared communal spirituality

      a. Gal. 3.28-29 (ESV) – There is neither Jew nor Greek, there is neither slave nor free, there is neither male nor female, for you are all one in Christ Jesus. And if you are Christ's, then you are Abraham's offspring, heirs according to promise.

      b. Col. 3.11 (ESV) – Here there is not Greek and Jew, circumcised and uncircumcised, barbarian, Scythian, slave, free; but Christ is all, and in all.

   2. We are to cultivate our "adoption," i.e., our belonging into the family of God.

      a. Eph. 1.5 (ESV) – . . . he predestined us for adoption through Jesus Christ, according to the purpose of his will.

      b. 1 John 3.1 (ESV) – See what kind of love the Father has given to us, that we should be called children of God; and so we are. The reason why the world does not know us is that it did not know him.

   3. Ownership: indigenously "owned and operated" structures and patterns

      a. We have a spiritual inheritance, Eph. 1.11 (ESV) – In him we have obtained an inheritance, having been predestined according to the purpose of him who works all things according to the counsel of his will.

b. Even the Corinthians are called to be saints of the Most High God, 1 Cor. 1.2 (ESV) – To the church of God that is in Corinth, to those sanctified in Christ Jesus, called to be saints together with all those who in every place call upon the name of our Lord Jesus Christ, both their Lord and ours.

c. There are no second class movements of the Spirit, James 2.5 (ESV) – Listen, my beloved brothers, has not God chosen those who are poor in the world to be rich in faith and heirs of the kingdom, which he has promised to those who love him?

4. Identity: The NT churches shared a fundamental oneness in apostolic faith and practice (i.e., shared the same colors, codes of conduct, and characteristics).

   a. 1 Cor. 4.17 (ESV) – That is why I sent you Timothy, my beloved and faithful child in the Lord, to remind you of my ways in Christ, as I teach them everywhere in every church.

   b. 1 Cor. 7.17 (ESV) – Only let each person lead the life that the Lord has assigned to him, and to which God has called him. This is my rule in all the churches.

   c. 1 Cor. 11.2 (ESV) – Now I commend you because you remember me in everything and maintain the traditions even as I delivered them to you.

   d. 1 Cor. 11.16 (ESV) – If anyone is inclined to be contentious, we have no such practice, nor do the churches of God.

   e. 1 Cor. 14.33 (ESV) – For God is not a God of confusion but of peace. As in all the churches of the saints.

   f. 1 Cor. 16.1 (ESV) – Now concerning the collection for the saints: as I directed the churches of Galatia, so you also are to do.

5. Answerability: incorporation, membership, promotion, demotion, and excommunication

C. Develop interrelated structures which connect in a systemic and integrated manner.

1. Movements involve *a plurality of leaders, congregations, and associations.*

2. Shared structures of organization: they remained steadfastly in *the apostles' teaching (i.e., their instruction about order and structure)*, see Acts 2.41-47.

3. Shared protocols of leadership identification and certification: *apostolic confirmation of the Holy Spirit's selection*

    a. 2 Tim. 1.6 (ESV) – For this reason I remind you to fan into flame the gift of God, which is in you through the laying on of my hands.

    b. Acts 20.28 (ESV) – Pay careful attention to yourselves and to all the flock, in which the Holy Spirit has made you overseers, to care for the church of God, which he obtained with his own blood.

D. Implications: Why must we strive to connect and integrate all our efforts in growing, mobilizing, and planting churches?

1. To invest in common ventures designed to enable and empower all of the member churches

2. To provide ongoing answerability and support to fledgling and growing churches

3. To join forces in specific projects and operations designed to advance the Kingdom of God in evangelism, outreach, and mission

4. To give care and edification to leaders, members, and congregations in significant felt-need operations and issues (e.g., leadership enhancement, family enrichment, camping, justice issues, etc.)

V. WHERE Ought We to Begin Such Efforts, and from What Venues Are We Likely to Find Champions to Stimulate in Such Church Planting Movements to American Inner-City Contexts?

Making the church the locus of all spirituality, authority, and governance eliminates the need for unnecessary and weighty bureaucracies, and ensures that the movements will be ecclesial and biblical in orientation. Furthermore, unlike many of the current mini-movements suggested as alternative venues for spiritual revolution, keeping the church as the center of spiritual vitality and mission allows for a new resuscitation of biblical language, a strident application of apostolic tradition, and a fresh rediscovery of the church's insights throughout its history.

1 Tim. 3.15-16 (ESV) – . . . if I delay, you may know how one ought to behave in the household of God, which is the church of the living God, a pillar and buttress of truth. Great indeed, we confess, is the mystery of godliness: He was manifested in the flesh, vindicated by the Spirit, seen by angels, proclaimed among the nations, believed on in the world, taken up in glory.

1 Pet. 2.4-5 (ESV) – As you come to him, a living stone rejected by men but in the sight of God chosen and precious, you yourselves like living stones are being built up as a spiritual house, to be a holy priesthood, to offer spiritual sacrifices acceptable to God through Jesus Christ.

A. The Church as the where of authentic kingdom spirituality and Spirit-directed growth: Twelve biblical reasons for starting a new church (from the Book of Acts) [Marlin Mull, p. 19]

1. A new church *brings the Kingdom of God to earth* (Acts 1.3; 8.12; 14.22; 19.8; 20.25; 28.23; 28.31).

2. A new church *helps fulfill the Great Commission* (Acts 1.8; Matt. 28.18-20; Mark 16.15-16; Luke 24.46-49; John 20.19-22).

3. A new church *provides a place of prayer to meet God with others* (Acts 1.14; 4.31; 12.5).

4. A new church *provides another public preaching place* (Acts 9.20; 10.42; 14.7; 16.10; 20.20).

5. A new church *is the most effective evangelistic tool* (Acts 2.38-39; 14.21).

6. A new church *teaches the Bible* (Acts 4.2; 5.19-21; 5.42; 8.4; 11.25-26; 18.11; 20.20; 28.31).

7. A new church *offers another place for Christian service* (Acts 6.3; 9.36; 11.25-26; 11.29-30; 17.15).

8. A new church *trains lay leaders to become preachers* (Acts 6.10; 14.23).

9. A new church *crosses cultural barriers* (Acts 8.35; 10.1-48; 16.9; 22.21).

10. A new church *mentors new believers* (Acts 9.26-28; 20.20; 20.31, 36; 20.34-36; 20.27).

11. A new church *supports worldwide missionary activity* (Acts 13.2-3; 16.9-10).

12. A new church *starts other churches* (Acts 13.2-3; 16.9-10).

B. The Church as the *where of district and locale church* cooperation and support

1. The concept of the Locale Church: "The presence and association of all Christ-honoring congregations in a particular geographical area, regardless of form, denomination, or structure (whether traditional, community, mega-churches, or cell or house churches) which together represent the body of Christ and kingdom witness in a region."

2. In the NT, the churches throughout Asia Minor and the Roman empire were connected and built upon the apostolic witness concerning the person and work of Jesus Christ; in every sense, the early Church was a united, universal church (i.e., it was not perceived in abstract language but real terms, concrete and visible).

3. The Nicene markers were there in the early church!

    a. One: Eph. 4.4-6 (ESV) – There is one body and one Spirit – just as you were called to the one hope that belongs to your call – one Lord, one faith, one baptism, one God and Father of all, who is over all and through all and in all.

b. Holy: 1 Pet. 2.9 (ESV) – But you are a chosen race, a royal priesthood, a holy nation, a people for his own possession, that you may proclaim the excellencies of him who called you out of darkness into his marvelous light.

c. Catholic: Titus 2.14 (ESV) – who gave himself for us to redeem us from all lawlessness and to purify for himself a people for his own possession who are zealous for good works.

d. Apostolic: Eph. 2.19-20 (ESV) – So then you are no longer strangers and aliens, but you are fellow citizens with the saints and members of the household of God, built on the foundation of the apostles and prophets, Christ Jesus himself being the cornerstone.

4. Note the distinctions in how the churches are identified in the NT.

a. According to their geographic location, 1 Thess. 2.14 (ESV) – For you, brothers, became imitators of *the churches of God in Christ Jesus that are in Judea*. For you suffered the same things from your own countrymen as they did from the Jews.

b. According to their cultural, linguistic, and social background, Rom. 16.3-4 (ESV) – "Greet Prisca and Aquila, my fellow workers in Christ Jesus, who risked their necks for my life, to whom not only I give thanks but all the churches of the Gentiles give thanks as well."

c. According to their place as assemblies of Messiah under the apostles' direction, Acts 15.41 (ESV) – "And he went through Syria and Cilicia, strengthening the churches."

C. The Church as the *where of regional and national*

1. Sometimes churches were considered in light of their shared conditions or experiences, whether good or bad, e.g., 2 Cor. 8.1 (ESV) – "We want you to know, brothers, about the grace of God that has been given among the churches of Macedonia."

2. Some markers seem to match our own descriptions of boundaries and place for churches, Rev. 1.4 (ESV) – "John to the seven churches that are in Asia: Grace to you and peace from him who is and who was and who is to come, and from the seven spirits who are before his throne."

3. Note templates and handouts: *Toward a Governing Structure for an Urban Church Planting Movement*

D. The Church as the *where of international interconnection, support, and growth*

E. Implications and conclusion: The Church is the essential element, structure, and reality of God, under the movement of the Holy Spirit, which God has selected for his glory to be seen, and his kingdom power to be demonstrated. The Church is both the locus and the agent of the Kingdom of God.

VI. WHEN Will Such Movements Be Most Likely to Start – What Are the Conditions and Requirements for the Igniting of New, Aggressive Church Planting Movements in Urban America?

In order for robust, dynamic urban church plant movements to occur in urban America, certain conditions will need to be met. These conditions relate to certain spiritual, structural, and missional dynamics which must be informed by the principles of Scripture, as well as the experience of movements abroad. The principle of the analogy of faith comes into play here. While God cannot be made subject to doing the same thing in the same way, we can however depend on God to be faithful to his truths in Scripture, and we can learn from the experience of history. When these truths are acknowledged and followed, we can expect his blessing and aid in our church growth and church planting efforts.

John 8.31-32 (ESV) – So Jesus said to the Jews who had believed in him, "If you abide in my word, you are truly my disciples, and you will know the truth, and the truth will set you free."

Hos. 6.3 (ESV) – Let us know; let us press on to know the Lord; his going out is sure as the dawn; he will come to us as the showers, as the spring rains that water the earth.

Matt. 13.11-12 (ESV) – And he answered them, "To you it has been given to know the secrets of the kingdom of heaven, but to them it has not been given. For to the one who has, more will be given, and he will have an abundance, but from the one who has not, even what he has will be taken away."

John 7.17 (ESV) – If anyone's will is to do God's will, he will know whether the teaching is from God or whether I am speaking on my own authority.

A. Vital church plant movements in urban America will be ignited when authentic spiritual dynamism is felt in the hearts and lives of those who have a burden to minister within it.

  1. The need for dynamic, focused, committed prayer (all of Garrison's research notices this important element in every vital movement)

  2. The power of God's Holy Spirit, Zech. 4.6 (ESV) – Then he said to me, "This is the word of the Lord to Zerubbabel: Not by might, nor by power, but by my Spirit, says the Lord of hosts."

  3. The rediscovery of the apostolic tradition, 2 Thess. 2.15 (ESV) – So then, brothers, stand firm and hold to the traditions that you were taught by us, either by our spoken word or by our letter.

  4. The readiness of a new cross-cultural missions company, Acts 13.2 (ESV) – While they were worshiping the Lord and fasting, the Holy Spirit said, "Set apart for me Barnabas and Saul for the work to which I have called them."

  5. The realization for a new level of spiritual warfare and combat, even in the face of persecution and rejection

B. Vital church plant movements in urban America will be ignited when we reaffirm the primacy and centrality of the Church in spiritual growth and mission.

  1. "The Church is like Noah's ark. If it weren't for the storm outside, you simply couldn't stand the stink *inside*."

2. God has raised up the Church in order to demonstrate his glory to the principalities and powers.

3. We simply cannot claim to be loyal to the Church with the big "C" if we are willing to ignore the church with the little "c."

4. We must recognize we will not be effective in planting churches if we in our hearts hold both disdain and disgust for the Church.

5. All strategies for vital spirituality and dynamic ministry must interface and intersect with the church in order to be both biblically credible and spiritually vital.

C. Vital church plant movements in urban America will be ignited when missionary efforts turn from seeking to do the entire work to becoming "fire-starters," "facilitators," and "gadflies" for authentic spiritual momentum.

1. The axiom of missions: Missionaries do not win nations; missionaries win and disciple people group champions who win their communities, their people, and their nations to the Lord.

2. Missionary activity must shift from doing the work to training indigenous people to do the work.

3. All authentic transformation of indigenous communities must be left to the Holy Spirit, who alone can and must raise up a new generation of believers to identify their gifts, and do the work of the ministry.

4. Missionary activity in urban America must determine to learn and emulate missionary activity in foreign contexts: *Missionaries coordinate strategies with indigenous laborers in order to maximize their ability to advance the gospel in their communities and cities.*

D. Vital church plant movements in urban America will be ignited when the churches that are planted are authentically indigenous, with full authority, oversight, and stewardship transferred to indigenous leaders who make the decisions and determine the directions.

1. The equipping of leaders is the single most important issue involved in the creation and sustaining of vital church planting movements among America's urban poor.

2. We must rediscover new, more biblical, less enculturated ways to raise up and release urban leaders for the work of leading the church, and advancing the Kingdom in mission.

3. While we must be careful not to lay hands on any person too quickly, we must also be careful to recognize that unless indigenous leaders fully receive the authority and responsibility to do the task, the Gospel will not penetrate the receiving culture.

VII. Conclusion

How do these views above coincide with the New Testament definition of the body of Christ, as well as the Nicene theology of the Church embodied in the creed, i.e., that which defines the church as one (biblical identity), holy (shared spirituality), catholic (historic roots and connectivity), and apostolic (representative authority)?

1 Thess. 5.21 (ESV) – but test everything; hold fast what is good.

A. Clarification between the *facts* and the *claims*

B. Evaluation of the *evidence* supporting the claims

   1. The facts of the matter

   2. The teachings of Scripture

C. *Re-evaluation of the claims* based on our understanding of the evidence

D. Conclusions to draw

Conclusion and Review of the Major Concepts

- Urban America can learn much from the experience of vital CPMs taking place around the world today.
- Because of its unique elements, however, urban America will demand its own unique "brand" of committed, critical, and open church planting wisdom and applications, taking seriously those elements of urban America that call for *a new kind of work for our time and place.*

Church Planting Movements, C1 Neighborhoods, and 80% Windows
The Importance of Vision

Rev. Dr. Don L. Davis • *Winning the World: Facilitating Urban Church Planting Movements. Foundations for Ministry Series*. Wichita: The Urban Ministry Institute, 2007.

> Now when Jesus came into the district of Caesarea Philippi, he asked his disciples, "Who do people say that the Son of Man is?" And they said, "Some say John the Baptist, others say Elijah, and others Jeremiah or one of the prophets." He said to them, "But who do you say that I am?" Simon Peter replied, "You are the Christ, the Son of the living God." And Jesus answered him, "Blessed are you, Simon Bar-Jonah! For flesh and blood has not revealed this to you, but my Father who is in heaven. And I tell you, you are Peter, and on this rock I will build my church, and the gates of hell shall not prevail against it. I will give you the keys of the kingdom of heaven, and whatever you bind on earth shall be bound in heaven, and whatever you loose on earth shall be loosed in heaven." Then he strictly charged the disciples to tell no one that he was the Christ.
>
> ~ Matthew 16.13-20 (ESV)

"To Facilitate Pioneer Church Planting Movements Among America's Unreached C1 Communities"

As a ministry of World Impact, TUMI is dedicated to generating and strategically facilitating dynamic, indigenous C1 church planting movements targeted to reach the 80% Window of America's inner cities.

I. The Always-Questioned Identity of Jesus

Matt. 16.13-20 (ESV) – Now when Jesus came into the district of Caesarea Philippi, he asked his disciples, "Who do people say that the Son of Man is?" And they said, "Some say John the Baptist, others say Elijah, and others Jeremiah or one of the prophets." He said to them, "But who do you say that I am?"

A. Question One: "Who do people say that the Son of Man is?"

B. Question Two: "But who do you say that I am?"

II. The Revelation of Peter: "You are the Messiah!"

Matt. 16.16 – Simon Peter replied, "You are the Christ, the Son of the living God."

A. Affirmation One: "You are the Messiah" (i.e., the anointed Servant of Yahweh foretold by the prophets who alone will rule over the Kingdom of God forever).

B. Affirmation Two: ". . . the Son of the Living God!" (i.e., the divine Son of God who reveals God's glory to us, and redeems us from the curse of sin and death)

III. On this Rock: The Centrality of the Church in the Cosmic Struggle for Humanity

Matt. 16.17-19 (ESV) – And Jesus answered him, "Blessed are you, Simon Bar-Jonah! For flesh and blood has not revealed this to you, but my Father who is in heaven. And I tell you, you are Peter, and on this rock I will build my church, and the gates of hell shall not prevail against it. I will give you the keys of the kingdom of heaven, and whatever you bind on earth shall be bound in heaven, and whatever you loose on earth shall be loosed in heaven."

A. Christ's Messianic identity occurs through divine revelation.

1 Cor. 12.3 (ESV) – Therefore I want you to understand that no one speaking in the Spirit of God ever says "Jesus is accursed!" and no one can say "Jesus is Lord" except in the Holy Spirit.

B. Christ's affirmation of "on this Rock"

1. On the Rock of the confession that Jesus of Nazareth is Messiah and Lord of all

Rom. 10.8-9 (ESV) – But what does it say? "The word is near you, in your mouth and in your heart" (that is, the word of faith that we proclaim); because, if you confess with your mouth that Jesus is Lord and believe in your heart that God raised him from the dead, you will be saved.

2. On this confession the Church of Jesus Christ is built.

   1 Cor. 3.10-11 (ESV) – According to the grace of God given to me, like a skilled master builder I laid a foundation, and someone else is building upon it. Let each one take care how he builds upon it. For no one can lay a foundation other than that which is laid, which is Jesus Christ.

3. Not even the gates of hell can withstand the onslaught of the Kingdom's advance through the Church of Jesus Christ.

   a. Our station and security are immovable.

      Ps. 125.1 (ESV) – Those who trust in the Lord are like Mount Zion, which cannot be moved, but abides forever.

   b. No weapon formed against us shall stand.

      Isa. 54.17 (ESV) – . . . no weapon that is fashioned against you shall succeed, and you shall confute every tongue that rises against you in judgment. This is the heritage of the servants of the Lord and their vindication from me, declares the Lord.

   c. Nothing can separate the church from the love of God.

      Rom. 8:33-39 (ESV) – Who shall bring any charge against God's elect? It is God who justifies. Who is to condemn? Christ Jesus is the one who died – more than that, who was raised – who is at the right hand of God, who indeed is interceding for us. Who shall separate us from the love of Christ? Shall tribulation, or distress, or persecution, or famine, or nakedness, or danger, or sword? As it is written, "For your sake we are being killed all the day long; we are regarded as sheep to be slaughtered." No, in all these things we are more than conquerors through him who loved us. For I am sure that neither death nor life, nor angels nor rulers, nor things present nor things to come, nor powers, nor height nor depth, nor anything else in all creation, will be able to separate us from the love of God in Christ Jesus our Lord.

4. The "keys of the Kingdom" are given to the Church: binding and loosing.

   Matt. 18.18 (ESV) – Truly, I say to you, whatever you bind on earth shall be bound in heaven, and whatever you loose on earth shall be loosed in heaven.

IV. Application to the Vision:

"To Facilitate Pioneer Church Planting Movements among America's Unreached C1 Communities. As a ministry of World Impact, TUMI is dedicated to generating and strategically facilitating dynamic, indigenous C1 church planting movements targeted to reach the 80% Window of America's inner cities."

A. TUMI seeks to generate and strategically facilitate *indigenous C1 church planting movements* (dynamic spiritual awakening and advancement of the Kingdom among the poorest of the poor in the cities of America and the world).

B. TUMI targets its activities on the *80% Window (those communities and urban areas where eighty percent of all urban poor residents in America dwell)*.

C. The rationale: four reasons why TUMI focuses on church planting among C1 populations

   1. The Church of Jesus Christ alone is the locus and agent of the Kingdom of God on earth during this Age, 2 Cor. 5.20.

   2. The urban poor (i.e., C1 neighborhoods) represent one of the most strategic and dynamic fields in the entire earth, James 2.5 cf. Luke 4.18.

   3. Facilitating movements that plant healthy churches in C1 neighborhoods is perhaps one of the greatest efforts anyone can make in fulfilling the Great Commission in our generation.

   4. Targeting the 80% Window could very well be the most strategic focus in mission that any urban ministry could have.

V. **The Power of Vision to Shape Culture and Achievement: Connecting the Dots of TUMI's Vision and Its Ongoing Operational Life and Mission**

A. The power of vision

Prov. 29.18 (ESV) – Where there is no prophetic vision the people cast off restraint, but blessed is he who keeps the law.

1. To give our enterprise meaning and direction

2. To guide our decisions and determinations

3. To determine our investments

4. To coordinate our efforts

B. Principles of vision: our responsibility to "run with the vision"

1. We must articulate clearly to ourselves and others what God has called us to be and do.

2. We are to recruit the right people at the right time to accomplish the right tasks alongside our team as we seek to accomplish our vision.

3. We must constantly dialogue about the vision's nature and significance.

4. We must apply ourselves in the most disciplined way to carry out our strategic initiatives and plans to accomplish our vision.

5. We must measure all we do according to the vision, and give one another feedback in how our efforts are helping and/or hindering our vision's accomplishment.

6. We must develop the courage to reject, remove, or change anything we have been doing as it relates to the vision.

7. We must invest all our time, money, and energy in those things that will help us accomplish our vision.

8. We must acknowledge the contribution of everyone who gave to the accomplishment of our vision, and ensure that they are rewarded for their efforts.

Understanding the Implications of Our Vision

- The Vision
- What the vision requires
- How our current people can contribute to the vision
- Where our gaps lie
- What we need to trust God for

> **The Last Word**
>
> And the Lord answered me: "Write the vision; make it plain on tablets, so he may run who reads it. For still the vision awaits its appointed time; it hastens to the end – it will not lie. If it seems slow, wait for it; it will surely come; it will not delay. "Behold, his soul is puffed up; it is not upright within him, but the righteous shall live by his faith.
>
> ~ Habakkuk 2.2-4 (ESV)

Discerning Valid Urban Church Planting Movements
Elements of Authentic Urban Christian Community

Rev. Dr. Don L. Davis

Core Evangelical Conviction
"What Is Our Confession?"

This circle represents *a movement's most fundamental convictions and commitments, i.e., its Affirmation of Faith*, its commitment to the Gospel and those truths contained in the early Christian creeds (i.e., The Nicene Creed). These convictions are anchored in the doctrinal teachings of the Word of God, and represent a movement's unequivocal commitment to historic orthodoxy.

As members of the one, holy, catholic (universal), and apostolic church, valid movements must *be ready and willing to die for the core evangelical convictions of the historic orthodox faith*. These convictions serve as the movement's connection to the historic Christian confession. As such, can never be compromised or altered.

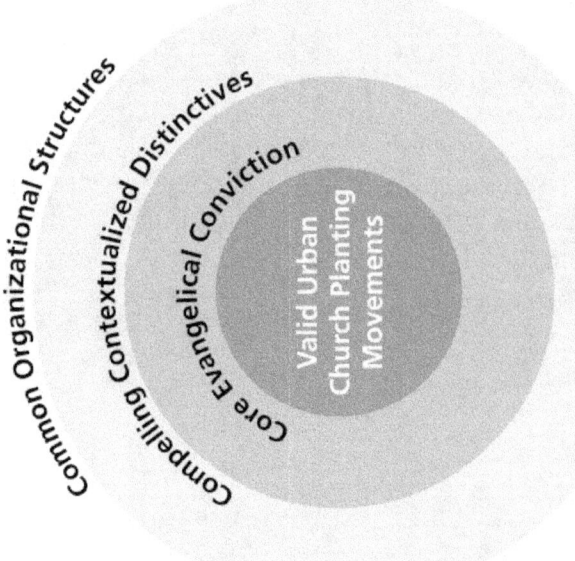

Common Organizational Structures
"What Is Our 'Way of Wisdom'?"

This circle represents the ways in which *valid urban church plant movements express their convictions and identity through their own distinct organizational structures and ministry programs*. Structures and programs should be designed and executed in light of the particular challenges and opportunities represented in a particular missions context. They must, by definition, be subject to change under the movement's constant search to find better, more effective ways to manage and organize for ministry. Such structures are therefore subject to the movement's self-defined processes to apply its accumulated wisdom in *how best to accomplish our purposes in the city*.

As communities of faith in Christ, urban church movements must *be encouraged to dialogue about their structures in order to discover and apply the best possible methods they can to contextualize the Gospel, edify their member churches, and advance the Kingdom of God among their neighbors*.

Compelling Contextualized Distinctives
"What Is Our Identity?"

This circle represents a movement's compelling distinctives, that is, those particular cultural, ethnic, and spiritual characteristics represented in the environment where a movement takes root. A simple example of such a distinctive is language. Evangelism and discipleship must be done in the language of the people who hear and receive the Gospel. Correspondingly, urban church planting movements will be impacted by spiritual and cultural distinctives in which the Spirit uses to gather the Lord's church together (i.e., note the power of pentecostal and charismatic movements among cultures with a strong sense of the powers and how they impact and affect everyday life). Such distinctives are often embodied and championed by leaders who represent these identities with particular clarity and force (e.g., Aimee Semple McPherson, Richard Allen, C. H. Mason, John Wesley, Martin Luther, Chuck Smith, John Wimber).

Specific traditions seek to express and live out this faithfulness to the Apostolic and Great Traditions through their worship, teaching, and service. They seek to make the Gospel clear within new cultures or sub-cultures, speaking and modeling the hope of Christ into new situations shaped by their own unique set of issues, concerns, questions and experience. These movements, therefore, are a form of *contextualization* of the Apostolic tradition, making that tradition real in such a way that new groups of people may come to faith in Jesus Christ, and be incorporated into the community of faith–obeying the teachings of Jesus and giving witness to his Kingdom to their neighbors.

Urban church plant movements must *be ready and willing to articulate and defend their unique distinctives as God's kingdom community in the city*.

The Church Planter and the Church Plant Team

How to PLANT a Church

Don L. Davis

Evangelize

> Mark 16.15-18 (ESV) – And he said to them, "Go into all the world and proclaim the gospel to the whole creation. [16] Whoever believes and is baptized will be saved, but whoever does not believe will be condemned. [17] And these signs will accompany those who believe: in my name they will cast out demons; they will speak in new tongues; [18] they will pick up serpents with their hands; and if they drink any deadly poison, it will not hurt them; they will lay their hands on the sick, and they will recover."

I. Prepare

Luke 24.46-49 (ESV) – and he said to them, "Thus it is written, that the Christ should suffer and on the third day rise from the dead, and that repentance and forgiveness of sins should be proclaimed in his name to all nations, beginning from Jerusalem. You are witnesses of these things. And behold, I am sending the promise of my Father upon you. But stay in the city until you are clothed with power from on high."

A. Form a church-plant team.

B. Pray.

C. Select a target area and population.

D. Do demographic and ethnographic studies.

II. Launch

Gal. 2.7-10 (ESV) – On the contrary, when they saw that I had been entrusted with the gospel to the uncircumcised, just as Peter had been entrusted with the gospel to the circumcised (for he who worked through Peter for his apostolic ministry to the circumcised worked also through me for mine to the Gentiles), and when James and Cephas and John, who seemed to be pillars, perceived the grace that was given to me, they gave the right hand of fellowship to Barnabas and me, that we should go to the Gentiles and they to the circumcised. Only, they asked us to remember the poor, the very thing I was eager to do.

A. Recruit and train volunteers.

   B. Conduct evangelistic events and door-to-door evangelism.

Equip

> Eph. 4.11-16 (ESV) – And he gave the apostles, the prophets, the evangelists, the pastors and teachers, [12] to equip the saints for the work of ministry, for building up the body of Christ, [13] until we all attain to the unity of the faith and of the knowledge of the Son of God, to mature manhood, to the measure of the stature of the fullness of Christ, [14] so that we may no longer be children, tossed to and fro by the waves and carried about by every wind of doctrine, by human cunning, by craftiness in deceitful schemes. [15] Rather, speaking the truth in love, we are to grow up in every way into him who is the head, into Christ, [16] from whom the whole body, joined and held together by every joint with which it is equipped, when each part is working properly, makes the body grow so that it builds itself up in love.

III. Assemble

Acts 2.41-47 (ESV) – So those who received his word were baptized, and there were added that day about three thousand souls. And they devoted themselves to the apostles' teaching and fellowship, to the breaking of bread and the prayers. And awe came upon every soul, and many wonders and signs were being done through the apostles. And all who believed were together and had all things in common. And they were selling their possessions and belongings and distributing the proceeds to all, as any had need. And day by day, attending the temple together and breaking bread in their homes, they received their food with glad and generous hearts, praising God and having favor with all the people. And the Lord added to their number day by day those who were being saved.

   A. Form cell groups, Bible studies, etc. to follow up new believers, to continue evangelism, and to identify and train emerging leaders.

   B. Announce the birth of a new church to the neighborhood and meet regularly for public worship, instruction and fellowship.

IV. Nurture

1 Thess. 2.5-9 (ESV) – For we never came with words of flattery, as you know, nor with a pretext for greed – God is witness. Nor did we seek glory from people, whether from you or from others, though we could have made demands as apostles of Christ. But we were gentle among you, like a nursing mother taking care of her own children. So, being affectionately desirous of you, we were ready to share with you not only the gospel of God but also our own selves, because you had become very dear to us. For you remember, brothers, our labor and toil: we worked night and day, that we might not be a burden to any of you, while we proclaimed to you the gospel of God.

A. Develop individual and group discipleship.

B. Fill key roles in the church: identify and use spiritual gifts.

Empower

> Acts 20.28 (ESV) – Pay careful attention to yourselves and to all the flock, in which the Holy Spirit has made you overseers, to care for the church of God, which he obtained with his own blood.
>
> Acts 20.32 (ESV) – And now I commend you to God and to the word of his grace, which is able to build you up and to give you the inheritance among all those who are sanctified.

V. Transition

Titus 1.4-5 (ESV) – To Titus, my true child in a common faith: Grace and peace from God the Father and Christ Jesus our Savior. This is why I left you in Crete, so that you might put what remained into order, and appoint elders in every town as I directed you –

A. Transfer leadership to indigenous leaders so they become self-governing, self-supporting and self-reproducing (appoint elders and pastors).

B. Finalize decisions about denominational or other affiliations.

C. Commission the church.

D. Foster association with World Impact and other urban churches for fellowship, support, and mission ministry.

How to PLANT a Church

Evanglize

PREPARE
- Form a church-plant team.
- Pray.
- Select a target area and population.
- Do demographic and ethnographic studies.

LAUNCH
- Recruit and train volunteers.
- Conduct evangelistic events and door-to-door evangelism.

Equip

ASSEMBLE
- Form cell groups, Bible studies, etc. to follow up new believers, to continue evangelism, and to identify and train emerging leaders.
- Announce the birth of a new church to the neighborhood and meet regularly for public worship, instruction and fellowship.

NURTURE
- Develop individual and group discipleship.
- Fill key roles in the church; identify and use spiritual gifts.

Empower

TRANSITION
- Transfer leadership to indigenous leaders so they become self-governing, self-supporting and self-reproducing (appoint elders and pastors).
- Finalize decisions about denominational or other affiliations.
- Commission the church.
- Foster association with World Impact and other urban churches for fellowship, support and mission ministry.

Pauline Precedents from Acts: The Pauline Cycle
1. Missionaries Commissioned: Acts 13.1-4; 15.39-40; Gal. 1.15-16.
2. Audience Contacted: Acts 13.14-16; 14.1; 16.13-15; 17.16-19.
3. Gospel Communicated: Acts 13.17-41; 16.31; Rom. 10.9-14; 2 Tim. 2.8.
4. Hearers Converted: Acts. 13.48; 16.14-15; 20.21; 26.20; 1 Thess. 1.9-10.

5. Believers Congregated: Acts 13.43; 19.9; Rom 16.4-5; 1 Cor. 14.26.
6. Faith Confirmed: Acts 14.21-22; 15.41; Rom 16.17; Col. 1.28; 2 Thess. 2.15; 1 Tim. 1.3.
7. Leadership Consecrated; Acts 14.23; 2 Tim. 2.2; Titus 1.5.
8. Believers Commended; Acts 14.23; 16.40; 21.32 (2 Tim. 4.9 and Titus 3.12 by implication).
9. Relationships Continued: Acts 15.36; 18.23; 1 Cor. 16.5; Eph. 6.21-22; Col. 4.7-8.
10. Sending Churches Convened: Acts 14.26-27; 15.1-4.

The "Pauline Cycle" terminology, stages, and diagram are taken from David J. Hesselgrave, *Planting Churches Cross-Culturally,* 2nd ed. Grand Rapids: Baker Book House, 2000.

"Evangelize, Equip, and Empower" and "P.L.A.N.T." schemas for church planting taken from *Crowns of Beauty: Planting Urban Churches Conference Binder* Los Angeles: World Impact Press, 1999.

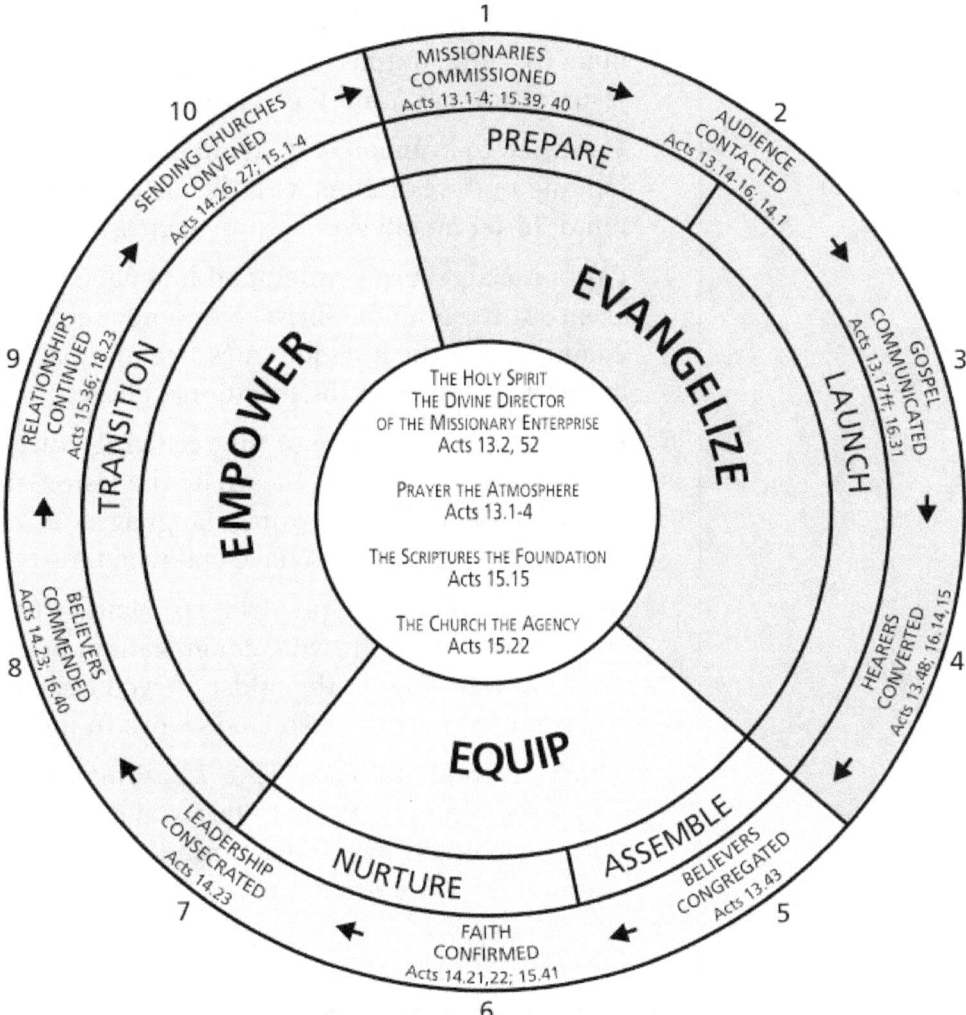

Ten Principles of Church Planting
1. **Jesus is Lord.** (Matt. 9.37-38) All church plant activity is made effective and fruitful under the watch care and power of the Lord Jesus, who himself is the Lord of the harvest.

2. **Evangelize, Equip, and Empower unreached people to reach people.** (1 Thess. 1.6-8) Our goal in reaching others for Christ is not only for solid conversion but also for dynamic multiplication; those who are reached must be trained to reach others as well.

3. **Be inclusive: whosoever will may come.** (Rom. 10.12) No strategy should forbid any person or group from entering into the Kingdom through Jesus Christ by faith.

4. **Be culturally neutral: Come just as you are.** (Col. 3.11) The Gospel places no demands on any seeker to change their culture as a prerequisite for coming to Jesus; they may come just as they are.

5. **Avoid a fortress mentality.** (Acts 1.8) The goal of missions is not to create an impregnable castle in the midst of an unsaved community, but a dynamic outpost of the Kingdom which launches a witness for Jesus within and unto the very borders of their world.

6. **Continue to evangelize to avoid stagnation.** (Rom. 1.16-17) Keep looking to the horizons with the vision of the Great Commission in mind; foster an environment of aggressive witness for Christ.

7. **Cross racial, class, gender, and language barriers.** (1 Cor. 9.19-22) Use your freedom in Christ to find new, credible ways to communicate the kingdom message to those farthest from the cultural spectrum of the traditional church.

8. **Respect the dominance of the receiving culture.** (Acts 15.23-29) Allow the Holy Spirit to incarnate the vision and the ethics of the Kingdom of God in the words, language, customs, styles, and experience of those who have embraced Jesus as their Lord.

9. **Avoid dependence.** (Eph. 4.11-16) Neither patronize nor be overly stingy towards the growing congregation; do not underestimate the power of the Spirit in the midst of even the smallest Christian community to accomplish God's work in their community.

10. **Think reproducibility.** (2 Tim. 2.2; Phil. 1.18) In every activity and project you initiate, think in terms of equipping others to do the same by maintaining an open mind regarding the means and ends of your missionary endeavors.

Resources for Further Study

Cornett, Terry G. and James D. Parker. "Developing Urban Congregations: A Framework for World Impact Church Planters." *World Impact Ministry Resources*. Los Angeles: World Impact Press, 1991.

Davis, Don L. and Terry G. Cornett. "An Outline for a Theology of the Church." *Crowns of Beauty: Planting Urban Churches* (Training Manual). Los Angeles: World Impact Press, 1999.

Hesselgrave, David J. *Planting Churches Cross Culturally: A Biblical Guide*. Grand Rapids: Baker Book House, 2000.

Hodges, Melvin L. *The Indigenous Church: A Handbook on How to Grow Young Churches*. Springfield, MO: Gospel Publishing House, 1976.

Shenk, David W. and Ervin R. Stutzman. *Creating Communities of the Kingdom: New Testament Models of Church Planting*. Scottsdale, PA: Herald Press, 1988.

Responsibilities of a Church Plant Team Leader
World Impact

- To *faithfully intercede* for oneself, one's members and volunteers, the community, and the entire effort during the Charter period
- To *relate and communicate regularly* with the Multiple Team Leader (MTL) and his/her Director and/or church authority on the status of the plant
- To commence the *John Mark Curriculum* and its prescribed courses for Team Leader development
- To attend *World Impact's Urban Church Plant School* with core team members and the MTL to develop a Team Charter
- To oversee *the formation and implementation of the team's church planting strategy*
- To insure that each team member has received *adequate orientation and training* for his/her role
- To care for *the spiritual and emotional welfare of the team*, both as individuals, and as a whole
- To *lead team meetings, and its processes* of planning, preparing, evaluating, and making adjustments to the Charter
- To help team members *resolve interpersonal conflict*
- To *secure resources, personnel, and counseling* for the team's ongoing challenges and opportunities
- To set an *example of service and spirituality* for the team

The Heartbeat of a Church Planter
Discerning an Apostolic/Pastoral Identity
Rev. Dr. Don L. Davis • *The Timothy Conference: Building Church Plant Teams*. Wichita: The Urban Ministry Institute, 2005.

> Gal. 1.1-5 (ESV) – Paul, an apostle – **not from men nor through man, but through Jesus Christ and God the Father, who raised him from the dead** – and all the brothers who are with me, To the churches of Galatia: Grace to you and peace from God our Father and the Lord Jesus Christ, who gave himself for our sins to deliver us from the present evil age, according to the will of our God and Father, to whom be the glory forever and ever. Amen.

I. **Definitions and Distinctions of the Apostleship**

   A. Linguistic considerations of *apostolos*: (the literal meaning "one sent forth," an envoy, messenger)

      1. Classical Greek: distinction between *aggelos* (messenger) and *apostolos* (a delegate or representative of the person who sent him)

      2. Later Judaism: *apostoloi* envoys sent by the elders in Jerusalem to collect tithe and tribute from the Jews of the Dispersion

> **New Testament Senses of Apostleship**
> The term apostles designates three different groups of people. Initially, only the original disciples (meaning "students, learners") of Jesus were called apostles (meaning "those sent forth with a mission"). Later, the name was given to missionaries involved in church planting who were also eyewitnesses of Christ's resurrection, such as Paul himself (1 Cor. 9.1-1) and a group of Jesus' followers other than the Twelve (1 Cor. 15.5,7). Finally, the designation was extended to people who had never seen Christ but who were involved with apostles in pioneer missionary efforts – Apollos (1 Cor. 4.6,9); Epaphroditus (Phil. 2.25); Silvanus and Timothy (1 Thess. 1.1, cf. 2.6). The definition of "apostles" as one of the higher gifts to be desired bears evidence to the continued accessibility to this ministry for qualified individuals (1 Cor. 12.28, cf. 31). Corinthian Christians could aspire to become apostles, prophets, or teachers. The term apostle was still used in this broad sense in the post-apostolic writings

> of the Didache. In his writings Paul also refers to some of his associates as his "co-workers" or his "fellow workers." Under his pen, this terms seems to have become a technical label to designate people who identified closely with him in his church-planting efforts as frontline, pioneer missionaries. Interestingly, the same people whom Paul calls "apostles" are also referred to as his "co-workers"– Barnabas (1 Cor. 9.5-6, cf. Acts 14.14; Col. 4.10-11), Epaphroditus (Phil. 2.25), Timothy (Rom. 16.21). In 2 Corinthians 8.23, Titus is a co-worker and his lesser companions are apostles. We can therefore deduce that there exists some interchangeability between the terms apostles and co-workers.
>
> ~ Gilbert Bilezikian.
> *Beyond Sex Roles: What the Bible says about a Woman's Place in Church and Family.* Grand Rapids: Baker Book House, 1986. pp 197-98.

B. Misconceptions about the Apostolic (i.e., Missionary) Pastor.

1. He must be a he.

    a. Biblical rebuttal: Phil. 4.2-3 (ESV) – I entreat Euodia and I entreat Syntyche to agree in the Lord. Yes, I ask you also, true companion, help these women, who have labored side by side with me in the gospel together with Clement and the rest of my fellow workers, whose names are in the book of life.

    b. The truth of the matter: God has called, anointed, and used both to be missionary pastors on the mission field as he has directed.

2. S/he must be endowed with all the gifts that the biblical apostles possessed in order to be competent to lead the effort.

    a. Biblical rebuttal: 2 Cor. 3.4-6 (ESV) – Such is the confidence that we have through Christ toward God. Not that we are sufficient in ourselves to claim anything as coming from us, but our sufficiency is from God, who has made us competent to be ministers of a new covenant, not of the letter but of the Spirit. For the letter kills, but the Spirit gives life.

    b. The truth of the matter: No missionary pastor is competent in and through themselves, regardless of their gifting or training; we are made competent ministers through the grace and provision of God alone.

3. S/he ought to perceive the role of church planting as a kind of ministry activity or programming emphasis, not as a life calling or commitment.

   a. Biblical rebuttal: Col. 1.24-27 (ESV) – Now I rejoice in my sufferings for your sake, and in my flesh I am filling up what is lacking in Christ's afflictions for the sake of his body, that is, the church, of which I became a minister according to the stewardship from God that was given to me for you, to make the word of God fully known, the mystery hidden for ages and generations but now revealed to his saints. To them God chose to make known how great among the Gentiles are the riches of the glory of this mystery, which is Christ in you, the hope of glory.

   b. The truth of the matter: Church planting is not merely a type of program or ministry; rather, to plant the Church of Jesus Christ is the heart of the Great Commission and the center of apostolic ministry.

4. S/he must be extroverted, outgoing, and wholly dynamic in personality and style.

   a. Biblical rebuttal: 2 Cor. 10.7-10 (ESV) – Look at what is before your eyes. If anyone is confident that he is Christ's, let him remind himself that just as he is Christ's, so also are we. For even if I boast a little too much of our authority, which the Lord gave for building you up and not for destroying you, I will not be ashamed. I do not want to appear to be frightening you with my letters. For they say, "His letters are weighty and strong, but his bodily presence is weak, and his speech of no account."

   b. The truth of the matter: The missionary pastor is based on God's authentic call and anointing by his Spirit, not on outward characteristics of appearance and personality expression.

5. S/he must assume all responsibility for the fruitfulness (or lack thereof) of a church planting endeavor.

   a. Biblical rebuttal: 1 Cor. 3.4-10 (ESV) – For when one says, "I follow Paul," and another, "I follow Apollos," are you not being merely human? What then is Apollos? What is Paul? Servants through whom you believed, as the Lord assigned to each. I planted, Apollos watered, but God gave the growth. So neither he who plants nor he who waters is anything, but only God who gives the growth. He who plants and he who waters are one, and each will receive his wages according to his labor. For we are God's fellow workers. You are God's field, God's building. According to the grace of God given to me, like a skilled master builder I laid a foundation, and someone else is building upon it. Let each one take care how he builds upon it.

b. The truth of the matter: Ultimately, only God gives the growth in ministry; we who are called use our gifts in the way and at the time that he dictates. We have no final control over either the number or timing of those who will respond to the Gospel.

6. S/he must have received training from a professional training academy, Bible college, seminary, or at least be credentialed by an accredited academic institution of higher learning.

   a. Biblical rebuttal: Acts 4.13-14 (ESV) – Now when they saw the boldness of Peter and John, and perceived that they were uneducated, common men, they were astonished. And they recognized that they had been with Jesus. But seeing the man who was healed standing beside them, they had nothing to say in opposition.

   b. The truth of the matter: Social standing, socio-economic background, or polished education mean nothing for the missionary pastor as do authentic calling and spiritual power from on high.

7. S/he must be eloquent and either endowed with or trained in the art of public speaking.

   a. Biblical rebuttal: 1 Cor. 2.1-5 (ESV) – And I, when I came to you, brothers, I did not come proclaiming to you the testimony of God with lofty speech or wisdom. For I decided to know nothing among you except Jesus Christ and him crucified. And I was with you in weakness and in fear and much trembling; and my speech and my message were not in plausible words of wisdom, but in demonstration of the Spirit and of power, that your faith might not rest in the wisdom of men but in the power of God.

b. The truth of the matter: God uses both men and women whose ministries are not primarily public in terms of speaking, but effective in terms of personal witness.

8. S/he must not be a person prone to weakness, insecurity, or neediness.

    a. Biblical rebuttal: 2 Cor. 12.9-10 (ESV) – But he said to me, "My grace is sufficient for you, for my power is made perfect in weakness." Therefore I will boast all the more gladly of my weaknesses, so that the power of Christ may rest upon me. For the sake of Christ, then, I am content with weaknesses, insults, hardships, persecutions, and calamities. For when I am weak, then I am strong.

    b. The truth of the matter: Missionary pastors are acquainted with their own weaknesses within and difficulties from without, and God demonstrates his power through them in spite of these weaknesses and hardships.

9. S/he must always be perceived by everyone in leadership as valuable, helpful and credible.

    a. Biblical rebuttal: Acts 15.35-40 (ESV) – But Paul and Barnabas remained in Antioch, teaching and preaching the word of the Lord, with many others also. And after some days Paul said to Barnabas, "Let us return and visit the brothers in every city where we proclaimed the word of the Lord, and see how they are." Now Barnabas wanted to take with them John called Mark. But Paul thought best not to take with them one who had withdrawn from them in Pamphylia and had not gone with them to the work. And there arose a sharp disagreement, so that they separated from each other. Barnabas took Mark with him and sailed away to Cyprus, but Paul chose Silas and departed, having been commended by the brothers to the grace of the Lord.

    b. The truth of the matter: Sometimes, the very one who appears the least likely to be used of God as a missionary pastor may become the very one whom the Lord calls to bear much fruit for the Kingdom.

II. The Profile of a Church Plant Team Leader

A. The Profile of the Apostolic Pastor

1. S/he maintains *a mature walk with Jesus Christ that is worthy to be imitated.*

    Phil. 4.8-9 (ESV) – Finally, brothers, whatever is true, whatever is honorable, whatever is just, whatever is pure, whatever is lovely, whatever is commendable, if there is any excellence, if there is anything worthy of praise, think about these things. What you have learned and received and heard and seen in me – practice these things, and the God of peace will be with you.

2. S/he represents the Lord through *a compelling personal witness and solid reputation among outsiders and among believers.*

    2 Cor. 6. 3-11 (ESV) – We put no obstacle in any one's way, so that no fault may be found with our ministry, but as servants of God we commend ourselves in every way: by great endurance, in afflictions, hardships, calamities, beatings, imprisonments, riots, labors, sleepless nights, hunger; by purity, knowledge, patience, kindness, the Holy Spirit, genuine love; by truthful speech, and the power of God; with the weapons of righteousness for the right hand and for the left; through honor and dishonor, through slander and praise. We are treated as impostors, and yet are true; as unknown, and yet well known; as dying, and behold we live; as punished, and yet not killed; as sorrowful, yet always rejoicing; as poor, yet making many rich; as having nothing, yet possessing everything. We have spoken freely to you, Corinthians; our heart is wide open.

3. S/he affirms with confidence *the calling of God to represent him* in pioneer church planting.

    Gal. 1.1 (ESV) – Paul, an apostle – not from men nor through man, but through Jesus Christ and God the Father, who raised him from the dead.

4. S/he *submits joyfully to their leaders* under the authority of Jesus Christ.

1 Tim. 1.18-19 (ESV) – This charge I entrust to you, Timothy, my child, in accordance with the prophecies previously made about you, that by them you may wage the good warfare, holding faith and a good conscience. By rejecting this, some have made shipwreck of their faith.

5. S/he possesses *a rich theological view of the Church, with an even deeper love for the body of Christ.*

    2 Cor. 11.2 (ESV) – I feel a divine jealousy for you, for I betrothed you to one husband, to present you as a pure virgin to Christ.

    Col. 1.24-27 (ESV) – Now I rejoice in my sufferings for your sake, and in my flesh I am filling up what is lacking in Christ's afflictions for the sake of his body, that is, the church, of which I became a minister according to the stewardship from God that was given to me for you, to make the word of God fully known, the mystery hidden for ages and generations but now revealed to his saints. To them God chose to make known how great among the Gentiles are the riches of the glory of this mystery, which is Christ in you, the hope of glory.

6. S/he *identifies fully and pastors sensitively (nurtures) the members* of his/her church plant team (apostolic band).

    Phil. 2.19-24 (ESV) – I hope in the Lord Jesus to send Timothy to you soon, so that I too may be cheered by news of you. For I have no one like him, who will be genuinely concerned for your welfare. They all seek their own interests, not those of Jesus Christ. But you know Timothy's proven worth, how as a son with a father he has served with me in the gospel. I hope therefore to send him just as soon as I see how it will go with me, and I trust in the Lord that shortly I myself will come also.

7. S/he *coordinates the gifted men and women under their care*, enabling the diverse members to make the maximum contribution possible to the church planting endeavor.

    Col. 4.10-17 (ESV) – Aristarchus my fellow prisoner greets you, and Mark the cousin of Barnabas (concerning whom you have received instructions – if he comes to you, welcome him), and Jesus who is called Justus. These are the only men of the circumcision among my fellow workers for the kingdom of God, and they have been a comfort to me. Epaphras, who is one of you, a servant of Christ Jesus, greets you, always struggling on your behalf in his prayers, that you may stand mature and fully assured in all the will of God. For I bear him witness that he has worked hard for you and for those in Laodicea and in Hierapolis. Luke the beloved physician greets you, as does Demas. Give my greetings to the brothers at Laodicea, and to Nympha and the church in her house. And when this letter has been read among you, have it also read in the church of the Laodiceans; and see that you also read the letter from Laodicea. And say to Archippus, "See that you fulfill the ministry that you have received in the Lord."

8. S/he **has a burden for the lost, and constantly seeks creative ways to share the good news of the Gospel with those who haven't heard**, with a passion to incorporate all those who respond in a local assembly of believers.

    Rom. 15.18-22 (ESV) – For I will not venture to speak of anything except what Christ has accomplished through me to bring the Gentiles to obedience – by word and deed, by the power of signs and wonders, by the power of the Spirit of God – so that from Jerusalem and all the way around to Illyricum I have fulfilled the ministry of the gospel of Christ; and thus I make it my ambition to preach the gospel, not where Christ has already been named, lest I build on someone else's foundation, but as it is written, "Those who have never been told of him will see, and those who have never heard will understand." This is the reason why I have so often been hindered from coming to you.

9. S/he **equips the Christian community to function as a congregation of believers**, training the leaders and members to grow in the grace of Jesus Christ.

    Gal. 4.12-19 (ESV) – Brothers, I entreat you, become as I am, for I also have become as you are. You did me no wrong. You know it was because of a bodily ailment that I preached the gospel to you at first, and though my condition was a trial to you, you did not scorn or despise me, but received me as an angel of God, as Christ Jesus. What then has become of the blessing you felt? For I testify to you that, if possible, you would have gouged out your eyes and given them to me. Have I then become your enemy by telling you the truth? They make much of you, but for no good purpose. They want to shut you out, that you may make much of them. It is always good to be made much of for a good purpose, and not only when I am present with you, my little children, for whom I am again in the anguish of childbirth until Christ is formed in you!

10. S/he allows the *emerging church to develop its own identity and destiny under the leadership of the Holy Spirit*.

Acts 20.25-32 (ESV) – And now, behold, I know that none of you among whom I have gone about proclaiming the kingdom will see my face again. Therefore I testify to you this day that I am innocent of the blood of all of you, for I did not shrink from declaring to you the whole counsel of God. Pay careful attention to yourselves and to all the flock, in which the Holy Spirit has made you overseers, to care for the church of God, which he obtained with his own blood. I know that after my departure fierce wolves will come in among you, not sparing the flock; and from among your own selves will arise men speaking twisted things, to draw away the disciples after them. Therefore be alert, remembering that for three years I did not cease night or day to admonish everyone with tears. And now I commend you to God and to the word of his grace, which is able to build you up and to give you the inheritance among all those who are sanctified.

B. Implications for the Apostolic Church Plant Team Leader

1. Of all the things listed above, nothing is as important as the *recognition of one's calling to plant churches*. Why?

    a. If you are called, *you'll be provided for*.

    b. If you are called, *the opportunities will come*.

    c. If you are called, *God will ensure your gifting and timing*.

2. Of all the gifts desired above, perhaps none is as important as these:

    a. Burden for *evangelism*

    b. Commitment to *love and nurture the team* as church

    c. *Ability to coordinate the gifts and efforts of team members* for maximum contribution in our mission outreach

III. Issues Surrounding the Missionary Apostleship

A. What level of *Preparation and Training* are necessary for someone to be missionary church plant team leader?

1. Ideally, the missionary apostle has *made disciples within their own cultural setting* before s/he has shifted to do the same cross-culturally in pioneer mission.

   2 Cor. 8.18-22 (ESV) – With him we are sending the brother who is famous among all the churches for his preaching of the gospel. And not only that, but he has been appointed by the churches to travel with us as we carry out this act of grace that is being ministered by us, for the glory of the Lord himself and to show our good will. We take this course so that no one should blame us about this generous gift that is being administered by us, for we aim at what is honorable not only in the Lord's sight but also in the sight of man. And with them we are sending our brother whom we have often tested and found earnest in many matters, but who is now more earnest than ever because of his great confidence in you.

2. More than anything else, the missionary apostle (the church plant team leader) must understand *his or her identity as God's called person* to lead a pioneer mission effort.

   Acts 20.24 (ESV) – But I do not account my life of any value nor as precious to myself, if only I may finish my course and the ministry that I received from the Lord Jesus, to testify to the gospel of the grace of God.

3. *Mastery of and being able to equip others with the Word of God* is the single most important asset needed to be possessed by a church plant team leader.

   2 Tim. 3.16-17 (ESV) – All Scripture is breathed out by God and profitable for teaching, for reproof, for correction, and for training in righteousness, that the man of God may be competent, equipped for every good work.

B. What is the relationship of a called missionary apostle and *Legitimate Partnerships* with others?

1. RMO is a *missionary apostolic class* devoted to pioneer mission.

2. No partnerships can ever eclipse or take the place of *the Missionary Apostle's call to go to the unchurched, proclaim the Good News, and establish congregations of disciples among them.*

3. As missionary apostles, *we go to the unchurched by compulsion of the Lord's call on our lives* first and foremost, not because of the willingness of any other group, however legitimate to go with us.

4. We ought to partner with others, not by losing our identity, but *joining forces for maximum impact.*

   Gal. 2.6-10 (ESV) – And from those who seemed to be influential (what they were makes no difference to me; God shows no partiality) – those, I say, who seemed influential added nothing to me. On the contrary, when they saw that I had been entrusted with the gospel to the uncircumcised, just as Peter had been entrusted with the gospel to the circumcised (for he who worked through Peter for his apostolic ministry to the circumcised worked also through me for mine to the Gentiles), and when James and Cephas and John, who seemed to be pillars, perceived the grace that was given to me, they gave the right hand of fellowship to Barnabas and me, that we should go to the Gentiles and they to the circumcised. Only, they asked us to remember the poor, the very thing I was eager to do.

C. What is the relationship between *assuming leadership and creating consensus* in your leading of a church plant team?

   1. The church plant team leader *challenges his/her team and others to follow him/her as s/he follows Christ.*

      1 Cor. 11.1 (ESV) – Be imitators of me, as I am of Christ.

   2. The church plant team leader must live by *his/her conviction under the direction of the Lord Jesus*, not by the opinions, whims, and threats of others.

      Gal. 1.10-12 (ESV) – For am I now seeking the approval of man, or of God? Or am I trying to please man? If I were still trying to please man, I would not be a servant of Christ. For I would have you know, brothers, that the gospel that was preached by me is not man's gospel. For I did not receive it from any man, nor was I taught it, but I received it through a revelation of Jesus Christ.

3. As a creator of community, however, the apostolic church plant team leader seeks to *help each member identify their gifts, discover their burdens, and utilize their resources to contribute to the planting of a healthy assembly of disciples*.

Eph. 4.11-16 (ESV) – And he gave the apostles, the prophets, the evangelists, the pastors and teachers, to equip the saints for the work of ministry, for building up the body of Christ, until we all attain to the unity of the faith and of the knowledge of the Son of God, to mature manhood, to the measure of the stature of the fullness of Christ, so that we may no longer be children, tossed to and fro by the waves and carried about by every wind of doctrine, by human cunning, by craftiness in deceitful schemes. Rather, speaking the truth in love, we are to grow up in every way into him who is the head, into Christ, from whom the whole body, joined and held together by every joint with which it is equipped, when each part is working properly, makes the body grow so that it builds itself up in love.

Rom. 12.4-8 (ESV) – For as in one body we have many members, and the members do not all have the same function, so we, though many, are one body in Christ, and individually members one of another. Having gifts that differ according to the grace given to us, let us use them: if prophecy, in proportion to our faith; if service, in our serving; the one who teaches, in his teaching; the one who exhorts, in his exhortation; the one who contributes, in generosity; the one who leads, with zeal; the one who does acts of mercy, with cheerfulness.

In a real sense, a church plant team member is playing the role of an apostle!

The designation of the Twelve as "the apostles," which occurs only here in Mark's Gospel, has specific reference to the mission they have just undertaken. In this context the term is descriptive of the disciple's function rather than an official title and could be rendered 'missionaries.' It was in consequence of their mission of preaching and exorcism in Galilee that the Twelve were designated 'apostles,' i.e., those who had been sent forth and empowered by Jesus.

~ William L. Lane. "The Gospel of Mark."
The New International Commentary on the New Testament.
Grand Rapids: William B. Eerdmans, 1974. p. 224.

Practical Steps in Church Planting
Knowing Your Call and Your Community
Rev. Dr. Don L. Davis

Abstract

The first step in effective cross-cultural church planting is becoming clear regarding your personal call from Christ to engage in this endeavor, discerning whom you are to partner with, and learning the people and community to which God has given you to reach. No one can be effective in the beginning stages of urban mission unless they take time to re-affirm their call, and study the people and place to which God has called them. This session gives guidelines for confidently knowing your call and your community.

I. Know Your Personal Call.

A. Begin by becoming familiar with the biblical vision and rationale for church planting.

1. The theology of the Church

2. The role of the Holy Spirit

3. The vitality of the apostolic band

B. Renew your personal commitment to the missionary vision, and to urban missions.

1. Recall your own "Damascus Road" experience: salvation, gifts, and ministry given to you from Christ.

2. Reconsider the nature of Christ's call on your life.

3. Assess your ministry life right now, and discern if God is still calling you to this kind of ministry.

4. Reaffirm your call to the gospel ministry: Is this God's particular call for you right now?

C. Circumcise your heart in dependence on God alone.

1. Acknowledge to the Lord your helplessness before him.

2. Acknowledge to your colleagues your helplessness before them.

3. Gird your mind to pay the price to see a church born in the community Christ has called you to serve.

D. Commit to play your position on the church plant team.

1. Buy wholeheartedly into the vision of church planting.

2. Have the courage to count the cost before you join the team.

3. Join the team – don't sit on the bench. (Remember John Mark.)

4. Make yourself available to be as involved in the church plant as you possibly can.

5. Commit yourself to fulfill the charter of the church plant team.

E. Recognize and submit to Christ's authority in your ministry.

1. Although the team must be semi-autonomous, it must also be fully accountable.

   a. Free to innovate in evangelical method

   b. Bound to the mandate of Christ and the vision of our ministry

2. Identify to whom you are accountable: Your church plant team leader, or your City Director or pastor.

3. Identify for whom you are accountable: those on the team and in the community.

4. Identify for what you are accountable: responsibilities and duties on the team.

II. **Know Your Call as a Church Plant Team.**

   A. From the start, commit ample time to living and learning as a community of servants.

      1. To grow together spiritually, socially, and interpersonally

      2. To discern one another's gifts, burdens, and skills

      3. To allow the team identity and "chemistry" to develop

      4. To develop a clear "modus operandi" as a team in its ongoing planning, doing, and reviewing together

   B. Plan special times for spiritual nurture and friendship (retreat, prayer, Bible study, social gatherings).

   C. Spend time before the Lord in prayer and supplication.

      1. For yourselves

      2. For the community

      3. For the Spirit's leading

   D. Spend time as a team in ministry preparation (training times, conferences, language study, Bible training, etc.).

      1. Need for ongoing training

      2. Important not to make any assumptions; over learning can be a blessing

      3. Allow for "blackboard battles" to be lost without blood: role play and simulation.

      4. Allow opportunity to practice skills and projects.

      5. Determine overall curricula based upon the particular needs of each individual team.

III. Know to Whom You Are Called: Your Community.

> I become all things to all people in order that I might win some.
>
> ~ The Apostle Paul

A. Do Your Homework before You Arrive in the Community.

1. Use standardized reference sources (demographic and statistical volumes).

2. Population, major newspapers, industry and commerce, museums, places of interest, universities, art galleries, museums, etc.

3. Do your library work to unearth data on your city.

    a. History and background

    b. Cultural distinctives

    c. Local personages and legends

    d. Ongoing neighborhood issues and concerns

    e. Places of importance

B. Enter the scene as a learner.

1. Adopt the mindset of a student of the community.

2. Keep a record of your experience and insights.

3. Formulate questions and seek to answer them.

4. Spend ample time learning about the city in general, and the history of the community to which you are called.

5. Judith Lingenfelter, Biola – set aside the first 3-6 months for learning the ethnographics of the community.

C. Early on adopt the role of "Participant Observer."

1. Gathering data and analyzing it is hard work.

2. "What am I supposed to be seeing?" – common query during first stage of ethnographic work

3. James Spradley, *Ethnographic Interviewing* (1980)

   a. Three parts: actor, activity, place

   b. Nine basic questions of observation in any context: space, object, act, activity, event, time, actor, goal, and feeling

4. Write down everything in detail – form hypotheses – test them

D. Learning the territory: mapping

1. "Determining what is where and why": its purpose?

   a. Helps us learn how people use space

   b. Builds rapport by asking non-threatening questions

   c. Learn indigenous terms, categories and points of interest and importance

2. Architectural maps – what is located where and why

3. Geographic areas – paths, landmarks, edges, districts, to help determine areas of safety and danger for specific persons

E. Getting the pulse: interviewing key members of the community

1. The importance of relationships for information: one relationship is worth a dozen surveys.

   a. Targets key members of influence

   b. Gain opportunity to get direct interpretation from someone who is from the culture

   c. Allow you to demonstrate interest and respect to people of the community

2. Importance: respect is absolutely critical.

3. Formal interviewing: (associations, groups, individuals) community survey

   a. Descriptive questions – "Grand Tour questions"

   b. Structural questions – seeking to determine what ethnic groups live where, and the differences between them

4. Informal interviewing: friendship and learning

5. The importance of recording and reflecting on all answers, and seeking to use information to better your ministry

6. The act of staying open to new information is as important as the interview process, formal or not.

7. Under all circumstances guard the dignity of the people you are researching; they are not bugs or microbes, but people for whom Christ died

F. Gleaning the field: spend time analyzing your data.

1. Never gather data without also scheduling some kind of feedback or evaluation setting.

2. Talk together as a team about what you are learning.

3. Constantly ask how your insights can serve your evangelism, compassion, and friend-making activities.

4. Make suggestions on how information can help your CPT efforts in ministering to the community.

G. Begin to walk circumspectly: become a good neighbor.

1. Appreciate the uniqueness of the community where you are.

2. Be discrete and respectful; do not become a tale-bearer.

3. Allow the Spirit to use your research to modify your methods and strategies of evangelism and justice.

4. Recognize that while you are in the community, you are a part of the community – watch out for the "aloof observer" mind set.

Traditions
(Paradosis)
Rev. Dr. Don L. Davis and Rev. Terry G. Cornett

> Remember the days of old; consider the years of many generations; ask your father, and he will show you, your elders, and they will tell you.
>
> ~ Deuteronomy 32.7

Strong's Definition
Paradosis. Transmission, i.e. (concretely) a precept; specifically, the Jewish traditionary law

Vine's Explanation
Denotes "a tradition," and hence, by metonymy, (a) "the teachings of the rabbis," . . .(b) "apostolic teaching," . . . of instructions concerning the gatherings of believers, of Christian doctrine in general . . . of instructions concerning everyday conduct.

I. **The concept of tradition in Scripture is rooted in the remembrance, celebration, enactment, and proclamation of the story of God's promise to redeem and save a people for his own.**

Every age of Christian testimony has given witness to their deep faith and hope in the salvation promise of the triune God to redeem a people out of the world for his own possession and service. The history of the Judeo-Christian faith is anchored in a hope which is renewed daily, weekly, monthly, and annually in the worship and service of the people of God. This hope is rooted in the work of Jesus of Nazareth, demonstrated in his perfect life, expressed in his death on the Cross, and vindicated by his resurrection from the dead and ascension to the Father's right hand. Rooted in the historical journey of God's people Israel, and made real in the life and service of the Church, tradition involves those acts, behaviors, customs, and practices which articulate, celebrate, enact, retell, defend, and embody the story of God's salvation in Jesus, those doctrines and practices whereby we sanctify the present by remembering the past so we can better live in light of the future, our true hope of glory in Christ.

Exod. 12.24-27 – "You shall observe this rite as a statute for you and for your sons forever. And when you come to the land that the Lord will give you, as he has promised, you shall keep this service. And when your children say to you, 'What do you mean by this service?' you shall say, 'It is the sacrifice of the Lord's Passover, for he passed over the houses of the people of Israel in Egypt, when he struck the Egyptians but spared our houses.'" And the people bowed their heads and worshiped.

Jer. 6.16 – Thus says the Lord: "Stand by the roads, and look, and ask for the ancient paths, where the good way is; and walk in it, and find rest for your souls. But they said, 'We will not walk in it'" (cf. Exod. 3.15; Judg. 2.17; 1 Kings 8.57-58; Ps. 78.1-6).

Deut. 26.5-11 – And you shall make response before the Lord your God, "A wandering Aramean was my father. And he went down into Egypt and sojourned there, few in number, and there he became a nation, great, mighty, and populous. And the Egyptians treated us harshly and humiliated us and laid on us hard labor. Then we cried to the Lord, the God of our fathers, and the Lord heard our voice and saw our affliction, our toil, and our oppression. And the Lord brought us out of Egypt with a mighty hand and an outstretched arm, with great deeds of terror, with signs and wonders. And he brought us into this place and gave us this land, a land flowing with milk and honey. And behold, now I bring the first of the fruit of the ground, which you, O Lord, have given me." And you shall set it down before the Lord your God and worship before the Lord your God. And you shall rejoice in all the good that the Lord your God has given to you and to your house, you, and the Levite, and the sojourner who is among you.

Exod. 13.8-9 – You shall tell your son on that day, "It is because of what the Lord did for me when I came out of Egypt." And it shall be to you as a sign on your hand and as a memorial between your eyes, that the law of the Lord may be in your mouth. For with a strong hand the Lord has brought you out of Egypt.

2 Chron. 35.25 (NIV) – Jeremiah composed laments for Josiah, and to this day all the men and women singers commemorate Josiah in the laments. These became a tradition in Israel and are written in the Laments (cf. Gen. 32.32; Judg. 11.38-40).

II. **Godly tradition edifies, grounds, and reinforces the truth and story of God in our lives. However, because of sinful habits and dead orthodoxy, not all tradition is godly.**

Any individual tradition must be judged by its faithfulness to the Word of God and its usefulness in helping people maintain obedience to Christ's example and teaching.* In the Gospels, Jesus frequently rebukes the Pharisees for establishing traditions that nullify rather than uphold God's commands.

Mark 7.8 – "You leave the commandment of God and hold to the tradition of men" (cf. Matt. 15.2-6; Mark. 7.13).

Col. 2.8 – See to it that no one takes you captive by philosophy and empty deceit, according to human tradition, according to the elemental spirits of the world, and not according to Christ.

III. **Without the fullness of the Holy Spirit among the people of God, the constant edification of the Scripture, and the passionate remembrance and celebration of God's works in history, tradition will inevitably lead to dead formalism.**

Those who are spiritual are filled with the Holy Spirit, whose power and leading alone provides individuals and congregations a sense of freedom and vitality in all they practice and believe. However, when the practices and teachings of any given tradition are no longer infused by the power of the Holy Spirit and the Word of God, tradition loses its effectiveness, and may actually become counterproductive to our discipleship in Jesus Christ.

Eph. 5.18 – And do not get drunk with wine, for that is debauchery, but be filled with the Spirit.

Gal. 5.22-25 – But the fruit of the Spirit is love, joy, peace, patience, kindness, goodness, faithfulness, gentleness, self-control; against such things there is no law. And those who belong to Christ Jesus have crucified the flesh with its passions and desires. If we live by the Spirit, let us also walk by the Spirit.

2 Cor. 3.5-6 – Not that we are sufficient in ourselves to claim anything as coming from us, but our sufficiency is from God, who has made us competent to be ministers of a new covenant, not of the letter but of the Spirit. For the letter kills, but the Spirit gives life.

---

* "All Protestants insist that these traditions must ever be tested against Scripture and can never possess an independent apostolic authority over or alongside of Scripture" (J. Van Engen, "Tradition," *Evangelical Dictionary of Theology*, Walter Elwell, Gen. ed.). We would add that Scripture is itself the "authoritative tradition" by which all other traditions are judged. See Appendix, *The Founders of Tradition: Three Levels of Christian Authority."

IV. Fidelity and reproduction to the Apostolic tradition (i.e., the testimony, teaching, and ethical vision of Christ and his kingdom) is the essence of Christian maturity.

Tradition for the Church is not misguided nor arbitrary. Rather, we draw our sense of identity and history from the story of Jesus of Nazareth based on the eyewitness testimony of the apostles, and their commentary and explanation of the meaning of the Christ event for our lives. The Church is a *messianic hermeneutical community*, drawing its life from its conviction, proclamation, celebration, and demonstration of the meaning of the person and work of Jesus as embodied in the history of Israel, as demonstrated through his incarnation and passion, and verified in his resurrection and ascension to the right hand of God. Their bold, clear proclamation of his coming again to complete his work on the Cross and to establish the reign of God in this world is the Church's hope and love. As so often said in the African American Christian worship communities, tradition makes this story and its hope "plain," telling to all in worship, ritual, celebration, and lifestyle that Jesus of Nazareth is the Chosen One of God, borne witness to by the apostles. Embracing and defending their witness is the heart of Christian maturity and discipleship.

2 Tim. 2.2 – and what you have heard from me in the presence of many witnesses entrust to faithful men who will be able to teach others also.

1 Cor. 11.1-2 – Be imitators of me, as I am of Christ. Now I commend you because you remember me in everything and maintain the traditions even as I delivered them to you (cf.1 Cor. 4.16-17; 2 Tim. 1.13-14; 2 Thess. 3.7-9; Phil. 4.9).

1 Cor. 15.3-8 – For I delivered to you as of first importance what I also received: that Christ died for our sins in accordance with the Scriptures, that he was buried, that he was raised on the third day in accordance with the Scriptures, and that he appeared to Cephas, then to the twelve. Then he appeared to more than five hundred brothers at one time, most of whom are still alive, though some have fallen asleep. Then he appeared to James, then to all the apostles. Last of all, as to one untimely born, he appeared also to me.

V. The Apostle Paul often includes to the churches an appeal to the tradition for support in both doctrinal and ethical practices.

The apostolic tradition was the yardstick and plumbline of authentic faith, genuine Christian love, and authentic demonstration of Christian hope in the church's faith and practice

1 Cor. 11.16 – If anyone is inclined to be contentious, we have no such practice, nor do the churches of God (cf. 1 Cor. 1.2; 7.17; 15.3).

1 Cor. 14.33-34 – For God is not a God of confusion but of peace. As in all the churches of the saints, the women should keep silent in the churches. For they are not permitted to speak, but should be in submission, as the Law also says.

VI. When a congregation uses received tradition to remain faithful to the "Word of God," they are commended by the apostles.

The apostles not only expected the churches to receive the traditions of faith and practice that they had given to the people of God, they were instructed to maintain and defend them, to hold fast to what they have been given, and to stand firm upon it for what it truly was, the authoritative word of God.

1 Cor. 11.2 – Now I commend you because you remember me in everything and maintain the traditions even as I delivered them to you.

2 Thess. 2.15 – So then, brothers, stand firm and hold to the traditions that you were taught by us, either by our spoken word or by our letter.

2 Thess. 3.6 – Now we command you, brothers, in the name of our Lord Jesus Christ, that you keep away from any brother who is walking in idleness and not in accord with the tradition that you received from us.

The Founders of Tradition: Three Levels of Christian Authority

Exod. 3.15 (ESV) – God also said to Moses, "Say this to the people of Israel, 'The Lord, the God of your fathers, the God of Abraham, the God of Isaac, and the God of Jacob, has sent me to you.' This is my name forever, and thus I am to be remembered throughout all generations."

I. The Authoritative Tradition: The Apostles and the Prophets (The Holy Scriptures)

> So then you are no longer strangers and aliens, but you are fellow citizens with the saints and members of the household of God, built on the foundation of the apostles and prophets, Christ Jesus himself being the cornerstone, in whom the whole structure, being joined together, grows into a holy temple in the Lord.
>
> ~ The Apostle Paul (Ephesians 2.19-21)

Those who gave eyewitness testimony to the revelation and saving acts of Yahweh, first in Israel, and ultimately in Jesus Christ the Messiah. This testimony is binding for all people, at all times, and in all places. It is the authoritative tradition by which all subsequent tradition is judged.

See Appendix, Defining the Great Tradition.

II. The Great Tradition: The Ecumenical Councils and their Creeds*

> What has been believed everywhere, always, and by all.
>
> ~ Vincent of Lerins

The Great Tradition is the core dogma (doctrine) of the church. It represents the teaching of the Church as it has understood the Authoritative Tradition (the Holy Scriptures), and summarizes those essential truths that Christians of all ages have confessed and believed. To these doctrinal statements the whole church, (Catholic, Orthodox, and Protestant)** gives its assent. The worship and theology of the church reflects this core dogma, which finds its summation and fulfillment in the person and work of Jesus Christ. From earliest times, Christians have expressed their devotion to God in its church calendar, a yearly pattern of worship which summarizes and reenacts the events of Christ's life.

**Even the more radical wing of the Protestant reformation (Anabaptists) who were the most reluctant to embrace the creeds as dogmatic instruments of faith, did not disagree with the essential content found in them. "They assumed the Apostolic Creed – they called it 'The Faith,' Der Glaube, as did most people." See John Howard Yoder, *Preface to Theology: Christology and Theological Method*, (Grand Rapids: Brazos Press, 2002), pp. 222-223.

III. Specific Church Traditions: The Founders of Denominations and Orders

> The Presbyterian Church (U.S.A.) has approximately 2.5 million members, 11,200 congregations and 21,000 ordained ministers. Presbyterians trace their history to the 16th century and the Protestant Reformation. Our heritage, and much of what we believe, began with the French lawyer John Calvin (1509-1564), whose writings crystallized much of the Reformed thinking that came before him.
> ~ The Presbyterian Church, U.S.A.

Christians have expressed their faith in Jesus Christ in various ways through specific movements and traditions which embrace and express the Authoritative Tradition and the Great Tradition in unique ways. For instance, Catholic movements have arisen around people like Benedict, Francis, or Dominic, and among Protestants people like Martin Luther, John Calvin, Ulrich Zwingli, and John Wesley. Women have founded vital movements of Christian faith (e.g., Aimee Semple McPherson of the Foursquare Church), as well as minorities (e.g., Richard Allen of the African Methodist Episcopal Church or Charles H. Mason of the Church of God in Christ, who also helped to spawn the Assemblies of God), all which attempted to express the Authoritative Tradition and the Great Tradition in a specific way consistent with their time and expression.

The emergence of vital, dynamic movements of the faith at different times and among different peoples reveal the fresh working of the Holy Spirit throughout history. Thus, inside Catholicism, new communities have arisen such as the Benedictines, Franciscans, and Dominicans; and outside Catholicism, new denominations have emerged (Lutherans, Presbyterians, Methodists, Church of God in Christ, etc.). Each of these specific traditions have "founders," key leaders whose energy and vision helped to establish a unique expression of Christian faith and practice. Of course, to be legitimate, these movements must adhere to and faithfully express both the Authoritative Tradition and the Great Tradition. Members of these specific traditions embrace their own unique practices and patterns of spirituality, but these unique features are not necessarily binding on the church at large. They represent the unique expressions of that community's understanding of and faithfulness to the Authoritative and Great Traditions.

Specific traditions seek to express and live out this faithfulness to the Authoritative and Great Traditions through their worship, teaching, and service. They seek to make the Gospel clear within new cultures or sub-cultures, speaking and modeling the hope of Christ into new situations shaped by their own set of questions posed in light of their own unique circumstances. These movements, therefore, seek to contextualize the Authoritative tradition in a way that faithfully and effectively leads new groups of people to faith in Jesus Christ, and incorporates those who believe into the community of faith that obeys his teachings and gives witness of him to others.

Defining the "Great Tradition"

The Great Tradition (sometimes called the "classical Christian tradition") is defined by Robert E. Webber as follows:

> [It is] the broad outline of Christian belief and practice developed from the Scriptures between the time of Christ and the middle of the fifth century.
> ~ Robert E. Webber. *The Majestic Tapestry*.
> Nashville: Thomas Nelson Publishers, 1986, p. 10.

This tradition is widely affirmed by Protestant theologians both ancient and modern.

> Thus those ancient Councils of Nicea, Constantinople, the first of Ephesus, Chalcedon, and the like, which were held for refuting errors, we willingly embrace, and reverence as sacred, in so far as relates to doctrines of faith, for they contain nothing but the pure and genuine interpretation of Scripture, which the holy Fathers with spiritual prudence adopted to crush the enemies of religion who had then arisen.
> ~ John Calvin. *Institutes*, IV, ix. 8

> . . . .most of what is enduringly valuable in contemporary biblical exegesis was discovered by the fifth century.
> ~Thomas C. Oden. *The Word of Life*.
> San Francisco: HarperSanFrancisco, 1989, p. xi

> The first four Councils are by far the most important, as they settled the orthodox faith on the Trinity and the Incarnation.
>
> ~ Philip Schaff. *The Creeds of Christendom, v. 1.*
> Grand Rapids: Baker Book House, 1996, p. 44.

Our reference to the Ecumenical Councils and Creeds is, therefore, focused on those Councils which retain a widespread agreement in the church among Catholics, Orthodox, *and Protestants*. While Catholic and Orthodox share common agreement on the first seven councils, Protestants tend to affirm and use primarily the first four. Therefore, those councils which *continue to be shared by the whole church* are completed with the Council of Chalcedon in 451.

It is worth noting that each of these four Ecumenical Councils took place in a pre-European cultural context and that none of them were held in Europe. They were councils of the whole church and they reflected a time in which Christianity was primarily an eastern religion in it's geographic core. By modern reckoning, their participants were African, Asian, and European. The councils reflected a church that ". . . has roots in cultures far distant from Europe and preceded the development of modern European identity, and [of which] some of its greatest minds have been African" (Oden, *The Living God*, SanFrancisco: HarperSanFrancisco, 1987, p. 9).

Perhaps the most important achievement of the Councils was the creation of what is now commonly called the Nicene Creed. It serves as a summary statement of the Christian faith that can be agreed on by Catholic, Orthodox, and Protestant Christians.

The first four Ecumenical Councils are summarized in the chart on the following page.

Name/Date/Location	Purpose
First Ecumenical Council 325 A.D. Nicea, Asia Minor	Defending against: *Arianism* Question answered: *Was Jesus God?* Action: *Developed the initial form of the Nicene Creed to serve as a summary of the Christian faith*
Second Ecumenical Council 381 A.D. Constantinople, Asia Minor	Defending against: *Macedonianism* Question answered: *Is the Holy Spirit a personal and equal part of the Godhead?* Action: *Completed the Nicene Creed by expanding the article dealing with the Holy Spirit*
Third Ecumenical Council 431 A.D. Ephesus, Asia Minor	Defending against: *Nestorianism* Question answered: *Is Jesus Christ both God and man in one person?* Action: *Defined Christ as the Incarnate Word of God and affirmed his mother Mary as theotokos (God-bearer)*
Fourth Ecumenical Council 451 A.D. Chalcedon, Asia Minor	Defending against: *Monophysitism* Question answered: *How can Jesus be both God and man?* Action: *Explained the relationship between Jesus' two natures (human and Divine)*

IV. Conclusion

> It is within the power of all, therefore, in every church, who may wish to see the truth, to contemplate clearly the tradition of the apostles manifested throughout the whole world. And we are in a position to reckon up those who were by the apostles instituted bishops in the churches, and the succession of these men to our own times. . . . For if the apostles had known hidden mysteries . . . they would have delivered them especially to those to whom they were also committing the churches themselves. For they were desirous that these men should be very perfect and blameless in all things, whom also they were leaving behind as their successors, delivering up their own place of government to these men.
>
> ~ Irenaeus (circa 180, E/W), 1.415.

- The apostolic tradition was the yardstick and plumbline of authentic faith, genuine Christian love, and authentic demonstration of Christian hope in the church's faith and practice.

- Valid church planting movements will all build upon, acknowledge and defend the apostolic tradition, expressed in the Great Tradition, and embodied in various worship communities which hold to the teaching of Christ faithfully and strongly, 2 Thess. 2.15 – So then, brothers, stand firm and hold to the traditions that you were taught by us, either by our spoken word or by our letter.

- Valid Christian faith cannot be wholly individualized; Christianity is a communitarian hope.

What Shall I Preach, How Shall We Grow?
The Urban Pastor's Dilemma
Rev. Dr. Don L. Davis • www.tumi.org/churchplanting

Recently, I met with a precious urban pastor who was wrestling with one of his greatest challenges of any pastor – what strategy should he use to lead the church toward spiritual maturity. He struggled with the trendy, odd kinds of themes used in churches today, and wondered if a more biblical alternative existed. He is not alone; many urban church pastors and their congregations have no clear plan to make disciples, and are often confused about content, that is, what themes and truths ought a growing vital congregation focus on to mature in Christ. For many, the choice of what to cover is a week-by-week decision, a hit-and-miss affair that all too often leaves both the preaching and discipleship subject to the whims of the latest fads and curiosities, without depth or focus.

In order to resolve this problem, TUMI has encouraged pastors to follow the Church Year, a Christ-centered, biblical approach to spiritual formation and Christian education. Also known as the Christian Year, the Church Year is a strategy used by Christians worldwide to help congregations concentrate on Jesus' life and ministry through specific seasons that correspond to the biblical drama: *Advent* (his coming), *Christmas* (his birth) *Epiphany* (his manifestation to the world), *Lent* (his lowliness and ministry), *Passion* (his death), *Easter* (his resurrection), and *Pentecost* (his sending of the Spirit and headship over the Church). When understood from an evangelical perspective, the Church Year encourages Christians to practice the spiritual disciplines throughout the year, and to integrate all preaching and activities together for the sake of participating in the life of Christ according to the storyline of the Bible!

TUMI's Annual Theme
As we do every year here at TUMI National, we are encouraging urban churches to follow Christ on the his journey from promise to incarnation to passion to resurrection and ascension through the Christian Year. On our website we are making available a host of resources (e.g., a Christian calendar, original artwork, a daily devotional guide, book readings, info on sermons, retreats, and meditations, etc.) to encourage pastors and their churches to probe the meaning of the Cross as they follow through the seasons of the Church Year. Through our classes, workshops, and consultations we hope to help urban pastors discover the power of a Christ-centered focus of the Church Year, filtered through the lens of the power and wonder of the Cross.

Here are some tips on equipping your Church Planters and disciples in the storyline of Jesus through the Church Year.

Understand the Church Year's Purpose
For centuries, the Christian church has employed the Seasons of the Church Year as a means of focusing on the promise, incarnation, passion, and resurrection of Jesus Christ. Following the Jewish tradition of celebration and festival rooted in Old Testament worship, Christians have used these seasons as a means of marking time, of establishing moments for remembrance, festivals, and holidays, as a way of worshiping God through the Story of Scripture, the hope of glory in our Lord Jesus Christ.

Used at least in part by virtually all traditions of the Church (including Catholic, Orthodox, Anglican, and Protestant traditions), the Christian Church year highlights and follows the prophecy, manifestation, and ministry of Jesus. The unfolding events on the calendar becomes an opportunity for worshipers to hear the prophets herald his coming, to kneel at the manger, to worship Christ with the Magi, and to hear his teaching to the multitudes. Through these events we see our Lord triumphantly come to Jerusalem, stand accused in a sham trial before his foes, be crucified with thieves on Golgotha, and rise from the dead on the third day! From his ascension to the coming of the Holy Spirit, from his exaltation to the mission of his Church in the world, the Church Year reminds us of the that Story which in fact is the Greatest Story Ever Told – the hope of salvation in Christ for the world.

The purpose of the Church Year, then, from ancient times to the present, has been to remember, reenact, and to be transformed by the major events of Jesus' life. In the course of our everyday lives, we redraw and relive the way of Jesus in real time, tracing his birth, death, resurrection, ascension, session and return through the course of the year. Our Church Year Calendar is a remarkable visual presentation of the Christian Year, and includes weekly lectionary texts, major Christian services and holy days, and commentary on their meaning. It is designed specifically to help urban pastors and their congregations avoid the pitfalls of idiosyncratic kinds of emphases that stray from the person of Christ, who is our life and the key to spiritual formation (Col. 3.1-4).

Discipline Your Attention and Practice
The key to character and discipline is focused attention, effort, and energy. Whatever subjects or directions upon which we concentrate our energies and efforts in a deliberate and disciplined manner, we grow and deepen. To use an analogy, honey is gathered by the bee, who draws out of a single blossom all the sweet nectars which it has to offer.

The butterfly, however, which flits around from bush to bush and plant to plant, may cover ground but gathers nothing sweet. In all things spiritual, we ought to strive to be like the bee and not the butterfly!

In all your counseling, prayer, and planning, strive to help your Church Plant Team integrate all of their devotions, preachings, worship liturgies, book readings, and spiritual exercises around the themes of the Church year (and, if you feel so inclined!) our TUMI annual theme. Through the theme, you can better revolve all of your shared spiritual pursuits of the Lord, and encourage each disciple or congregation to select specific missional projects and events consistent with those themes. that we sponsor and host. Each year TUMI creates a comprehensive spiritual formation guide we call our "TUMI Annual." It is a treasury of devotional readings, prayers, spiritual discipline suggestions, chronological Bible readings, and other rich goodies all anchored in the seasons of the Church Year. It is suitable for individuals, groups, and congregations to use and share a spiritual walk that is informed by the Church year, and this year's theme, the Cross.

Help your Church Plant Team to stay focused, to "keep the main thing the main thing" by settling down day by day on the anchored, biblical, and overarching concept that can shape, direction, and substance to their personal and corporate practice of the spiritual disciplines.

Focus on Christ
Finally, an evangelical appropriation of the Church Year will unashamedly focus on Christ. As Paul could say to the Corinthians, "He is the source of your life in Christ Jesus, whom God made our wisdom and our righteousness and sanctification and redemption" (1 Cor. 1.30, ESV). In the history of the Christian Church, no other story, no other event, no other symbol has been so integral and definitive to our faith, devotion, and worship as the Cross. Over the centuries this visual representation of the Tree on which our Savior died for the sins of the world has become arguably Christianity's signature and primary image. This year, we will explore not only the bare facts (as listed above) but also explore the larger sense of what it means for the redeemed to be identified with Jesus in his suffering and death, and in his resurrection and new life. Indeed, both the start and continuation of Christian discipleship (from our confession of faith and baptism, to carrying our Cross daily and following our Master), depend on our understanding and appropriating the power of the Cross in our lives. This is why Paul the apostle can center his gospel ministry on the proclamation of the Cross to his various audiences: "For I decided to know nothing among you except Jesus Christ and him crucified" (1 Cor. 2.2.).

The Church Year: Your Invitation to a Shared Spiritual Journey
Do not be afraid, especially if this emphasis on the Church Year seems overwhelming! It is being practiced as the ground of spiritual formation by hundreds of thousands of congregations on every continent where the Church worships Christ. Begin small; go to our website and explore the abundant resources we have on this subject, and see how helpful a Christ-centered, biblically based spiritual formation informed by the Church Year can be to eliminate the distraction and confusion in both pulpit and pew today in so many of our urban congregations and Christian families.

Forming the Church Plant Team and Understanding the Roles

Excerpted from *The Nehemiah Team Training Materials*

I. **The Team (four types of members)**

   A. Core members (the primary job of the core member is church planting): four to six people

      1. Meet for planning, outreach, and worship at least two weekday evenings and some weekend time

      2. Stay in active service with the team for a minimum of two years

      3. Called by God and willing to engage in cross-cultural evangelism

      4. The team leader must be a core team member

   B. Support team members

      1. Stay in active service for a minimum of 3 months

      2. Meet weekly with the team for planning and prayer

      3. Give at least one weekday evening and/or some weekend time to serve church plant

   C. Volunteers: Individuals or groups

      1. Serve as needed on a project-by-project basis

      2. Are invited to planning meetings and projects that pertain to them, but do not function as week-to-week team members

   D. Indigenous leaders

      1. The goal of all core team members, support team members and volunteers is replacement by indigenous leadership.

      2. The team function moves from doing to equipping.

3. As the church plant progresses, more and more of the team becomes people won to Christ during the church planting process.

   a. Avoid dependency.

   b. Think reproducibility.

II. Leadership of the Team

A. The leader of the church plant team is appointed by the leadership of the sending church.

   1. He or she is co-leader with World Impact's staff member assigned to lead the team through the church planting process. Together they:

      a. Lead the team in prayer, strategy formulation, execution of plans, and evaluation of progress

      b. Train the team

      c. Regularly inform sending church and World Impact of progress and needs

   2. Specific responsibilities of team leader:

      a. Facilitate meetings

      b. Make sure that there is excellent communication among the team

      c. Maintain excellent communication with leadership of sending church regarding progress and needs

      d. Meet regularly with World Impact coach (separate from the team)

      e. Provide pastoral care for team members

      f. Maintain team unity

      g. Provide leadership for the church that is planted (assume role as pastor) until replacement is trained

B. Specific responsibilities of World Impact coach:

1. Train the team in principles of urban church planting

2. Provide practical ongoing guidance for how to accomplish each step of the church planting process

3. Meet regularly with team leader

4. Provide expert counsel to team in planning meetings

5. Help the team execute plans

6. Help the team evaluate programs and make adjustments

7. Help team utilize World Impact support ministries for enhancing their church planting efforts

C. The sending church is ultimately responsible for the spiritual accountability and oversight of their appointed leader and church plant members.

D. The core members, support members, volunteer members, and indigenous leaders will be expected to submit to the authority of the team leader and the World Impact coach.

III. Beginning Activities to Build Team Cohesion

A. Get to know each other.

1. Eat together.

2. Share testimonies.

3. Share individual visions.

4. Pray for each other.

5. Retreat together.

B. Work on forging a common vision and strategy for this project and training each team member to articulate it.

C. Pray together for the target community.

1. Pray for the establishment of God's Church and Kingdom.

2. Pray against strongholds of evil.

D. Worship God corporately.

Discipling the Faithful
Establishing Leaders for the Urban Church
Rev. Dr. Don L. Davis

	Commission	Character	Competence	Community
Definition	Recognizes *the call of God* and replies with prompt obedience to his lordship and leading	Reflects *the character of Christ* in his/her personal convictions, conduct, and lifestyle	Responds in *the power of the Spirit* with excellence in carrying out their appointed tasks and ministry	Regards multiplying disciples in *the body of Christ* as the primary role of ministry
Key Scripture	2 Tim. 1.6-14; 1 Tim. 4.14; Acts 1.8; Matt. 28.18-20	John 15.4-5; 2 Tim. 2.2; 1 Cor. 4.2; Gal. 5.16-23	2 Tim. 2.15; 3.16-17; Rom. 15.14; 1 Cor. 12	Eph. 4.9-15; 1 Cor. 12.1-27
Critical Concept	The Authority of **God**: God's leader acts on God's recognized call and authority, acknowledged by the saints and God's leaders	The Humility of **Christ**: God's leader demonstrates the mind and lifestyle of Christ in his or her actions and relationships	The Power of the **Spirit**: God's leader operates in the gifting and anointing of the Holy Spirit	The Growth of the **Church**: God's leader uses all of his or her resources to equip and empower the body of Christ for his/her goal and task
Central Elements	A clear call from God Authentic testimony before God and others Deep sense of personal conviction based on Scripture Personal burden for a particular task or people Confirmation by leaders and the body	Passion for Christlikeness Radical lifestyle for the Kingdom Serious pursuit of holiness Discipline in the personal life Fulfills role-relationships and bond-slave of Jesus Christ Provides an attractive model for others in their conduct, speech, and lifestyle (the fruit of the Spirit)	Endowments and gifts from the Spirit Sound discipling from an able mentor Skill in the spiritual disciplines Ability in the Word Able to evangelize, follow up, and disciple new converts Strategic in the use of resources and people to accomplish God's task	Genuine love for and desire to serve God's people Disciples faithful individuals Facilitates growth in small groups Pastors and equips believers in the congregation Nurtures associations and networks among Christians and churches Advances new movements among God's people locally
Satanic Strategy to Abort	Operates on the basis of personality or position rather than on God's appointed call and ongoing authority	Substitutes ministry activity and/or hard work and industry for godliness and Christlikeness	Functions on natural gifting and personal ingenuity rather than on the Spirit's leading and gifting	Exalts tasks and activities above equipping the saints and developing Christian community
Key Steps	Identify God's call Discover your burden Be confirmed by leaders	Abide in Christ Discipline for godliness Pursue holiness in all	Discover the Spirit's gifts Receive excellent training Hone your performance	Embrace God's Church Learn leadership's contexts Equip concentrically
Results	Deep confidence in God arising from God's call	Powerful Christlike example provided for others to follow	Dynamic working of the Holy Spirit	Multiplying disciples in the Church

Spiritual Service Checklist

Rev. Dr. Don L. Davis

1. *Salvation*: Has this person believed the Gospel, confessed Jesus as Lord and Savior, been baptized, and formally joined our church as a member?

2. *Personal integrity*: Are they walking with God, growing in their personal life, and demonstrating love and faithfulness in their family, work, and in the community?

3. *Equipped in the Word*: How equipped is this person in the Word of God to share and teach with others?

4. *Support of our church*: Do they support the church through their presence, prayer for the leaders and members, and give financially to its support?

5. *Submission to authority*: Does this person joyfully submit to spiritual authority?

6. *Identification of spiritual gifts*: What gifts, talents, abilities, or special resources does this person have for service, and what is their paritcular burden for ministry now?

7. *Present availability*: Are they open to be assigned to a task or project where we could use their service to build up the body?

8. *Reputation amongst leaders*: How do the other leaders feel about this person's readiness for a new role of leadership?

9. *Resources needed to accomplish*: If appointed to this role, what particular training, monies, resources, and/or input will they need to accomplish the task?

10. *Formal commissioning*: When and how will we make known to others that we have appointed this person to their task or project?

11. *Timing and reporting*: Also, if we dedicate this person to this role/task, when will they be able to start, and how long ought they serve before we evaluate them.

12. *Evaluate and re-commission*: When will we evaluate the performance of the person, and determine what next steps we ought to take in their leadership role at the church?

Models of Church Planting

Overview PLANT to Birth Models

Rev. Dr. Don L. Davis

World Impact Model	Phases of Church Planting Compared to Childbirth	Emphasis During Particular Phase of Childbearing
Prepare	Commitment to Parent	Commitment to give birth and to parent secured from qualified parents
	Conception	Core team, volunteers gathered/prepared, parenting church engaged, target population and community selected, studied, canvassed
Launch	Prenatal Care	Ongoing outreach, small group community, structured in-reach of nucleus
Assemble	Birth	Announcement of Public Gathering and Worship, Celebration of gathered groups
Nurture	Growth toward Maturity	Building foundations, developing vital ministries, forming systems, achieving leadership autonomy
Transition	Reproduction	Congregational "adulthood," new church as Kingdom outpost: spiritual DNA planting new congregations

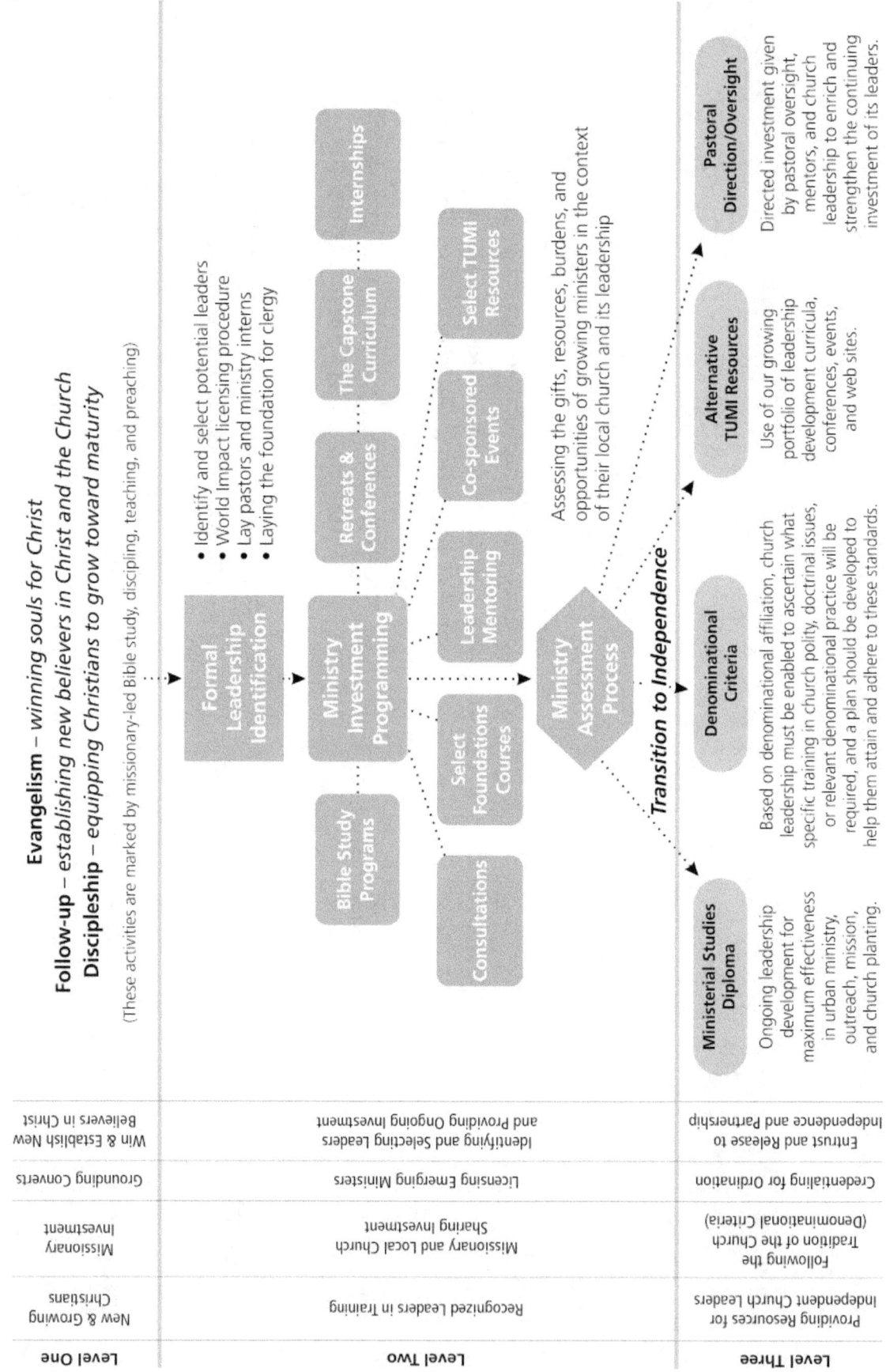

Six Types of Neighborhoods

Warren & Warren. 1977. *The Neighborhood Organizer's Handbook*. Notre Dame, Indiana: University of Notre Dame Press, pp. 96-97

Integral
A cosmopolitan as well as a local center. Individuals are in close contact. They share many concerns. They participate in activities of the larger community.

Parochial
A neighborhood having a strong ethnic identity or homogeneous character. Self-contained, independent of larger community. Has ways to screen out what does not conform to its own norms.

Diffuse
Often homogeneous setting ranging from a new subdivision to an inner city housing project. Has many things in common. However, there is no active internal life. Little local involvement with neighbors.

Stepping Stone
An active neighborhood. A game of "musical chairs." People participate in neighborhood activities because they identify with the neighborhood but often to "get ahead" in a career or some other nonlocal point of destination.

Transitory
A neighborhood where population change has been or is occurring. Often breaks up into little clusters of people – frequently "old-timers" and newcomers are separated. Little collective action or organization takes place.

Anomic
It's really a non-neighborhood. Highly atomized; no cohesion. Great social distance between people. No protective barriers to outside influences making it responsive to some outside change. It lacks the capacity to mobilize for common actions from within.

Advancing the Kingdom in the City
Multiplying Congregations with a Common Identity
Rev. Dr. Don L. Davis • *Winning the World: Facilitating Urban Church Planting Movements. Foundations for Ministry Series.* Wichita: The Urban Ministry Institute, 2007.

> Acts 2.41-47 (ESV) – So those who received his word were baptized, and there were added that day about three thousand souls. [42] And they devoted themselves to the apostles' teaching and fellowship, to the breaking of bread and the prayers. [43] And awe came upon every soul, and many wonders and signs were being done through the apostles. [44] *And all who believed were together and had all things in common.* [45] And they were selling their possessions and belongings and distributing the proceeds to all, as any had need. [46] And day by day, attending the temple together and breaking bread in their homes, they received their food with glad and generous hearts, [47] praising God and having favor with all the people. *And the Lord added to their number day by day those who were being saved.*

koinonia (pronunciation: [koy-nohn-ee'-ah])

Trinitarian Principle: Unity • Diversity • Equality

World Impact seeks to plant churches that are kingdom-oriented communities where Christ is exalted as Lord and the Kingdom of God is advanced in every facet of community life, and, we seek to do this in a way that respects and acknowledges the validity and significance of incarnating this community life in the receiving culture. In order to ensure the viability, protection, and flourishing of these congregations, we ought to explore forming close-knit associations between congregations where a common identity, confession, and faith are practiced, under a common oversight and governance, that connects in a fundamental way the resources and visions of each church without lording over them.

Following is a chart that sketches what might be the elements of such a common coalition of churches which would link their lives in a strategic way for the well-being and enrichment of the entire fellowship of churches. (Cf. *Imagining a Unified, Connected C1 Church Planting Movement* [see www.tumi.org/Capstone under the header *Appendices*] which in a comprehensive way suggests what may be included along ecclesial and missional, liturgical, and catechetical lines in such a fellowship).

Sharing a Common Identity, Purpose, and Mission	
A Common Name and Association	Understanding the churches as fundamentally linked in history, identity, legacy, and destiny
A Common Confession of Faith	Developing a common theological and doctrinal vision
A Common Celebration and Worship	Practicing a common liturgy with shared worship approaches
A Common Discipleship and Catechism	Sharing a common curriculum and process for welcoming, incorporating, and discipling new believers into our fellowship
A Common Governance and Oversight	Answering to a common accountability for leadership and care
A Common Service and Missionary Outreach	Developing integrated processes and programs of justice, good works, outreach, evangelism, and missions, both at home and throughout the world
A Common Stewardship and Partnership	Combining resources through consistent mutual contribution to maximize impact for the entire association

Benefits of a Common Movement
1. Sense of belonging through a shared faith and identity
2. Efficiency and economy of effort
3. Ability to plant multiple plants in many different venues and populations
4. Cultivating genuine unity and diversity, with a spirit of mutuality and equality among the congregations
5. Increased productivity and viability within our missions efforts and churches
6. Interchangability and cross pollination
7. Ongoing support and encouragement of our leaders
8. Provide leverage for new projects and new initiatives
9. Standardized processes and procedures for incorporation and training

10. Greater opportunities for convocation and exposure to other like-minded believers
11. Exploration of new connections with other associations with similar vision
12. Assistance in jump starting WI RMO spirituality and unity

Church Planting Models

Rev. Dr. Don L. Davis

The following models represent a spectrum of models which have been associated with evangelical church planting. Questions are designed to help us explore the various options available to the cross-cultural urban church planter in establishing congregations among the poor. Our dialogue today hopefully will isolate some of the critical issues necessary for a church plant team to think through in order to make its selection as to what particular kind of church they ought to plant, given the culture, population, and other factors encountered in its particular mission field.

1. What is the definition of the phrase "church planting models"? Why might it be important to consider various options in planting a church among the poor in the city?

2. How would you characterize the various models (or other) which have been allowed or employed in traditional church planting? What would you consider to be its strengths and/or weaknesses, and should we use any of them in our planting of churches among the poor in the city?

    a. Founding Pastor Model – a leader moves into a community with a commitment to lead and shepherd the church that is planted.

    b. Church Split Model?! – a new church is formed due to fundamental disagreement over some issue of morality, Bible interpretation, or schism.

    c. Nucleus Model – (sometimes referred to as the "colonization" model). This model involves a central assembly commissioning a smaller nucleus from its group (usually with leadership and members already organized) to leave the larger assembly and relocate into an unreached community as a kind of ready-made nucleus of the church which is to be formed.

    d. Beachhead or Mother Church Model – a strong, central congregation determines to become a kind of sending center and nurturing headquarters for new churches planted through its oversight and auspices, in the immediate area and/or beyond.

e. Cell Church Model – once centralized assembly which considers the heart of its life and ministry to occur in the cells which are connected structurally and pastorally to the central congregation; their participation together constitutes the church.

f. Home Church Model – a church, which although similar to a cell church model, is intentionally planted with greater attention given to the authority and autonomy of the gathering of Christians who meet regularly in their respective homes.

g. Missionary Model – a church where a cross-cultural church planter seeks to plant a church among an unreached people with an intent from the beginning to help the church to be self-propagating, self-governing, and self-supporting.

3. Instead of models language, World Impact recognizes three distinct "expressions" of church planting, out of which various models can be considered and employed.

The Small Church Expression (or "house church," 20-50 people). The small (or house) church can be understood as a *small store in a shopping mall*. Needs the connections to other small churches to both survive and thrive. Small churches are able to meet virtually anywhere and can operate with a tiny footprint with little to no financial burdens. They can focus on a specific block, housing development, or network of families. This expressions allows for a strong discipleship focus of indigenous leadership development can take place in this smaller connected group.

The Community Church Expression (60-150 people)
The community church is the most common expression of church, numerically speaking, in the world today. This expression can be understood as a *grocery or convenience store in a neighborhood or community*. This expression focuses on a particular geographic identity and proximity, highlighting both the, affinity, connection, and unique context of the congregation and the surrounding community. It is developed around a deep calling and connection to a particular neighborhood, and typically requires a semi-stable place to meet (e.g., a park, community center, or school). Partnership with other community churches is important.

The Mother Church Expression (200+ people)
The mother church (or "hub church") represents a larger assembly of believers, and can be understood as *a Walmart Superstore or Super*

Target, a store which houses a number of select entities that supply its patrons with many choices and opportunities. This kind of church, which has both the economic and spiritual resources for multiplication, can leverage its resources and capabilities to become both a sending/empowering church which reproduces itself many times over. Ideally, a mother or hub church is a congregation that is led by clear missional intents that allow it to leverages its capabilities and gifts to become a center of compassion, mercy, and justice ministries. It can also come to serve as the nurturing headquarters for church planters and ministry starters, and can easily operate as an incubator of other effective ministries among the unreached urban poor. Such an expression usually is more rooted in a particular built-to-suit facility that allows it to leverage these kinds of capabilities.

4. What are the critical issues (e.g., culture, the tradition of the church planters, and contextualization) which ought to be factored most into selecting the appropriate model or expression for use in planting a church cross-culturally in the city?

5. Of all the things which a church planter may be aware of, what do you believe is the central element he or she must understand in order to choose the "right" option for them?

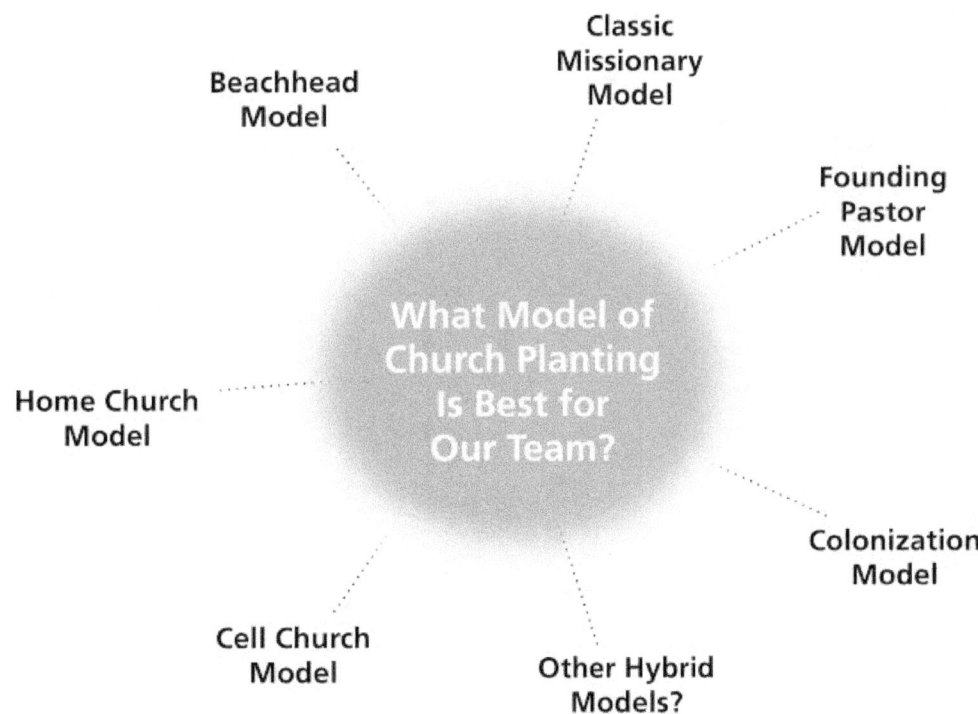

Overview of Church Plant Planning Phases

Rev. Dr. Don L. Davis

	Prepare	Launch	Assemble	Nurture	Transition
Definition	Forming a team of called members who ready themselves to plant a church under the Holy Spirit's direction	Penetrating the selected community by conducting evangelistic events among the target population	Gathering the cells of converts together to form a local assembly of believers, announcing the new church to the neighbors in the community	Nurturing member and leadership discipleship, enabling members to function in their spiritual gifts, and establishing solid infrastructure within the Christian assembly	Empowering the church for independence by equipping leaders for autonomy, transferring authority, and creating structures for financial independence
Purpose	Seek God regarding the target population and community, the formation of your church plant team, organizing strategic intercession for the community, and doing research on its needs and opportunities	Mobilize team and recruit volunteers to conduct ongoing evangelistic events and holistic outreach to win associates and neighbors to Christ	Form cell groups, Bible studies, or home fellowships for follow-up, continued evangelism, and ongoing growth toward public birth of the church	Develop individual and group discipleship by filling key roles in the body based on burden and gifting of members	Commission members and elders, install pastor, and foster church associations
Parent-Child Metaphor	Decision and Conception	Pre-natal Care	Childbirth	Growth and Parenting	Maturity to Adulthood
Question Focus During Dialogue	Questions about: • Preparing your team • The target community • Strategic prayer initiatives • Demographic studies	Questions about: • Character and number of evangelistic events • Communication and advertisement of events • Recruiting and coordinating volunteers • Identity and name of the outreach	Questions about: • Follow-up and incorporation of new believers • Make-up of small group life • The character of public worship • Initial church structures and procedures • Initial body life and growth • Cultural friendliness of church	Questions about: • Discipling individuals and leaders • Helping members identify gifts and burdens (teams) • Credentials for leadership • Church order, government and discipline	Questions about: • Incorporation • Affiliations and associations • Transferring leadership • Missionary transition • Ongoing reproduction
Cardinal Virtue	Openness to the Lord	Courage to engage the community	Wisdom to discern God's timing	Focus upon the faithful core	Dependence on the Spirit's ability
Cardinal Vices	Presumption and "paralysis of analysis"	Intimidation and haughtiness	Impatience and cowardice	Neglect and micromanagement	Paternalism and quick release
Bottom Line	Cultivate a period of listening and reflecting	Initiate your engagement with boldness and confidence	Celebrate the announcement of your body with joy	Concentrate on investing in the faithful	Pass the baton with confidence in the Spirit's continued working

The Role of Women in Ministry

Rev. Dr. Don L. Davis • *Focus on Reproduction. Module 12, The Capstone Curriculum.*
Wichita: The Urban Ministry Institute, 2005

While it is clear that God has established a clearly designed order of responsibility within the home, it is equally clear that women are called and gifted by God, led by his own Spirit to bear fruit worthy of their calling in Christ. Throughout the NT, commands are directed specifically to women to submit, with the particular Greek verb *hupotasso*, occurring frequently which means "to place under" or "to submit" (cf. 1 Tim. 2.11). The word also translated into our English word "subjection" is from the same root. In such contexts these Greek renderings ought not to be understood in any way except as positive admonitions towards God's designed framework for the home, where women are charged to learn quietly and submissively, trusting and working within the Lord's own plan.

This ordering of the woman's submission in the home, however, must not be misinterpreted to mean that women are disallowed from ministering their gifts under the Spirit's direction. Indeed, it is the Holy Spirit through Christ's gracious endowment who assigns the gifts as he wills, for the edification of the Church (1 Cor. 12.1-27; Eph. 4.1-16). The gifts are not given to believers on the criteria of gender; in other words, there is no indication from the Scriptures that some gifts are for men only, and the others reserved for women. On the contrary, Paul affirms that Christ provided gifts as a direct result of his own personal victory over the devil and his minions (cf. Eph. 4.6ff). This was his own personal choice, given by his Spirit to whomever he wills (cf. 1 Cor. 12.1-11). In affirming the ministry of women we affirm the right of the Spirit to be creative in all saints for the well-being of all and the expansion of his Kingdom, as he sees fit, and not necessarily as we determine (Rom. 12.4-8; 1 Pet. 4.10-11).

Furthermore, a careful study of the Scriptures as a whole indicates that God's ordering of the home in no way undermines his intention for men and women to serve Christ as disciples and laborers together, under Christ's leading. The clear NT teaching of Christ as head of the man, and the man of the woman (see 1 Cor. 11.4) shows God's esteem for godly spiritual representation within the home. The apparent forbidding of women to hold teaching/ruling positions appears to be an admonition to protect God's assigned lines of responsibility and authority within the home. For instance, the particular Greek term in the highly debated passage in 1 Tim. 2.12, *andros*, which has often times been translated "man," may also be translated "husband." With such a translation, then, the teaching would be that a wife ought not to rule over her husband.

This doctrine of a woman who, in choosing to marry, makes herself voluntarily submissive to "line up under" her husband is entirely consistent with the gist of the NT teaching on the role of authority in the Christian home. The Greek word *hupotasso*, which means to "line up under" refers to a wife's voluntary submission to her own husband (cf. Eph. 5.22, 23; Col. 3.18; Titus 2.5; 1 Pet. 3.1). This has nothing to do with any supposed superior status or capacity of the husband; rather, this refers to God's design of godly headship, authority which is given for comfort, protection, and care, not for destruction or domination (cf. Gen. 2.15-17; 3.16; 1 Cor. 11.3). Indeed, that this headship is interpreted in light of Christ's headship over the church signifies the kind of godly headship that must be given, that sense of tireless care, service, and protection required from godly leadership.

Of course, such an admonition for a wife to submit to a husband would not in any way rule out that women be involved in a teaching ministry (e.g., Titus 2.4), but, rather, that in the particular case of married women, that their own ministries would come under the protection and direction of their respective husbands (Acts 18.26). This would assert that a married woman's ministry in the church would be given serving, protective oversight by her husband, not due to any notion of inferior capacity or defective spirituality, but for the sake of, as one commentator has put it, "avoiding confusion and maintaining orderliness" (cf. 1 Cor. 14.40).

In both Corinth and Ephesus (which represent the contested Corinthian and Timothy epistolary comments), it appears that Paul's restriction upon women's participation was prompted by occasional happenings, issues which grew particularly out of these contexts, and therefore are meant to be understood in those lights. For instance, the hotly contested test of a women's "silence" in the church (see both 1 Cor. 14 and 1 Tim. 2) does not appear in any way to undermine the prominent role women played in the expansion of the Kingdom and development of the church in the first century. Women were involved in the ministries of prophecy and prayer (1 Cor. 11.5), personal instruction (Acts 18.26), teaching (Titus 2.4,5), giving testimony (John 4.28,29), offering hospitality (Acts 12.12), and serving as co-laborers with the apostles in the cause of the Gospel (Phil. 4.2-3). Paul did not relegate women to an inferior role or hidden status but served side-by-side with women for the sake of Christ "I urge Euodia and I urge Syntyche to live in harmony in the Lord. Indeed, true companion, I ask you also to help these women who have shared my struggle in the *cause of* the gospel, together with Clement also and the rest of my fellow workers, whose names are in the book of life" (Phil. 4.2-3).

Furthermore, we must be careful in subordinating the personage of women *per se* (that is, their nature as women) versus their subordinated role in the marriage relationship. Notwithstanding the clear description of the role of women as heirs together of the grace of life in the marriage relationship (1 Pet. 3.7), it is equally plain that the Kingdom of God has created a dramatic shift in how women are to be viewed, understood, and embraced in the Kingdom community. It is plain that in Christ there is now no difference between rich and poor, Jew and Gentile, barbarian, Scythian, bondman and freemen, as well as man and woman (cf. Gal. 3.28; Col. 3.11). Women were allowed to be disciples of a Rabbi (which was foreign and disallowed at the time of Jesus), and played prominent roles in the NT church, including being fellow laborers side by side with the apostles in ministry (e.g., see Euodia and Syntyche in Phil. 4.1ff), as well as hosting a church in their houses (cf. Phoebe in Rom. 16.1-2, and Apphia in Philem. 1).

In regards to the issue of pastoral authority, I am convinced that Paul's understanding of the role of equippers (of which the pastor-teacher is one such role, cf. Eph. 4.9-15) is not gender specific. In other words, the decisive and seminal text for me on the operation of gifts and the status and function of offices are those NT texts which deal with the gifts (1 Cor. 12.1-27; Rom. 12.4-8; 1 Pet. 4.10-11, and Eph. 4.9-15). There is no indication in any of these formative texts that gifts are gender-specific. In other words, for the argument to hold decisively that women were never to be in roles that were pastoral or equipping in nature, the simplest and most effective argument would be to show that the Spirit simply would never even consider giving a woman a gift which was not suited to the range of callings which she felt a calling towards. Women would be forbidden from leadership because the Holy Spirit would never grant to a woman a calling and its requisite gifts because she was a woman. Some gifts would be reserved for men, and women would never receive those gifts.

A careful reading of these and other related texts show no such prohibition. It appears that it is up to the Holy Spirit to give any person, man or woman, any gift that suits him for any ministry he wishes them to do, as he wills (1 Cor. 12.11 "But one and the same Spirit works all these things, distributing to each one individually as he wills"). Building upon this point, Terry Cornett has even written a fine theological essay showing how the NT Greek for the word "apostle" is unequivocally applied to women, most clearly shown in the rendering of the female noun, "Junia" applied to "apostle" in Romans 16.7, as well as allusions to co-laboring, for instance, with the twins, Tryphena and Tryphosa, who "labored" with Paul in the Lord (16.12).

Believing that every God-called, Christ-endowed, and Spirit-gifted and led Christian ought to fulfill their role in the body, we affirm the role of women to lead and instruct under godly authority that submits to the Holy Spirit, the Word of God, and is informed by the tradition of the Church and spiritual reasoning. We ought to expect God to give women supernatural endowments of grace to carry out his bidding on behalf of his Church, and his reign in the Kingdom of God. Since both men and women both reflect the *Imago Dei* (i.e., image of God), and both stand as heirs together of God's grace (cf. Gen. 1.27; 5.2; Matt. 19.4; Gal. 3.28; 1 Pet. 3.7), they are given the high privilege of representing Christ together as his ambassadors (2 Cor. 5.20), and through their partnership to bring to completion our obedience to Christ's Great Commission of making disciples of all nations (Matt. 28.18-20).

Ordination of Women Q and A

Rev. Dr. Don L. Davis

Question

Hello Dr. Davis! I am writing you to get your insights into ordination, particularly ordination of women. We are privileged to have a strong sister who is a member of our congregation, who is a committed worker here at our church and is incredibly dedicated to building God's kingdom!

We understand it would be advantageous for her if she was ordained; it would help her navigate through the secular areas where she ministers without so much difficultly. We are wrestling with the issue of what the Scriptures teach regarding women being ordained, and in particular leadership over men. Our church is closely associated with a more conservative church movement, and it is not typical for us to ordain women (none of our other churches have done this that I can recall), but if we are only doing so because of tradition, we are open to examining the Scriptures to see this issue more clearly.

Please share with us (the elders of our church) your understanding of this issue. God will use this sister regardless of any titles she is given by men; we only want to do what glorifies God and pleases Him!

Answer

Thank you so much for your note on ordination, and, more specifically, on the ordination of women. Being a part of a historically Black denomination, as well as an inter-denominational urban missions organization, I have been a part of and am aware of evangelical communions which wholeheartedly affirm a more egalitarian understanding (over against a more complimentarian vision) of the role of women in ministry, specifically in both missions and church polity. In the AME church (African Methodist Episcopal communion) in which I was raised, the ordination of women was a fundament in its clergy life, being a denomination that was deeply informed from the 18th century onwards by the black-white disparity in American society, and the recognition of godly, gifted, and anointed females whom the communion assessed to be able and willing to accept the role of pastoral care.

Even in light of this, I totally appreciate your questions, issues, and concerns about women being ordained, and, as this is a question where Bible-believing evangelicals have sparred over for many years, I hope my opinion and input can bring at least the evidence and arguments for my view. You will find attached a document that we use routinely in our TUMI training entitled "The Role of Women in Ministry" which lays out transparently our notion of women spirituality and ministry. Essentially, we argue that with the coming of our Lord and the transformation and union with Christ of all who believe, the traditional societal roles of class, gender, and race have been superseded. Now in Christ "There is neither Jew nor Greek, there is neither slave[a] nor free, there is no male and female, for you are all one in Christ Jesus" Galatians 3.28. In the body of Christ now "Here there is not Greek and Jew, circumcised and uncircumcised, barbarian, Scythian, slave, free; but Christ is all, and in all" (Col. 3.11). As the key foundational texts on the nature of difference in culture and gender, these texts are read as exegetical lens to think critically over the controversial texts in the NT which seem to restrict the roles of women in ministry, most specifically 1 Timothy 2 and 1 Cor. 14.

Rather than retrace the argument already made in the essay, let me summarize by saying the issue for me has been less of the role of women in ministry as the freedom of the Holy Spirit. 1 Corinthians 12 is clear that the Holy Spirit. Excuse me while I insert the verses 4-11:

> Now there are varieties of gifts, but the same Spirit; and there are varieties of service, but the same Lord; and there are varieties of activities, but it is the same God who empowers them all in everyone. To each is given the manifestation of the Spirit for the common good. For to one is given through the Spirit the utterance of wisdom, and to another the utterance of knowledge according to the same Spirit, to another faith by the same Spirit, to another gifts of healing by the one Spirit, to another the working of miracles, to another prophecy, to another the ability to distinguish between spirits, to another various kinds of tongues, to another the interpretation of tongues. All these are empowered by one and the same Spirit, who apportions to each one individually as he wills.

This last verse, "All these are empowered by one and the same Spirit, who apportions to each one individually as he wills" is decisive for me in this issue. The Holy Spirit is free, able to apportion to any individual any endowment, gift, calling, or dispensation he desires, based solely on his sovereign grace and election. None of the gifts or offices are restricted per se to any person of any gender, meaning in my reading that the Spirit may confer on any believer any gifting or charismata he chooses. Women are heirs together of God's grace, able to receive and therefore exercise whatever gift the Spirit provides. The issue is not whether women are categorically restricted because of gender from certain callings; the plain readings of the text put the ability to use a gift in the Spirit's election, not in the believer's gender.

I go into depth in these questions in the essay, and it deals specifically into the questions of women not speaking in church, or exercising authority over men, which frankly, I believe are more rightly understood in the context of the Ephesian and Corinthian contexts rather than binding principles for all time on the church through this age. For what it is, I seek to address these and other issues in the short essay, and I trust you will find it helpful.

Thanks so much for your gracious and warm offer to dialogue and share our views. I have always chuckled at our evangelical sensibilities; we rarely if ever challenge women's roles in ministry on the mission field, but we enthusiastically challenge them in our own back yards! I have sought over the years to consistently embrace the role of the Spirit's freedom and our union with Christ, and building on those foundational truths.

Defining the Leaders and Members of a Church Plant Team
World Impact, Inc.

CD - City Director   TL - Team Leader   MTL - Multiple Team Leader   CPT - Church Plant Team

	Church Plant Team Member	**Church Plant Team Leader**	**Multiple Team Leader**
Definition	Member of cross-cultural church planting team	Leader of cross-cultural church planting team	Facilitator and coordinator of multiple church planting teams
Responsibility	To employ gifts to enhance the ministry of the team as it plants a viable church	To facilitate and manage the effective operation of the team in order to plant a church	To provide counsel, resources, and support to all teams in a given area
Training	Church Plant School, initial training, ongoing team input (John Mark Curriculum)	Specialized training curriculum, personal mentoring and TUMI	TUMI course work, regional training, and specialized input
Accountable to Whom?	Team Leader	City Director (support from MTL)	City Director and Regional VP
Time Commitments	Accredited to plant for specified period of charter as primary or support member	Throughout the duration of the church plant's charter	Regular review and substantive ministry assessment at end of CPT Time
Resources	Church Plant School, Team members and leaders, CPT "kit"	Team members, ministry budget, access to MTL and City Director	Transportation to CPTs, access to City Director and Regional VP
Authority	To pursue those steps necessary to evangelize, disciple, and plant	To lead the team in all of its operations as it seeks to plant a church in a given period of time	To support the team during its charter, and decide whether at the end the plant warrants further time and effort
Assignment	By CD and TL for particular time and role	By CD for duration of the church plant	By CD and Regional VP as they determine necessary
Composition	Primary members, support members, and/or volunteers	Individual or co-leaders	Individual selected by CD and Regional VP

Engaging the Community

Selecting a Target Area
Bryan Cullison

I had the luxury of a clean slate and no expectations when I began the process of picking an area to start in. I had no team members and no idea where to start. I knew only that we were to go into an area where we had done no previous ministry, both for the sake of branching out as a ministry where we had done 90% of our work within about a one-square-mile radius, and also as a bold statement that testified to our staff the seriousness of our vision to plant churches across Los Angeles County wherever the urban poor were. I was frustrated and convicted that we as a ministry talked about the abundance of people groups in Los Angeles and how the world had come to our doorstep, yet we were only in reality ministering to a fraction of these people groups, rendering those statistics interesting at best and misleading at worst.

At the Timothy Conference in July of 2002, I met a young woman on staff in Wichita named Stacy Waddle who had lived and ministered in the Hollywood area. Stacy was a wealth of information on the ins and outs of that community, its flavor, essence, spiritual climate, needs, history, direction, people groups, demographics, and physical structures. More importantly, she displayed an infectious burden for the city of Hollywood, one that my heart was already feeling previous to meeting her. She painted quite an attractive picture for me, citing the diversity of the area, the plentiful and rich opportunities to develop relationships through the means of basketball (my best and favorite sport) with the young men, and the obvious favor towards media (my other passion) that would be particularly relevant and useful in reaching non-Christians there. I returned to Los Angeles after the conference with an excitement to learn as much as I could about the Hollywood community, prematurely committing my heart to this area without going through the necessary steps of seeking God's heart or doing the legwork or academic research to validate the choice. Through wise leadership, I was compelled to pull back a bit and go through some more formal decision-making in committing to an area where the ministry as a whole would be investing for such a long time in the future. I am thankful for that.

So, at this point I had identified Hollywood as one possibility. I was also given the suggestion of an area just northeast of the LA Office which was particularly dense and close to our ministry center which could capitalize on the resources already available and established here. A major street running through the middle of this second area was Westmoreland Avenue, so this area was dubbed Westmoreland for reference purposes.

The next step was to develop a few more possibilities based on the criteria that were suggested to me by Fred Stoesz, my MTL, and Tim Goddu, my City Director. The two driving characteristics we were seeking in a community were that they be both dense in population and poor. Using these as standards, I began researching Census 2000 data for a period of approximately a week on the Internet. Considering all 2054 census tracts in Los Angeles County, I eliminated all those tracts not containing 30% or more families in poverty and 23,000 or more people per square mile. This reduced the number to approximately 250 tracts for each category. I then tightened the standard to 45% or more families in poverty and 50,000 people per square mile, which effectively isolated the top 1-2% of all census tracts in LA County for each category. Having this, I cross-referenced each list to see which tracts fit both standards. Three new clusters of census tracts emerged, giving me three areas in the county to consider. Two of them were on either side of Vermont Avenue on the north end of Koreatown. Due to the number of businesses and a street near both of these areas named Shatto, I labeled these two areas West Shatto and East Shatto. The third area was in Long Beach.

I now had five total areas born of personal experience, reference, suggestion, and research. Out of these five areas there were 26 census tracts represented. These 26 census tracts were compared and ranked against each other in the following categories:

- population
- population density
- ethnicity
- number of households
- number of families
- number of housing units
- transiency
- English proficiency levels
- household income level
- % earning wages
- per capita income
- % in poverty
- occupancy status
- gross rent

With each category weighted according to our standards of desirability in what we were looking for (i.e. high in population, poor, low transiency, low gross rent), a rank was assigned to each tract so the 5 areas could distinguish themselves from each other. Now, what was God doing in these areas? Church planting is more an art than a science, and to go about this spiritual work in a completely cerebral fashion would be folly. To see what God was doing in these communities would take some footwork, personal observation, prayerwalking, discernment, and guidance from him. The first step was to explore each area and recognize/map where the schools, churches, and social service centers were. This would give a great picture into the health, cohesiveness, and activity of a community. After a fairly thorough foray into each neighborhood, I had a good idea of how churched each area was.

Seeing in West Shatto an area almost entirely comprised of Koreans with a glut of Korean churches (many of which had been some other church previously), I had a good idea that, although this fit our criteria of urban poor, dense, and statistically desirable, it did not have a high need for more church plants. Had these been African-American churches or Latino storefront churches, I would have come to a different conclusion, but these Korean churches would most certainly be more effective in reaching their neighborhood than a new church plant by a Caucasian missionary who did not speak their language.

I encountered the same type scenario in the Westmoreland area seeing many Korean churches and Hispanic churches (mostly storefront – indicating a new and active movement) in an area fairly evenly mixed between Koreans and Hispanics population-wise.

So, after prayer walking and taking community-inventory forays into each area, it seemed like the right decision to eliminate both the West Shatto and Westmoreland areas and to decide between Long Beach, East Shatto, and Hollywood.

Long Beach had a great community feel and was extremely diverse and integrated. There were very few churches in the area, but the ones that were there seemed to be actively evangelizing and reaching out to their neighbors. On one Saturday of prayer walking, the group I was with encountered three different churches who were street preaching, passing out tracts, and door to door canvassing. They told me they did this regularly, if not weekly. The church going door to door was made up of three different congregations, and was very well integrated and active in the community.

East Shatto did not seem like a community as much as Hollywood or Long Beach. It did have some churches, a YMCA, and a park, but there was a disjointed feel to the whole area, a random smattering of commercial, industrial, and residential, but no definable boundaries or flavor.

Hollywood, on the other hand, where my heart was pulling, had the unique combination of being incredibly unchurched, a strong community feeling and culture, fairly populous and diverse, and urban poor. The only caveat with this area was being careful exactly where to minister. There is an interesting intermixing of rich and poor here which skews the statistical data. There is a huge urban poor population here, with an especially high concentration of homeless, runaways, addicts, prostitutes, and ex-cons in transitional housing. There are also many urban poor families here, but around each corner are also financially well-off households. The stigma of Hollywood as a rich area and very glitzy to outsiders is certainly one presupposition which will have to be addressed, but the stark reality is that much of what is considered Hollywood proper is as broken and poor as any area we have worked in within the South Central area, without the negative reputation.

Four things happened in the same week, however, that nailed down the choice for me. At one meeting for "The Call" taking place at Lake Avenue Congregational Church, a man came up to me afterwards and asked if I worked for World Impact. After I said yes, he said that he felt God wanted him to talk to me. In the midst of that conversation, he told me about a new church plant which was going on right in the area where I had been focusing my prayerwalks and exploration, one which had a similar vision to mine regarding the use of media and the arts, one which not only welcomed the homeless and prostitutes of the neighborhood, but actively sought out the broken.

The second thing was the visit I had with that same church – Gateway City Center. This talk with them was encouraging in learning that they were so like-minded with me, they had a heart for the community of Hollywood, and they stressed the need that there was absolutely a need for more churches in the area – I was in no way intruding. In fact, they said that in their opinion there could be a church on every single block and it still would not be enough. This was confirmed to me by another pastor in the area of a first-generation Korean church, who both welcomed me and another church plant, and affirmed that there were plenty of urban poor in the area.

The third significant confirmation was the meeting I had with some Biola students I was hooked up with via a connection through Jim Parker and Dr. Judith Lingenfelter, the intercultural studies professor at Biola. Three students from one of her classes were on a team together with the assignment to pick an area in LA County to research in depth, explore, observe, participate in, then report on. These three students not only scrapped the work they had been doing in another area to come work with me and start over in Hollywood, they were also excited to do so, had a disproportionately large amount of experience in missions work for their young age, and committed to working with me and helping me through the entire school year in whatever way they could (way beyond the limits and responsibilities of their research project).

Lastly, John Suarez, a powerfully evangelistic and prayerful brother in the Lord with me was interceding for me in a group prayer meeting on Friday of that same week. The group was specifically praying for me and for what area God might lead me to in my church plant. John relayed to me how while he was praying and listening to what God might have to say about this, all he could hear from him repeatedly was "Hollywood." This was the strongest and most overwhelming confirmation to me of all of them.

After confirming Hollywood through these means and having it approved of by the leadership, all of which took about six months, the specific target area within Hollywood had to be chosen. After a few months of processing through all the issues with leadership which go hand in hand with the seriousness of choosing a brand new church plant area for the Los Angeles ministry, in January of 2003 the official and final stamp of approval was given to the Church Plant Team (CPT) to go ahead with Hollywood as the target area. The CPT at that point consisted of myself and Susie Kook, but we had a generous helping of volunteers, intercessors, and a few support members (who were also interested in possibly joining the team when the time was right). In February of 2003, over the course of two Saturdays, two different groups of 10 people each gathered to canvas 5 different areas of South Hollywood. A week of survey development and strategic neighborhood location scouting was done before this in preparation. The goal was to get a good idea, through surveying a goal of 500 households, which neighborhoods were the most open, fitting the category of urban poor, with the least representation of existing churches and church members. The five areas canvassed were the "Tropicana area," "LeConte MS area," "Hollywood Rec Center area," "Lemon Grove Park area," and the Ramona Street ES area." Teams of two went to each area to collect as many surveys as possible in the course of a few hours. The goal in this was quantity, not necessarily relationships. We were open to seeing what doors might be open in the future to develop relationships, but our primary goal was to get a good snapshot of each area. After the two Saturdays were over, the surveys were compiled, summarized, and studied, given consideration of the personal encounters experienced with the community residents by our surveys as well. This data and the conclusions made from it led us to choose an area in the 90029 zip code, and centered in the 1911.20 census tract, geocentric and within easy walking distance (5 blocks or less) to LeConte MS, Ramona Street ES, the Tropicana, and Lemon Grove Park. It also led us to focus on one particular apartment complex, and two men of peace.

These two men are named Lamar and Rolando, African-American and Hispanic, respectively. Both Christian, one walking closer with God than the other, and more mature, these men were very open and friendly in the initial dealings with us, and seemed to indicate a desire to pursue friendship. From March until now, these conclusions have been verified by deeper and deeper relationships being formed with both of them, and with even extremely vulnerable accountability and prayer with Rolando, and regular prayerwalking around the Tropicana building, which we have now dubbed "The House of Prayer."

In addition to these two men, during the course of our prayerwalking, Susie and I have met a network of homeless individuals, men and women, upwards of 10 or so, with one particular man named Carl who knew Stacy Waddle, mentioned above. This man showed a lot of promise early on, and walked with the Lord at some point in his life, but in the last few months he has been increasingly sporadic and absent, and relationship with him has been at a stall.

Lastly, through a series of false starts and delays, and another friendship and great connection in the community to Rene, the apartment manager of the complex we had been focusing our interest and attention on, I was about to move in to the very apartment we had our eyes on, which would have put me in the most poor, multicultural, and strategically located apartment in the area (in our vision). With the late addition of a new roommate for me though, for accountability and emotional support purposes, I had to forgo this one-bedroom apartment option in the quest for a two-bedroom apartment. God blessed this search though, because within two weeks of looking, my roommate, John Comfort, and I, both found one, built a relationship with the manager, and secured the apartment. We actually found and were approved for two different 2-bedroom apartments, both of them financially reasonable, both strategic in location, and both to our liking, but the apartment complex of the one we eventually chose, on Lexington (almost exactly right between where Lamar and Rolando live), was much more community-feeling, and friendly, with a warmer atmosphere and look.

Researching Your Community

Rev. Dr. Don L. Davis, expanded, amended, and adapted from *You and Your Community*, National Council of Churches

The following questions were designed in order of a parish or community based church or Christian service/mission organization to study carefully and learn more of the precise nature of the needs and potentials its community possesses. These questions are comprehensive but not exhaustive, and are meant to provoke your mind to explore the various situations, experiences, needs, and critical concerns that are intrinsic to the community where you live, work, and witness. Each broad question area could easily be delegated to a researcher or task force that would investigate this area and present information regarding the community's overall condition.

I. What Area of the City or County Do You Regard as Your Target Community?

1. What does your community call itself?
2. What is the extent and what are the boundaries of your natural geographical parish?
3. What are your community's chief characteristics?
4. What are its traditions, histories, legacies; how did this community come to be, who founded it, when and how?
5. What is the predominant character of it – industrial, commercial, agricultural, educational, recreational, or residential?
6. What are the "natural" boundaries which outline your community, i.e., major streets or highways, railroad lines, parks, industrial or business districts, rivers or bodies of waters, etc.?
7. What is its relationship to its neighboring communities, town/city at large?
8. What is the general accepted opinion or attitude towards the community and its residents? What is it known/famous for?
9. What is the unit you regard as your community (precinct, ward, village, town, city, county)? What is its total area and population?
10. What is the nature of its adjoining communities? What nearby cities influence the life of your community? (Is it rural, village, urban, suburban)?
11. Describe the various physical characteristics and general well-being or status of your community?

II. Who Lives in Your Community?

1. How many people live within your target area?
2. What is the density of the population, i.e., its socioeconomic, racial, religious, cultural/ethnic, age, gender, educational distribution?
3. What are the differing cultures, races, nationalities, ethnicities represented in your community, and how are they distributed within it? What areas of the community do these differing people groups reside?
4. How long have the majority of residents lived in your community?
5. How fast are your community's residents either moving in or exiting your area?
6. How large are the average family units, and what kind of families make up the majority of homes in the community (single parent, two parent, with or without children, etc.)?
7. What are the current birth and death rates for the community?
8. What are the current rates of divorce, legal separation, broken families, etc.?
9. What are the some the predominant kinship patterns in the community?
10. What percent of the population would be considered "alternative" or even considered as "deviant" by the majority culture's standards (homosexual community, some particular minority community, etc.)?
11. Where did most of the residents come from (where did they live before they moved into the neighborhood)?
12. Where do most people who exit this community go?
13. How do the majority of residents view as their community's strengths and/or weaknesses?
14. How cohesive and unified are the members of the community?

III. What Is the Character of the Housing Within the Community?

1. What percentage of the families or individuals own or lease their home?
2. What do these homes cost and/or what is the average rental fee?
3. Who are the land and property owners for most of the community?
4. What is the general condition of the rental housing in the community?

5. To what extent is the property adequately repaired and maintained? Why?
6. How many of the residents of the community lack adequate housing? What is the number of homeless people in this neighborhood?
7. How many hotels, rooming houses, trailer camps, and other facilities exist for transients and the homeless?
8. How does the housing opportunities in your neighborhood compare to dwellings in neighboring communities?
9. Who are the individuals in charge of public housing administration in this area? Who are the key Realtors and realty agencies here?
10. What is the number of government units and housing in the area? Are there any government housing projects? If so, how many currently live in these homes/apartments/duplexes?
11. What are the current building projects taking place in the community that have the potential to change the current housing situation?
12. What innovate housing alternatives exist for the poor and needy in this area?
13. According to population trends, what will the community need in obtain or change in light of its future housing needs?

IV. What Is the Economic Condition and Character of the Community?
1. What is the income range of the people in our community? What tax brackets are represented within it?
2. How do most of its residents earn their living?
3. What percentage of the communities working population commute outside of the community to work?
4. What percentage of community residents are unemployed? Stratify your answer according to population differences in race, gender, ethnicity, education level, etc.
5. What is the standard of living in the community compared to other communities nearby, and the city at large?
6. What opportunities and/or problems do most residents encounter in finding or maintaining employment?
7. Are commercial interests running high here? Why or why not?

8. How do entrepreneurs or other financial investors see this community? Have the banks redlined this area, or which banks are offering money to its residents for business, home, and other financial opportunities?
9. What is the relationship of the community to the overall business community in the city (e.g., the Rotary club, the Chamber of Commerce, Business groups, etc.)?
10. Who are the key economic and business leaders in the community? What are their assets and key economic enterprises?
11. How much illegal activity (drugs, gambling, prostitution, etc.) takes places in the community, and how do these activities affect the community financially?
12. Are there any examples of blatant economic injustices within the community? If so, how did they arise and what groups or events are responsible?
13. Are there any locally based economic groups seeking to bring renewal to this community? Who are they and what kind of projects are they engaged in?
14. What special hardships have affected the community's economic condition adversely, or what special opportunities have affected it positively in the last 5 years?
15. What do the leading economic indicators show for the economic future of the community?
16. What kind of industries or businesses exist within or border the community (e.g., grocery stores, convenience, fast-food, offices, malls, government, construction, etc.)? What are the major employers, businesses, or industries within the community?

V. What Is the Quality of Education Provided to Your Residents?

1. How many of the residents within your community boundary are of school age?
2. What is the average amount of schooling most adults have in the community? Where were most of the community's residents educated?
3. What are the literacy rates for the adults in the community?
4. What are the major schools in the area (e.g., preschools, grammar schools, middle schools, secondary schools, trade or vocational schools, colleges, institutes, etc.)?

5. How old and in what condition are the various educational institutions in the area?
6. What caliber of teachers are employed in the various levels here, and what sort of facilities are provided at institutions within this community?
7. How do students of various grades rank academically with neighboring communities, in the city or town at-large, and nationally?
8. What are the current teacher-student ratios in the schools at present? What is the level of expertise and experience for the average administrators in the various educational institutions?
9. Who are the key individuals in charge of the administration of the schools at the various levels in the community? Who are the members of the school board and what has been their performance of late?
10. What is the current dropout/truancy rate for the various schools?
11. What is the overall character of the schools, that is, their safety, cleanliness, organization, support? What are the best/worst schools in the community?
12. What teacher or parent-teacher organizations exist that are making an impact on the quality of the education provided in the schools?
13. To what degree is equal privileges open to all children and adults of the area?
14. How many of the communities high school graduates go on to college? What kind of colleges or advanced institutions do they attend?
15. What opportunities exist for remedial or continuing education for adults and young people after they leave high school?

VI. How Is the Community Organized and Governed Politically?
1. How many of the community are of voting age? What percentage of the community typically participates in local and national referendums and voting?
2. How is the local community organized politically? What are the precincts, districts, or zoning sections set up?
3. How many representative slots does the community have on the city council, state government, and national political bodies? Who is responsible for drawing up these districts?

4. Who are the current officials representing the community locally, statewide, and nationally (aldermen, city council members, state representatives, state senators, congressional persons, senators)? How involved/informed have they been of the community's needs and potentials?

5. Who are the civic leaders for the community?

6. What are the organizations and/or institutions that have been associated with resisting injustice and inequality within the community? What are the premier advocacy organizations in the community, and who are their leaders?

7. What are the key political action groups or committees within the community? Who is in charge of these groups and what are their political agendas for the community?

8. How much of the cities resources and goods (dollars, personnel, projects, urban improvements, street maintenance, public services, etc.) have been allocated to this community, and how have those allocated resources been spent and distributed within it? Who are the liaisons serving as "middle-persons" in charge of this distribution?

9. What are the primary political affiliations of the residents within the community? What is the political history of the affiliation of the community at-large?

VII. How Does the Community Dispense Justice by the Law and the Courts?

1. How do most residents describe the status of law enforcement and the administration of justice in the community?

2. Who are the current leaders in the administration of justice in the community (Chief ofpolice, District attorney, etc.)?

3. What courts are located within the community? Who are the key public prosecutors and judges within the community? What is their record regarding the protection of the community and enforcement of the law on behalf of the community?

4. What are the latest statistics regarding the numbers and types of crimes committed within the community, and/or delinquency?

5. What are the numbers of residents currently being incarcerated in city, state, and federal jails or prisons?

6. What provision is made for the treatment and rehabilitation of offenders? What level of provision has been made regarding the offenders families during the incarceration of the offenders?

7. What level and caliber of legal representation is provided for and offered to residents of the community? Who are the key attorneys in the community?

8. How many police and city law enforcement officers are assigned to the community for its service and protection?

9. What is the current relationship of the police department to the residents in the community? What steps have been taken to strengthen community-police relations?

10. To what degree have the courts protected the civil rights and liberties of the people in the community?

VIII. What Is the State of the Community's Health and Health Providing Services?

1. How do local health providing institutions characterize the general status of your community's health?

2. Who gets sick most in the community, and why?

3. What are the birth and death rates per thousand? How does this number compare to neighboring communities, the city, and the nation?

4. What are the clinics, hospitals, and medical facilities located in the community? What are the current number of physicians, dentists, specialists, and other medical personnel per capita?

5. Who are the key physicians and care providers in the community?

6. What is the price and quality of care at these various hospitals and clinics in the community?

7. How is the community staffed in terms of ambulance, paramedical, and fire department protection? In other words, how many of these units are assigned to the community? How do the numbers in the community compare with the services used by other communities or the city at large?

8. Who is the fire chief in the community, and who are the key fire prevention officials in the community?

9. What provision has been made in the community for its vulnerable populations, i.e., the elderly, the disabled, the poor and indigent, the mentally retarded, the mentally ill, etc.? Do these populations have access to this provision?

10. What kind of services does the community provide for those who have either been victims of abuse (e.g., children, battered women), or those struggling with addictions (e.g., alcoholism, drugs)? What are the half-way houses or community placement homes available for those in need of such care?

11. What is currently being done in terms of illegitimacy and issues surrounding family planning and care in the community?

12. What provision is being made for the lowering the numbers of people exposed to contagious disease, especially STD's and the AIDS virus?

13. What (if any) are special medical needs or problems confronted by the community? Who has been placed in charge of alleviating these problems, and what is their current rate of success in doing so?

14. What sort of programs exist for the education of the general public regarding safety and health issues in the community?

IX. How Do People Recreate and Spend Their Leisure in the Community?

1. What recreational facilities, hangouts, or spots exist in the community (parks, zoos, pedestrian malls, exercise facilities, music places, clubs, public swimming pools, bowing alleys, sports complexes, etc.)? What are the key commercial amusement centers in the community?

2. Who frequents these various places? Do certain members of the community tend to frequent only special places of interest?

3. What places of recreation or association are not necessarily wholesome or are associated with problem or delinquent activity in the community?

4. What needs does the community have in terms of providing acceptable entertainment under wholesome conditions for its residents, especially its youth?

5. Are the more wholesome places of recreation accessible to all members of the community?

6. Is there sufficient variety and opportunity for play and leisure for all age groups within the community?

7. What is the condition and availability of the parks and public places in the community?

8. What social activities/organizations exist organized either as women's or men's groups, youth groups, groups organized on the basis of age or hobbies or other similar interests?
9. What are the key activities that teens and children participate in during their spare time?
10. What kinds of festivals, traditional meetings, parades, or celebrations does the community participate in each year?
11. What music groups, bands, drama and theater groups, or cultural groups (poets, sculptors, artists) exist and are well known within the community?
12. What kind of sports leagues exist for the community's participation?
13. What kinds of activities and resources are available to the community in its various community centers (Boys or Girls clubs, Boys Scouts or Girl Scouts, YMCA, etc.)?

X. What Are the Key Media Centers Based within the Community?
1. What are the key community voices of media present (newspapers, newsletters, radio stations, television stations, publishing centers, etc.)? Who owns these and what are their circulation and audience numbers?
2. Who are the key persons consulted by the media as spokespersons for the community?
3. What are the key organizations, individuals, or institutions within the community that give voice to its opinions, views, and positions?
4. How does the media depict the community – what issues, themes, stories, personalities does the media tend focus upon in its analysis of the community?
5. What kinds of community programming is made available for the community's discretion on radio and television?
6. Who are the reporters or journalists assigned to deal with issues related to the needs and life of the community?
7. What neighborhood-based community newspapers or newsletters address the particular concerns of members of the community? Who owns them? How often are they published, and how great is their staffs?

XI. How Does the Community Address Its Residents with Special Needs?

1. What are the most vulnerable populations in the community right now?
2. What level of awareness exists regarding these populations among its residents, its leaders, its care providers, etc.?
3. What are the key bureaus, councils, and agencies in the community set up to deal with people in crisis (whether financial, legal, medical, etc.)?
4. What kind of problems or needs cause the greatest amount of difficulty and concern for the residents within the community?
5. What community-based organizations exist that target the special needs of some particular population group struggling with some particular problem or issue (e.g., Alcoholics Anonymous, volunteer groups, D.A.R.E., etc.)?
6. What kinds of networks exist that enable or help the community and its people helping agencies coordinate its helping activities?
7. What are the ten most used public agencies dealing with residents with special needs and problems? What is the phone number and addresses of these agencies, and who among them are in charge?
8. What role have the churches taken in dealing with some of the pressing concerns of the community or its parishes? What churches or church leaders have special programs designed to meet the needs of those who are most vulnerable in the community?
9. What kinds of money, scholarships, grants, fellowships, endowments, or allocations are available locally, statewide, or nationally to remedy some of the community's problems?
10. Who is in charge of administering or allocating these resources and funds?

XII. What Is the Status of Minority Groups within the Community?

1. What racial, ethnic, national, and cultural groups or families are represented in the community?
2. What section(s) of the community do these groups currently reside?
3. What has been the past legacy or relationship that the community has had with minority groups in the past? What is the history of the community in regard to its care for minority groups?

4. What is the predominant perception of the various minority groups towards their community and their life within it?
5. Is there ill-will between the majority culture and minorities within the community? If so, how has this ill-will been expressed?
6. What evidences of injustice, segregation, mistreatment, and/or discrimination can be found in the life of the community (e.g., in the schools, hospitals, places of entertainment, etc.)?
7. Do equal opportunities exist for housing, police protection, employment, and leadership within community posts?
8. What churches, organizations, or community centers do minorities within the community frequent and congregate?
9. How does the media depict the minority population within the community?

XIII. What Is the Religious Character and Expression within the Community?

1. How does the community envision its own religious identity?
2. What are the major religious affiliations within the community (e.g., Christian, Judaism, Islam, Buddhism, Taoism, etc.)? How many belong to each affiliation, how long has the tradition been present within the community, and who are the respective leaders of each tradition within the community?
3. What percentage of the community attends some type of religious event regularly on daily, weekly, monthly, or annually?
4. What is the predominant religious group in the community?
5. What kind and number of Christian churches (Catholic, Protestant, or Orthodox) exist in the area?
6. How much does cultic or sectarian behavior influence the residents of the community (i.e., Jehovah's Witnesses, Mormons, Black Muslims, etc.)?
7. How does the community celebrate major religious holidays/events/festivals?
8. Who are the key religious figures in the community? What is the nature of the relationship and dialogue among them?
9. What kind of missionizing and religious outreach activities are currently taking place within the community?
10. To what degree is religious life and affiliation associated with cultural, racial, economic, or lifestyle lines of the greater secular community?

11. What evidence exists to affirm or deny the community's spiritual readiness and openness to the gospel?

12. What opportunities exist for Christian care-givers to cooperate in their outreach and people-helping ministries within the community?

13. How many Christian organizations are based and operate out of the community? What are they and what needs or problems do they seek to address? Who are the leaders of these various organizations?

XIV. What Is the Community's Awareness of the Larger Community of Which it Is a Part?

1. To what degree are the citizens aware or interested and informed of local, state, national or international events?

2. What issues of neighboring communities are of central importance for the residence of your community?

3. Comparatively speaking, what percentage of the city's overall resources and goods are used by the residents within the community?

4. What is the city's overall perception of the life and potential of the community?

5. What kind of partnerships and alliances exist between political and financial leaders of this community and leaders of other communities citywide?

6. What issues are of special weight or importance in the community's involvement in city, state, and national issues?

7. How have city policies directly influenced or shaped the ongoing life of the community in the last few years?

8. Who are the key liaisons or representatives of local or state governments assigned to the community? Where are city and state offices located within the community?

9. What organizations and institutions promote involvement in citizenship issues, political action, and education about national and world affairs?

10. What interest groups from outside the community have fought for the allegiance of the residents within the community? How have these interest groups been able to shape and influence community opinion?

11. What percentage of residents have been actively involved in civic affairs that are of importance to the overall community and city's welfare? What is the nature of their involvement and participation?
12. How often do the leaders within the community interact with other community leaders regarding their needs, perceptions' and concerns?

XV. Who Is Meeting the Existing Needs of the Community?
1. What are the key organizations and institutions at work in the community overall in meeting the community's most critical needs?
2. In what ways are these groups currently cooperating to meet its needs?
3. What is the current role of churches in this effort?
4. Who are the key pastors, and what is their opinion as to the need for the church to be involved in community advancement?

XVI. What Is Our Christian Responsibility to Our Community?
1. In light of the available information and resources at our disposal, what is our obligation to this community?
2. What specific community ministry should our organization, congregation, or alliance explore further and undertake for the community in the immediate future?

The Oikos Factor: Spheres of Relationship and Influence

Rev. Dr. Don L. Davis

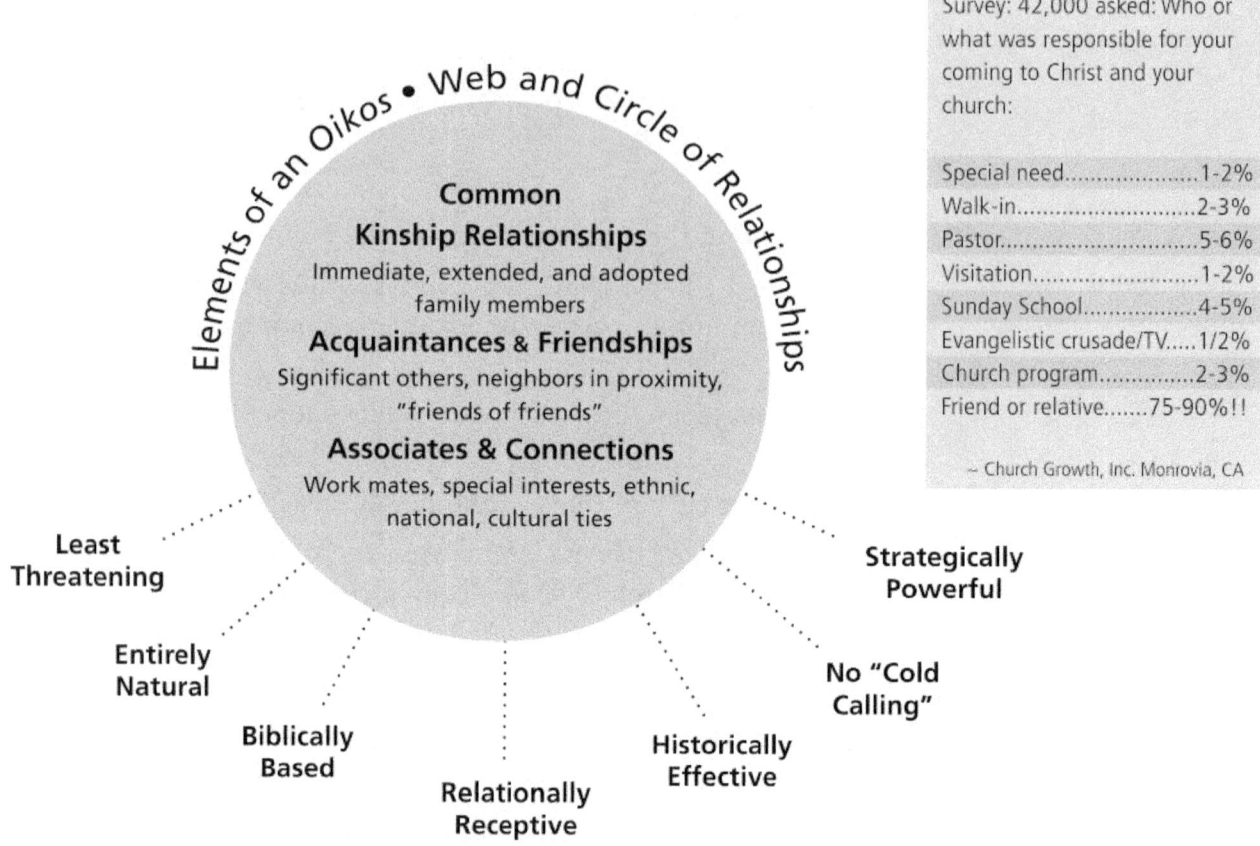

Survey: 42,000 asked: Who or what was responsible for your coming to Christ and your church:

Special need	1-2%
Walk-in	2-3%
Pastor	5-6%
Visitation	1-2%
Sunday School	4-5%
Evangelistic crusade/TV	1/2%
Church program	2-3%
Friend or relative	75-90%!!

~ Church Growth, Inc. Monrovia, CA

Oikos (household) in the OT

"A household usually contained four generations, including men, married women, unmarried daughters, slaves of both sexes, persons without citizenship, and 'sojourners,' or resident foreign workers."

— Hans Walter Wolff, *Anthology of the Old Testament*.

Oikos (household) in the NT

Evangelism and disciple making in our NT narratives are often described as following the flow of the relational networks of various people within their *oikoi* (households), that is, those natural lines of connection in which they resided and lived (c.f., Mark 5.19; Luke 19.9; John 4.53; 1.41-45, etc.). Andrew to Simon (John 1.41-45), and both Cornelius (Acts 10-11) and the Philippian jailer (Acts 16) are notable cases of evangelism and discipling through *oikoi*.

Oikos (household) among the urban poor

While great differences exist between cultures, kinship relationships, special interest groups, and family structures among urban populations, it is clear that urbanites connect with others far more on the basis of connections through relationships, friendships, and family than through proximity and neighborhood alone. Often times the closest friends of urban poor dwellers are not immediately close by in terms of neighborhood; family and friends may dwell blocks, even miles away. Taking the time to study the precise linkages of relationships among the dwellers in a certain area can prove extremely helpful in determining the most effective strategies for evangelism and disciple making in inner city contexts.

Receptivity Scale
Arn and Arn, *The Master's Plan for Making Disciples*

The Holmes-Rahe Social Readjustment Scale indicates different events, in approximate order of their importance, that have an effect in producing periods of personal or family transition. The numbers on the right indicate the importance of the event relative to other transition-producing events. Various events may compound each other when an individual experiences more than one incident over a relatively short period of time. The higher the number, the more receptive the person is to the Gospel. For example, someone who was just married and is also having trouble with his or her boss will be more receptive than if either event had occurred separately. Also, the larger the number or accumulation of numbers, the longer the period of transition will last and the more intense it will be.

~ Win Arn and Charles Arn.
The Master's Plan for Making Disciples. 2nd ed.
Grand Rapids: Baker Books, 1998. pp. 88-89.

The Holmes-Rahe Social Readjustment Scale

Event	Value
Death of Spouse	100
Divorce	73
Marital Separation	65
Jail Term	63
Death of Close Family Member	63
Personal Injury or Illness	53
Marriage	50
Fired from Work	47
Marital Reconciliation	45
Retirement	45
Change in Family Member's Health	44
Pregnancy	40
Sex Difficulties	39
Addition to Family	39
Business Readjustment	39
Change in Financial Status	38
Death of Close Friend	37
Change in Number of Marital Arguments	35
Mortgage or Loan over $75,000	31
Foreclosure of Mortgage or Loan	30
Change in Work Responsibilities	29
Son or Daughter Leaving Home	29
Trouble with In-Laws	29
Outstanding Personal Achievement	28
Spouse Starts Work	26
Starting or Finishing School	26
Change in Living Conditions	25
Revision of Personal Habits	24
Trouble with Boss	23
Change in Work Hours or Conditions	20
Change in Residence	20
Change in Schools	20
Change in Recreational Habits	19
Change in Social Activities	18
Mortgage or Loan under $75,000	18
Easter Season	17
Change in Sleeping Habits	16
Change in Number of Family Gatherings	15
Vacation	13
Christmas Season	12
Minor Violation of the Law	11

Living as an Oikos Ambassador
Rev. Dr. Don L. Davis

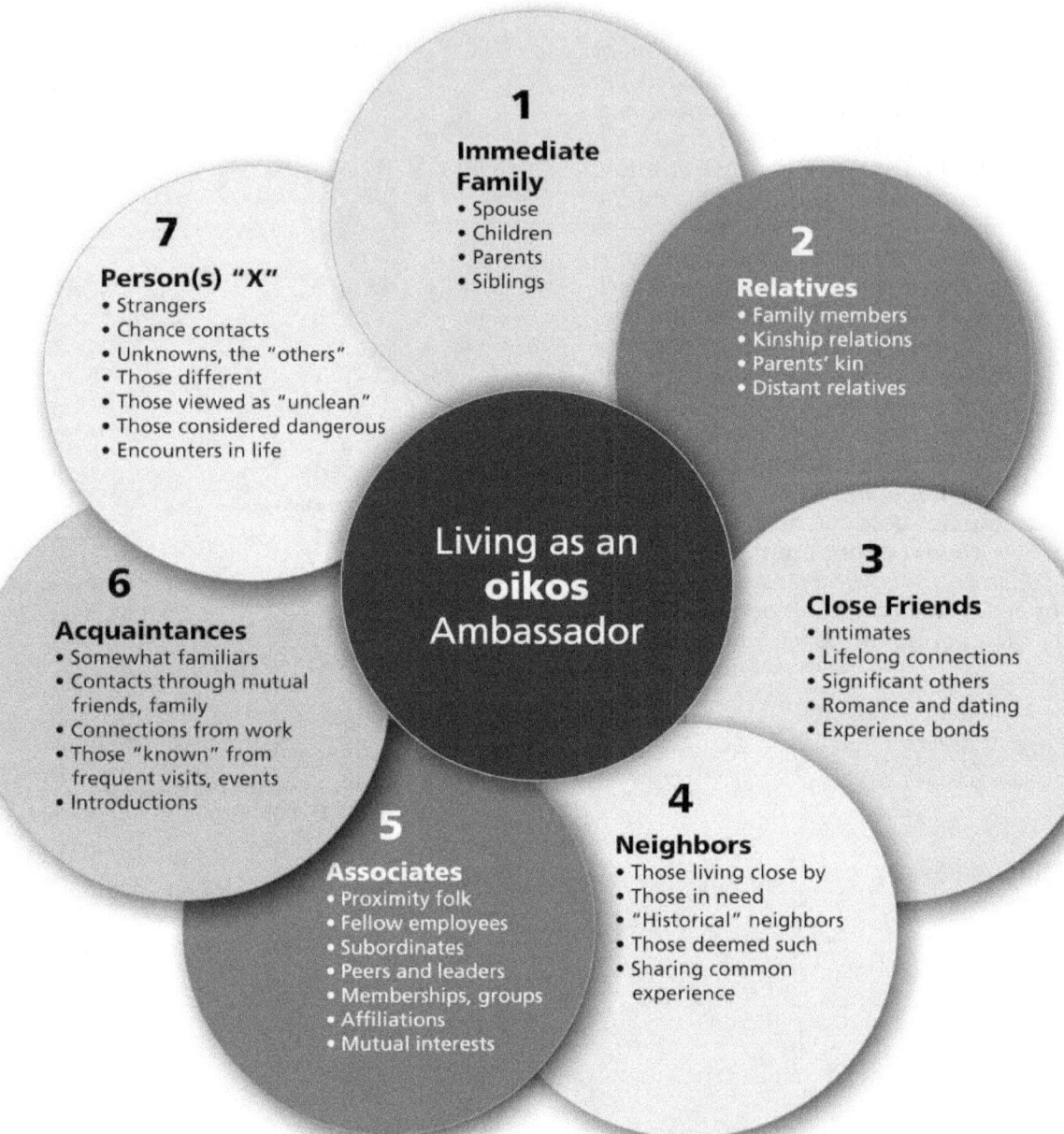

Apostolic Band: Cultivating Outreach for Dynamic Harvest
Rev. Dr. Don L. Davis

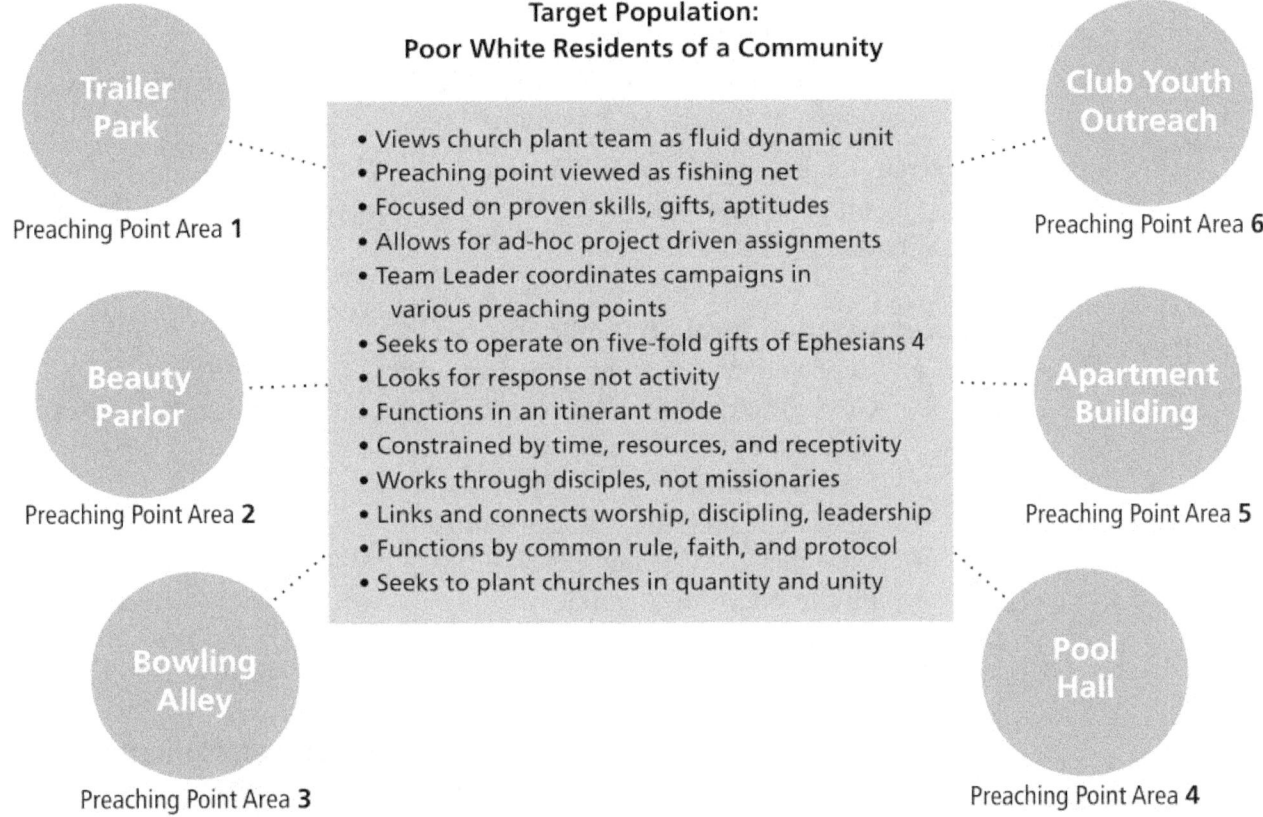

Target Population: Poor White Residents of a Community

- Views church plant team as fluid dynamic unit
- Preaching point viewed as fishing net
- Focused on proven skills, gifts, aptitudes
- Allows for ad-hoc project driven assignments
- Team Leader coordinates campaigns in various preaching points
- Seeks to operate on five-fold gifts of Ephesians 4
- Looks for response not activity
- Functions in an itinerant mode
- Constrained by time, resources, and receptivity
- Works through disciples, not missionaries
- Links and connects worship, discipling, leadership
- Functions by common rule, faith, and protocol
- Seeks to plant churches in quantity and unity

Preaching Point Area **1** – Trailer Park
Preaching Point Area **2** – Beauty Parlor
Preaching Point Area **3** – Bowling Alley
Preaching Point Area **4** – Pool Hall
Preaching Point Area **5** – Apartment Building
Preaching Point Area **6** – Club Youth Outreach

Principle Concepts

1. Itinerancy- an apostolic band functions <u>in multiple-contexts simultaneously</u> organized around a common target population
2. Commonality- an apostolic band uses <u>similar forms, methods, and protocols</u> to win and build converts
3. Authority- an apostolic band functions under a <u>common authority structure</u> and <u>leadership core</u>
4. Identity- an apostolic band plants <u>churches of a kind</u> with shared doctrine, practice, structures and traditions
5. Gifting- an apostolic band is organized around <u>the proven gifts of the band,</u> not availability and assignment alone
6. Fluidity- an apostolic band invests in <u>contacts who respond in preaching points,</u> giving <u>the receptive</u> their critical attention
7. Coordination- an apostolic band will <u>draft and employ select individuals for contribution</u> at critical times for particular projects
8. Consolidation- an apostolic band <u>consolidates the fruit in an area</u> with an eye toward movement and growth, not permanence
9. Discipline- an apostolic band functions according to an <u>order and structure</u>, equipping disciples in the disciplines of the faith
10. Germinal- an apostolic band seeks to <u>inaugurate and initiate spiritual birth and formation,</u> entrusting the lion's share of the congregation's growth and maturity to pastoral oversight

DEFINITION OF TERMS:

Apostolic Band – a fluid team of gifted, available, and committed workers assigned to play particular roles or accomplish specific tasks contributing to the <u>outreach to a population</u>

Preaching Point – a distinct area, venue, or place where people of the <u>target population live or gather</u>

Team Charter – a fluid agreement based on the prospective time and resources necessary to <u>present the Gospel credibly to a target population</u> in a given venue

Project Management – putting together a temporary group of people, strategies, and resources to <u>complete a particular task, outreach, or event</u>

Resources for Studying Your Community
Richard Carlson

Books for a General Overview

Bryant, Marcus and Charles Kemp. 1977 *The Church and Community Resources*. St. Louis, MO: Bethany Press.

Warren, Rachelle and Donald Warren. 1977 *The Neighborhood Organizer's Handbook*. Notre Dame, IN: University of Notre Dame Press.

Documentation through Public Sources
- Census data (by community and tract)
- Governmental libraries (e.g. Cal State Fullerton is a U.S. Govt. Depository library nearby)
- Public libraries
- Historical societies and museums
- Chambers of Commerce
- Public Planning Agencies
- Local Newspapers
- Maps

People Who Might Be a Good Source of Community Information
- Government officials (aldermen, precinct workers)
- School principals (esp. elementary)
- Other church leaders
- PTA presidents and school volunteer organizers
- Presidents of clubs and organizations
- Leaders of homeowners associations
- Scouts, Little League, etc.
- Neighborhood and community leaders
- Realtors
- Local business people
- Chronic gripers
- Service agencies
- Deviants
- Representatives of all age/ethnic groups
- Police
- Social service workers at hospitals
- Bankers
- Workers (those who live within the community and those who do not)
- "The person on the street"

Ideas about Neighborhood Evangelism

Rev. Dr. Don L. Davis

These are just ideas – they are just to provoke your thinking and discussion together. Happy brainstorming!

1. Map out an area or neighborhood you would like to begin your outreach. Set the boundaries.

2. Engage in a prayer walk through the community, praying on behalf of the community.

3. Create a brochure about your church that could be used as an opener in conversation with people on why you are making the visit.

4. Recruit members from your church to make a commitment to (X) number of weeks of door-to-door evangelism, and climax the visits by inviting interested people to a church open house or community picnic.

5. Create a ledger of responses, or survey that can be used at the various homes and households you visit. Keep careful record of openness and follow-up all interested parties.

6. Gather list of households and visit them.

7. Make special return visits to those who are interested with other members of the body, or invite them to a special event that allows us to continue contact with them.

8. Buy simple, appropriate tracts that could be left with each family that you visit that would tell of the gospel and/or your church family.

9. Host something for those interested in local park area (church open house).

10. Pray faithfully in the cells for all families who are interested, and follow up interested parties regularly.

Canvassing Dos and Don'ts

Rev. Dr. Don L. Davis

Critical Assumptions of Communicating Christ with Our Neighbors

- **The Lord will accompany us as we go in His name.**

   Matt. 28.18-20 – "Then Jesus came and spoke to them, saying, 'All authority has been given to Me in heaven and on earth. Go therefore and make disciples of all the nations, baptizing them in the name of the Father and of the Son and of the Holy Spirit, teaching them to observe all things that I have commanded you, and lo, I am with you always, even to the end of the age.'"

- **The Lord will create divine appointments with those He directs us to meet.**

   Acts 8.26-39 – "Now an angel of the Lord spoke to Philip, saying, 'Arise and go toward the south along the road which goes down from Jerusalem to Gaza.' This is desert. So he arose and went. And behold, a man of Ethiopia, an enuch of great authority under Candace the Queen of the Ethiopians, who had charge of all her treasury, and had come to Jerusalem to worship, was returning. And sitting in his chariot, he was reading Isaiah the prophet. Then the Spirit said to Philip, 'Go near and overtake this chariot.'"

- **The Lord will give us the appropriate word for each person with whom we speak.**

   Mark 13.9-11 – "But watch out for yourselves, for they will deliver you up to councils, and you will be beaten in the synagogues. And you will be brought before rulers and kings for My sake, for a testimony to them. And the gospel must first be preached to all the nations. But when they arrest you and deliver you up, do not worry, beforehand, or premeditate what you will speak. But whatever is given you in that hour, speak that; for it is not you who speak, but the Holy Spirit."

- **The Lord will honor His word and our testimony of His grace with fruit.**

   John 15.16 – "You did not choose Me, but I chose you and appointed you that you should go and bear fruit, and that your fruit should remain, that whatever you ask the Father in My name He may give you."

The Dos of Canvassing:

1. Be *prayerful*: Only the grace of God can make our contacts fruitful (Matt. 9.35-38).
2. Be *prepared*: Represent Christ and the gospel with clarity and integrity (1 Pet. 3.15,16).
3. Be *expectant*: Christ Jesus will accompany us as we go in His name (Matt. 28.20).
4. Be *faithful*: Respect your commitments and honor your dates (Prov. 20.6).
5. Be *alert*: Stay aware of your environment, your purpose, and your audience (1 Pet. 5.8-9).
6. Be *yourself*: God can use anyone to be His ambassador (2 Cor. 5.20).

The Don'ts of Canvassing:

1. Don't be *anxious*: Worry about nothing, but bathe the enterprise in prayer (Phil. 4.6-7).
2. Don't be *intimidated*: We go forth in the name and authority of Christ (Matt. 28.18-19).
3. Don't be *apologetic*: God gives us the privilege and duty to share (John 15.16).
4. Don't be *isolated*: Even Christ sent out his apostles in pairs (Mark 6.7).
5. Don't be *pushy*: God makes all things beautiful in His time (Eccles. 3.11).
6. Don't be *insensitive*: Study and know the people with whom you interact (1 Cor. 9.19-21).

Door-to-Door
Starting the Conversation
Rev. Dr. Don L. Davis

The sentences before the questions are meant to be primers, suggestions to transition into asking the questions.

1. We're out sharing about our new church, Anyname Fellowship, with our neighbors here. **Do you currently attend church anywhere?**

2. *So, you don't/do have some beliefs about spiritual things?*

3. Regardless of what people think about God, nearly everybody has some idea about why we are here. **Do you believe that there's some ultimate purpose for our lives?**

4. Also, most religions (and most people, too) have some idea about life after death. **If YOU were to die tonight, where do you think YOU would go?**

5. You've really been so open to talk about these things. **Do you have a moment to hear what the Bible says about these things?**

"Yes": Continue on with the conversation

"No": Thank you so much for your time. We really appreciate your willingness to talk briefly with us about these things. Again, if you have any questions about our new church, AF, please don't hesitate to call us. Our number is listed on the brochure.

Body Life and Spiritual Formation

Using Wisdom in Ministry
The PWR Process
Rev. Don Allsman

God Is a Purposeful God

Matt. 28.19 (ESV) – Go therefore and make disciples of all nations, baptizing them in the name of the Father and of the Son and of the Holy Spirit.

Acts 1.8 (ESV) – But you will receive power when the Holy Spirit has come upon you, and you will be my witnesses in Jerusalem, and in all Judea and Samaria, and to the end of the earth.

Matt. 24.14 (ESV) – And this gospel of the kingdom will be proclaimed throughout the whole world as a testimony to all nations, and then the end will come.

John 15.8 (ESV) – By this my Father is glorified, that you bear much fruit and so prove to be my disciples.

How Can We Fulfill God's Purpose?
Using Wisdom in Ministry

The Dialectic: Wisdom is choosing what is best between viable truths.

Wisdom not ivory tower experience, but found in *engagement*.

Eph. 5.15-17 (ESV) – Look carefully then how you walk, not as unwise but as wise, making the best use of the time, because the days are evil. Therefore do not be foolish, but understand what the will of the Lord is.

Prov. 24.3-6 (ESV) – By wisdom a house is built, and by understanding it is established; by knowledge the rooms are filled with all precious and pleasant riches. A wise man is full of strength, and a man of knowledge enhances his might, [6] for by wise guidance you can wage your war, and in abundance of counselors there is victory.

Barriers to Using Wisdom in Ministry Tasks
". . . we are not unaware of his schemes" (2 Cor. 2.11)

- **"We've never done it that way before."** God has no use for traditions that block his progress. Just because it has been done a certain way does not indicate it remains a wise option (Acts 10).
- **"We're doing fine."** Apparent (or real) success can keep you from greater fruitfulness (John 15.2).
- **"Being organized doesn't allow for the leading of the Holy Spirit."** God had a plan and is working his plan through us. We should not be ashamed to have a plan and work that plan.
- **"It doesn't matter what we do – God will bless it. We will face it when we come to it."** While there are some things that are better left later, sometimes this attitude reflects a lack of discipline.
- **"We can do it" rather than "we should do it."** – basing decisions on emotion, expediency, or available resources.
    - ~ Keep a clear focus on the vision.
    - ~ Engage activities which contribute to that vision.
    - ~ Many good things to invest in, but only a few *contribute to the vision*.
    - ~ Poor stewardship to be driven by opportunities rather than by vision.
    - ~ Wisely consider the implications of decisions, not the easiest path.
    - ~ Emotions can easily deceive us. "Be clear-minded and self-controlled so you can pray" (1 Pet. 4.7).
    - ~ The path of least resistance often carries a price to pay.
    - ~ CONTRIBUTION TO VISION.
- **Fatigue.** "Fatigue makes cowards of us all." When we get tired, we are more resistant to new ideas and anything which will tap our already-low resources. This resistance can result in missed opportunities.
- **Fear of failure, fear of change, fear of losing supporters**
    - ~ Mediocrity is preferable because it is safer.
    - ~ Risk brings the prospect of personal failure and humiliation ("For God gave us a spirit not of fear but of power and love and self-control," 2 Tim. 1.7).
    - ~ Natural to dread change, but we are constantly being transformed (Rom. 12.2; 2 Cor. 3.18).

- Flexibility (openness to change) is critical to exercising wisdom (God does things we don't expect).
- Wisdom may dictate action resulting in controversy, but if it is in the best interest of the vision, you must act courageously and sensitively.

- **Willingness to be in a protracted conflict**
  - Armies continue fighting even when they know they will be defeated.
  - Prolonging the war reduces the humiliation of defeat.
  - You need help to be victorious but also when to minimize your losses.
  - "Encouraging people to pledge themselves to survival is an admission of defeat" (George Barna).

- **Experience.** "I've been here a long time and I know what's been going on. I've been in this community for twelve years and I know this isn't going to work."

Process that addresses barriers and benefits, and is both deliberate and emergent:

- Deliberate: Decide now, before it's too late.
- Emergent: Face when it comes.

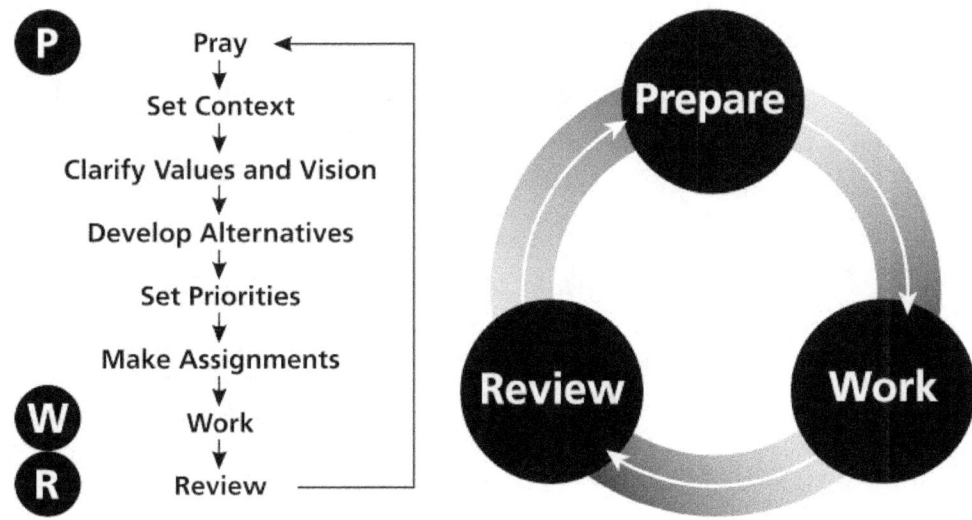

PWR

PREPARE

- *Pray* (Discover his plan).

    "We start not with a plan, but a passion. Motion flows from emotion" (Wheatley).

- *Set context* (God is God of history).

    Good decisions are made in the proper context.

    Be reflective. "In everything the prudent acts with knowledge, but a fool flaunts his folly" (Prov. 13.16).

- ***Clarify the values and vision.***

    Values: 3-5 driving forces to find consensus (Abilene Paradox ~ J. Harvey, 1988).

    Who, what, when, how (Great Commission, Moses, Noah, Joshua, Nehemiah).

    Be discerning. "The wisdom of the prudent is to discern his way, but the folly of fools is deceiving" (Prov. 14.8).

- *Develop alternatives* (Don't go with the first, most obvious answer).

    Dream, get counsel.

    Be imaginative. "Plans are established by counsel; by wise guidance wage war" (Prov. 20.18).

- *Set priorities* (Don't just try all the alternatives).

    Be prudent. "The simple believes everything, but the prudent gives thought to his steps. . . . The prudent sees danger and hides himself, but the simple go on and suffer for it" (Prov. 14.15, 22.3).

- *Make assignments* (Don't leave people guessing about the specifics of their assignment).

    Be decisive. ". . . He gave me understanding in all the details of the plan . . . be strong and courageous and do the work" (1 Chron. 28.19-20).

WORK (Stop talking and start doing.)
- Be bold; innovate; "Give the boundaries in which people are free to live out their spiritual gift without asking for permission." ~ Bill Easum
- Friction: things seldom go as planned.
- Better to execute a poor plan than poorly execute a great plan.
- *Be creative.* (Matt. 25.14-30).
- Two extremes: rigidity and lack of discipline.

REVIEW (Don't assume what you did was effective.)
- Make half-time adjustments (Sanballat, Cornelius, Gideon, Macedonian vision).
- Check the fruit (John 15.2).
- "The most important part of any mission is the debrief."
- *Be reflective.* "Poverty and disgrace come to him who ignores instruction, but whoever heeds reproof is honored. . . . Whoever ignores instruction despises himself, but he who listens to reproof gains intelligence" (Prov. 13.18; 15.32).
- Celebrate! (Remember Ed Delahanty's 65.4% failure rate.)

What Is PWR?

We will spend time this week in Preparation, but don't be deceived. No formula or good plan will plant a church; not a analytic process.

Bobby Bowden on blending control with improvisation: *"You may work all week on a game plan, then get four plays into the game and realize the plan's no good. You have to be able to adjust. You have to build flexibility into your people and strategies."*

Robert McNamara: *"We must first determine what our foreign policy is to be, formulate a military strategy to carry out that policy, then build the military forces to successfully conduct this strategy"* (Failed Vietnam Strategy).

PWR Is About	PWR Is Not About
Adapting	Being organized
Wisdom (wisely pursuing vision)	Goals
Adjustment	Checking off tasks
Learning	Planning
Contribution to vision	Calculated analysis
Fruit checking (John 15.2)	Bean counting
Dreaming and scheming	Paperwork
"Rapid assessment and adaptation to a complex and rapidly changing environment that you can't control" ~ John Boyd, OODA Loop	Being linear
Prepare, Work, Review	Pain Without Reward

Applications for PWR

Dimensions: leading a choir, leading a worship service, leading a cell group, planning Church Plant School, elder meetings, worship services, retreats, evangelistic events.

PWR is not World Impact; PWR represents biblical principles of wisdom.

Victory is found when:
There is wise preparation
    . . . creatively executed under the guidance of the Holy Spirit
        . . . and rigorously reviewed.

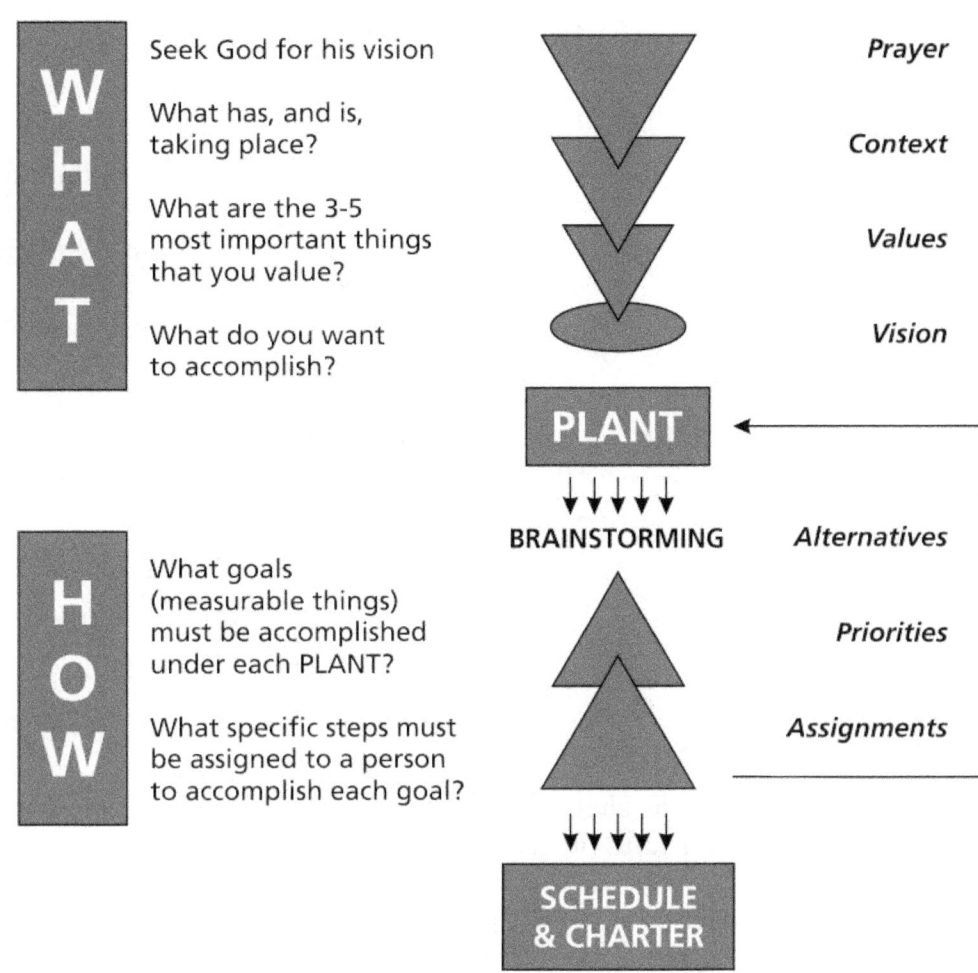

Schedule and Charter

End result of the preparation phase of PWR is the charter form
- Captures the entirety of the plan on one sheet
- Helps the team members, the multiple team leader, potential volunteers, and other interested parties see a snapshot of the intentions of the church plant enterprise
- Becomes the means by which the team is given authority, signed off by the Deans, Multiple Team Leader and City Director (World Impact only)

No charters are open-ended.
- Due date for charter review
- Review may determine if:
  - an additional length of time should be authorized to continue the effort
  - there is not sufficient fruit from the effort and the team should be disbanded
  - there may need to be wholesale changes in the vision, the team structure, or strategies

The charter makes the team semi-autonomous.
- Allows team to carry out its vision within the stated guidelines without micro-management
- Creates intensive scrutiny of the team's vision and methods
  - at the front end of charter development
  - at the back end during charter review
- Less scrutiny in the middle during implementation

The charter is the culmination of the strategic planning process and equips the team to proceed with wisdom and authority.

Benefits of Using Wisdom in Ministry Tasks
- Clear vision helps everyone clearly see *if the team is doing well* or not.
- Clear direction *minimizes confusion* giving a sense of confidence and hope.
- Everyone knows *their assignment*.
- People can decide if they want to stay and *help fulfill the vision* or move on to something else. You do not want people on your team who are not supporting the vision. If they stay they will either become inactive or will cause problems.
- *Wasteful activities* are minimized (stay focused on vision, not opportunities).
- An environment is created where you can *say "no" to opportunities* that do not contribute to the vision.
- Opportunities that contribute to the vision *can be anticipated* and recognized quickly. Nehemiah was ready when the opportunity arose to explain his vision to the king.

- Clarity and direction *minimizes hurting or discouraging the troops*. Soldiers die from lack of clarity and direction.
- Wisdom demands a balance between *vision (faith) and reality (prudence)*.
- Clear direction inspires people and sets them *free to innovate*.
- It provides the tools to be pro-active, *minimizing becoming a "victim of circumstances."*
- The principles can be applied to *many areas of the team's activities*. Developing a habit of using wisdom will make every activity, large or small, more effective.

Discern God's Vision

Prepare Plan of Attack

Spiritual & Tactical Readiness • Contribution to Vision

Engage the Enemy

Check the Fruit

Prepare New Plan of Attack

Our Commitments (Non-negotiables)

- Bible
  - ~ As our basis for life and ministry

- Team
  - ~ Church Plant Teams
  - ~ Leadership and oversight

- Wisdom
  - ~ Led by the Holy Spirit
  - ~ Choosing what's best among viable alternatives
  - ~ Engaging the enemy
  - ~ Adjustment and flexibility

Your Solemn Pledge

Although I will spend a lot of time in planning this week . . .

- I understand that PWR is about wisely *adapting* and making *adjustments*, not organization, goals, or tasks.
- It's about *learning*, not planning.
- It's about *vision and fruit checking*, not analysis and bean counting.
- It's about *dreaming and scheming*, not paperwork.

Getting a Good Team Rhythm
Time Management and Ministry Stewardship
Rev. Dr. Don L. Davis

Basic Theological Assumptions

- The Kingdom of God is the framework of all ministry.
- The Church is both foretaste and agent of the Kingdom of God.
- Through our witness and actions we proclaim Christ's reign through the Church to the world.
- As a Team, we are to seek God's face regarding our ministry endeavors and strive to accomplish them efficiently and excellently.
- God desires his people to be wise in their proclamation of the Kingdom.

Ministry Management Strategy

I. **Clarify Your Identity and Mission**
   A. What is our ultimate purpose and identity?
   B. What are our key ministry areas (worship, witness, learning, mission, justice, service)?
   C. What are our ultimate commitments (to God in Christ, to Scripture, to the Church, to the world)?
   D. What are our ultimate convictions, ideals, and values?

II. **Understand Your Particular Field of Mission**
   A. What is the history of our particular field of mission?
   B. For whom and to whom are our efforts directed?
   C. What are the critical needs, and how are they currently being met?
   D. What programs/activities currently exist to meet them?
   E. How effective have they been to alleviate these needs?
   F. What conditions currently demand attention or relief?

III. Appraise Your Resources (Situational Analysis)

A. What is the level of our commitment and burden to this need?

B. Who is currently working on these problems or available to work (people and personnel)?

C. What facilities, equipment, and materials do we have?

D. What kind of budget and monies do we currently have?

E. What training or preparation do we offer?

F. What factors help (opportunities) or hinder (threats) us in seeking to address these needs?

IV. Formulate Goals to Meet Needs

A. Set a planning cycle (six months to one year is recommended).

B. State your goals in terms of one clear statement and idea (Clarity).

C. Make certain that your goals are able to be done (Feasibility).

D. State your goals in terms of end results: how much and how many (Specificity).

1. How many (number)?
2. How well done (quality)?
3. How much (quantity)?

E. Determine how long or what date you expect these to take place.

V. Establish Clear Priorities

A. Does this goal relate to our ultimate purposes and objectives?

B. Of all possible goals, which are most important to us now?

C. Of the important goals, which ones must be done immediately?

D. Of the important goals, which ones should be done sometime soon?

E. Which goals ought to be postponed for later consideration?

VI. Determine Plans and Strategies

A. Outline step-by-step strategies for each important goal.

B. What precisely are the steps and phases for this project?

C. What specific courses of action does this project require?

D. Who is responsible for this project (for what, for whom, to whom)?

E. What training will the participants require, and where will they obtain it?

F. What resources do we need, and how will we get it (people, money, facilities, equipment, training, counsel)?

VII. Execute Your Plans according to Schedule

A. Create a project schedule.

B. Communicate to all parties their roles and responsibilities.

C. Coordinate activities at appropriate times.

D. Set dates for review and feedback.

E. Set up appointments for accountability, review, and assessment.

VIII. Review and Evaluate Effectiveness in Light of Goals

A. What did we hope to accomplish?

B. Did we accomplish our goals? Why or why not?

C. Should this or another goal be repeated? Why or why not?

D. How did those responsible perform?

E. Did these efforts bring us any closer to our ultimate goal, or did these activities deter and distract us?

IX. Revise Goals, Priorities, and Strategies for New Cycle

Use information received to assess needs more clearly, to set better goals, formulate better strategies, and obtain better results for the glory of God.

Commissioning of Our Elders

The Urban Ministry Institute • *Church Resources CD*. Wichita: The Urban Ministry Institute, 2004

Charge to the Elders

Our congregation, the members of *Anyname Fellowship*, has chosen you to fill the office of elders to further the cause of Christ and his Kingdom, as well as to strengthen and guide the congregation to maturity in him. Now, in the presence of God, and before these saints, I charge you to this task in the name of Jesus Christ.

1. Do you all reaffirm your commitment to Christ and His kingdom, to walk with Him as His disciple, doing His will as His Holy Spirit leads and enables?

   Answer: I do

2. Are you willing to assume the office of Elder with its varied duties, and do you pledge with God's help to carry out the duties of this office for the glory of God, and the welfare of the entire congregation and its individual members?

   Answer: I am willing, with God's help

3. Finally, will you further pledge yourself to be an example to the members of this flock, to pray consistently for the welfare of its members, and to continue to grow toward Christian maturity through your obedience to Christ, fellowship within the Body, prayer, worship, nurturing from the Word of God, and instruction from others?

   Answer: I will

Charge to the Congregation

You the members of *Anyname Church* have called these leaders to serve in the office of Elder on the Council of this church. These leaders have now declared their willingness to take on this important responsibility. Now I ask you to declare your willingness to cooperate with and to give your loyal support to these men in their work. Will you declare this by standing now together as a congregation as the office is being conferred?

Commission

In the name of Christ and his church I confer upon you the office of Elder of *Anyname Fellowship* with its duties and responsibilities for the term of office determined by the congregation. May our Lord Jesus Christ, the Great Shepherd of the sheep, give you grace as you guide and shepherd this congregation under His leadership. May the Lord bless you and your families in every way, and through the enabling of His Spirit, make you a blessing in all you say and do as Elders of Anyname Fellowship Church. Let us pray.

Order of Service
Sample 1
The Urban Ministry Institute

Anyname Fellowship Church

Theme of Service . . . . Press on Toward the Prize

Welcome, Call to Worship . . . . Rebecca

Psalm Reading . . . . Psalm 42.1-5

Prayer of Invocation . . . . Shelby

Worship Songs
   Well I Woke Up This Morning
   In the Name of Jesus
   I'll Do My Best
   Victory in Jesus
   We Will Triumph in the Lord
   We Choose the Fear
   More Precious Than Silver
   Turn Your Eyes upon Jesus
   Singing a Song to You

Prayer for the Body, Offering, and Announcements . . . . . Russ

Old Testament Reading . . . . Jeff

New Testament Reading . . . . Shanequa

Gospel Reading . . . . Roberto

Offertory Music . . . . Jesus in the Morning

Sermon and Scripture Passage . . . . Maurice
                                                       Phil. 3.12-14

Closing Song . . . . All I Once Held Dear

Benediction . . . . Maurice

Order of Service
Sample 2
The Urban Ministry Institute

**Blessed Hope Missionary Fellowship
Order of Service**

LIGHTING OF CANDLES . . . . *Carolyn*

> *Ascribe to the Lord*
> *O, you mighty ones*
> *Ascribe to the Lord*
> *Glory and strength*
> *Sing praise to the Lord,*
> *Come, worship the LORD Most High*
> *Now enter his gates*
> *With gladness and praise*
>
> *Hallelujah, Hallelujah*
> *Hallelujah to the Lord!*
> *Hallelujah, Hallelujah*
> *Hallelujah to the Lord!*
>
> *Come, worship the Lamb*
> *Raise up your songs of joy*
> *With off'rings of love*
> *Exalt the Most High!*
> *Come, shout to the Lord*
> *Applaud him for all he's done*
> *Come into his courts*
> *And bring sacrifice!*

WELCOME AND INVOCATION . . . . *Beth*

ACCLAMATION . . . . *All*

> *Blessèd are You, O God,*
> *Father, Son, and Holy Spirit,*
> *And blessèd is Your Kingdom.*
> *Amen! (repeat)*

Both now and forever,
Blessèd be Your Name.
And blessèd is Your Kingdom.
Amen!
And throughout the endless ages
Evermore the same
And blessèd is Your Kingdom
Amen!

Worship in Song . . . . All

All Hail the Power of Jesus' Name
Everything Cries Holy
For Me to Live Is Christ
Above All
I Surrender All
My All in All

Collect for the Day . . . . Don

The Psalm . . . . Beth
Psalm 45.10-17 (ESV)

Hear, O daughter, and consider, and incline your ear: forget your people and your father's house, and the king will desire your beauty.

Since he is your lord, bow to him.

The people of Tyre will seek your favor with gifts, the richest of the people.

All glorious is the princess in her chamber, with robes interwoven with gold.

In many-colored robes she is led to the king, with her virgin companions following behind her.

With joy and gladness they are led along as they enter the palace of the king.

In place of your fathers shall be your sons; you will make them princes in all the earth.

[all]
> I will cause your name to be remembered in all generations;
> therefore nations will praise you forever and ever.

SUMMARY OF THE LAW . . . . *Beth*
Celebrant
I am the LORD your God, who brought you out of Egypt, out of the land of slavery.

People
You shall have no other gods before me.
You shall not make for yourself an idol in the form of anything in
   heaven above or on the earth beneath or in the waters below.
You shall not misuse the name of the LORD your God, for the LORD
   will not hold anyone guiltless who misuses his name.
Remember the Sabbath day by keeping it holy.
Honor your father and your mother, so that you may live long in the
   land the LORD your God is giving you.
You shall not murder.
You shall not commit adultery.
You shall not steal.
You shall not give false testimony against your neighbor.
You shall not covet . . . anything that belongs to your neighbor.

Celebrant
Jesus said, "You shall love the Lord your God with all your heart and with all your soul and with all your mind. This is the great and first commandment. And a second is like it: You shall love your neighbor as yourself. On these two commandments depend all the Law and the Prophets" (Matt. 22.37-40 ESV).

OLD TESTAMENT READING . . . . *Brian*
Reader
Our Old Testament reading is Genesis 24.34-38, 42-49. 58-67. [Text is read.]
This is the Word of God.

People
The word of the Lord endures forever. Amen.

Gospel Reading . . . . *Carolyn*

Reader
Our Gospel reading is Matthew 11.16-19, 25-30. [Text is read.]
This is the Gospel of the Lord.

People
Lord Jesus, Your words are spirit and life. Amen.

New Testament Reading . . . . *Dan*

Reader
Our New Testament reading is Romans 7.15-25a. [Text is read.]
This is what the Spirit says to the churches.

People
Your word is a lamp to my feet and a light to my path. Amen.

Gloria Patri . . . . *All*

> *Glory be to the Father,*
> *And to the Son*
> *And to the Holy Spirit:*
> *As it was in the beginning,*
> *Is now, and ever shall be,*
> *World without end.*
> *Amen, amen.*

Teaching . . . . *Davis*

The Nicene Creed . . . . *All*

WE BELIEVE in one God, the Father Almighty, maker of heaven and earth and of all things visible and invisible.

WE BELIEVE in one Lord Jesus Christ, the only begotten Son of God, begotten of the Father before all ages, God from God, Light from Light, True God from True God, begotten not created, of the same essence as the Father, through whom all things were made.

WHO FOR US men and for our salvation came down from heaven and was incarnate by the Holy Spirit and the Virgin Mary and became human. Who for us too, was crucified under Pontius Pilate, suffered and was buried. The third day he rose again according to the Scriptures, ascended into heaven and is seated at the right hand of the Father. He will come again in glory to judge the living and the dead, and his Kingdom will have no end.

We believe in the Holy Spirit, the Lord and life-giver, who proceeds from the Father and the Son. Who together with the Father and Son is worshiped and glorified. Who spoke by the prophets.

We believe in one holy, catholic, and apostolic church.

We acknowledge one baptism for the forgiveness of sin, and we look for the resurrection of the dead and the life of the age to come. Amen.

Evermore . . . . *All*

Ever ancient, ever new
Ever mythic, ever true
Ever future, ever near
Ever wondrous, ever clear

Ever gracious, ever pure
Ever lovely, ever sure
Ever bless-ed, ever blessed
Ever trusted and confessed

Ever triune, ever one
Ever forming, ever done
Ever recent, ever old
Ever humble, ever bold

Ever veil-ed, ever known
Ever mystic, ever shown,
Ever legend, ever lore
Ever lasting, evermore.

Testimony of the People . . . . *Brian*
Close together with the Lord's Prayer:
Our Father who art in heaven, hallowed be thy name. Thy Kingdom come, thy will be done in earth as it is in heaven. Give us this day our daily bread and forgive us our debts as we forgive our debtors. And lead us not into temptation, but deliver us from evil. For thine is the Kingdom, and the power, and the glory for ever. Amen.

Confession of Sin, The Peace, Holy Communion . . . . *Carolyn*
Celebrant and People (sing)

> Kyrie eleison, Christe eleison,
> Kyrie eleison.
> Lord, have mercy, Christ, have mercy,
> Lord, have mercy.
>
> O Lamb of God, who takes away
> The sin of Adam's race,
> O, incline Your ear,
> And hear our prayer—
> Lord, have mercy!
>
> O Lamb of God, whose precious blood
> Was shed upon the Tree,
> O, incline Your ear,
> And hear our prayer—
> Lord, have mercy.

Confession of Sin
Celebrant
Let each of us now confess our sins to God and receive mercy and grace to help in our time of need.

(Time of silent confession and repentance)

Celebrant
I announce forgiveness to you now, according to the promise of God's Word. Having faithfully confessed and renounced your sin, Christ also has been faithful to forgive your sins and to purify you from all unrighteousness. It is certain, that there is One who has spoken to the Father in your defense, Jesus Christ, the Righteous One who is the atoning sacrifice for our sins and for the sins of the whole world. His grace and peace are with you now. Amen.

The Peace
Celebrant
Greet one another in the love of Christ. And if you have anything against a brother or sister, reconcile with them as we prepare to eat together, as one family, around the table of the Lord.

CHRISTUS VICTOR
Celebrant and People (sing)

> *Child of a lowly birth*
> *Hero of the wayward earth*
> *Righteous One ere dawn of time*
> *In full flesh and all divine*
> *Spotless Lamb for sinners slain*
> *True and Faithful is his name*
> *Undoer of all ill-done things*
> *Savior, Master, King of kings*
>
> *Vanquisher of hell and death*
> *Includer of the lowliest*
> *Crusher of the serpent's head*
> *Terminating woe and dread*
> *Opener of heaven's door*
> *Reigning Victor evermore*

HOLY COMMUNION
Celebrant
It is truly right to glorify you Father, and to give you thanks; for you alone are God, living and true, dwelling in light inaccessible from before time and forever.

Fountain of life and source of goodness, you made all things and fill them with your blessing; you created them to rejoice in the splendor of your radiance.

Countless throngs of angels stand before you to serve you night and day; and, beholding the glory of your presence they offer you unceasing praise. Joining with them, and giving voice to every creature under heaven, we acclaim you and glorify your Name, as we sing:

Celebrant and People (sing)

> *Holy Lord, most holy Lamb*
> *Son of God, the Great I Am*
> *Rabbi and Priest, our dearest Friend*
> *Walk with us today, walk with us today*
>
> *Mighty King, exalted high*
> *Savior Prince, and Lord of light*
> *Ascended Lord, now glorified*
> *Fill our hearts today, fill our hearts today*

> *Immanuel, God's Word made flesh*
> *Filled with truth and holiness*
> *Our glorious Head, our Source and Life*
> *Reveal Yourself today, reveal Yourself today*
>
> *Holy Lord, most holy Lamb*
> *Beautiful Seed of Abraham*
> *Our coming King, Who'll rule and reign*
> *Reign o'er us today, reign o'er us today*
>
> Celebrant
> We acclaim you, holy Lord, glorious in power. Your mighty works reveal your wisdom and love. You formed us in your own image, giving the whole world into our care, so that, in obedience to you, we might rule and serve all creatures.
>
> People
> When our disobedience took us far from you, you did not abandon us to the power of death. In your mercy you came to our help, so that in seeking you we might find you.
>
> Celebrant and People (sing)
>
> > *A Fountain that brings healing*
> > *And it prompts the Spirit's sealing*
> > *It's the Blood that will not lose its power*
> > *O, the precious Blood of Christ.*
>
> Celebrant
> Again and again you called us into covenant with you, and through the prophets you taught us to hope for salvation. Father, you loved the world so much that in the fullness of time you sent your only Son to be our Savior. Incarnate by the Holy Spirit, born of the Virgin Mary, he lived as one of us, yet without sin.
>
> People
> To the poor he proclaimed the good news of salvation; to prisoners, freedom; to the sorrowful, joy. To fulfill your purpose, he gave himself up to death; and, rising from the grave, destroyed death, and made the whole creation new.
>
> Celebrant and People
> And, that we might no longer live for ourselves, but for him who died and rose for us, he sent the Holy Spirit, his own first gift for those who believe, to complete his work in the world and to bring to fulfillment the sanctification of us all.

Celebrant and People (sing)

> *A Stream from veins so holy*
> *From the crown of thorns dripped slowly*
> *It's the Blood that Jesus shed to save me*
> *O, the precious Blood of Christ.*

Celebrant [breaks the bread and places a hand on the bread and cup]
Lord, we pray that in your goodness and mercy your Holy Spirit may descend upon us and upon these gifts, sanctifying them and showing them to be holy gifts for your holy people, the bread of life and the cup of salvation, the Body and Blood of your Son, Jesus Christ.

Celebrant and People (sing) [Celebrant distributes bread]

> *From Cross so coarse, not handsome*
> *From the Cross, Blood flowed, did ransom*
> *It's the Blood that purchased all my pardon*
> *O, the precious Blood of Christ.*

Celebrant
When the hour had come for Christ to be glorified by You, his heavenly Father, having loved his own who were in the world, he loved them to the end; at supper with them he took bread, and when he had given thanks to you, he broke it, and gave it to his disciples, and said, "Take, eat: this is my Body, which is given for you. Do this for the remembrance of me." [everyone eats the bread]

Celebrant and People (sing) [the Celebrant distributes the cup]

> *Let heav'n and earth exalt him*
> *He was slain, God's Lamb, for our sin*
> *For the Blood has overcome the dragon*
> *O, the precious Blood of Christ.*

Celebrant
After supper he took the cup of wine, and when he had given thanks, he gave it to them, and said, "Drink this, all of you: this is my Blood of the New Covenant, which is shed for you and for many for the forgiveness of sins. Whenever you drink it, do this for the remembrance of me." [everyone takes the cup]

Celebrant
Father, we celebrate this memorial of our redemption. Recalling Christ's death and his descent among the dead, proclaiming his resurrection and ascension to your right hand, awaiting his coming glory; and offering to you the gifts he has given us, we praise you and we bless you.

Celebrant and People (sing)

> *And for all time, its power*
> *It will keep us from wrath's hour*
> *It's the Blood that washes and redeems us*
> *O, the precious Blood of Christ.*

Celebrant
Jesus said, "I am the bread that came down from heaven . . . I tell you the truth unless you eat the flesh of the Son of Man and drink his blood, you have no life in you . . . For my flesh is real food and my blood is real drink . . . The Spirit gives life, the flesh counts for nothing. The words I speak to you are Spirit and they are life."

Grant that all who share this bread and cup may become one body and one spirit, a living sacrifice in Christ, to the praise of your Name. Amen.

Celebrant and People (sing)

> *Praise God from whom all blessings flow.*
> *Praise Him all creatures here below.*
> *Praise Him above ye heavenly host.*
> *Praise Father, Son, and Holy Ghost, Amen.*

SURSUM CORDA AND EXTINGUISHING OF CANDLES . . . . *All*

> *The Lord be with you,*
> *And with your spirit.*
> *Come, raise your hearts,*
> *We lift them to the Lord.*
> *Let us give thanks to the LORD, our Lord,*
> *It is good and right to give him thanks.*

BENEDICTION . . . . *Don*

SENDING FORTH . . . . *Don*

Small Groups
Ten Principles and Their Implications for Open Christian Gatherings

The Urban Ministry Institute

1. *Loving the Lord God is the center* of our gathering (Deut. 6.4-9; Matt. 22.37-39).

    a. The Father is glorified and adored
    b. Jesus is known and worshiped
    c. The Spirit is sought and obeyed

2. *Freedom and liberty* in the Spirit reigns (2 Cor. 3.17-18).

3. *Every Christian* is encouraged to minister and participate; everyone is free to share, exhort, speak, and participate as God leads (1 Cor. 14.26).

4. *Nobody hogs* or dominates, but all contribute for the upbuilding of the body of Christ (1 Cor. 14.31-33).

5. *Real needs in the body* are shared and prayed for openly together in Christian love (Gal. 6.2; James 5.13-16).

6. The *Word of God* is spoken, heard, and applied to life (1 Cor. 14.1-25).

7. *Supplications, intercessions, and petitions* are made to God in the name of Jesus (1 Tim. 2.1-8).

8. *The ordinances* (Baptism and the Lord's supper) are regularly held and celebrated together. (Rom. 6.1-4; 1 Cor. 11.17-34).

9. *Discovering and using one's gifts and callings* is encouraged, expected, and nurtured; these are confirmed by testified experience and by official appointment in the church (Rom. 12.3-8; 1 Pet. 4.7-11; 1 Cor. 12.1-27; 2 Cor. 13.1; 1 Tim. 1.18; 4.14).

10. *The authority of godly servant-leaders* is exercised, *order* is maintained, and *limits* recognized, all for the edification of the church (2 Cor. 13.9-10; 1 Cor. 14.26-33, 39-40).

Implications for Healthy Small Group Life

1. Every believer in Christ is *joined to the body of Christ*, and should be welcomed into God's forever family (Rom. 15.5-6; John 1.12-13).

2. Every Christian is a *minister*, called by God, and has been given *gifts by the Spirit* to build up the body (Rom. 12.5-8; 1 Cor. 12.4-11).

3. Healthy discipleship and church life requires *three important dimensions of belonging* (relationships):

    a. Personal friendships
    b. Small group care and ministry
    c. Large group celebration and convocation

4. *Dynamic cells* where disciples of Jesus are made and grow do four things well:

    a. They *love* the Lord and each other (Matt. 22.37ff.; John 13.34-35)
    b. They *learn* of Christ together (Matt. 11.29)
    c. They *serve* each other and those in need, whether in the body or their neighbors (James 2.17; 1 John 4.7-8)
    d. They *reach* others with the good news of the gospel, and reproduce themselves in Christ (Matt. 28.18-20)

5. Growing cells are *Spirit-led* and *leader-served*, emphasizing these different components as God leads them, all to bear one another's burdens (Gal. 6.2).

6. Healthy groups *reproduce themselves*, raising up new leaders to lead new cells, and divide and multiply as they continue to grow under God's leading (Eph. 4.11-15).

The Service of Believer's Baptism

Rev. Dr. Don L. Davis

The following is a model of a Believer's Baptism Service. The general outline is as follows:

Opening Prayer and Invocation
Hymn, Chorus, or Anthem
Brief Explanation of Baptism
Scripture Reading
Presentation and Examination of the Candidates
The Baptismal Covenant
Personal Words of Testimony and Affirmation
Prayers for the Candidates
Baptism of the Candidates
Hymn, Song, Final Word of Exhortation, and Benediction

Depending on the church tradition, certain items as the Baptismal Covenant (a recitation of the Apostles' Creed by the congregation) may be omitted, and other elements may be arranged differently. Still, these above essential elements of invocation, song, Scritpure, examination, personal testimony, prayer, baptism, and benediction are used in various forms throughout the Church of Jesus Christ today.

An Outline for a Believer's Baptism Service

OPENING PRAYER AND INVOCATION

HYMN, CHORUS, OR ANTHEM

BRIEF EXPLANATION OF BAPTISM
The Celebrant (i.e., minister officiating the service) provides a brief explanation of the role and significance of Baptism in the life of the new Christian, and its place in the Church of Jesus Christ.

Example:
Believer's Baptism is the act of obedience commanded by Christ on all who come to him in faith. When we are baptized we acknowledge our repentance from sin, our faith and trust in the death and resurrection of Jesus Christ on our behalf, and testify to those present our commitment to follow Christ as Lord and Master. Through our act of obedience to Christ through water baptism we confess our faith in Jesus, ask for the strength of his Holy Spirit to glorify God in all we are and do, and

express desire to walk in unition with Christ's Body the Church. Through baptism and through faith God establishes a bond with us, himself, and his people that cannot be broken.

We ask that each candidate for Believer's Baptism be sponsored by one or more baptized persons, those who can vouch for their faith and new life and Christ. Sponsors of adults and older children present their candidates and thereby signify their endorsement of the candidates and their intention to support them by prayer and example in their Christian life.

Infants may be dedicated by their parents, who select sponsors commonly called godparents, who present their little ones to the Lord, with their godparents making promises to guide, watch, and protect those so dedicated until they come of age to place their faith in Christ in voluntary faith.

Every candidate for Baptism signifies in their obedience their commitment to grow in the grace and the knowledge of Jesus Christ in the Church, to seek God as Christ's follower, and to fulfill with zeal and love their responsibilities as members of Christ's Church.

Scripture Reading

The Celebrant (or someone appointed) reads select Scriptures relevant to the theme of Baptism in the presence of those gathered:

Matthew 28.18-20 (ESV) – And Jesus came and said to them, "All authority in heaven and on earth has been given to me. Go therefore and make disciples of all nations, baptizing them in the name of the Father and of the Son and of the Holy Spirit, teaching them to observe all that I have commanded you. And behold, I am with you always, to the end of the age."

Romans 6.1-8 (ESV) – What shall we say then? Are we to continue in sin that grace may abound? By no means! How can we who died to sin still live in it? Do you not know that all of us who have been baptized into Christ Jesus were baptized into his death? We were buried therefore with him by baptism into death, in order that, just as Christ was raised from the dead by the glory of the Father, we too might walk in newness of life. For if we have been united with him in a death like his, we shall certainly be united with him in a resurrection like his. We know that our old self was crucified with him in order that the body of sin might be brought to nothing, so that we would no longer be enslaved to sin. For one who has died has been set free from sin. Now if we have died with Christ, we believe that we will also live with him.

PRESENTATION AND EXAMINATION OF THE CANDIDATES
(Please note: the presentation and examination of candidates differs among the Church traditions. What all share, however, is a clear opportunity for the candidates to affirm their faith in Christ, their renunciation of the world, and their commitment to follow Christ as faithful members of his Church. The following presentation, examination, and covenant can be amended based on the tradition sponsoring the service).

Celebrant: **The Candidate(s) for Holy Baptism will now be presented.**

[Adults and Older Children – The candidates who are able to answer for themselves are presented individually by their Sponsors, as follows:]

Sponsor: I present _____ to receive the Sacrament of Baptism.

[The Celebrant asks each candidate when presented:]

Celebrant: **Do you desire to be baptized?**

Candidate: I do.

[Infants and Younger Children – The candidates who are unable to answer for themselves are presented individually by their parents and godparents, as follows:]

Parents and
godparents: I present _____ to receive the Sacrament of Baptism.

[When all have been presented the Celebrant asks the parents and godparents:]

Celebrant: **Will you be responsible for seeing that the child you present is brought up in the Christian faith and life?**

Parents and godparents: I will, with God's help.

Celebrant: **Will you by your prayers and witness help this child to grow into the full stature of Christ?**

Parents and
godparents: I will, with God's help.

[The Celebrant asks the following questions of the candidates who can speak for themselves, and of the parents and godparents who speak on behalf of the infants and younger children:]

Question:	Do you renounce Satan and all the spiritual forces of wickedness that rebel against God?
Answer:	I renounce them.
Question:	Do you renounce the evil powers of this world which corrupt and destroy the creatures of God?
Answer:	I renounce them.
Question:	Do you renounce all sinful desires that draw you from the love of God?
Answer:	I renounce them.
Question:	Do you turn to Jesus Christ and accept him as your Savior?
Answer:	I do.
Question:	Do you put your whole trust in his grace and love?
Answer:	I do.
Question:	Do you promise to follow and obey him as your Lord?
Answer:	I do.

[When there are others to be presented, the Celebrant says:]

Celebrant:	The other Candidate(s) will now be presented.

Presenters:	I present these persons for Confirmation.
	    - or -
	I present these persons to be received into this Communion.
	    - or -
	I present these persons who desire to reaffirm their baptismal vows.

[The Celebrant asks the candidates:]

Celebrant:	Do you reaffirm your renunciation of evil?

Candidate: I do.

Celebrant:	**Do you renew your commitment to Jesus Christ?**
Candidate:	I do, and with God's grace I will follow him as my Savior and Lord.

[After all have been presented, the Celebrant addresses the congregation, saying:]

Celebrant:	**Will you who witness these vows do all in your power to support these persons in their life in Christ?**
People:	We will.

[The Celebrant then says these or similar words:]

Celebrant:	**Let us join with those who are committing themselves to Christ and renew our own baptismal covenant.**

The Baptismal Covenant

Celebrant:	**Do you believe in God the Father?**
People:	I believe in God, the Father almighty, creator of heaven and earth.
Celebrant:	**Do you believe in Jesus Christ, the Son of God?**
People:	I believe in Jesus Christ, his only Son, our Lord. He was conceived by the power of the Holy Spirit and born of the Virgin Mary. He suffered under Pontius Pilate, was crucified, died, and was buried. He descended to the dead. On the third day he rose again. He ascended into heaven, and is seated at the right hand of the Father. He will come again to judge the living and the dead.
Celebrant:	**Do you believe in God the Holy Spirit?**
People:	I believe in the Holy Spirit, the holy catholic Church, the communion of saints, the forgiveness of sins, the resurrection of the body, and the life everlasting.
Celebrant:	**Will you continue in the apostles' teaching and fellowship, in the breaking of bread, and in the prayers?**
People:	I will, with God's help.

Celebrant: Will you persevere in resisting evil, and, whenever you fall into sin, repent and return to the Lord?

People: I will, with God's help.

Celebrant: Will you proclaim by word and example the Good News of God in Christ?

People: I will, with God's help.

Celebrant: Will you seek and serve Christ in all persons, loving your neighbor as yourself?

People: I will, with God's help.

Celebrant: Will you strive for justice and peace among all people, and respect the dignity of every human being?

People: I will, with God's help.

Personal Words of Testimony and Affirmation
[The Candidate(s) for Holy Baptism are asked to give a personal word of testimony about their belief in Christ, their desire to trust and obey him, and their commitment to follow him fully, as the Spirit leads.]

Prayers for the Candidates

[The Celebrant then says to the congregation:]

Celebrant: Let us now pray for these persons who are to receive the Sacrament of new birth [and for those (this person) who have renewed their commitment to Christ.]

[A petitioner (person appointed for prayer) asks God's blessing and provision on the candidates for baptism with this or a similar prayer:]

Petitioner: Grant, O Lord, that all who are baptized into the death of Jesus Christ your Son may live in the power of his resurrection and look for him to come again in glory; who lives and reigns now and forever. Amen.

BAPTISM OF THE CANDIDATES
[The Celebrant turns to the Candidate, having prepared them for immersion into the water, and pronounces the following words over them:]

Celebrant: And now, _____, upon your public confession of faith in our Jesus Christ as both Lord and Savior, and in light of your professed desire to obey Christ by giving yourself to be baptized here in the presence of these witnesses, I now baptize you in the name of the Father, and the Son, and the Holy Spirit. Amen.

[The Celebrant baptizes the candidate, and asks the congregation to greet the newly baptized Christian as full member of the Church of Jesus Christ.]

FINAL WORD OF EXHORTATION, CLOSING HYMN OR SONG, AND BENEDICTION

Sample Follow-up Card
World Impact

Name: _____

Names of relatives:

Brother: Uncle:

Sister: Aunt:

Mother: Cousin:

Father: Other:

Address: _____ **Phone:** _____

Notes	What Needs to Be Done	By Whom	By When

Church Plant Team Responsive Reading
World Impact

Leader
As church-planting missionaries, it is your task to proclaim, by word and deed, the Gospel of Jesus Christ and to build his Church. You are to call people to repentance and faith, announcing God's forgiveness to those who repent and believe. You are to love and serve the people you work among. You are to be faithful in preaching and teaching the Word of God to them. You are to baptize and disciple them so that they learn to obey everything that Christ commanded.

Teams
We commit ourselves to the task of establishing new churches among the unreached in urban America.

Leader
So now, go forth in his name and make disciples.

Teams
We will seek to respect and be guided by our appointed leaders, and serve our fellow team members with love and humility.

Leader
Go, and bear witness to the Gospel of Jesus Christ.

Teams
We will strive to be diligent in our reading and study of the Scriptures and faithfully teach and defend sound doctrine.

Leader
Go, and sow the seeds of eternal life.

Teams
We will trust the Holy Spirit to help us to faithfully shepherd all whom we are called to serve, laboring together with them and with our fellow ministers to build up the Church of God.

Leader
Go, and declare the name of Jesus to the lost.

Teams
We will do our best to pattern our lives in obedience to Christ's teachings so that we may be an example to the churches we plant.

Leader

Go, and advance the Kingdom of God among the poor.

Teams

We will seek in all things the prompting of the Holy Spirit, exercising the wisdom he provides us in all things and persevering in prayer, both public and private.

Leader

O God, we make ourselves available to you as your instruments to bring the freedom, wholeness, and justice of your Kingdom to all those served by our ministry.

All

Make us instruments of your gospel, your peace, and your Kingdom, to the glory of your name.

Key Roles of a Church Planting Team
World Impact

- Evangelist (good at developing relationships with new people to lead them to God)
- Worship leader
- Children's ministry leader
- Shepherd/care-giver (good at nurturing the believers)
- Organizer (organizes special projects and builds systems to turn vision into reality)
- Administrator (administrates systems to help team accomplish goals)
- Church Planter (roles that can't be delegated)
  - ~ Spiritual leadership and vision casting
  - ~ Team building and supervision
  - ~ Modeling pastoral care and evangelism
  - ~ Overall leadership of small group ministry

The Power of Multiplication
The 2 Timothy 2.2 Principle
Rev. Dr. Don L. Davis

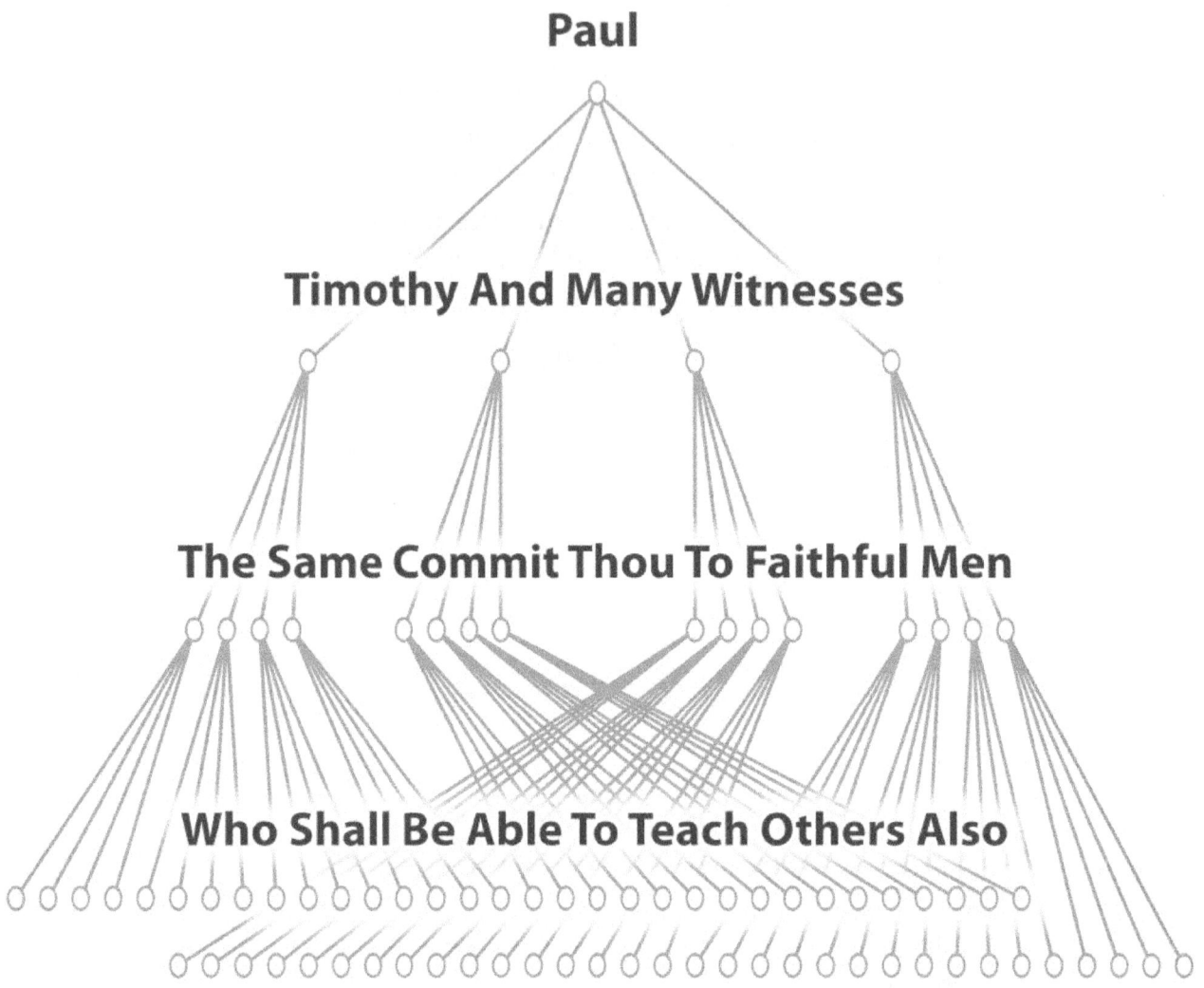

2 Tim. 2.2 (ESV) - And what you have heard from me in the presence of many witnesses entrust to faithful men who will be able to teach others also.

Developing Ears That Hear: Responding to the Spirit and the Word
Rev. Dr. Don L. Davis

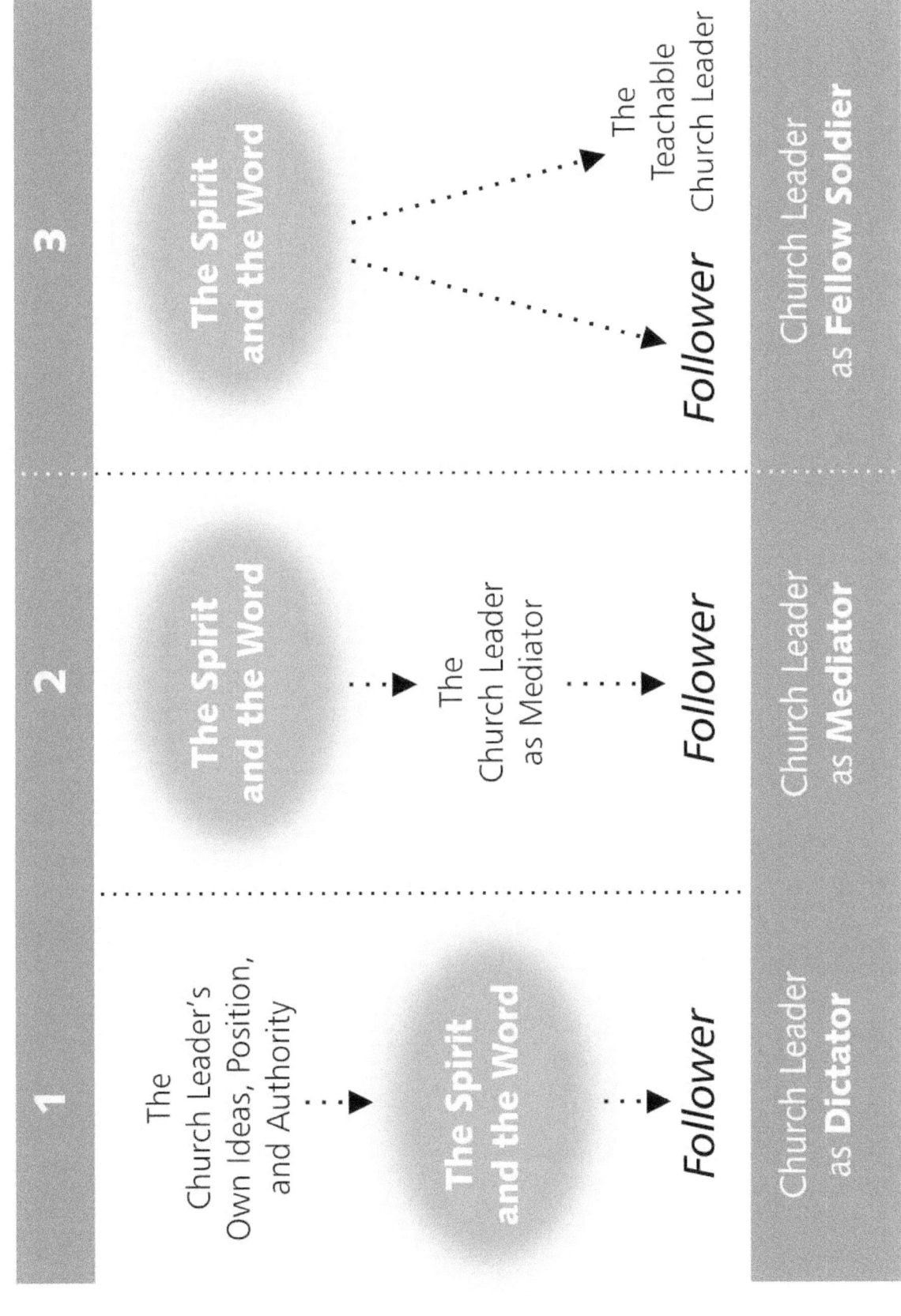

Appendix
**Twenty-five Years of
Urban Church Planting among the Poor:**
A Report

Twenty Five Years of Urban Church Planting Among the Poor: A Report

Dr. Hank Voss
National Director for Church Planting

January 31, 2015

The Urban Ministry Institute
National Office for Church Planting

Table of Contents

I. Introduction 4
II. Executive Summary of World Impact's Church Plant History 5
    A. Church Plants and Churches 5
    B. Training: 6
    C. Missional Partnerships 6
III. Regional Reports 8
    A. Introduction 8
    B. East Coast 8
    C. Midwest 9
    D. West Coast 11
IV. World Impact Church Planting Environmental Assessment 14
    A. General 14
    B. World Impact Strengths 14
    C. Weaknesses (Icebergs below surface) 14
V. Four Recommendations for 2015 15
    A. Present research 15
    B. Identify agreed upon language for WI church planting nationally. 15
    C. Develop Certification for Church Planters in Ministry Context 16
    D. Church Planting Resource Table at 13 conferences in 2015. 16
VI. Appendixes 17
    A. Appendix 1: Strategic Objectives of the National Office of Church Planting 17
    B. Appendix 2: "Healthy churches" Defined 18
    C. Appendix 3: "Napkin" Budget 19
    D. Appendix 4: Frequently Asked Questions 20
    E. Appendix 5: Three Components of a Urban Church Plant Movement .. 21
    F. Appendix 6: WI Church Planting Partnerships: Denominations 22
    G. Appendix 7: WI Church Plant Partnerships: Associations 23
    H. Appendix 8: WI Church Planting Partnerships: "Movements" 23
    I. Appendix 9: WI Church Planting Partnership Totals 23
    J. Appendix 10: Abbreviations Used in Report 24
    K. Appendix 11: Current Regional Church Planting Assignments 26

L. Appendix 12: Movement sample: "Christ is Lord" (Rev. Hector Cedillo)..... 31
M. Appendix 13: World Impact Church Planting Resources. 33

Twenty Five Years of Urban Church Planting Among the Poor: A Report

I. **Introduction**

    A. World Impact is a Christian missions organization committed to planting healthy urban churches, especially among the poor.

    B. In 1990, World Impact's National Board announced a ministry philosophy change emphasizing the importance of planting urban churches as a core part of World Impact's mission. In 1991, the first church plant efforts were officially launched by World Impact as "Celebration Churches."[1]

    C. In the twenty-five years between 1991 and January 1, 2015 World Impact and its partners have commissioned over 150 church plants. More than half of these bodies are currently advancing the Kingdom of God among the poor.

        1. During this time, World Impact has also trained nearly 6,000 leaders through church planting conferences, church plant schools, and the TUMI satellite network.

        2. World Impact has also partnered with more than 30 denominations, associations, and movements to plant churches.

    D. In October of 2014, World Impact's second president, Rev. Efrem Smith announced a new vision for World Impact's church planting initiative, "Crowns of Beauty."[2]

        1. By the end of 2021, World Impact's 50th year of ministry, World Impact will have planted or partnered to plant three hundred new healthy churches in America's under-resourced communities.

        2. Gideon's story provides an example of how God used 300 to bring freedom, wholeness, and justice to a people who were "powerfully oppressed" (Judges 6:2) and it informs World Impact's church planting vision.

---

[1] The three foundational papers for World Impact's move into church planting are currently available on World Impact's Intranet. They are: Terry Cornett and Don Davis, "Developing Urban Congregations: A Framework for World Impact Church Planters" (World Impact Press, 1991), 69 pages; Terry Cornett and Don Davis, "Missionary and Culture" (Wichita, KS, 1991), 37 pages; Don Davis and Terry Cornett, "Empowering People for Freedom, Wholeness, and Justice," reprinted in *Foundations for Christian Mission*, ed. Don Davis, vol. 4, Capstone Curriculum (Wichita, KS: The Urban Ministry Institute, 2005), 310–39.

[2] Efrem Smith, *World Impact Strategic Plan 2014 - Efrem Smith*, 2014, https://www.youtube.com/watch?v=5eOxhp_1FzU&feature=youtu.be.

3. World Impact's Church Planting Initiative is known as "Crowns of Beauty." The prophet Isaiah predicted a time when God himself would come and make beautiful a people in bondage and exile (Isaiah 60:4). The Lord would make ashes into a "Crown of Beauty" (Isaiah 61:10). He would do this amazing work so that his beauty would be displayed (Isaiah 60:21; Eph 3:10).

II. Executive Summary of World Impact's Church Plant History

A. Church Plants and Churches[3]

1. Totals: 156 church plant teams commissioned by World Impact and its partners since 1991.

    a) 1990–1999 = 25 Church Plants

    b) 2000–2009 = 82 Church Plants

    c) 2010–2015 = 49 Church Plants.

2. Generations:

    a) 17 Second Generation Church Plants

    b) 1 Third Generation Church Plant

    c) 2 Fourth Generation Church Plants

3. Church Plant Sizes:

    a) 11 are Simple Church size (3-19 people)

    b) 93 are Small "House" Church size (20–50 people)

    c) 53 are Community Church size (51–150 people),

    d) 0 are Hub Church size (200+)

4. Active Churches:

    a) 82 (at least) are currently active (82/137 CPs or 60% of total church plant efforts, 19 unknown status)

    b) 0 simple churches are active (0/11 CPs or 0%)

---

[3]A "church plant" is a formally commissioned church plant team which has not yet completed the "Transition" phase of a church plant cycle. A "church" is a church plant that has completed the "T" or "Transition" phase of church planting as evidenced by the commissioning of "elders" (Titus 1:5).

c) 50 Small "House" Churches are active (50/89 CPs or 56%, 4 unknown status)

   d) 31 Community churches are active (31/38 CPs or 82%, 15 unknown status)

B. Training

   1. More than 3,600 leaders trained through four national conferences:

      a) **The Jericho Conference** (Los Angeles, 1996). World Impact's first Church Planting conference trained some 200 missionaries and urban leaders in the foundations of urban church planting.

      b) **The Crowns of Beauty Conferences** I(1999), II (2001), and III (2004) in Los Angeles brought together over 3,200 urban church leaders from more than thirty denominations in order to launch new churches and church plant movements among the poor.

      c) **The Timothy Conference** (Wichita, 2004) brought together some 200 urban church leaders to challenge them to pursue Church Planting in their own communities.

   2. More than 300 leaders and some 80 church plant teams trained through 15 national and regional church plant schools.

   3. More than 2,000 Urban Church Leaders trained in church planting through the TUMI satellite network:

      a) Over 200 urban church leaders have taken the eight-week *Vision for Mission: Nurturing an Apostolic Heart* Foundations course on the heart of a church planter.

      b) Over 1,600 urban leaders have taken the eight-week Capstone Course on Church Planting (*Module 12: Focus on Reproduction*).

      c) Over 200 urban church leaders have taken the eight-week *Winning the World* Foundations course on Church Plant Movements.

C. Missional Partnerships

   1. World Impact has partnered with more than 30 denominations, associations, and movements to plant churches.

      a) These denominations include the Christian Missionary and Alliance, the Reformed Church in America, Converge, Evangelical Free Church, Evangelical Lutheran Church of America and many others (see Appendix 6).

- b) 119 partnership church plants have resulted in 50 active church plants and 42 active churches.

- c) One fruitful example of partnership is World Impact's work with the Urban Church Association of Los Angeles. This partnership has resulted in 32 church plants, twenty five of which are currently active. Seven TUMI satellites have also been launched through the LA UCA.

2. While World Impact has partnered to launch more than 195 TUMI satellites, at least 37of these TUMI satellites were started by church planting denominations, associations, and movements (28 currently active in TUMI satellite network).

    - a) An example would be the Manantial Church Association in Cuba. Manantial de Amor is an American Baptist church in Los Angeles that has planted twenty-five churches in Cuba. Manantial has started three TUMI satellites, one in Los Angeles (2014) and two in Cuba (2015) in order to train their church leaders and church planters.

    - b) Minister Joel (site coordinator for Manantial Church) is pictured at right with TUMI materials he brought to Cuba in January of 2015.

Twenty Five Years of Urban Church Planting Among the Poor: A Report

III. Regional Reports

A. Introduction

Information for World Impact's three regions is summarized in the table below. Definitions for categories and abbreviations used in the report can be found in Appendix 3.

	ECR	MWR	WCR
Total # of Church Plant Efforts	21	27	107
Total # of Active Churches and Church Plants	9	8	58
Primary Ministry Assignment (PMA) as Church Planters (RMO and Ministry Staff)	0	0	12
Primary Ministry Assignment (PMA) as Church Planters (Associates)	3	0	1
Primary Ministry Assignment (PMA) "Ministry Developers"		7	
Currently Active MTLs	1	2	6
Currently Active TLs	3	1	12
Church Plant "Movements"	0	2	2
Denomination and Association Church Planting Partnerships	4	10	20
Approximate # of Active TUMI Satellites	13	36	80
Approximate # of Active TUMI Students	150	350	1,200

B. East Coast

1. **Summary:** The East Coast Region has planted or partnered in 21 church plant efforts since 1990. Nine of these church plants and churches are currently active. There are currently no staff assigned to full time church plant activities, but there is 1 MTL (RMO with a SMA) and 3 TL (WI Associates) currently active in the region.

2. Church Plants:

    a) 21 Church Plant efforts since 1990

    b) 9 currently active church plants or churches (2 status unknown)

3. Church Planting Staff

Currently no WI staff are serving full time in church planting roles on the East Coast.

4. East Coast Region Church Planting Story

a) 24/7 Community Church

The 24/7 Community Church (pictured left) grew out of the first Crowns of Beauty Conference in 1999. Dr. Fred Clark served as a "midwife" for the team which was planted out of a church in Montvale, NJ by Pastor Ron Robinson.

Pastor Robinson had been serving as a deacon previously. Some of the early members of 24/7 had been in Ron's Bible study and helped launch the church. Ron named the church "24/7" because he wanted the church to make Jesus available 24 hours per day, seven days per week in the community. The church regularly has held summer evangelistic festivals and continues to minister 24/7 in Newark, NJ.

C. Midwest

1. **Summary:** The Midwest Region has planted or partnered in 27 church plant efforts since 1990. Fourteen of these church plants and churches are currently active. There are two possible movements in the region (Christ the Victor [6 churches/church plants] and Iglesia Del Maestro [2 churches]. There are currently no staff assigned to full time church plant activities.

2. Church Plants:

a) 21 Church Plant efforts since 1990

b) 8 currently active church plants or churches (6 status unknown)

3. Church Planting Staff

Currently no WI staff are serving full time in church planting roles in the Midwest Region, but there are 2 MTLs (2 RMO) and 1 TL (WI Ministry Staff) currently active in the region. The Midwest Region has developed a new position called "Ministry Developer." There are 7 "full-time" (core) people serving on the "Ministry Developer" team and 17 "part-time" (support) people on this team.

4. Midwest Church Planting Stories

a) Restored Community Church: The Story of a Church with a Vision

Pastor Rob Danz is a TUMI graduate who planted Restored Community Church. He is also the Site Coordinator of TUMI Restored. He and the elders at his church have a vision and dream that Restored Community Church would become a Church Planting Movement. Pastor Rob is one of hundreds of TUMI students who have caught the vision of seeing God's kingdom advanced in every neighborhood in every city through the local church.

b) Christ the Victor Churches: The Story of a New Movement of Churches

Christ the Victor is a movement of churches launched by World Impact Missionaries in 2008. There are currently four churches in the network. The CTV movement has developed a number of resources to aid church planters in their movement (See right).

Twenty Five Years of Urban Church Planting Among the Poor: A Report

c) Iglesia Del Maestro: A Church with International Impact

Pastors Juan Pablo and Sol Herrera have planted two churches in the Dallas area. Their first church began working with a church plant in Guadalajara, Mexico. That church began training church planters using TUMI. The church has now planted three churches through TUMI students who have been trained as church planters.

D. West Coast

1. **Summary:** The West Coast Region has planted or partnered in 107 church plant efforts since 1990. Fifty eight of these church plants and churches are currently active. There are two possible movements in the region (Powerhouse [3 church plants] and Christ is Lord [16 churches/ church plants]). World Impact currently has 15 staff assigned to full time church plant activities in the region. Church Plant Resources for the region are:

   a) 6 MTLs

   b) 12 Team Leaders (3 full time)

   c) 21 PTM (8 full time)

   d) 17 STM (0 full time)

2. Church Plants:

   a) 107 Church Plant efforts since 1990

   b) 58 are currently active church plants or churches (9 status unknown)

3. Church Planting Staff

The West Coast Region has six Church Plant Coaches (formally called "Multiple Team Leaders"), 12 church plant Team Leaders (TL) and 21 staff serving as Primary Team Members (PTMs) on church plant teams. Thirteen West Coast staff have church planting as their Primary Ministry Assignment (PMA).

4. Stories

   a) Powerhouse Church: A Story of Denominational Partnership and Kingdom Compassion and Justice (2006)

   (1) Rev. Dr. Todd Grant and his wife Jennifer Grant joined staff with World Impact in 2006 after having pastored and planted several churches. After attending church plant school in 2006 they were commissioned to lead a Church Plant Team in Watts, CA.

   (2) Today Powerhouse Church operates a free Christian medical clinic, a free dental clinic, free medical and counseling services for those facing unexpected pregnancies, a men's home, a food distribution ministry, and a variety of youth programs. The church plant's transformational impact on the Watts community is currently the subject of doctoral research and has been reported on in a number of media outlets. For a short video on Powerhouse and on the Grant's story click here.

b) Church by the Lake: A Story of Church Plant Multiplication through Equipped and Empowered Leaders (2000)

The Church by the Lake was planted by Pastor Hector Cedillo in partnership with a team of World Impact Missionaries beginning in 1999. In January of 2004, The Church by the Lake planted its first church. Hector is believing God for at least 343 (7x7x7) daughter, granddaughter, and great granddaughter churches to be planted from Church by the Lake before he dies.

A third church was planted through the ministry of The Church by the Lake in July of 2007 under the leadership of Pastor Enrique Juarez. A fourth church planter, Gonza Gonzalas was sent out to plant a church near Mexico City in the Fall of 2007. Both Enrique and Gonza were licensed by World Impact for ministry in October of 2007 and Pastor Hector was ordained through World Impact on Oct. 14, 2006.

More than twenty leaders from the Church by the Lake have become TUMI students, and as of the end of 2014, Hector and his TUMI students have seen 16 church plants commissioned in five countries (See list in Appendix). Two of the church plant team leaders whom Hector currently supervises (Pastors Douglas and Octavio) were saved and began their formal theological training at the TUMI satellite in Pitches County Jail where Hector currently serves as a TUMI mentor. Pastor Hector is pictured center right with Pastor Al (far right) and three TUMI students who began their TUMI studies in Los Angeles County Jails.

IV. **World Impact Church Planting Environmental Assessment**

　　A.　General

　　　　1.　World. The Church is rapidly losing its privileged place in the West's post-Christendom context. This change of position presents both crisis and opportunity.

　　　　2.　Church Planting. In the last twenty years the Holy Spirit has raised up an increased emphasis on church plants and church plant movements. The larger movement toward church planting has resulted in many new organizations (Launch), associations (LA-CPM, Association of Related Churches, etc.) and conferences (Verge, Exponential, African American Church Planting Initiative, etc.) which focus on church planting. More than twenty organizations, conferences and training programs in church planting have begun during the last twenty years.

　　B.　World Impact Strengths

　　　　1.　TUMI. A movement of movements with thousands of urban leaders being trained for mission and ministry through the local church

　　　　2.　Church Planting President with cultural competence

　　　　3.　Highly disciplined and committed staff

　　　　4.　Large support base and well respected forty year history

　　C.　Weaknesses (Icebergs below surface)

　　　　1.　Identity Confusion

　　　　　　a)　Lack of clarity across our ministry on core identity. Are we first a Religious Missionary Order (form of the church) or first a non-profit (like other associations above)? Current policies reflect state of confusion and competing understandings of mission's core identity.

　　　　　　b)　Lack of clarity across our ministry on culture issues. Is WI first a cross-cultural missions organization or first a missional order working among the poor?[4]

　　　　2.　Communication and Competency Issues

---

[4] I am thinking here to some of the issues discussed in Leroy Barber and Velma Maia Thomas, *Red, Brown, Yellow, Black, White—Who's More Precious In God's Sight?: A Call for Diversity in Christian Missions and Ministry* (New York: Jericho Books, 2014).

a) Some leaders and staff lack competencies and/or training for assigned tasks.

b) Communication needs to remain a continued priority as misunderstandings abound.

3. Ongoing purge of "old culture" demons

a) Internal challenges related to race and culture

b) Internal issues related to gender (especially women and current policies)

c) Inappropriate uses of spiritual authority[5]

V. **Four Recommendations for 2015**

A. Present research to regional and national leaders. Publish publically accessible reports on World Impact's first 25 years of church planting.

1. Begin Monthly "National News and Notes for Urban Church Planters"

2. Solicit Internal Feedback and Revise Internal Report

3. Publish National Church Planting Report (for external communication; June 1), "Twenty Five Years of Urban Church Planting Among the Poor: A Report." This would be a white paper available at www.tumi.org

B. Identify agreed upon language and qualifications for WI church planting nationally.[6]

1. Publish *Ripe for the Harvest: A Manual for Urban Church Planters* (2015).

2. Publish *A Fresh Harvest: A Manual for Cross-cultural Church Planters* (2015).

---

[5]As illustrated by the influence of Howard Butt's, *The Velvet Covered Brick: Christian Leadership in an Age of Rebellion* (New York: Harper & Row, 1973) on Dr. Keith Philips, who once described the book as his "favorite book on leadership."

[6]Examples of this language include "charters," job descriptions for roles ("Coach," "Team Leader," etc.) and levels of training for each role (e.g. "provisional," "senior"). Most of this language is already documented in *The John Mark Curriculum* (Los Angeles: World Impact Press, 2000), 500 pages.

C. Develop Certification for Church Planters in Ministry Context

1. Develop Church Plant Certification Process for TUMI Satellites and Partners[7]

2. Launch **Church Plant Coach Training,** and publish new manual for Church Plant Coaches (update of *Feeding and Leading: A Manual for Coaching Church Planters*)

3. Hold Evangel Church Plant School in new three day format (Nov 2015)

4. Develop Training and Certification process for Deans of Evangel so that regional schools can be offered beginning in 2016.

D. World Impact Church Planting Resource Table and church planting information at 13 conferences in 2015.

1. Seven World Impact Conferences

    1. EC Men's Conference
    2. MW Men's Conference
    3. WC Men's Conference
    4. TUMI Summit
    5. EC Staff Conference
    6. MW Staff Conference
    7. WC Staff Conference

2. Six Urban Ministry/Church Planting Conferences

    1. Together LA (Feb 26-28)
    2. Exponential East (April 27-30), Orlando.
    3. UYWI (May 14-16)-LA, Efrem Smith (Keynote)
    4. Legacy (July 23-25)
    5. Flavor Fest (October 8-11). Efrem Smith (Keynote)
    6. CCDA (November 11-14)

---

[7]The goal is eventually to send 300 church plant Team Leaders (TLs), plus five team members (PTMs) per team, through Evangel Church Plant School. Thus vision is to send six urban leaders from 300 teams (1,800 church leaders) through Evangel in next seven years.

VI. Appendixes

A. Appendix 1: Strategic Objectives of the National Office of Church Planting

1. Reestablish annual Church Plant School on a national or regional basis (Evangel Church Plant School).

2. Establish a national system for identifying, accessing, training, and commissioning church plant team leaders.

3. Support regions in their mission of chartering three hundred church plant team leaders.

4. Partner with other groups (Associations, Movements and Denominations) to reach church planting vision.

5. Research urban church planting among the poor at World Impact and at other organizations.

6. Centralize use of TUMI's resources by World Impact Church Planters.

7. Develop resources for urban church planting.

8. Ensure regular communication within network.

B. Appendix 2: "Healthy Churches" Defined

"We Believe in One, Holy, Catholic and Apostolic Church"

An outline for healthy churches can be found in the Nicene Creed.

1. "One"

    a) Churches value obedience to God's Word (Psa 119; e.g. *Equip*; *Master the Bible, Bible Blossom Project*).

    b) Churches value the Great Tradition (e.g. *Sacred Roots*, Capstone's Nicene foundations).

2. "Holy"

    a) Churches value the freedom, justice, and wholeness of the Kingdom of God (Kingdom of God theme in Capstone).

    b) Churches value our participation in Christ's royal priesthood (Seven essential practices of the royal priesthood).

3. "Catholic"

    a) Churches value the catholicity of the church (committed to connection with other churches).

    b) Churches value and embrace the gifts of different cultures; (*Post Black-Post White; Black and Human*).

4. "Apostolic"

    a) Churches value proclaiming the gospel especially among the poor (e.g. *Evangelize*, Capstone's Urban Mission modules, Pauline Cycle).

    b) Churches value empowering missional leaders who reproduce themselves (*Empower;* Capstone Curriculum; Evangel Church Plant School).

C. Appendix 3: "Napkin" Budget

    1. Proposed 2015 Budget = $52,000

        a) $11,700- National Office of Church Planting Expenses
        b) $5,000- Coaches Training (1 School, Ten Coaches)
        c) $35,300 National Evangel School (1 School, 10 Teams)
        d) Salary
            (1) Director = Missionary Support
            (2) Administrator = ?

    2. Proposed Cost for Evangel Church Plant School Teams (6 People)

Materials	$300	$50 * 6 persons
Food and Lodging	$1,800	$300 * 6 persons for three nights and nine meals
Coach and Dean Expenses	$600	Cost of lodging for two coaches.
Travel	$300	50 per person
Miscellaneous	$200	
Total per team	$3200	

    3. Number of Schools Needed (Average of 10 Teams per School)

	Number of Schools	Number of Teams	Deans Needed	Coaches Needed
2015	1	10	2	10
2016	3	30	6	30
2017	4	40	8	40
2018	5	50	10	50
2019	5	50	10	50
2020	6	60	12	60
2021	7	70	14	70
Total	31	310	14	70

D. Appendix 4: Frequently Asked Questions

1. What is the difference between a church and a church plant? A "church plant" is a formally commissioned church plant team which has not yet completed the "Transition" phase of a church plant cycle. A "church" is a church plant that has completed the "T" or "Transition" phase of church planting as evidenced by the commissioning of "elders" (Titus 1:5).

2. What is a church plant "movement"? Church plant movements are defined differently by different organizations. In this report, the term is used for a local church which has planted at least one daughter church and which has a clearly defined vision for launching more churches with Contextualization, Commonality and Connectivity (See Appendix 5 for definitions).

3. How will the 300 churches be counted? Regional leadership has suggested we begin counting the "300" as church plants in progress or commissioned after Jan 1, 2014. Thus any church plants that have been going since that date, or which will be commissioned between now and the end of 2021 can be counted as one of the 300.

E.   Appendix 5: Three Components of a Urban Church Plant Movement

The Threefold Cord of Urban Cross-Cultural Church Planting Movements
Rev. Dr. Don L. Davis

Urban Church Plant Movement

- Contextualization
- Commonality
- Connectivity

Ecc. 4.12 (ESV) - *And though a man might prevail against one who is alone, two will withstand him—a threefold cord is not quickly broken.*

Contextualization – (the <u>cultural</u> essential) "an urban church planting movement must be grounded in the culture, experience, leadership, and identity of a particular people group who come to embrace the Gospel holistically in such a way that those within the culture both understand and accept as their very own."

Commonality – (the <u>spiritual</u> essential) "an urban church planting movement must be rooted in a shared spirituality, theology, liturgy, and praxis that empowers its members to practice a common spiritual discipline, to submit to a shared governance and order, to recognize and affirm its unique theological and spiritual distinctives, to incorporate and confirm its members and leaders according to a common protocol, and to integrate the efforts of its congregations together into a coherent, unified movement."

Connectivity – (the <u>structural</u> essential) "an urban church planting movement must connect its leaders, members, and congregations through integrated structures that enable its congregations and leaders to gather regularly for convocation and fellowship, that combine resources and funds for cooperation and mutual support, and that provide oversight that protects and equips the members of the movement for dynamic reproduction."

TUMI

F. Appendix 6: WI Church Planting Partnerships: Denominations

Name	Pri.	YFP	MRP	WICPP	CPsA	CA	TS	TSA	ECR	MWR	WCR
American Baptist	A	2015	2015	1	1	1	1	1			1
Assemblies of God	C	2005	2005	1	0	1	0	0			1
Baptist General Conference	C	2000		1	0	1	0	0			1
Brethren	C	*2003*	2003	1			1	1		1	
Calvary Chapel	C	2005	2005	1	0	1	0	0			1
Charismatic Episcopal Church (ICCEE)	A	2015					1	1			
Christian and Missionary Alliance	A	2006	2013	4	3	1	0	0	1	.	1
Christian Church	C	2009		1	0	0	0	0		1	
Church of God (Cleveland)	C	2002	2002	1							
Church of God in Christ (COGIC)	A	2015	2015	0	0	0	6	5		1	
Converge	A	2009	2014	2	0	2	1	1			1
Dallas Baptist Association	B	2006	2014	2	1	1	1	1		1	
Evangelical Covenant Church	A	2015	2015	0	0	0	1	1			1
Evangelical Free Church	A	2000		2	1	1	6	1			1
Evangelical Lutheran (ELCA)	C	2003	2005	8			0	0		1	1
Four Square	C	1999	2013	4	1	1	1	1	1		1
Grace Communion International	C	1999		1	0	1	0	0	1		
Mennonite Brethren	C	2000		2	0	1	0	0		1	
Praise Chapel	C	2012	2012	1	0	1	0	0			1
Presbyterian Church	C	2006		1	0	0	0	0		1	
Presbyterian Church USA	C	2013	2013	1	1	0	0	0			1
Reformed Church of America	A	2008	2014	3	1	2	0	0			1
Salvation Army	C	*2005*	2005	1	0	0	0	0			1
Southern Baptist	A	2007	2014	3	2	1	1	1			1
Vineyard	A	2014	2015	2	2	0	0	0			1
Denomination Totals				44	13	16	20	14	3	6	12

Twenty Five Years of Urban Church Planting Among the Poor: A Report

G. Appendix 7: WI Church Plant Partnerships: Associations

Name	YS	YFP	T#C	Pri.	WICPP	CPsA	CA	TS	TSA	ECR	MWR	WCR	I
UCA-1—LA	2007	2007	30	A	32	17	8	7	6			1	
Launch	2011	2015	30	A	1	1	1	0	0			1	
UCA-4—LA	2012	2012	15	A	3	0	1	0	0			1	
UCA-6—LA	2006	2006	4	A	5	1	3	1	0			1	
UCA-3--Wichita	2011	2011	4	A	4		4				1		
Christian Transformation Association--Newark	2015	2015	30	A						1			
Honduras Church Association	2000	2012	30	A	5	5		1	1				1
Manantial Church Association --Cuba	1990	2014	25	A				3	3				1
Totals					50	24	17	12	10	1	1	4	2

H. Appendix 8: WI Church Planting Partnerships: "Movements" and Partnership Totals

Name	YS	YFP	T#C	Pri.	WICPP	CPsA	CA	TS	TSA	ECR	MWR	WCR
Christ the Victor	2008	2008	6	A	4	2	2	1	1		1	
Christ is Lord	1999	1999	16	A	16	7	6	2	1			1
Powerhouse	2006	2006	3	A	3	3						1
Iglesia Del Maestro	2006	2006	2	A	2	1	1	2	2		1	
Totals					25	13	9	5	4		2	2

I. Appendix 9: WI Church Planting Partnership Totals

World Impact Church Planting Partnership Totals

Name	WICPP	CPsA	CA	TS	TSA	ECR	MWR	WCR	I
Denomination Totals	44	13	16	20	14	3	7	16	
Association Totals	50	24	17	12	10	1	1	4	2
Movement Totals	25	13	9	5	4		2	2	
Combined Totals	119	50	42	37	28	4	10	22	2

J. Appendix 10: Abbreviations Used in Report

!	Needs Charter Renewal
#AC	Number of Active Churches
#TC	Number of Total Churches who have been involved
*	Current Charter on Record
**	Completed Charter on Record
A	Assemble Phase in P.L.A.N.T. Cycle.
Act	Church is currently Active
CC	Community Church (50-150)
C-CP-MA	Current Church Plant Ministry Assignment
CPS	Church Plant School
D.	Done. Church Independent with Elders Established
ECR	East Coast Region
EE	Elders Established
HC	House Church (20-50 people)
Hub	Hub Church (200+)
Int	International
L	Launch Phase in P.L.A.N.T. Cycle.
M	Merged with another church. Date indicates year of merge.
MTL	Multiple Team Leader (Church Plant Coach)
MWR	Midwest Region
N	Nurture Phase in P.L.A.N.T. Cycle.
NA	Not Active
P	Prepare Phase in P.L.A.N.T. Cycle.
P-CB	Partner- Crowns of Beauty
P-CPS-N	Partner-Church Plant School-National
P-CPS-R	Partner Church Plant School Regional
P-CPS-S	Partner-Church Plant School Spanish
PMA	Primary Ministry Assignment (usually <50 hours per week)
Pre-UCA	Pre Urban Church Association
Ps.	Phase of PLANT cycle
PTM	Primary Team Member
P-TNT	Partner- The Nehemiah Team
P-TUMI	Partner-The Urban Ministry Institute
P-UCA	Partner-Urban Church Association
P-WIA	Partner World Impact Associate
P-WIC	Partner-World Impact Chartered
P-WILM	Partner-World Impact Licensed Minister of the Gospel
P-WIOM	Partner-World Impact Ordained Minister of the Gospel
RCP	Reproduced Church Plant
Reg.	Region
SC	Simple Church Model (3-19)

Twenty Five Years of Urban Church Planting Among the Poor: A Report

SMA	Secondary Ministry Assignment (usually <15 hours per week)
STM	Support Team Member
T	Transition Phase in P.L.A.N.T. Cycle.
TL	Team Leader for Church Plant
TNT	The Nehemiah Team. WI Church Plant Coaching Strategy.
TUMI-M-C	TUMI Modules Completed
TUMI-M-M	TUMI Modules Mentored
UCA	Urban Church Association
UCA-1	Urban Church Association-Los Angeles
UCA-2	Urban Church Association-Fresno
UCA-3	Urban Church Association-LA Simple Church
VMA	Volunteer Ministry Assignment
VTM	Volunteer Team Member (Body Life Assignment, <5 hrs/wk)
WCR	West Coast Region
WCR-BA	West Coast Region-Bay Area
WCR-F	West Coast Region -Fresno
WCR-LA	West Coast Region -Los Angeles
WCR-SD	West Coast Region -San Diego
WI	World Impact
WIA	World Impact Associate
WICP	World Impact Church Plant
WI-Gen	World Impact Generation of Church Plant
WI-IC	World Impact Independent Contractor
WI-MS	World Impact Ministry Staff
WIR	World Impact Region
WI-RMO	World Impact Religious Missionary Order
WI-V	World Impact Volunteer
YC	Year Commissioned
YE	Year Ended
YT	Year Transitioned

K. Appendix 11: Current Regional Church Planting Assignments

1. East Coast Region

   a) 1= Multiple Team Leader (MTLs) in Region (currently active)
      (1) 1 = RMO Staff
         (a) 0 = Primary Ministry Assignment (PMA)
         (b) 1 = Secondary Ministry Assignment (SMA)
         (c) 0 = Volunteer Ministry Assignment (VMA)

      (2) 0 = Ministry Staff
         (a) 0 = Primary Ministry Assignment (PMA)
         (b) 0 = Secondary Ministry Assignment (SMA)
         (c) 0 = Volunteer Ministry Assignment (VMA)

      (3) 0 = Associate Staff
         (a) 3 = Primary Ministry Assignment (PMA)
         (b) 0 = Secondary Ministry Assignment (SMA)
         (c) 0 = Volunteer Ministry Assignment (VMA)

      (4) 0 = Volunteer Staff (or other)
         (a) 0 = Primary Ministry Assignment (PMA)
         (b) 0 = Secondary Ministry Assignment (SMA)
         (c) 0 = Volunteer Ministry Assignment (VMA)

   b) 3 = Team Leaders (TLs) in Region
      (1) 0 = RMO Staff
         (a) 0 = Primary Ministry Assignment (PMA)
         (b) 0 = Secondary Ministry Assignment (SMA)
         (c) 0 = Volunteer Ministry Assignment (VMA)

      (2) 0 = Ministry Staff
         (a) 0 = Primary Ministry Assignment (PMA)
         (b) 0 = Secondary Ministry Assignment (SMA)
         (c) 0 = Volunteer Ministry Assignment (VMA)

      (3) 0 = Associate Staff
         (a) 0 = Primary Ministry Assignment (PMA)
         (b) 3 = Secondary Ministry Assignment (SMA)
         (c) 0 = Volunteer Ministry Assignment (VMA)

Twenty Five Years of Urban Church Planting Among the Poor: A Report

            (4)   0 = Volunteer Staff (or other)
                 (a)   0 = Primary Ministry Assignment (PMA)
                 (b)   0 = Secondary Ministry Assignment (SMA)
                 (c)   0 = Volunteer Ministry Assignment (VMA)

       c)   VTM
            (1)   ? = RMO
            (2)   ? = Ministry Staff

       d)   0 = Primary Team Members (PTMs) in Region
            (1)   0 = RMO Staff
                 (a)   0 = Primary Ministry Assignment (PMA)
                 (b)   0 = Secondary Ministry Assignment (SMA)
                 (c)   0 = Volunteer Ministry Assignment (VMA)

            (2)   0 = Ministry Staff
                 (a)   0 = Primary Ministry Assignment (PMA)
                 (b)   0 = Secondary Ministry Assignment (SMA)
                 (c)   0 = Volunteer Ministry Assignment (VMA)

            (3)   0 = Associate Staff
                 (a)   0 = Primary Ministry Assignment (PMA)
                 (b)   0 = Secondary Ministry Assignment (SMA)
                 (c)   0 = Volunteer Ministry Assignment (VMA)

       e)   Support Team Members in Region
            (1)   ? = RMO
            (2)   ? =Ministry Staff

2.   Midwest Region

       a)   2= Multiple Team Leader (MTLs) in Region (currently active)
            (1)   2 = RMO Staff
                 (a)   0 = Primary Ministry Assignment (PMA)
                 (b)   2 = Secondary Ministry Assignment (SMA)
                 (c)   0 = Volunteer Ministry Assignment (VMA)

            (2)   0 = Ministry Staff
                 (a)   0 = Primary Ministry Assignment (PMA)
                 (b)   0 = Secondary Ministry Assignment (SMA)
                 (c)   0 = Volunteer Ministry Assignment (VMA)

(3) 0 = Associate Staff
　　(a) 0 = Primary Ministry Assignment (PMA)
　　(b) 0 = Secondary Ministry Assignment (SMA)
　　(c) 0 = Volunteer Ministry Assignment (VMA)

(4) 0 = Volunteer Staff (or other)
　　(a) 0 = Primary Ministry Assignment (PMA)
　　(b) 0 = Secondary Ministry Assignment (SMA)
　　(c) 0 = Volunteer Ministry Assignment (VMA)

b) 1 = Team Leader (TLs) in Region
　(1) 0 = RMO Staff
　　(a) 0 = Primary Ministry Assignment (PMA)
　　(b) 0 = Secondary Ministry Assignment (SMA)
　　(c) 0 = Volunteer Ministry Assignment (VMA)

　(2) 1 = Ministry Staff
　　(a) 0 = Primary Ministry Assignment (PMA)
　　(b) 1 = Secondary Ministry Assignment (SMA)
　　(c) 0 = Volunteer Ministry Assignment (VMA)

　(3) 0 = Associate Staff
　　(a) 0 = Primary Ministry Assignment (PMA)
　　(b) 3 = Secondary Ministry Assignment (SMA)
　　(c) 0 = Volunteer Ministry Assignment (VMA)

　(4) 0 = Volunteer Staff (or other)
　　(a) 0 = Primary Ministry Assignment (PMA)
　　(b) 0 = Secondary Ministry Assignment (SMA)
　　(c) 0 = Volunteer Ministry Assignment (VMA)

c) 2 = Primary Team Members (PTMs) in Region
　(1) 0 = RMO Staff
　　(a) 0 = Primary Ministry Assignment (PMA)
　　(b) 0 = Secondary Ministry Assignment (SMA)
　　(c) 0 = Volunteer Ministry Assignment (VMA)

　(2) 0 = Ministry Staff
　　(a) 0 = Primary Ministry Assignment (PMA)
　　(b) 2 = Secondary Ministry Assignment (SMA)
　　(c) 0 = Volunteer Ministry Assignment (VMA)

(3) 0 = Associate Staff
   (a) 0 = Primary Ministry Assignment (PMA)
   (b) 0 = Secondary Ministry Assignment (SMA)
   (c) 0 = Volunteer Ministry Assignment (VMA)

d) Support Team Members in Region
   (1) ? = RMO
   (2) ? = Ministry Staff

e) VTM
   (1) ? = RMO
   (2) ? = Ministry Staff

3. West Coast Region

   a) 6 = Multiple Team Leader (MTLs) in Region (currently active)
      (1) 3 = RMO Staff
         (a) 0 = Primary Ministry Assignment (PMA)
         (b) 2 = Secondary Ministry Assignment (SMA)
         (c) 1 = Volunteer Ministry Assignment (VMA)

      (2) 1 = Ministry Staff
         (a) 0 = Primary Ministry Assignment (PMA)
         (b) 1 = Secondary Ministry Assignment (SMA)
         (c) 0 = Volunteer Ministry Assignment (VMA)

      (3) 1 = Associate Staff
         (a) 0 = Primary Ministry Assignment (PMA)
         (b) 1 = Secondary Ministry Assignment (SMA)
         (c) 0 = Volunteer Ministry Assignment (VMA)

      (4) 1 = Volunteer Staff (or other)
         (a) 0 = Primary Ministry Assignment (PMA)
         (b) 0 = Secondary Ministry Assignment (SMA)
         (c) 1 = Volunteer Ministry Assignment (VMA)

   b) 12 = Current Team Leader (TLs) in Region
      (1) 3 = RMO Staff
         (a) 3 = Primary Ministry Assignment (PMA)
         (b) 0 = Secondary Ministry Assignment (SMA)
         (c) 0 = Volunteer Ministry Assignment (VMA)

(2) 3 = Ministry Staff
    (a) 1 = Primary Ministry Assignment (PMA)
    (b) 1= Secondary Ministry Assignment (SMA)
    (c) 1 = Volunteer Ministry Assignment (VMA)

(3) 1 = Associate Staff
    (a) 1 = Primary Ministry Assignment (PMA)
    (b) 0= Secondary Ministry Assignment (SMA)
    (c) 0 = Volunteer Ministry Assignment (VMA)

(4) 5 = Volunteer Staff (or other)
    (a) 0 = Primary Ministry Assignment (PMA)
    (b) 0 = Secondary Ministry Assignment (SMA)
    (c) 5 = Volunteer Ministry Assignment (VMA)

c) 21 = Primary Team Members (PTMs) in Region
   (1) 21 = RMO Staff
      (a) 7 = Primary Ministry Assignment (PMA)
      (b) 14 = Secondary Ministry Assignment (SMA)
      (c) 0 = Volunteer Ministry Assignment (VMA)

   (2) = Ministry Staff
      (a) = Primary Ministry Assignment (PMA)
      (b) = Secondary Ministry Assignment (SMA)
      (c) = Volunteer Ministry Assignment (VMA)

   (3) 0 = Associate Staff
      (a) 0 = Primary Ministry Assignment (PMA)
      (b) 0 = Secondary Ministry Assignment (SMA)
      (c) 0 = Volunteer Ministry Assignment (VMA)

d) Support Team Members in Region
   (1) = RMO
   (2) =Ministry Staff

e) VTM
   (1) = RMO
   (2) = Ministry Staff

L. Appendix 12: Movement sample: "Christ is Lord" (Rev. Hector Cedillo)

WI-Gen	WICP Type	YC	YT	YE or Act.	Church Name	UCA (yes/no)	Reg.	Address or Area	Coach/MTL	Team Leader(s)	World Impact or Partner Church	Origin of Church
1	CC	1999	2004	Act	Cristo Salva (Church By the Lake)	UCA-1	WCR-LA	Central LA	Fred Stoesz	Hector Cedillo (1999-2013)	WI	Parent Church
2	HC	2004	.	2007	La Luz	UCA-1	WRC-LA	Central LA		Hector Cedillo	P-TUMI, P-CPS-S	Church by the Lake
2	HC	2005	2010	Act	One Time Baptist Church	UCA-6	WCR-LA		Hector Cedillo	Fidencio Vasquez	P-CPS-S	Church by the Lake
2	HC	2007		2008	Set Free Church	UCA-1	WRC-LA	Skid Row	Hector Cedillo	Victor Patzán	P-TUMI, P-CPS-S	Church by the Lake
2	HC	2007	2009	Act	Iglesia Nueva Vida		I	Cuatitlan, Yzcalli, Mexico	Hector Cedillo	Pastor Neto		Church by the Lake
2	HC	2010	2011	Act	Iglesia Cristiana Tierra de Dios		I	San Juan del Río, Mexico	Hector Cedillo	Gonzalo Gonzalez	P-TUMI, P-CPS-S	Church by the Lake
2	HC	2011	2011	Act	Iglesia Evangelica de Jesu Cristo	n	I	Tella, Honduras	Hector Cedillo	Norris Beltran	P-TUMI P-TUMI	Church by the Lake
2	HC	2012	2012	Act	Ministerios Internationales de Jesus	n	WRC-LA	Mac Arthur Park	Hector Cedillo	Carlos Mendoza	Grad, P-WILM, P-WIC	Church by the Lake
2	CC	2013		Act	Pitchess Jail Church	UCA-1	WRC-LA	Castaic, CA		Hector Cedillo	P-TUMI	Church by the Lake
2	HC	2013		Act	Lighthouse Spanish Congregation		WRC-LA	20th and Wilshire	Hector Cedillo	Peter Ceaser		Church by the Lake
2	HC	2013		2013	JCT Jesus Christ Tabernacle		WRC-LA	Action, CA		Hector Cedillo	P-TUMI	Church by the Lake

Twenty Five Years of Urban Church Planting Among the Poor: A Report

2	HC	2013	Act	Gracia Inaculada	UCA-1	WRC-LA	Burlington and 8th	Hector Cedillo	Enrique Juarez	P-TUMI, P-WILM	Church by the Lake
2	CC	2013	Act	Men's Central Jail Church	UCA-1				Hector Cedillo		
2	CC	2014	Act	Twin Towers Jail Church	UCA-1				Hector Cedillo		
3	HC	2014 (2/23)	Act	Christ the Lord Bilingual Ministries	UCA-1	WCR-LA	Venice, CA	Hector Cedillo	Daniel Orozco		Pitchess Prison Church
4	HC	2014 (6/?)	Act	La Iglesia de Jesus Cristo		N	Morelos, Mexico	Hector Cedillo	Pastor Ulices		Christ the Lord Bilingual Ministries

M. Appendix 13: World Impact Church Planting Resources.

FAQ's on World Impact and TUMI
Church and Church Planting Resources

The Urban Ministry Institute (TUMI) has developed more than seven hundred resources for equipping church leaders to engage in urban ministry and mission. Currently these resources are being used in hundreds of churches and urban ministries around the globe. This report reviews some of the more important resources in three categories: Church Planting, Spiritual Formation and Discipleship, and Leadership Development.

I. **Church Planting**

    A. What resource is the single most important practical tool for World Impact Church Plant Coaches and Team Leaders?

        1. *Leading and Feeding Urban Church Plant Teams*

        2. *Leading and Feeding* covers World Impact's basic expectations for Church Plant Charters, Church Plant Team Leaders, and other church plant team members.

    B. What are the two most important theological books for WI Church Planters?

        1. Davis, Don. *Sacred Roots: A Primer on Retrieving the Great Tradition*. Wichita, KS: The Urban Ministry Institute, 2010.

        2. Smith, Efrem. *The Post-Black and Post-White Church: Becoming the Beloved Community in a Multi-Ethnic World*. Vol. 59. San Francisco: Jossey-Bass, 2012.

    C. How many courses are available from TUMI on Church Planting?

        1. *Focus on Reproduction*

            a) One of four Capstone Curriculum Urban Missions Courses, this eight segment course covers the foundational principles of church planting.
            b) This is the most important course available for WI Church Planters.

2. *Winning the World*

   a) The focus of the course is on Church Plant Movements.
   b) (This course can be downloaded and taken for free at www.biblicaltraining.org)

3. *Vision for Mission: Nurturing an Apostolic Heart*

   a) A TUMI Foundations Class.
   b) Significantly impacted numerous World Impact missionaries to pursue church planting. http://www.tumistore.org/foundations-nurturing-an-apostolic-heart-course/

D. What is Evangel Church Plant School?

   1. World Impact's church plant schools have chartered more than eighty church plant teams. The next one is tentatively planned for November, 2015. Watch for more information on the *Evangel Church Plant School*.

   2. Look for *Evangel Church Plant School* at a location near you. Contact Hank Voss if you or a church plant team leader you know is interested in a school in your region (hvoss@worldimpact.org).

E. What system was used to train World Impact missionaries, church planters, team leaders and church plant team coaches from 2000 through 2007?

   1. The *John Mark Curriculum*. This five hundred page resource provided thirty three training modules on discreet topics related to urban mission including modules on Culture, Counseling, Evangelism, Team Leadership, Coaching a Church Plant Team, etc.

   2. This resource is now out of print although hard copies are available in all WI cities.

F. What is a sample resource developed by a World Impact Church Plant?

   1. Christ the Victor is a church in the Midwest region that has started reproducing church plants. Its Church Resource Guidebook is available from Amazon here.

   2. Contact Ryan Carter form more on Christ the Victor resources, church planting conferences, etc.

G. In 2015 look for two new manuals on church planting to be released by The Urban Ministry Institute.

II. **Spiritual Formation and Discipleship**

   A. Sermons and Preaching Resources

      1. More than 500 sermons, lectures, and conference presentations are available for free download at two TUMI websites:

         a) As of October 10, 2014 there are 72 sermons available for download at https://soundcloud.com/tumimedia/sets
         b) At http://www.tumimedia.org
            (1) More than 450 sermons, lectures and conference presentations.
            (2) More than 90 topics are addressed and can be searched easily using topical search tool.

      2. What kind of series are available for free download?

         a) Revised Common Lectionary Year A (More than fifty sermons).
         b) Revised Common Lectionary Year B (More than fifty sermons).
         c) Revised Common Lectionary Year C (More than fifty sermons)
         d) Effective Worship Leading (12 messages)
         e) *Revelation* (22 Sermons), and Many More.

   B. Songs and Worship Resources

      1. Doctor Davis has written more than 500 songs, many of which are available for free (As of October 10, 2014 there are 44 songs and soundtracks available for free download at https://soundcloud.com/tumimedia/sets

      2. See the 12 session course on Effective Worship Leading at http://www.tumimedia.org. See also the TUMI's technical resource for learning the guitar entitled *Making Joyful Noises*.

   C. Spiritual Discipline Resources

      1. TUMI Annual (http://www.tumistore.org/church-resources/)

         a) A devotional guide to prayer and reading Scripture. Published every year by TUMI.
         b) Each year focuses on a different theme.

      2. TUMI Calendar (http://www.tumistore.org/church-resources/)

         a) TUMI's Scripture Texts for the Preaching, Reading, and Prayer taken from the RCL each year.
         b) Each year redesigned with new artwork. .

3. Master the Bible (http://www.tumistore.org/master-the-bible/)

   a) Four Year Plan to memorize more than 800 scripture passages. See a review here.
   b) Resource for Churches to plan how to help their people memorize Scripture. Includes, book, dvds, bookmarks, posters,

4. Prayer Resources

   a) Prayer Mountain! Free Retreat Center at World Impact's Oaks Conference Center for all church planters taking a personal spiritual retreat.
   b) Let God Arise Prayer Network Resources
      (1) Don Davis, *Let God Arise* (TUMI, 2000)
      (2) www.letgodarise.com.

D. Discipleship Resources

   1. *Fighting the Good Fight: Playing Your Part in God's Unfolding Drama* is now available (Jan 1, 2015). It is a new believers follow-up curriculum based on the book of Ephesians and can be purchased at http://www.tumistore.org/fight-the-good-fight/ .

   2. *Fit to Represent: Vision for Discipleship Seminar* is available now at http://www.tumistore.org/fit-to-represent-vision-for-discipleship-seminar/

E. What are the best Men's and Women's Discipleship tools developed by TUMI and World Impact to date? (http://www.tumi.org/siafu)

   1. Don Davis, *The SIAFU Network Guidebook: Standing Together for Christ in the City* (TUMI, 2013).

   2. Don Davis, *The SIAFU Chapter Meeting Guide* (TUMI, 2013)

F. More than 700 resources developed for urban churches and leaders engaged in urban ministry available at www.tumistore.org and at http://www.cafepress.com/tumi .

   1. Resources include artwork, videos, clothing, books, etc.

   2. More than 30 resources available in Spanish.

III. Leadership Development

  A. Books

  1. Don Davis, *Sacred Roots: A Primer on Retrieving the Great Tradition* (Wichita, KS: The Urban Ministry Institute, 2010).

  2. Don Allsman, *Jesus Cropped from the Picture: Why Christians Get Bored and How to Restore Them to Vibrant Faith* (CreateSpace Independent Publishing Platform, 2010).

  3. Efrem Smith, *The Post-Black and Post-White Church: Becoming the Beloved Community in a Multi-Ethnic World*, vol. 59, Jossey-Bass Leadership Network Series (San Francisco: Jossey-Bass, 2012).

  B. Leadership Development Classes

  1. The Urban Ministry Institute Satellite (TUMI) Network

     a) Currently more than 180 urban ministries, churches, and denominations have launched TUMI leadership training institutes for training leaders in their ministry context.

     b) Learn how to start a satellite at your ministry by visiting www.tumi.org/satellite.

  2. The Capstone Curriculum

     a) TUMI's premier leadership training program. Sixteen classes usually taken over a four year period with courses in four subject areas: Biblical Studies; Christian Ministry; Urban Mission; and Christian Theology.

     b) The Capstone Courses can be transferred to several accredited colleges and universities for those interested in continuing their education. For more information on Capstone, visit www.tumi.org/capstone .

  3. Foundations Classes (13 currently available)

     a) Sample courses include *Church Matters*. A course that covers the major periods of the church and emphasizes how evangelical churches can be renewed by a retrieval of the Great Tradition and the pursuit of a shared spirituality.http://www.tumistore.org/foundations-church-matters-course/

b) Sample Courses include *Marking Time: Forming Spirituality Through the Christian Year*. This course introduces evangelicals to a theology of time rooted in the practice of the Christian Year. The course looks at the way a shared spirituality can equip churches working among the poor with vital resources for discipleship, preaching, and worship. http://www.tumistore.org/foundations-marking-time-course/

C. Conferences

1. Annual TUMI Summit. More than two hundred leaders from around the globe who are involved with urban leadership development through the TUMI satellite network. Next summit is May 15–17, 2015 in Wichita, KS. Information will be posted soon at http://www.tumistore.org/satellite-summit/

2. Men's and Women's SIAFU Conferences. Regional men's and women's conferences to encourage missional outreach in the cities. See http://www.tumi.org/siafu for more information.

An Abridged Church Planting Bibliography

An Abridged Church Planting Bibliography

The Urban Ministry Institute

Allen, Roland. *Missionary Methods: St. Paul's or Ours?* Grand Rapids: Wm. B. Eerdmans Publishing Company, 2001.

Arn, Win, and Charles Arn. *The Master's Plan for Making Disciples*, 2nd ed. Grand Rapids: Baker Books, 1998.

Banks, Robert. *Paul's Idea of Community*, rev. ed. Peabody, MA: Hendrickson Publishers, 1994.

Becker, Paul. *Dynamic Church Planting: A Complete Handbook*. Vista, Calif.: Multiplication Ministries, 1992.

Bessenecker, Scott A. *Overturning Tables: Freeing Missions from the Christian-Industrial Complex*. Downers Grover, IL: InterVarsity Press, 2014.

Black, Vicki K. *Welcome to the Church Year: An Introduction to the Seasons of the Episcopal Church*. Harrisburg, PA: Morehouse Publishing, 2004.

Carter, Ryan, ed. *Christ the Victor Church: The Guidebook: Ancient Faith for an Urban Movement*. N.P.: CreateSpace, 2014.

Chaney, Charles L. *Church Planting at the End of the Twentieth Century*. Revised and expanded. Wheaton: Tyndale House Publishers, 1991.

Conn, Harvie M. *Planting and Growing Urban Churches: From Dream to Reality*. Grand Rapids, MI: Baker Books, 1997.

Davis, Don L. *Vision for Mission: Nurturing an Apostolic Heart*. Wichita, KS: The Urban Ministry Institute (World Impact, Inc.), 1999.

———. *Focus on Reproduction*. Vol. 12, 16 vols. *The Capstone Curriculum*. Wichita, KS: The Urban Ministry Institute (World Impact, Inc.), 2005.

———. *Marking Time. Forming Spirituality through the Christian Year*. Wichita, KS: The Urban Ministry Institute (World Impact, Inc.), 2007.

———. *Ministry in a Multi-Cultural and Unchurched Society*. Wichita, KS: The Urban Ministry Institute (World Impact, Inc.), 2007.

———. *Winning the World: Facilitating Urban Church Planting Movements*. Wichita, KS: The Urban Ministry Institute (World Impact, Inc.), 2007.

———. *Master the Bible Guidebook: Charting Your Course through Scripture Memorization*. Wichita, KS: The Urban Ministry Institute (World Impact, Inc.), 2008.

———. *Church Matters: Retrieving the Great Tradition*. Wichita, KS: The Urban Ministry Institute (World Impact, Inc.), 2010.

———. *Sacred Roots: A Primer on Retrieving the Great Tradition*. Wichita, KS: The Urban Ministry Institute (World Impact, Inc.), 2010.

———. *The Most Amazing Story Ever Told*. Wichita, KS: The Urban Ministry Institute (World Impact, Inc.), 2011.

Davis, Don L. and Terry Cornett. *The Capstone Curriculum*. 16 vols. Wichita, KS: The Urban Ministry Institute (World Impact, Inc.) 2005.

ETA (Evangelical Training Association). *Perspectives from Church History*. Wheaton, IL: Evangelical Training Association, 1996.

Fairchild, Samuel D. *Church Planting for Reproduction*. Grand Rapids: Baker Book House, 1991.

Francis, Hozell C. *Church Planting in the African-American Context*. Grand Rapids, MI: Zondervan Publishing House, 1999.

Garrison, David. *Church Planting Movements*. Midlothian, VA: WIGTake Resources, 2004.

Gonzales, Justo L. *Church History: An Essential Guide*. Nashville: Abingdon Press, 1996.

Greenway, Roger S., and Timothy M. Monsma. *Cities: Missions' New Frontier*, 2nd Ed. Grand Rapids, MI: Baker Books, 2000.

Hauerwas, Stanley and Willian H. Willimon. *Resident Aliens: Life in the Christian Colony*. Nashville, TN: Abingdon Press, 1989.

Hesselgrave, David J. *Planting Churches Cross-Culturally*, 2nd Ed. Grand Rapids, MI: Baker Books, 2000.

Hickman, Hoyt L, Don E. Saliers, Laurence Hull Stookey, James F. White. *The New Handbook of the Christian Year*. Nashville, TN: Abingdon Press, 1992.

Hiebert, Paul G. *Anthropological Insights for Missionaries*. Grand Rapids, MI: Baker Books, 1985.

Hiebert, Paul G. and Eloise Hiebert Meneses. *Incarnational Ministry: Planting Churches in Band, Tribal, Peasant, and Urban Societies*. Grand Rapids, MI: Baker Books, 1995.

Jennings, Willie James. *The Christian Imagination: Theology and the Origins of Race*. New Haven: Yale University Press, 2010.

Kreider, Larry. *House Church Networks*. Ephrata, PA: House to House Publications, 2001.

Kyle, John E. ed. *Urban Mission: God's Concern for the City*. Downers Grove, IL: InterVarsity Press, 1988.

Ladd, G. E. *Gospel of the Kingdom*. Grand Rapids, MI: Eerdmans, 1959.

Liele, George. "An Account of Several Baptist Churches, Consisting Chiefly of Negro Slaves: Particularly of One at Kingston, in Jamaica; and Another at Savannah in Georgia (1793)." In *Unchained Voices: An Anthology of Black Authors in the English-speaking World of the Eighteenth Century*. Edited by Vincent Carretta. Lexington: University Press of Kentucky, 2004.

———. "The Covenant of the Anabaptist Church: Began in America 1777, in Jamaica, Dec. 1783." 1796. British Baptist material, Angus Library of Regents Park College, Oxford, England, reel 1, no. 14.; Publication (Historical Commission, Southern Baptist Convention), MF # 4265.

Liele, George and Andrew Bryan. "Letters from Pioneer Black Baptists." In *Afro-American Religious History: A Documentary Witness*. Edited by Milton C. Sernett. Durham, NC: Duke University Press, 1985.

———. "Letters Showing the Rise and Progress of the Early Negro Churches of Georgia and the West Indies." Comprised of "An Account of Several Baptist Churches, Consisting Chiefly of Negro Slaves: Particularly of One at Kingston, in Jamaica; and Another at Savannah in Georgia," and "Sketches of the Black Baptist Church at Savannah, in Georgia: And of Their Minister Andrew Bryan, Extracted from Several Letters." *Journal of Negro History* 1 no. 1 (Jan. 1916): 69-92.

Logan, Robert E., and Steven L. Ogne. *Church Planter's Toolkit*. Pasadena: Charles E. Fuller Institute of Evangelism & Church Growth, 1991.

Logan, Robert E., and Neil Cole. *Beyond Church Planting: Pathways for Emerging Churches*. St. Charles, IL: ChurchSmart Resources, 2005.

Malphurs, Aubrey. *Planting Growing Churches for the 21st Century: A Comprehensive Guide for New Churches and Those Desiring Renewal*. 2nd ed. Grand Rapids: Baker Books, 1998.

Mannoia, Kevin. *Church Planting the Next Generation: Introducing the Century 21 Church Planting System*. Indianapolis: Light and Life Press, 1994.

Miley, George. *Loving the Church, Blessing the Nations: Pursuing the Role of Local Churches in Global Mission*. Waynesboro, GA: Authentic Media, 2003.

Montgomery, Jim. *DAWN 2000: 7 Million Churches to Go*. Pasadena: William Carey Library, 1989.

Mull, Marlin. *A Biblical Church Planting Manual from the Book of Acts*. Eugene, OR: Wipf and Stock Publishers, 2003.

Nebel, Tom, and Gary Rohrmayer. *Church Planting Landmines: Mistakes to Avoid in Years 2 through 10*. St. Charles, IL: ChurchSmart Resources.

Niebuhr, H. Richard. *Christ and Culture*. New York, NY: HarperSanFrancisco, 1951.

Noll, Mark A. *Turning Points: Decisive Moments in the History of Christianity*. Grand Rapids, MI: Baker Academic (Baker Book House), 1997, 2000.

Overstreet, Don. *Sent Out: The Calling, the Character, and the Challenge of the Apostle/Missionary*. Bloomington, IN: Crossbooks, 2009.

Overstreet, Don, and Mark Hammond. *God's Call to the City*. Bloomington, IN: Crossbooks, 2011.

Phillips, Keith. *Out of Ashes*. Los Angeles, CA: World Impact Press, 1996.

Ratliff, Joe S., and Michael J. Cox. *Church Planting in the African-American Community*. Nashville: Broadman Press, 1993.

Romo, Oscar I. American Mosaic: *Church Planting in Ethnic America*. Nashville: Broadman Press, 1993.

Schaller, Lyle. *44 Questions for Church Planters*. Nashville: Abingdon Press, 1991.

Schwarz, Christian A. *Natural Church Development*. St. Charles, IL: ChurchSmart Resources, 2000.

Searcy, Nelson, and Kerrick Thomas. *Launch: Starting a New Church from Scratch*. Ventura, Calif.: Regal Books, 2007.

Shenk, David W., and Ervin R. Stutzman. *Creating Communities of the Kingdom: New Testament Models of Church Planting*. Scottdale: Herald Press, 1988.

Smith, Efrem. *Raising Up Young Heroes: Developing a Revolutionary Youth Ministry*. Downers Grove: InterVarsity Press, 2004.

———. *Jump into a Life of Further and Higher*. Colorado Springs: David C. Cook, 2010.

———. *The Post-Black and Post-White Church: Becoming the Beloved Community in a Multi-Ethnic World*. San Francisco: Jossey-Bass Publishers, 2012.

Smith, Efrem and Phil Jackson. *The Hip-Hop Church: Connecting with the Movement Shaping our Culture*. Downers Grove: InterVarsity Press, 2005.

Snyder, Howard A. *Kingdom, Church, and World*. Eugene, OR: Wipf and Stock, 1997.

---. *The Community of the King*, Rev. ed. Downers Grove, IL: InterVarsity Press, 2004.

Stetzer, Ed. *Planting New Churches in a Postmodern Age.* Nashville: Broadman & Holman Publishers, 2003.

---. *Planting Missional Chruches.* Nashville: B & H Publishing Group, 2006.

---. "Books/Resources on Ethnic Groups in the U.S. and Canada." *The Exchange.* April 15, 2008. *http://www.christianitytoday.com/edstetzer.*

---. "Church Planting Bibliography." *The Exchange.* April 20, 2009. *http://www.christianitytoday.com/edstetzer.*

Surratt, Geoff, Greg Ligon, and Warren Bird. *The Multi-Site Church Revolution: Being One Church in Many Locations.* Grand Rapids: Zondervan, 2006.

Teja, Gary, and John Wagenveld, eds. *Planting Healthy Churches.* Sauk Village, IL: Multiplication Network Ministries, 2015.

Wagner, C. Peter. *Church Planting for a Greater Harvest: A Comprehensive Guide.* Ventura: Regal Books, 1990.

Webber, Robert E. *Ancient-Future Time: Forming Spirituality through the Christian Year.* Grand Rapids, MI: Baker Books, 2004.

Woodson, Carter Godwin. *The History of the Negro Church.* Washington, D.C.: Associated Publishers, 1921.

The Urban Ministry Institute:
Polishing the Stones That the Builders Reject
How You Can Equip Leaders for Your Church and Ministry

The Urban Ministry Institute:
Polishing the Stones That the Builders Reject
How You Can Equip Leaders for Your Church and Ministry

Rev. Dr. Don L. Davis • April 18, 2015

The Stone the Builders Rejected Has Become the Capstone!
Ps. 118.22-23 (ESV) – The stone that the builders rejected has become the cornerstone. This is the Lord's doing; it is marvelous in our eyes.

Inspired by text above (and Jesus' quotation of it in Matthew 21.42), *The Urban Ministry Institute* has formulated a precise vision regarding God's selection and preparation of urban leaders. We believe that this text captures the gist of God's intention to raise up laborers for his harvest among the urban poor.

Jesus Himself is the Pattern for Urban Leadership Development
Most scholars believe this to be a proverb, but with a huge amount of an ironic twist: a stone was rejected for building purposes by the very builders themselves. However, this rejected stone proves to be of inestimable value and worth. This despised stone turns out on further inspection to be the chief cornerstone, often called the bondstone or the capstone, the corner of the foundation, the crowning stone of all. In light of the plain NT references, this text alludes to Christ Jesus,* the Stone of Stumbling. The so-called "builders" in Israel, who rejected his lordship, ignored the very one who has now been exalted through the anointing and election of God. As the Stone laid in Zion by Yahweh himself, Jesus is the Capstone, the Chief and Precious Cornerstone, whom believed in and relied upon never disappoints (Isa. 28.16).

* Matthew 21.42;
Mark 12.10;
Luke 20.17;
Acts 4.11;
Ephesians 2.20;
1 Peter 2:4, 7

This powerful messianic prophecy has a corollary truth conjoined to it that lies at the heart of both the Old and New Testament citations about God's choice and our rejection of it. A principle emerges that illustrates the complexity of God's divine irony in leadership selection. This principle clearly reveals the precise nature of God's choice of men and women to represent him.

God's Choice of the Poor
God has chosen the poor to be rich in faith, and heirs of the Kingdom to come (James 2.5). God chooses the broken to confound the whole, the foolish to shame the wise, and the poor to astound the rich. He has elected what is base and despised to shame the honorable, and what is weak and pathetic to humble the strong. God chooses and exalts what

men tend to reject and despise (cf. 1 Corinthians 1.26-29). Throughout church history, this principle proves to be true. Only the Lord can determine what vessels he will use for the honor of his Son, and the advancement of his Kingdom. It is his choice alone; and, whomever he elects, so does he empower and direct!

TUMI: Affirming God's Call for the Poor to Lead

This is the heart of the irony of God's use of men and women, and is testified in virtually every narrative involving God's choice. While we tend to judge based on a person's appearance or background, God looks to a person's character and call. He does not often elect on the basis of one's training, pedigree, socioeconomic background, or education. Rather, God looks on the heart (1 Sam. 16.7). Whomever God calls and empowers accomplishes his task, and he tends to select those who even the most experienced find detestable. The strength and wisdom of God are best displayed through human vessels which are weak and foolish, and his grace is made perfect through weakness. Those who appear to be useless to the keenest eye of the most experienced builders, may easily become the select vessel of God. By his grace and preparation, even the despised may become the very cornerstone of God's enterprise. This is the heart of the divine irony of God's selection of his leaders.

Towards a New Paradigm and Structure of Urban Leadership Development

For more than twenty years, *The Urban Ministry Institute* (TUMI), has been the training arm of *World Impact*. We design resources, programs, and tools that can equip servant leaders to plant and lead healthy, evangelical churches and movements which will advance the Kingdom in the cities of America and beyond. Our distinctive is that we concentrate our efforts of empowering those who seek to reach the lost among the urban disadvantaged. We are convinced that God will raise up an army of laborers who will transform their communities through the Gospel, and its corollary acts of compassion, justice, and witness to the Kingdom.

We desire, therefore, to provide the kind of theological, pastoral, and spiritual formation that will allow so-called despised people to access credible, affordable, and life-changing training where they live and minister. In order to attain this goal, we seek to transform both the content and method of theological education to make our structures conducive to empowering the urban poor.

While traditional theological education and seminaries have been the mainstays of most Christian leadership development, the urban poor are often overlooked or completely ignored in their programs. As successful as traditional seminaries have been in raising up qualified leaders for suburban contexts, much traditional theological education programs are simply too cumbersome and out of sync for urban leadership development.

Unfortunately, most urban leaders do not qualify for the Christian leadership education available today. It is too expensive, usually offered in venues far from the context of urban churches and their neighborhoods, and tends to disqualify urban candidates because of academic qualifications. Finally, much of traditional theological development training remains culturally distant from the experience and work of most urban spiritual laborers, and proves not conducive to the needs and issues of contemporary urban life.

From Idea to Revolution:
Equipping Leaders for Ministry around the Globe
Since 1995, we have sought to redesign Christian leadership education for the poor. We have taught dozens of seminars, conferences, and seminary-level courses, graduated hundreds of men and women through our academic Certificate program, and created numerous ministry resources for use by urban churches around the world. Our passion is to multiply this excellent training for every urban context, making our resources as affordable, biblically credible, missionally reproducible, and culturally sensitive as possible. At the time of this writing, we have nearly 200 satellites in fourteen countries, representing more than 2,000 students who are being equipped for frontline ministry in some of the most dangerous and neglected neighborhoods on earth.

Our structures are designed to enhance this burden for multiplication and accessibility to urban churches and their leaders. Of course, all of our courses, conferences, seminars, and workshops are facilitated by experienced, qualified TUMI faculty, many whom hold terminal degrees in major seminaries and universities, having many years in pastoral care and urban ministry experience.

Empowerment: A New Strategy to
Develop Leaders without Debt Where They Live
Our strategy is to establish a system that allows local churches and organizations to establish satellite training centers in their own venue and locale. Our intent is to facilitate sound, solid biblical training through our support of churches in their ministry environment. After extensive study of theological and leadership education in America, we have designed processes and mechanisms to allow churches to form training centers which are Christ-centered, Scripture-formed, and ministry-focused.

While we do give considerable attention to providing resources to urban churches to help them ground new and growing Christians in Christ, the heart of our vision is to equip leaders for the urban church. This entails two things: 1) providing new and emerging Christian leaders and workers in urban churches with the essential theological resources and support necessary for effective urban ministry, and 2) to provide on-going investment for seasoned urban church leaders who intend to sharpen their ministry and train others for ministry as well.

Join Us: Help Equip Leaders Affordably In Your Own Locale
The staff and faculty of *The Urban Ministry Institute* wholeheartedly believe that God is raising up in significant numbers men and women among the urban poor who serve his Kingdom in extraordinary ways, across the nation and world. In order to facilitate this emergence of leaders, we have established an effective administrative structure that permits qualified churches and organizations to provide excellent, affordable, and accessible training in the context of their own church and ministry. If you are interested in establishing a training center in your church, ministry, association, or denomination, please contact us at *www.tumi.org*.